Boundary-Spanning in Organizations

In more recent times, the essence of the gatekeeper's role has moved to that of the 'boundary spanner'—a systems thinker who understands the specific needs and interests of the organization and whose greatest asset is their ability to move across and through the formal and informal features of the modern organization.

There are many types of boundaries associated with an organization, for example, horizontal (function and expertise), vertical (status, hierarchy), geographic, demographic, and stakeholder. Boundaries are "the defining characteristic of organizations and, boundary roles are the link between the environment and the organization" (Aldrich and Herker 1977), with functions crucial to the effectiveness and success of the organization.

Despite being a critical success factor for an organization, beginning in the 1970s, the term *boundary-spanning* has had an intermittent research history: there has been no systematic body of research that has evolved over time. This book aims to invigorate, excite, and expand the literature on boundary-spanning in a diverse range of disciplines such as sociology, organizational psychology, management, medicine, defense, health, social work, and community services. The book serves as the first collection of reviews on boundary-spanning in organizations.

Janice Langan-Fox is professor of management at Swinburne University of Technology. She started her career in industry where she worked for ten years in manufacturing, shipping, distribution, travel, and law, prior to entering academia as a lecturer at RMIT University teaching organizational behavior. In 2007, she was made an Honorary Principal Fellow by the psychology department, the University of Melbourne. Janice's research spans several disciplines: psychology, management, health, and human factors.

Cary L. Cooper is Distinguished Professor of Organizational Psychology and Health at Lancaster Management School. He is currently founding editor of the *Journal of Organizational Behavior* and editor-in-chief of the medical journal *Stress & Health*. Professor Cooper is also the president of the Institute of Welfare, president of the British Association of Counselling and Psychotherapy, president of RELATE, a national Ambassador of the Samaritans, and a Patron of the Anxiety UK.

Routledge Studies in Management, Organizations, and Society

This series presents innovative work grounded in new realities, addressing issues crucial to an understanding of the contemporary world. This is the world of organized societies, where boundaries between formal and informal, public and private, local and global organizations have been displaced or have vanished, along with other nineteenth-century dichotomies and oppositions. Management, apart from becoming a specialized profession for a growing number of people, is an everyday activity for most members of modern societies.

Similarly, at the level of enquiry, culture and technology and literature and economics, can no longer be conceived as isolated intellectual fields; conventional canons and established mainstreams are contested. **Management, Organizations, and Society** addresses these contemporary dynamics of transformation in a manner that transcends disciplinary boundaries, with books that will appeal to researchers, students, and practitioners alike.

Boundary-Spanning in Organizations

Network, Influence, and Conflict

Edited by Janice Langan-Fox
and Cary L. Cooper

Routledge
Taylor & Francis Group
NEW YORK   LONDON

First published 2014
by Routledge
711 Third Avenue, New York, NY 10017

Simultaneously published in the UK
by Routledge
2 Park Square, Milton Park, Abingdon, Oxon OX14 4RN

*Routledge is an imprint of the Taylor & Francis Group,
an informa business*

Library of Congress Cataloging-in-Publication Data

Boundary-spanning in organizations : network, influence, and conflict / edited by
  Janice Langan-Fox and Cary L. Cooper.
    pages cm. — (Routledge studies in management, organizations,
  and society)
    Includes bibliographical references and index.
  1. Organizational change.   2. Organizational behavior.   I. Langan-Fox,
Janice, 1946–.   II. Cooper, Cary L.
  HD58.8.B673   2013
  302.3'5—dc23
  2013009102

ISBN: 978-0-415-62883-9 (hbk)
ISBN: 978-0-415-48805-8 (ebk)

Typeset in Sabon
by Apex CoVantage, LLC

Printed and bound in the United States of America by Publishers Graphics,
LLC on sustainably sourced paper.

For Caroline and Julian

—Janice Langan-Fox

Contents

Introduction

Forty or more years ago, the "gatekeeper" (not to be confused with Zuul, the gatekeeper of Gozer in the movie *Ghostbusters*) was the point of contact for external sources of information for an organizational team or department. However, the development of the Internet made the role of the gatekeeper redundant, and nowadays, everyone is expected to keep up to date and abreast of pertinent information through their computer.

In more recent times, the essence of the gatekeeper's role has moved to that of the 'boundary-spanner'—a systems thinker who understands the specific needs and interests of the organization and whose greatest asset is their ability to move across and through the formal and informal features of the modern organization: boundary-spanners have a diverse knowledge base, draw on a wide range of expertise, are change agents, are flexible, mobile, multiskilled, and more than anything, connected and networked across a wide range of people in departments and units, both inside and outside the organization. Such individuals become legend and folklore in organizations: they are individuals who everyone wants to know, or, would like to know and to be seen to be with. Influence and power accrues to the effective boundary-spanner.

Despite being a critical success factor for an organization, beginning in the 1970s, the term *boundary-spanning* has had an intermittent research history: there has been no systematic body of research that has evolved over time, as has happened with more familiar concepts, such as job satisfaction; in general, then, the literature, being only thirty to forty years old, is somewhat spartan. Scholars on the topic of boundary-spanning have given attention to a range of variables, including organizational structure, roles, networks, communication, teamwork, and decision making. With some exceptions, this literature has been North American.

There are many types of boundaries associated with an organization, for example, horizontal (function and expertise), vertical (status, hierarchy), geographic, demographic, and stakeholder. Boundaries are "the defining

Aldrich H and Herker D (1977) Boundary spanning roles and organizational structure. Academy of Management Review. 2 (2), 217–230 characteristic of organizations, and, boundary roles are the link between the environment and the organization" (Aldrich and Herker 1977), with functions crucial to the effectiveness and success of the organization, and forming the basis for strategic jobs at a senior level.

Many management and leadership roles can be conceptualized as boundary-spanning, and an important capability across all levels of leadership but perhaps all individuals working in organizations have some aspect of boundary-spanning contained in their role because there has been a global increase in networked forms of organizational structures. Also, there is a parallel growing challenge for organizations to enhance their performance and stakeholder engagement through identifying and rewarding individuals and teams who can effectively perform boundary-spanning roles and who are able to operate across multiple internal and external boundaries, build relationships, identify threats and opportunities, and return insights back to the organization. The drive for innovation and creativity requires leaders to be more effective at spanning multiple boundaries, in cross-functional, cross-generational, and cross-country/region learning and coordination, which hopefully will lead to breakthrough insights. Boundary-spanning roles are part of competitive business practices and market developments, and have been at the heart of cutting-edge advances in space exploration and hand-held technology.

Typically, the concept has been concerned with how organizations can maximize talent in their workforces, how they can be competitive in a global market, and in general, is positively oriented. But, there is a *dark* side to boundary-spanning. Common in organizations these days, there is a greater level of job insecurity; a complex web of politics; and barriers associated with vested interests in the professions, unions, departments, and sometimes senior management. Such dynamics are often accompanied by imbalances of power, lack of meaningful engagement and communication, inability to think laterally, and an endemic lack of trust, which results in conflict, collusion, and sometimes hatred of those in boundary-spanning roles. Those 'sent to Coventry,' and those employed in contract and casual jobs, for whatever reason, are kept outside the box, and are not carried along by the boundary-spanning individual or team engaged in developing the goals of the organizations. Such individuals may find they need to develop a unique form of boundary-spanning *themselves*: trying to develop organizational ties and relationships to avoid being ostracized and disenfranchised from the organization; or, develop a boundary-spanning style where the internal aspect of their organizational relationship partially dissolves, and they develop boundary-spanning activities more concerned with external factors, whether that is collusion with colleagues in other organizations or closer involvements with family and outside interests. Such boundary-spanning is not in the typical form found in the literature, but of someone struggling to survive organizational change, ferment, and chaos. These stories are not available in the boundary-spanning literature, but we need to know about them.

This book aims to invigorate, excite, and expand the literature on boundary-spanning, because we believe the concept provides a wealth of richness and opportunity to developing research into important problems relevant to communities and modern organizations, in a diverse range of disciplines such as sociology, organizational psychology, management, medicine, health, social work, and community services. The book serves as the *first* collection of reviews on boundary-spanning in organizations. The reviews are written by researchers who have experience or publication in boundary-spanning and therefore bring a strong level of expertise to discuss this important topic.

The book is divided into four sections: Individuals and Concepts, Groups and Teams, Management, and Organizations. Section 1—Chapter 1, by Linda Hobb, describes learning possibilities by teachers; Chapter 2, by Jacob Vakkayil, is focused on boundary objects in boundary-spanning; Chapter 3, by Preeta Banerjee and Rafael Corredoira, discusses individual and collective boundary-spanning. Section 2 includes Chapter 4, by Susan Gasson, who presents details about enterprise system innovation project groups; Chapter 5, by Anit Somech and Anat Drach-Zahavy, describes intra- and inter-team contextual facilitators; Chapter 6, by Thomas Calvard, discusses about the difficulties of boundary-spanning by inter-organizational teams; Chapter 7, by Fiona Buick, addresses boundary-spanning in Indigenous disadvantage; Chapter 8, by Janice Langan-Fox, Sharon Grant, and Vikas Anand, relates collusion in organizations and the role of the boundary-spanner. Section 3 includes Chapter 9, by Philip Riley, presenting data on the boundary-spanning activities of school principals; Chapter 10, by Charles Palus, Donna Chrobot-Mason, and Kristin Cullen, describes boundary-spanning leadership; and Chapter 11, by David Wilemon, presents data on boundary-spanning in three organizational functions. Section 4 has Chapter 12, by Frens Kroeger and Reinhard Bachmann, on trust in boundary-spanning; Chapter 13, by Natalia Levina and Emmanuelle Vaast, describes transactive and transformative boundary-spanning practices; Chapter 14, by Peter Rosenweg and Janice Langan-Fox, discusses the difficult issue of compliance in infection control and boundary-spanning in hospitals; and finally, Chapter 15, by Anandasivam Gopal and Sanjay Gosain, describes organizational controls and boundary-spanning in software development outsourcing.

We hope you will enjoy this richly diverse book on the unusual topic of boundary-spanning—the first of its kind. The book should be attractive to social workers, administrators, managers, psychologists, teachers, academics, community workers, and policy makers.

Janice Langan-Fox

Part I
Individuals and Concepts

1 Boundary Crossings of Out-of-Field Teachers

Locating Learning Possibilities amid Disruption

Linda Hobbs

As with many work environments, schools contain boundaries that are being constantly negotiated by teachers. Subject specialization at the secondary level has resulted in teachers who are trained in specific disciplines, who then take on the task of translating disciplinary knowledge, practices, and modes of inquiry into school curriculum. The question for this chapter is in relation to the boundary negotiations involved for teachers who move from an in-field subject to out-of-field subjects, that is, subjects for which they hold no formal qualification in either the discipline or teaching method. Such teachers have conceptualized learning and teaching within the field of their specialist area, but are required to take on new knowledge, and find ways to translate or transform what they already know into another subject. Despite the obvious discontinuity relating to new content knowledge for the teacher, there are many factors that disrupt the 'rhythm' of a teacher when teaching out-of-field. This chapter focuses on the need to define the 'field' and resultant discontinuity in order to identify where learning can take place during a boundary crossing.

A research program focusing on the subject-specific nature of teaching has drawn attention to the complexity of teaching out-of-field and the influence of boundary crossings on teacher professional identity. This research (Hobbs 2012a, 2012b) has highlighted relationships between school governance and teacher autonomy, and between support mechanisms within the environment, teachers' attitudes toward their out-of-field subject, and teachers' personal resources. These various factors have a bearing on: a teacher's desire to become a capable and innovative teacher of the out-of-field subject; opportunities for learning; and the likelihood of identity development.

In this chapter I draw on the experiences of a number of teachers in order to demonstrate that it is important to examine the field when investigating issues around teaching out-of-field in order to identify if and where discontinuity arises. I begin with a discussion on the emergence of the 'subject' as a defining element of teachers' work and identity, and situate the subject as 'field.' I then describe the theoretical framework of *boundary crossings* as a language for describing possibilities for learning at the boundary between in-field and out-of-field spaces. I then draw from previous research in order to present a series of snapshots of teachers' experiences with teaching out-of-field, focusing explicitly on the boundary and fields, and the discontinuities and possibilities for learning, which are then discussed using Akkerman and Bakker's (2011) mechanisms of learning.

A REVIEW OF THE LITERATURE

This research uses a theoretical lens informed by the boundary crossing literature (e.g., Star 1989; Akkerman and Bakker 2011), which recognizes the heterogeneous nature of workplaces and the role of different actors who represent different cultures. Boundaries between practices and knowledge domains are "constitutive of what counts as expertise or as central participation" (Akkerman and Bakker 2011, 1). The notion of boundaries between different fields, or domains, is a move away from the idea that contexts within workplaces are bounded and singular. Akkerman and Bakker define boundaries as "sociocultural differences leading to discontinuities in action and interaction" (2011, 21), rather than any move between different practices. Boundaries simultaneously are marked by a sameness and continuity in some ways.

The boundary crossing concept became rarefied in the late 1980s through the work of Engeström (e.g., Engeström, Engeström, and Kärkkäinen 1995), Star (1989), and Suchman (1994), and is gaining prominence in research in the educational sciences and educational psychology (Akkerman and Bakker 2011). The boundaries concept has become a key component of two current learning theories: Engeström's (1987) cultural historical activity theory on expansive learning, which enables exploration of relationships within and between activity systems; and Wenger's (1998) situated learning theory on communities of practice, which enables exploration of membership to a community based on participation.

The discussion in the chapter aligns more closely with the communities of practice perspective rather than activity theory because the former enables theorization around varying degrees of participation in the practices that constitute the community of subject teaching. In the context of my research exploring out-of-field teachers, the boundary crossing lens enables:

- examination of the movement of teachers from in-field to out-of-field teaching spaces;
- a focus on discontinuities that are expected to arise; and
- learning and shifts in professional identity that are expected to ensure productive boundary crossings.

Whether in-field or out-of-field, sameness and continuity reside in the fact that both fields involve such things as pedagogy, curriculum and meeting learning outcomes. However, teachers can experience discontinuity when experiences result in shifts in degrees of confidence and competence in their ability to effect positive learning outcomes for their students. The use of the boundary crossings lens provides a platform for re-conceptualizing these experiences as opportunities for professional learning occurring within schools as communities of practice, where teachers are supported and enabled to adapt to new fields and expand their professional identity (van Manen 1990). My focus on intersecting social worlds is not on the intersection of groups of people as with any of the employing boundary crossing subjects, such as with collaboration between different groups within a problem space. Instead, my focus is on the need to adapt practice as people move between different communities of practice, and the dialogical interchanges between knowledge domains, what I call 'fields,' that enable a teacher to change practice and construct identities that are commensurate with the new field. These communities of practice are situated around the school 'subject,,' which I describe in the following section.

The Subject as "Field"

Secondary schooling (ages 12–18) in Australia tends to be based on a departmental model, where teaching involves engaging students in the knowledge, practices and activities of a 'subject,' and teachers usually refer to themselves as teachers of specific subject areas. The subject became a unit of analysis of school cultures in the 1990s as researchers explored subjects as defining elements of secondary teachers' work, showing that subject departments act as the locus around which teachers gather, collaborate, develop identities, and support each other. Siskin (1994), for example, found that teachers from the selected subject departments of English, science and mathematics spoke different 'languages.' These language differences were more than simply "idiosyncratic appearances of technical jargon; rather, the discipline's language and epistemology in the ways teachers—as subject-matter specialists—conceptualise the world, their roles within it, and the nature of knowledge, teaching and learning" (Siskin 1994, 152).

Subjects by their nature, are epistemologically, ontologically, and philosophically different. They are defined by the disciplines from which they come (Dorfler and McLone 1986), as well as the subject-specific knowledge that forms the curriculum, and ways of thinking, doing, and being. Subject specificity may apply to subject matter knowledge, experiential knowledge, pedagogy, orientation, beliefs, and interests. Teacher specialization ensures that teaching is informed by deep knowledge of the area (Goodson 1993).

A teacher's identity and work, according to van Manen (1982), are organically bound up in what teachers know about their subject. Teachers describe themselves as teachers according to what they know:

> To know a particular subject means that I know something in this domain of human knowledge. But to know something does not mean to

just know just anything about something. To know something is to know what that something is in the way that it is and speaks to us. (van Manen 1982, 295)

As a teacher takes on the role as subject teacher, they participate in what Gee calls the "discourse" of what it means to teach that subject, which requires learning the "ways of combining and integrating language, actions, interactions, ways of thinking, believing, valuing, and using various symbols, tools and objects to enact a particular socially recognizable identity" (Gee 2010, 29). Professional identity develops not just through this participation but also through the interpretation or recognition of that participation by self or others. A sociocultural framing of identity describes it not as fixed, but as an ongoing process of becoming (Beijaard, Meijer, and Verloop 2004) where context plays a crucial role (Beijaard et al. 2004; Connelly and Clandinin 1999). Therefore, teachers' socio-historical interactions with their subject equip them with competence and confidence in their teaching.

At a fundamental level, the 'field' refers to this bounded system of knowledge, attitudes, beliefs, and practices specific to the subject. However, as with many workplaces, a school is a heterogeneous workplace (Akkerman and Bakker 2011), involving multiple actors representing different professional cultures (Suchman 1994). Layers of management, varying and changing roles, changing work spaces, and different actors mean that teachers are constantly moving between different practices, domains of knowledge, rules of engagement, and layers of expertise. Because of this changing nature of teachers' work, out-of-field teaching is often perceived as an expected part of the profession, which perhaps explains why McConney and Price (2009) claim that it remains under-theorized.

Teachers are considered in-field when they have the necessary qualifications to teach that subject. The secondary teacher degree in Australia usually includes at least two method areas, such as general science and senior physics, or physical education and mathematics. To undertake these method studies as part of their teaching degree they must have a major or minor in those areas.

So, what does it mean to be teaching *technically* out-of-field? Teachers who are teaching out-of-field usually have neither a major nor minor in that discipline, nor a teaching method in that subject. However, teachers can *feel* out-of-field for a number of reasons, even if they are technically in-field, or qualified to teach that subject. Also, teachers can *feel* in-field when technically out-of-field. These *feelings* are significant in situations where a principal is assigning technically out-of-field teachers to a subject when a qualified teacher is not available. These feelings are also significant because a teachers' approach to their subject will influence their willingness to engage with professional learning, invest time in preparation, and engage in professional dialogue (Hobbs 2012). Teachers who consider themselves as just filling in are less likely to seek professional development in an out-of-field subject than those teachers who have requested an out-of-field subject because of their personal interest in it.

Certainly teaching out-of-field can place a teacher in unfamiliar territory and lead to feelings of being unqualified. Suchman (1994 25) states that "crossing boundaries involves encountering difference, entering into territory in which we are unfamiliar and, to some significant extent therefore, unqualified." A teacher's willingness to engage with learning at the boundary can make the difference between an out-of-field teacher delivering an inspiring mathematics class, and an out-of-field teacher who actively builds new knowledge because he or she takes seriously the learning contract between teacher and student.

However, it is important to recognize the continuity between in-field and out-of-field contexts when ascertaining feelings of "out-of-field"-ness. Teaching is defined by more than just the demands of the subject. "I teach students, not the subject" is a common declaration of secondary teachers. Knowledge of and care for the learner are part of a teacher's 'toolkit.' In addition, knowledge of how to use curriculum, manage a group of learners, deal with junior versus senior learners, deal with parents, and participate as part of a teaching team is generic in nature, and is part of the broader field of education. However, the nature of a subject may change the dynamic of relationship with students (Darby 2009). The teacher's expectations of student behavior and normal mode of relating with students can become compromised such that a once confident teacher is made to feel incompetent. So while it is hoped that an out-of-field teacher maintains some degree of continuity through a knowledge base that underpins all teaching, even this seemingly "generic" knowledge can be surprisingly affected by the practices and demands of the subject.

Learning at the Boundaries

According to Griffiths and Guile (2003), "Crossing boundaries requires construction or transformation of new knowledge, identities and skills rather than only taking advantage of constructions transported from other contexts." They are not simple transfers occurring in one-time, one-sided transitions, but are ongoing, two-sided actions and interactions between contexts (Akkerman and Bakker 2011). An adaptable teacher transforms and transports knowledge from one subject to another. Their learning involves both transforming current knowledge from their in-field teaching practice so that it becomes applicable to their out-of-field teaching, as well as the construction of new knowledge. This new knowledge may or may not be brought back to their in-field subject depending on how flexible that knowledge is.

A boundary arises when a move from one field of practices and knowledge to another results in discontinuity (Akkerman and Bakker 2011). The emphasis here is on the resultant discontinuity that arises for the individual "rather than sociocultural diversity per se" (Akkerman and Bakker 2011, 21). According to this view, for out-of-field teachers, a boundary exists when the differences between the practices and perspectives required to teach the subject are "discontinuous." Such discontinuities can be overcome through a process of "reestablishing action or interaction" (2011, 5), leading to learning, and which ultimately leads to identity development.

Teachers can be seen to utilize boundary objects to support negotiation between subjects. As support mechanisms, these boundary objects act as bridges between in-field and out-of-field spaces. Star and Griesemer (1989) describes boundary objects as bridges or anchors between "intersecting social worlds." In relation to his work on communities of practice, Wenger describes boundary objects as "forms of reification around which communities of practice can organize their interconnections" (Wenger 1998, 105). They refer to the object of learning for teachers, and can be human or non-human, and come in the form of artifacts (tools), discourses (as a common language), or processes that allow coordination of actions (Wenger 1998). Boundary objects are central to professional identity development because they improve the likelihood of learning through the boundary crossing event.

To illustrate the learning that can take place as teachers negotiate boundaries between subjects, I draw on the work of Akkerman and Bakker (2011). In their analysis of the boundary-crossing literature, they discern four dialogical learning mechanisms of boundaries: identification, coordination, reflection, and transformation. "Identification" refers to learning that involves determining relationships between the practices of each site. This identification dialogical process can be called *othering* in the sense that it emphasizes "encountering and reconstructing the boundary, without necessarily overcoming discontinuities" (Akkerman and Bakker, 2011, 12). Learning arises out of recognizing and appreciating the different practices and identities. "Coordination" refers to learning at the boundary as coordination of objects. Overcoming the boundary involves establishing continuity, in order to "[facilitate] future and effortless movement between different sites" (Akkerman and Bakker 2011, 13). "Reflection" emphasizes the potential of the boundary to enhance reflection on practice that can lead to a new construction of identity that can inform future practices. The boundary crossing is seen to play a role in "coming to realize and explicate differences between practices and thus to learn something new about their own and others' practices" (13–14). "Transformation" often involves some confrontation that arises as a result of the intersection of social worlds. This confrontation can lead to a reconsideration of practice. A process involved is recognizing a shared problem space where, using Star and Griesemer's (1989) original conceptualization, boundary objects act as mediating artifacts. "Transforming current practices . . . is motivated by and directed toward the problem space that binds the intersecting practice together" (17). The "boundaries and crossing of boundaries mediate a deliberate target of change" (17).

ILLUSTRATING DISCONTINUITIES AND LEARNING POSSIBILITIES FOR OUT-OF-FIELD TEACHERS

I use the above mechanisms as a framework for exploring the learning potential for out-of-field teachers. I will refer to the mechanisms in the following way: Identification of the discontinuities experienced by teachers, coordination of boundary objects that assist in negotiating boundaries, reflection on practice and identity, and transformation of identity and practices.

Data Collection

In 2009 I undertook a pilot study exploring the issues around teaching out-of-field. The study involved single individual semistructured interviews (Hitchcock and Hughes 1989) with twenty-three teachers, administrators, and support staff from three rural and regional schools. Teacher interviews focused on their out-of-field teaching experiences, why they felt they were out-of-field, and the support mechanism that they have drawn on. Teachers were selected on the basis that they had taught mathematics or science at some point in their teaching career. Interviews with a principal or support staff provided information about the broader context. In the interviews, probing was used to establish the meanings of questions and responses (Fontana and Frey 2005). The interviews relied purely on self-report, although there was some corroboration as interviewees confirmed the stories of other interviewees. Given that the data was generated through only a single interview of about fifty to sixty minutes, this analysis provides a snapshot of individual's experiences rather than providing a comprehensive analysis of the context and complex interactions between actors within the school's communities of practice. However, for the purpose of the analysis presented in this chapter, the individual interviews provided some insight into teachers' immediate orientations toward the subjects they have taught. While discussions on teachers' feeling of "confidence and competence" are potentially threatening, teachers were assured that their interviews were confidential and findings presented anonymously. The following discussion draws on interviews with teachers who could elaborate on the *process* of moving into an out-of-field subject, that is, the boundary crossing process, the discontinuities, the processes of learning, and identity shifts.

Three Victorian rural or regional secondary schools were involved in the study (School A, School B, and School C). Strategic sampling (Neumann 2003) was used to select schools based on school type (Prep–Year 12, or Year 7–12), and rurality (rural or regional). School A and B were rural schools offering Prep–Year 12. At the time of the research School A had an enrolment of 142 students and School B had 220 students. School A was in a predominantly wheat-growing area and serviced mainly a farming community. School B had students from both town and farming communities. School C was in a major regional town, offered Years 7–12 only, and had an enrolment of 732 students. At the time of the research, School C was undergoing an amalgamation of two campuses into a single site.

Data from three teachers of mathematics are included here as short snapshots of their out-of-field experience, two from School A and one from School B. In order to explore the potential for learning at the boundary between subjects, three teachers who have had positive experiences were selected, at varying stages of career. In constructing the snapshots, I rely mostly on carefully selected excerpts from the interview transcripts that demonstrate their rationale for teaching out-of-field, the discontinuity, and impact on their learning, practice and identity.

Table 1.1 provides details on the three teachers: qualifications, subjects they have taught throughout their teaching career as identified during the interviews, and their in-field and out-of-field subject areas. "In-field teaching" refers to the subjects for whom teachers had undergraduate and teaching qualifications; "out-of-field teaching" refers to those subjects for whom teachers did not have undergraduate and teaching qualifications. The bolded subjects indicate where teachers disagreed with these labels.

Teacher 1: Seral

Seral was a graduate teacher who chose to teach mathematics even though it is technically out-of-field. Seral experienced a high degree of success

Table 1.1 Participants' teaching experience, qualifications and self-assessment of in-field or out-of-field

Name	Code	Yrs	Qualifications	In-Field Teaching	Out-of-Field Teaching
SERAL	A4	1	B.A. (Hons), GDE[1] (Humanities, Psychology methods)	Psychology (11, 12)#	Math (7)*
SIMEON	A5	20	Dip Teach (Math major, English minor); B.Ed. (4th yr) (Math, Computers methods)	Primary teacher	Math (7)
KEVIN	B4	34	B.Econ, GDE (Economics, History methods)	Economics (11, 12); Commerce (11, 12); Geography (7-8); Australian Studies (7-9)	**Math (VCAL[2])**

#Year level in parentheses
*Bolded subjects are where teachers have self-assessed themselves differently to the technical definition.
[1]Graduate Diploma of Education.
[2]Victorian Certificate of Applied Learning.

with mathematics at high school. As a result, she felt capable of teaching mathematics and did not *feel* out-of-field. Restrictions to teaching methods imposed by her teaching qualifications are negated by her own self-efficacy—being "good at it" and "comfortable" with the content is central to whether she feels in-field or out-of-field.

> [19][1] I was interested in doing Maths as a method for my DipEd anyway, but I technically wasn't able to, but I did a lot of it in school, so I was keen to teach Maths anyway. So I was glad that I was able to get some Maths classes. [23] In Year 12 I did Methods and Specialist (middle and advanced Mathematics), so I pretty much went as high as you could get. So I felt that I certainly had enough qualifications to teach. At least junior Maths in schools, even though I didn't do much Maths in uni. [25] I guess I just felt like I knew enough about Maths, and was proficient enough, particularly from the 7–10 level that I could teach it. Even though I haven't technically done Maths as a method for my DipEd. [27] I like teaching it; I like the sort of the structure you get of teaching Maths . . . [122] To be honest, I think the method training gets more credit than it should . . . It's certainly helpful, but I don't think any subject should be ruled out just because you haven't done it as a method. I find it easy enough to move between subject areas. So maybe you would have a few other ideas if you did it as a method. But I don't think you're too overly disadvantaged if you don't.

In addition, she receives support from her mother, who is a highly successful specialist mathematics teacher, who was employed as a mathematics coach by the education department for a number of years. She also cites a number of other support mechanisms that enable her to feel confident and competent in her teaching: supportive teaching staff at the school and access to and development of a number of resources. As a result of these factors, she feels in-field teaching mathematics, even though technically out-of-field.

> [30] Well the textbook's telling you what you have to teach specifically. So it's easy to follow the VELS. And everything we have studied I remember how to do so I felt confident. [32] I try and mix it up a bit with group work and a bit of computer work and things like that, but I probably just stick to the standard. You know, showing stuff on the whiteboard and then get them to do exercises most of the time. But, yeah, I try and explore different ways if I can, if I come up with any ideas. And that's probably one of the only areas that I try and seek help for, is just to get different ideas so I'm changing it up a bit. [34] I've got a mentor, being my first year and just a senior Maths teacher here, so she's very helpful . . . I sometimes call my mum 'cause she's done heaps of Maths teaching in her time. So I ask her for ideas, mainly just ask people for their ideas. But also I've just been able to collect heaps of resources from

different areas that give me ideas. [70] . . . I enjoy Maths because I find it easy to teach in a way . . . [156] I would describe myself . . . I would say Psychology and Maths. Just because those are the two subjects I teach. And, even though I did humanities as a method, I wouldn't mention it at this stage. No, I would definitely describe myself as both. [124] I think the one area that I'd feel out of field would be Science. It's something I didn't enjoy at school at all, didn't do much of. [126] I just wouldn't feel comfortable with the content that I'd have to teach and the various practical exercises that you would have to. So I'd feel I have to work a lot to be able to get good at it. And I'd sort of be teaching myself along the way.

Teaching outside of her method areas seems unproblematic to Seral, where her learning appears to be an unfolding map where she relies on her cognitive abilities to navigate her way through, one step ahead of the students.

[134] [Competency needed to teach outside of a method area] you need just general intelligence is just helpful in a way because technically you really only have to be one lesson ahead of the students . . . As long as you're capable of being able to teach yourself before you have to teach the kids I feel like that's all that's really necessary. Obviously it would be ideal if you didn't have to do that, but I think that's all you really need.

Teacher 2: Simeon

Simeon is a primary-trained teacher (5–12 year olds) with experience as a classroom generalist teacher, as well as mathematics specialist in the primary years, teaching mathematics to various year levels between Years 2–6. Due to a shortage of qualified mathematics teachers available to teach the junior secondary classes, Simeon was asked to take a Year 7 class. Simeon described his motivation for undertaking further studies to qualify him as a Mathematics specialist.

[95] Mathematics I feel very comfortable with. [103] I did my fourth year . . . to find newer, better ways. Because I think you can get stuck in an environment . . . A disadvantage of teaching [in] rural schools is often . . . you're "the Grade 4–6 person" to most kids and you don't get a chance to change . . . So probably you think, "I'll stick to the safe way, I'll keep doing it the same way." If it works for the majority that's fine . . . but it probably comes to the point where you think, well maybe I can do things a little better.

Simeon described teaching in the secondary context after years teaching in the primary context, recognizing that primary mathematics is a richer context and more focused on core competencies for which flexible planning is important.

> [34] [Primary teaching is] more children-teacher based, you get a better chance to develop more of a relationship with the kids. Your day is not as structured. Secondary I see as really subject-orientated, whereas in primary you adapt to what's happening and you're flexible. You've got more freedom in the fact that, yes, if you don't do it now, you can do it later. Whereas, secondary, well, that's your Mathematics lesson for the day, and you can't diversify. [38] Probably in primary mathematics you've got to do a lot more ground-work . . . You're probably not isolating the different parts of the Mathematics curriculum, more like integrating them. Whereas, if you get a Year 7 text book, well you've got Chapter 1 is this topic, and Chapter 2 is that topic—so you're more topic-based in the secondary part, whereas you've got more chance to intermingle those concepts in the primary part—probably because you've got the freedom—you've got the timetable freedom. . . [48] I teach the Year 7s but I've also had them in Year 5 and 6. We've built up [their problem solving skills] so it's probably less visuals around the room [in secondary classrooms]. They've seen all the problem-solving strategies [in primary school].

He felt out-of-field not because of the content, but because of the different pedagogical practices that are expected at the secondary level: how to teach the more complex concepts, dealing with teenage students, use of a text-book, and timetable constraints.

> [117] It's probably the way you deal with kids. The content wasn't a worry because my initial studies were mathematics and we did mathematics up to Year 12. It was probably just how you deal with the kids, so they're 13, 14-year-olds, they're not 8 and 9 year olds, so strategies that work with an 8 and 9 don't work with a 13-year-old. [147] The textbook was a bit daunting at first, because that becomes your bible; it becomes a lot more prescriptive. Whereas primary, you've got an overall view of what you're going to put in to the year, but . . . you can sort of vary it a little bit if something pops up. Whereas these are the ten chapters you've got to cover; and you've got five lessons a week. [149] Last semester we had last two lessons on a Friday and I think the last thing most kids want to do on a Friday is Mathematics, so that was a challenge to keep them interested, motivated.

With support from teachers from the secondary school, Simeon has gained insights into student learning that has influenced his practice. His final comment points to the potential for enrichment of practice within his in-field space as a result of the out-of-field experience,

[119] Probably asking [125] how you deal with teenagers that really don't want to do something. [131] [I've had to learn] people-management skills. Managing their learning, behavior and attitudes. 'Cause some of the issues you have with 13, 14, 15-year-olds, you don't have with 9 and 10-year-olds . . . emotional and social and peer start to kick in in your teenage years. [99] [I've changed] in how I do it. Because if you come from a strong Mathematics background especially when you're starting off, it's sometimes hard to work out why kids aren't getting it. Because you think it's easy . . . so I think you need sometimes to take a step back and work out what they aren't getting . . . I've got to try and do as many different ways to help them. [135] A lot of the problems come because they haven't got the grounding. Like if there's big gaps there. [137] It's probably made me more aware of what some kids need to be guided toward and sometimes they're lacking that, so you probably put extra work into making sure that they know all this stuff before you get [to secondary school].

Teacher 3: Kevin

Kevin was a mature teacher with 34 years teaching experience who was willing to take on a new challenge teaching Victorian Certificate of Applied Learning (VCAL) Mathematics to small groups of Year 10 students. As an applied Mathematics course, he has drawn on his own experiences of using Mathematics in everyday life.

[52] Oh, it's just a new discipline, completely new discipline. I mean you are talking about the concepts [54] and methodology. I'm not a trained Mathematics teacher, and obviously there are different ways of delivering the content, and so I'm just relying on my experience, which is drawn from my traditional teaching areas, and I apply and adapt that to the new area. And I believe it's worked successfully . . . [56] But there's always that, you know, how would a qualified Mathematics teacher of some years' experience approach this? So you're really relying on your nous, your innate experience . . . [64] I was told that it was an applied form of learning, an applied Mathematics and you could use real life examples, and I thought, then okay if that's the case, then I can draw on my experience and my learning experience and life experience, and come up with activities which would not only reflect this but at the same time benefit the kids and further their education. [60] Something they could relate to. Because . . . I think these kids would have struggled with Pythagoras or trigonometry, which is a pretty abstract form of Mathematics and probably would have been too challenging for them. So my aim is to develop units that apply to real life situations; and at the same time equip them with some skills.

Having crossed the boundary into mathematics teaching after years of teaching his in-field subjects, commerce and economics, Kevin recognized that efficiency can lead to feelings of comfort, which can make movement across boundaries more daunting.

> [50] [When picking up an out of-field subject after thirty years of teaching] I think the challenges are probably created because over a period of time you become settled in the areas for which you are qualified and feel comfortable. Then suddenly, you find years later, perhaps you are moving into another area, it is a challenge. But I think that's what teaching is all about, a challenge, and certainly if you're working in a bush school I think you've got to be fairly adaptable and where possible try and accommodate the needs of the school, more so the needs of the students. And I believe I do it competently and I think the school would say that. [124] Because you can get into a comfort zone, I guess, and stay there. But if you move into a totally new area you've got to be obviously more resourceful and you've certainly got to adapt.

Kevin has found that such challenges can lead to its own rewards. Being a late-career boundary crosser means that he has an appreciation for the capabilities required to move between subjects: adaptability, flexibility in methodologies, confidence in your abilities, and the continuity of relationships with students across subjects. Authentic engagement with the boundary leads to rewards, such as seeing student learning from a new perspective.

> [102] You've got to be open-minded, confident in your own ability to do that . . . and if you haven't got that confidence from the outset, then obviously you are going in very much behind the eight ball. . . . Having a rapport with the students is terribly important. . . . [104] You apply that and use that to further your educational outcomes. Respect for the students, respect their abilities and if you've got that common respect then obviously I think you are able to take on board new areas of learning that may be outside your comfort zone. [126] [I have learned about] the way kids learn. You look back and say "Gee, perhaps I should step back a bit" . . . I'm learning at the same time. I've never done that before. So I'm learning from that point of view, I enjoy watching the kids learn and how they learn.

While there was initial apprehension, experience, support, and acknowledgement by others has provided Kevin with a renewed sense of his own capability:

> [44] I've generally found that [when] you are coming into a new area for which you haven't been trained, there's a bit of apprehension at first, but once you get your teeth into it, and with the support you receive

from the school, you can approach it more confidently. [48] But certainly I've really enjoyed it and of course in the first year it was audited and that probably—hehe, gosh only the first year and it's being audited and there's a process involved there, but it came through with flying colors. And that tick of approval certainly was very helpful. [84] It's fantastic; this school really thrives in terms of professional development and support. I mean, if there are any issues you've got any number of staff that would be only too willing to help. It is a small staff that is very collegiate—it's very supportive and the principal is very big on professional development.

REDEFINING OUT-OF-FIELD TEACHING AS OPPORTUNITIES FOR LEARNING

These three teachers are boundary crossers, although they present three different experiences of being out-of-field. Seral is a graduate psychology and humanities teacher who decided to pursue mathematics teaching, which is technically out-of-field; however, a history of success in the subject and a strong support network enables her to identify with the label of mathematics teacher as much as her in-field subject of psychology. On the other hand, Kevin is an end-of-career economics and commerce teacher who decided to accept the challenge of teaching mathematics out-of-field. Unlike Seral, who has had no chance to become established in her field of psychology before teaching out-of-field, Kevin had over thirty years teaching in-field before crossing the boundary into this applied Mathematics class; therefore, his crossing of the boundary between subjects involved both a shift from efficiency and an opportunity to do something different. Simeon's out-of-field experience was not between subjects, but the same subject at a different year level. Simeon was also late-career, and crossing the boundary from primary to secondary mathematics teaching presented challenges in terms of student behavior and demands of the subject culture that differed from his in-field context, as well as new insights into how best to prepare students in the lower years.

The four mechanisms of learning described by Akkerman and Bakker (2011) present a methodological framework to explore these experiences.

Identification of Discontinuities

Discontinuities were present for each teacher; however, they were identified to varying degrees. Seral did not identify with the discontinuity that might be present for a teacher with less support or positive background experiences. Her disposition toward boundary was one of pursuing an interest, therefore, the challenge was invited and considered surmountable. Discontinuity lies in the didactic knowledge of how to make the subject more interesting and challenging for students, however, her confidence and perceived competence in her content knowledge borne from a history of positive experiences with the subject means that her professional identity embraces the role of mathematics teacher. There appears to be a high degree of learning occurring as she draws from her support network. Interestingly she indicated science as an area she would definitely feel out-of-field in because of less positive experiences as a learner. The content and practices of the *other* subject were perceived as too discontinuous with her knowledge, skills and interests. "Being just one step ahead" of the students would require too high an investment, which suggests that proficiency in teaching for Seral requires more than simply reading the textbook and knowing the procedures.

The boundary for Kevin was between mainstream education to an applied learning mathematics context. This boundary crossing might have been vastly different if the move had been into a mainstream mathematics classroom with more challenging content. Within this applied learning context, the typical academic approach to his commerce and economics subject teaching through the use of textbooks and normal classroom teaching is discontinuous with the need to develop practical and hands-on learning experiences in contexts that students recognize. Discontinuity arises out of a background of dealing predominantly with students in a mixed mainstream classroom, and limited opportunity to cater specifically to the type of learning required in applied learning classes.

The boundary for Simeon was between primary and secondary learning environments. Continuity lay in the content as the mathematics presented little challenge. In-field for Simeon was primary mathematics, and out-of-field was secondary mathematics. Discontinuity lay in the pedagogical practices, student learning needs and behavior, and culture of teaching mathematics at that secondary level. Discontinuity arose out of his background in building learning environments and use of pedagogical practices at the primary level that are discontinuous with those expected at the secondary level. Learning therefore focuses on learning practices commensurate with the subject culture (Darby 2009) within secondary year levels.

Akkerman and Bakker (2011) use the term *othering* to denote difference, which can determine membership or not to a community of practice. Unlike Kevin and Simeon, who had strong identifies in relation to their in-field areas and who saw clearly the boundary as they shifted into new demands on practice, Seral felt legitimized in her positioning within the mathematics teaching community. Differences in the positioning of the three teachers lay in level of teaching experience, with Seral building her teacher expertise while teaching in-field and out-of-field at the same time. For Seral, qualifications are the only measure of in-field-ness, and she distances herself from these as determinants of her identity and self-efficacy in her teaching. Kevin and Simeon, however, have qualifications and years of experience to construct strong identities in relation to their in-field areas: for Kevin it is teaching commerce and economics to mainstream students, and for Simeon it is generalist primary teacher with a specialization in mathematics. Identifying and learning from difference in perspectives and practices was a more intense process for Simeon and Kevin.

Coordination of Boundary Objects

Boundary objects provide a bridge between social worlds, or fields. All teachers utilized boundary objects to negotiate the boundary between their in-field and out-of-field teaching. For learning to occur through coordination of these objects there needs to be a communicative connection between the diverse practices or perspectives that are established by objects that are shared by people within multiple worlds. In the case of the three teachers, curriculum documents and syllabuses are recognizable within all subject areas and levels of schooling. The textbook, however, while a boundary object for Seral, was not for Simeon or Kevin. For Seral, the textbook was common to psychology and mathematics, although effective use of these objects depended on her perception of the cultural demands or traditions in each subject, that is, use of the psychology textbook as a resource to support teaching compared with use of the mathematics textbook more or less a guide to practice. For Simeon, however, the textbook was a foreign object that was not used in his in-field area, primary mathematics teaching, and it actually presented as a discontinuity that led to new insights into other ways of teaching mathematics. For Kevin, the absence of the textbook provided freedom to be creative and resourceful, and have a greater degree of autonomy in curriculum development. Kevin's general unit and lesson planning skills acted as boundary objects that enabled a degree of continuity in practice and sense of self as a capable teacher. So, Seral's textbooks and Kevin's planning skills enabled translation between different worlds because they entailed both an intersubjective ground (being understood in both worlds), and a diversity of possible understandings (flexibility enabling application or use in both worlds).

People were also important boundary objects for the three teachers. All referred to colleagues from the out-of-field community as key resources. Simeon spoke to secondary mathematics teachers, Kevin indicated a supportive and collegiate environment, and Seral had a mentor (a requirement for graduate teachers) who was in her out-of-field area and also called on other mathematics teachers at her school and family members who taught the subjects. Apart from the mentor, which was a provision of support, the colleagues were actively sought out by the teachers, and were important in assisting them to overcome and learn through the discontinuity. For example, Simeon sought assistance in how to deal with teenage students, and Seral sought interesting activities that moved her away from the more typical textbook teaching approach. While there is dialogue between the teacher and these boundary objects, the evidence suggests that the focus is on building efficacy of the teacher to reconcile differences between practices, rather than building bridges between the practices of people within different worlds.

Akkerman and Bakker (2011) state that boundary objects can increase boundary permeability, so that a boundary crosser is not even aware of different practices simply because actions and interactions run smoothly without costs and deliberate choice. In addition, permeability can be enhanced where there is repeated crossing of different practices. This is an argument for placing teachers in an out-of-field subject multiple times to maximize re-establishment of competence and confidence. Kevin mentioned this when he identified the initial apprehension that accompanies a move into a new area, but that confidence builds 'once you get your teeth into it' and with support. Being immersed in the new field, understanding the landscape, working out what can be translated from one's current set of knowledge, skills and attitudes, constructing new knowledge sets, and being supported in these processes, are determinants of boundary permeability. For Seral, however, there was immediate permeability because in her mind the boundary presented limited discontinuity because of her strong sense of herself as a proficient mathematician and her limited teaching experience generally.

Reflection on Practice

This mechanism emphasizes the potential of the boundary to enhance reflection on practice. Learning about themselves and their practice was one of the advantages teachers associated with out-of-field teaching. While all three teachers were approached and invited to teach the subjects, they all accepted the challenge willingly because it was within the realms of what they considered possible for themselves (explored further in the following section), but also because they recognized benefits to themselves professionally.

Seral volunteered to teach mathematics because she felt capable, despite being unable to include mathematics as one of her methods. For her, teaching mathematics provided an opportunity to pursue an interest, something that she thought she could do well and enjoy. In terms of reflection, she has less to gain from this experience than the other two teachers because, in some ways, she is at a baseline in her longitudinal experience of teaching. For her, just knowing the content and how to teach it is the main requirement, 'being one step ahead of the students' is enough. She recognizes her practice as aligning with her view of the mathematics teaching Discourse, which, in her view does not need to be understood through tertiary qualifications.

Both Kevin and Simeon saw opportunities for learning when one moves out of their comfort zone. Kevin perceived teaching to by typified by 'challenge,' requiring a teacher to be adaptable and resourceful. Simeon appreciated that each day is different and enjoyed the diversity of teaching.

Kevin's belief in the need to respect students' abilities regardless of the subject opened up possibilities for him to gain a renewed appreciation of the ways students learn. Working in this applied learning environment with students who typically are aliens within a mainstream environment where they tend to exhibit problem behavior and experience limited success, has enabled Kevin to 'step back' and reconsider his understanding of how students learn.

Similarly, Simeon mentioned that the boundary has prompted him to 'step back' and see students in this new context in two different ways. The first is that he realized the need to develop new ways of teaching the more difficult mathematical concepts so that students understood them, whereas previously his teaching of concepts to the younger year levels was not so problematic. The second is that he became aware of problems that some Year 7 students experienced due to gaps in their mathematical understanding. His teaching in the lower-year levels has changed to more adequately prepare students for their future studies.

Boland and Tenkasi (1995) concluded that 'perspective making' and 'perspective taking' are ways of making visible the perspectives of others in order to facilitate shared understanding. In education, teaching is largely an activity involving a teacher and their students, although interaction between teachers occurs at an organizational and planning level. Perspective-making (developing more coherent meaning structures as individual and groups work together) is not evident in my data, although it is possible where teachers work in teams and there is a requirement to develop new perspectives together. The more traditional mode of teachers working independently in the classroom as represented by the participants of this research presents opportunities for perspective-taking (seeing other peoples' perspective). Both Kevin and Simeon have been able to gain a glimpse across the boundary at practices and perspectives that might have remained peripheral or even 'off radar.' Simeon has come to appreciate the various constraints imposed on teachers by the structure of secondary school: timetabling constraints such as mathematics lessons on Friday afternoons, set lesson times and frequency; inability to diversify and link with other subject areas; and different demands and conditions for developing relationship with students. Through reflecting on these distinctions, he has differentiated the practices and perspectives of secondary and primary teaching activities. For Simeon, perspective taking has involved examining his assumptions about teaching as he came to appreciate and learn from colleagues about how to deal with student behavior and learning difficulties. He, therefore, reached the point of imagining the perspective of others within the community of secondary mathematics teachers. Whether this has been a dialogical process is not clear as the data only shows the taking of perspective in one direction, toward the out-of-field teacher. True perspective-taking is where differences between all actors involved in the interaction are recognized, acknowledged and valued.

Transformation of Identity and Practices

Akkerman and Bakker (2011, 17) stated that "boundaries and crossing of boundaries mediate a deliberate target of change." All three teachers accepted the challenge of teaching out-of-field willingly because it was deemed possible to learn the necessary content and teaching approaches. After some initial apprehension, and with support, coordination of boundary objects, and successful experiences, they have broadened their identity to encompass the new role. So while Kevin progresses tentatively, wondering how a 'real' mathematics teacher might approach the teaching of some concepts, reflection on practice transforms his understanding of students and learning. Simeon's transformation lies in his keener understanding of what students need to be successful in mathematics, as well as a stronger appreciation for what it means to be a secondary teacher. Seral, while 'change' is not really the issue as she transitions into teaching, she resists the technical label imposed by her qualifications and appears to be experimenting with what Ibarra (2009) calls 'provisional' versions of a new self on her way to developing a fully elaborated professional identity that includes teacher of mathematics.

CONCLUSIONS AND FUTURE RESEARCH

This analysis has demonstrated that, when crossing subject boundaries, beginning and early career teachers who are still establishing themselves may face challenges that are different to challenges faced by mid or late career teachers who have established and reified versions of themselves. Certainly research has shown that teaching out-of-field can lead to a compromising of 'teaching competence' and disruption to a teacher's identity, self-efficacy, and well-being (Pillay, Goddard, and Wilss 2005; Ingersoll 2002). However, my analysis has demonstrated that such boundary crossings also present learning opportunities for the teacher if there is space to identify the discontinuities, sufficient boundary objects to re-establish action and interactions in the out-of-field space, reflection that draws on the perspectives of members of the community, and there is time to build on experience in order to increase the permeability of the boundary.

Research also shows that out-of-field teaching can place additional strain on graduate teachers as they contend with the added pressure of planning and implementing curriculum for an unfamiliar subject (McConney and Price 2009). Watson's (2006) study of early career science teachers, in fact, found that the greatest attrition rates were with beginning teachers. However, this analysis of Seral's experience demonstrates that when adequate support is provided, when the teacher' self-efficacy is strong, and the discontinuity between the two social worlds appear surmountable, then teaching out-of-field can present opportunities for new teachers to establish flexible professional identities.

While opportunities for teacher learning may exist, I have not taken into account the effect of this boundary-crossing period on student learning. Reliance on more traditional and less effective teaching approaches can be the default for teachers who teach without the passion to research and seek out engaging and enriching activities or contemporary approaches to teaching. There is also a question of whether they achieve a deep appreciation of the epistemological basis of the subject and the culture within which the discipline is practiced. Further, lacking a coherent understanding of the concepts and course structure can lead to disjointed or ineffective learning practices. However, for the teachers included here, it appears that in placing them into otherwise unfilled positions, the school has benefited from a teacher that has a renewed and deeper understanding of how to adequately prepare his primary students for secondary mathematics learning, a graduate teacher who has enough interest in mathematics and has enough success in the subject to seek out and develop interesting curriculum materials and undertake professional development in the area, and a teacher who has an appreciation for the diversity of students and a transformed sense of how students learn.

A final point is about the nature of the 'field' and its relationship to discontinuities that can arise at the boundary between fields. In each case, the field was the subject, but it needs to be seen as "subject-in-context" such that the teachers' moves were to: the same context, an applied learning context, or different year level or primary/secondary contexts. Seral's case was perhaps the most typical where the type of students and context are the same in the in-field and out-of-field subjects, although her case was somewhat atypical given her perceived strong background in mathematics. The data demonstrates that context can be the locus of discontinuity, rather than subject matter. Being attentive to where discontinuity lies is important when devising a program of support. Conversely, identifying continuity between fields is an important step in identifying boundary objects that can assist in re-establishing action.

So, rather than assuming a deficit position toward out-of-field teaching, my approach to the issue recognizes the possibilities for identity expansion and a reconceptualization of practice if teachers are supported at their point of need. Knowing this discontinuity can inform the focus of support in the enhancement of learning possibilities. This exploration of discontinuities associated with boundary crossings has the potential to highlight the black spots (problematic areas) and blind spots (unknowns) in pre-service teacher education and in-service professional development.

As a methodological framework, a classification of learning mechanisms has the potential to inform approaches to investigating issues around out-of-field teaching. This analysis has highlighted a need to gain better understanding of differences between out-of-field graduate and experienced teachers. Also, without examining the actual practices of these teachers it was difficult to ascertain if the out-of-field teaching experience resulted in deep learning and a transformation of practices. Future research should take account of interactions between multiple actors, including students, teachers and school leadership. For example, research could examine students' learning and attitudes when taught by in-field and out-of-field teachers, school leadership approaches to assigning and supporting teachers, or teacher-in-action where classroom practice is accounted for. Longitudinal studies that monitor change over time have great potential in understanding the effects of out-of-field teaching, mechanisms for learning, and factors within the community of practice that ensure safe and productive boundary crossings. Such research advances theoretical understandings of the boundaries between fields, and how to afford those mechanisms that lead to learning and identity development,

NOTES

Linda Hobbs has published previously as Linda Darby.

The funding for this research was provided by The National Centre of Science, Information and Communication Technology, and Mathematics Education for Rural and Regional Australia (SiMERR).

1. Denotes paragraph from transcript

REFERENCES

Akkerman, Sanne F., and Bakker, Arthur. 2011. "Boundary crossing and boundary objects" *Review of Educational Research* 81: 132–169.

Beijaard, Douwe, Meijer, Paulien C., and Verloop, Nico. 2004. "Reconsidering research on teachers' professional identity" *Teaching and Teacher Education* 20: 107–128.

Boland, Richard J., and Tenkasi, Ramkrishnan V. 1995. "Perspective making and perspective taking in communities of knowing," Organization Science 6: 350–372.

Darby, Linda. 2010. *Subject cultures and pedagogy: Comparing secondary mathematics and science.* Saarbrücken, Germany: LAP Lambert Academic Publishing.

Connelly, F. Michael, and Clandinin, D. Jean. 1999. *Shaping a professional identity: Stories of experience.* New York, NY: Teachers College Press.

Engeström, Yrjo, Engeström, Ritva, and Kärkkäinen, Merja. 1995. "Polycontextuality and boundary crossing in expert cognition: Learning and problem solving in complex work activities" *Learning and Instruction* 5: 319–336.

Engeström, Yrjo. 1987. *Learning by expanding. An activity-theoretical approach to developmental research.* Helsinki, Finland: Orienta-Konsultit.

Fontana, Andrea, and Frey, James H. 2005. The Interview. In *The Sage Handbook of Qualitative Research,* ed. Norman K. Denzin and Yvonna S. Lincoln, 695–727. London: Sage.

Gee, James P. 2010. *An introduction to discourse analysis: theory and method.* London: Routledge.

Goodson, Ivor. 1993. *School subjects and curriculum change* (3rd ed.). Bristol: Falmer Press.

Griffiths, Toni and Guile, David A. 2003. "Connective model of learning: the implications for work process knowledge," *European Educational Research Journal* 2: 56–73.

Hitchcock, Graham, and Hughes, David. 1989. *Research and the teacher*. London: Routledge.

Hobbs, Linda. 2012. "Teaching 'out-of-field' as a boundary-crossing event: Factors shaping teacher identity." *International Journal of Science and Mathematics Education*. Online first

Ingersoll, Richard M. 2002. *Out-of-field teaching, educational inequity, and the organization of schools: An exploratory analysis*. Washington, DC: Centre of the Study of Teaching and Policy.

McConney, Andrew and Price, Anne. 2009. *An assessment of the phenomenon of "teaching out-of-field" in WA schools*. Perth: Western Australian College of Teaching.

Neumann, W. Lawrence. 2003. *Social research methods. Qualitative and quantitative approaches*. Boston: Allyn Bacon.

Pillay, Hitendra, Goddard, Ricahrd, and Wilss, Lynn. 2005. "Well-being, burnout and competence: Implications for teachers," *Australian Journal of Teacher Education* 30: 22–33.

Siskin, Lee. S. 1994. *Realms of knowledge: Academic departments in secondary schools*. London: The Falmer Press.

Star, Susan. L. 1989. The structure of ill-structured solutions: Boundary objects and heterogeneous distributed problem-solving. In *Distributed artificial intelligence Vol. II*, ed. Les Gasser and Michael N. Huhns, 37–54. London: Pitman.

Star, Susan L., and Griesemer, James R. 1989. "Institutional ecology, 'translations' and boundary objects: Amateurs and professionals in Berkeley's museum of vertebrate zoology," *Social Studies of Science* 19: 387–420.

Suchman, Lucy. 1994. "Working relations of technology production and use," *Computer Supported Cooperative Work* 2: 21–39.

van Manen, Max. 1982. "Phenomenological pedagogy," *Curriculum Inquiry* 12: 283–299.

van Manen, Max. 1990. *Researching lived experience; Human science for an action sensitive pedagogy*. London: Althouse Press.

Watson, Scott W. 2006. "Novice science teachers: Expectations and experiences," *Journal of Science Teacher Education* 17: 279–290.

Wenger, Etienne. 1998. *Communities of practice: Learning, meaning and identity*. Cambridge: Cambridge University Press.

2 Boundary Objects in Boundary-Spanning

Jacob D. Vakkayil

INTRODUCTION

Many attempts to understand social phenomena have pointed to the importance of "objects" in human action and have striven to incorporate them firmly into their analysis (Law and Singleton 2005). Objects have often been found useful devices for studying social interaction and innovation (Prasad 1993) and in studies of technology, where there have been many attempts at highlighting the importance of materialistic aspects on action (Orlikowski 2007). Objects are treated as central, taken-for-granted entities within communities of practice, and achievement of membership in these communities involves developing capabilities to use them in certain ways (Lave and Wenger 1991). Objects have also been central to studies of information systems development (Wastell 1999, Levina and Vaast 2005) and in management and organization studies (Engeström and Blackler 2005, Bechky 2003b).

In these attempts, the words *objects*, *tools*, and *artifacts* are used to refer to a class of varied entities. Often physical artifacts such as computer systems or networks may be considered as objects, while at other times virtual entities such as software programs and intangible entities such as concepts or theories might also be considered as objects.

> An object is something people (or, in computer science, other objects and programs) act toward and with. Its materiality derives from action, not from a sense of prefabricated stuff or "thing"-ness. So, a theory may be a powerful object. Although it is embodied, voiced, printed, danced, and named, it is not exactly like a car that sits on four wheels. (Star 2010, 603)

In this chapter, such a broad meaning of objects is retained to include "stuff and things, tools, artifacts and techniques, and ideas, stories and memories" (Bowker and Star 2000, 298).

Latour (1992) pointed to the necessity of objects for ensuring lasting and robust social connections. As studies explore complex human action, involving multiple social units far removed by their divergent perspectives and approaches, the study of objects becomes more challenging. Objects are found to travel across communities and interact in ways that are often unpredictable. The fact that they retain a certain amount of commonality across these communities despite vast differences in fundamental perspectives was interesting for keen observers of their action. The necessity of analyzing moving objects across time and space has led to viewing them as *immutable mobiles* (Latour 1987). The concept of "boundary objects" (Star and Griesemer 1989) evolved as a result to further understand the work of such objects that seem to be adaptable to different types of action and yet retain certain commonalities across communities that employ them. Since its introduction, the concept has been popularly applied in a number of domains, including sociology of science, organization and management studies, technology and work, etc.

BOUNDARY OBJECTS

Susan L. Star and James R. Griesemer coined the term "boundary objects" while studying the establishment and development of Berkeley's Museum of Vertebrate Biology from 1907 to 1939 (Star and Griesemer 1989). According to them, boundary objects "are objects which are both plastic enough to adapt to local needs and the constraints of the several parties employing them, yet robust enough to maintain a common identity across sites" (393). They visualized the museum as a boundary object that linked different communities in the society such as university administration, conservation activists, etc. Bowker and Star (2000) elaborate on the features of boundary objects as below:

> They are weakly structured in common use and become strongly structured in individual-site use. These objects may be abstract or concrete . . . Such objects have different meanings in different social worlds but their structure is common enough to more than one world to make them recognizable, a means of translation. (Bowker and Star 2000, 297)

Boundary objects thus help communities to interact profitably toward a purpose that is perceived as useful by each. Further, they might play an important role in coordination of varied perspectives and by agreeing on aspects of meaning that are common enough to enable such coordination. "The creation and management of boundary objects is a key process in developing and maintaining coherence across intersecting communities" (Bowker and Star 2000, 297). Though they possess interpretive flexibility (Bijker, Hughes, and Pinch 1987), they are stabilized enough temporarily to enable meaningful communication and common action.

The idea of boundary objects has been found to be useful in works employing many theoretical perspectives. In studies that utilize the conceptual repertoire of actor-network theory, it is recognized that elements can belong to multiple networks and can undergo translations in each with the resultant attribution of meanings. A focus on boundary objects brings these phenomena to the foreground, enabling greater understanding of the processes involved. In activity theory, human action is conceptualized as mediated by tools of various kinds. These tools can often be shared by multiple activities, and the linking mechanisms involved are interesting avenues of exploration.

In the literature centered on the theme of practice, objects that cross boundaries have been treated as important carriers of knowledge and expertise across communities. According to Wenger (1998, 107), boundary objects are "artefacts, documents, terms, concepts, and other forms of reification around which communities of practice can organize their interconnections." They have four important characteristics. The first is *modularity*, which means that one particular group can cater to a single portion of the overall boundary object and yet the object will be coherent. The second characteristic is *abstraction*. This denotes the commonness that boundary objects possess after the deletion of particularities associated with each group that is involved. The third property is *accommodation*. This means that boundary objects are capable of lending themselves to various activities in different communities. The last property is labeled *standardization*, which implies that there is a prespecified format with regard to the information content of boundary objects. Because of standardization, various groups are able to deal with it locally in an effective manner.

TYPOLOGIES

Star and Griesemer (1989) describe four types of boundary objects. The first type is called *repositories*, which consist of entities ordered and indexed in particular ways. They handle heterogeneity by using a standard indexing or classification system and have the characteristic of modularity. The second category is called *ideal types*. These can fit into more than one context because they are vague or specified very broadly. These include objects such as maps, which are abstracted from complex and diverse sets of information. They can be adapted locally because of intentional nonspecification. The third category consists of objects with *coincident boundaries*. These have different internal contents, although they share similar boundaries. They are useful for aggregation work since they serve to resolve diverse goals across different areas of operation. The last type is labeled *standardized forms*. These are effective for ensuring communication across different contexts and can deal with local variations and uncertainties.

To the above four types, Briers and Chua (2001) added a fifth category, i.e., *visionary objects*. This refers to "conceptual objects that have high levels of legitimacy within a particular community" (Briers and Chua 2001, 242). People respond to them emotively and these objects seem to possess a sacred quality that makes them irresistible. One example is the idea of efficiency of work practices; the precise nature of this is difficult to pin down, but the concept itself is understood widely by managers.

Wenger (2000) proposes another typology delineating three categories. The first is labeled *artifacts* and includes entities such as tools, models, documents, and so forth. Examples include medical records that connect multiple groups such as doctors, nurses, and insurers, and architectural blueprints that enable architects, city planners, and contractors to collaborate. He describes the second category as *discourses*. This points to a common language employed to ensure that people are able to communicate across boundaries and negotiate meanings across communities. He calls the final category *processes*. These include routines and procedures that seek to achieve coordination across various groups.

Other typologies for boundary objects have been suggested in further work on the subject by various authors. Garrety and Badham (2000) differentiated between primary and secondary boundary objects. They classified basic technology used in interaction across communities as primary objects, while further devices such as contracts that facilitated easy communication across communities were treated as secondary boundary objects. Carlile (2002, 2004) differentiated three types of boundaries, namely syntactic, semantic, and pragmatic boundaries, and a good boundary object was conceptualized as one that is effective in crossing three categories of boundaries. Syntactic boundaries focus on the availability of a common syntax to aid information flow across units. Semantic boundaries focus on differing meanings and how boundary objects can aid in the development of common meanings. Pragmatic boundaries focus on the differences of interests, and here, the role of boundary objects would be of help in developing common interests. Levina and Vaast (2005) differentiated between two types of boundary objects. The first is referred to as *designated boundary objects* and indicates those objects that are supposed to serve the function of boundary objects by virtue of their design properties. The second category is called *boundary objects in-use* and signifies objects that have been utilized by diverse groups to support collaborative work. Like typologies of any kind, efforts to categorize boundary objects have helped in making their analysis richer and more nuanced. Zeiss and Groenewegen (2009) observe that the tendency to resort to typologies seems to be more pronounced in management and organization studies, where "the [mere extension of a] typology is seen as a contribution to the literature" (Zeiss and Groenewegen 2009, 95). They note that this is not the case in fields such as science and technology studies and suggest that the importance attached to practical applications of boundary objects in management studies might be an important reason for this.

KEY FOCUS THEMES

The popularity of the concept has resulted in its employment in a large number of studies in multiple fields of inquiry. These studies approach boundary objects with different themes as the focus of their inquiry. In this varied literature, three prominent themes of focus can be identified in the way the functions and usage of boundary objects are approached.

Enabling Coordination

Many studies focus on tools of coordination in organizations as boundary objects. Physical objects of coordination have been identified as boundary objects in a number of studies. Objects such as proposal documents, work plans, flowcharts, and documents outlining objectives can aid in clarifying interdependencies and thus shape the direction of work (Garrety and Badham 2000). Levina and Vaast (2005) explored standardized forms as boundary objects, while Eckert and Boujut (2003) consider spreadsheets and sketches transferred between designers and toolmakers as boundary-crossing objects or intermediary objects. Yakura (2002) focused on Gantt Charts, which facilitate flexible yet robust interpretation of time across units and enable different units to coordinate their activities. They are labeled "temporal boundary objects," and it is pointed out that their narrative quality "distinguishes them from other organizational artifacts and explains some of their unique properties as tools for temporal coordination" (Yakura 2002, 956).

The idea of coordination is particularly evident in object-oriented activities as specified in activity theory. Though the term 'object' has a different meaning in the literature in activity theory, the role of boundary objects has been discussed in many activity-theoretical studies. For example, Engeström, Engeström, and Kärkkäinen (1995) describe the case of interaction between units in an industrial manufacturing plant. When parts do not comply with specifications, a host of problems arise. The dialogue between representatives from both units gave rise to standards that were used as boundary objects that enable better coordination of action.

Aiding Knowledge Flow

A number of studies have highlighted the knowledge component of objects and point to how boundary objects can lead to transfer of knowledge across communities. Carlile's works (2002, 2004) have advanced a number of propositions with this focus. He found that to be effective they should be able to represent different types of knowledge and must be tangible and concrete to enable easy manipulation and problem solving; they must be accessible, evolving over time and absorbing the information necessary for interaction; and they must be specified in a broad, nonspecific manner to be able to adjust to varied information and knowledge needs. His work also examined the evolution of boundary objects in the context of competing influences of challenging and defending parties in times of change. The application of knowledge across occupational communities is influenced by these dynamics.

Focusing on the same attention on knowledge, Bechky (2003a) demonstrate how domain-specific knowledge can be transformed in ways such that it can be used by multiple communities toward a common goal. Studying the activity of production, ways in which boundary objects reduce differences in meaning between various professional teams are explored. Along the same lines, Boland and Tenkasi (1995) declare that "once a visible representation of an individual's knowledge is made available for analysis and communication, it becomes a boundary object and provides a basis for 'perspective taking'" (362). Pawlowski and Robey (2004) examine the process of knowledge brokering between information technology professionals using information systems as boundary objects in a large company engaged in manufacturing and distribution. They found that knowledge brokering was influenced by the structure of the organization and the technical conditions that helped transfer knowledge. Swan et al. (2007) found that treating certain types of knowledge as a boundary object and pursuing it as a desirable goal to achieve might be required in some cases to result in the wider acceptance of the object across communities.

Facilitating Differences in Collaboration

The third focus theme that can be identified in many works relates to how boundary objects facilitate collaboration across significant differences. Large scientific and technical enterprises often involve collaborations of different types of organizations, including communities, firms, social movements, etc. These participants are able to interact despite fundamental differences in orientation and perspectives. Often they share a superordinate goal, and this facilitates minimal collaboration (O'Mahoney and Bechky 2008). Boundary objects contribute to this also by enabling multiple definitions of the way in which this superordinate goal is defined. In Star and Griesemer's original work (Star and Griesemer 1989), multiple objectives seem to drive the groups involved in collaboration for the establishment and development of Berkeley's Museum of Vertebrate Biology. To the curator, the museum was a means of supporting and explaining the theory of evolution by demonstrating how natural selection was influenced by changes in the environment. For conservationists it was a means of preserving the vast flora and fauna of California that was quickly disappearing. To the university administration the project was an opportunity to serve California and its people and to compete with well-known eastern universities.

Fujimura (1992) argued that the ambiguity inherent in boundary objects makes them poor facilitators of consensus across communities. This, however, does not mean that collaboration in various forms is not possible. Henderson (1999) explored engineering design drawings as boundary objects and found that different groups of persons involved in the final construction interpreted the drawings varyingly according to their perspectives, often filling in missing information in ways that were peculiar to their communities. The work of Yakura (2002) on timelines in organizations found that although they seem to be inflexible, they allowed organizational subgroups to employ different assumptions to negotiate and manage project time. Levina and Vaast (2005) also uses the idea of boundary objects to examine how diverse stakeholders collaborate in information systems development. She proposed the idea of the *collective-reflection-in-action cycle* to illustrate how different agents interact in varied ways during the process of design. Lee (2007) also observes that the operation of boundary-negotiating artifacts does not presuppose high levels of coordination. They can function as flexible, empty, and vague support structures for local and collaborative action. D'Adderio (2004) highlights how boundary objects possess the capacity for flexible localization. The same theme is affirmed by Sapsed and Salter (2004) in their study of a global program in a major computing firm. "Boundary objects may provide informational support but denote no intrinsic meaning. They are, in this sense, empty vessels to be filled with whatever is the preferred local beverage." (Sapsed and Salter 2004, 1519)

Changes within communities that use boundary objects can have different types of impact on these objects. While Briers and Chua (2001) identified boundary objects in an organization's accounting system and examined how a network of these is involved in effecting changes within the system, Subrahmanian et al. (2003) explored how existing common grounds for interaction can be disrupted by changes, leading to a debate on the role of existing boundary objects. These again point to how inherent multiplicities of perspectives and differences arising from changes impact and are impacted by boundary objects functioning within the system of interacting units. Often the promise of boundary objects points to possibilities of collaboration without common objectives or common understanding of meanings. The quality of boundary objects in facilitating these differences is one of their most valued characteristics.

BOUNDARY INFRASTRUCTURES IN PRACTICES

The usefulness of boundary objects as an analytical device prompted more complex conceptualizations of intercommunity interactions focusing on objects and material artifacts. Research informed by actor-network theory often explores large-scale collaborative efforts involving a network of scientific and technical objects and how they stabilize over time. Such efforts involve organizations of various types, such as firms, universities, social movements, etc. In these settings focusing on single objects is unlikely to provide a comprehensive and rich picture of what is going on. Realizing this, Engeström (2000) proposes that we should analyze a whole system of tools, instead of analyzing single tools as stand-alone artifacts. Karsten et al. (2001) studied the role of technical specifications of a paper machine delivery project as a boundary object and maintained that a boundary object is always located in a larger system of interacting objects. Many studies of information systems refer to their infrastructural properties that incorporate a large number of individual interacting components and the organizational and social elements that go into their usage as systems that support action (Bowker, Timmermans, and Star 1995; Turner et al. 2006). Star and Ruhleder (1996) define the key characteristics of infrastructure as follows:

- Embeddedness: Infrastructure is embedded in social structures and arrangements of various kinds.
- Transparency: Infrastructure supports work in a transparent yet invisible way and can be repeatedly used without the necessity for reassembly each time it is used.
- Reach or scope: Infrastructure possesses temporal or spatial reach that helps it to be used beyond a single event or practice.
- Learned as part of membership: Usage of infrastructure in communities is learned as a part of the socialization of members into these communities.
- Linked with practice: Infrastructure shapes and is shaped by practices as it is used and worked upon continuously.
- Embodiment of standards: Infrastructures can plug into other infrastructures, tools and objects in a standardized way.
- Built on an installed base: Infrastructures cannot be created on a clean slate. They are affected by the inertia of the base on which they are founded.
- Becomes visible upon breakdown: Infrastructure is normally invisible when it functions as intended, but becomes visible when it breaks down.
- Is fixed in modular increments, not all at once or globally: Infrastructures are complex arrays of objects, and therefore they evolve in a layered manner and never change all at once through hierarchical efforts. Changes involve negotiation and mutual adjustment of multiple objects involved.

This visualization of infrastructures makes it possible to view boundary objects as a constantly evolving setup of multiple artifacts, the old tools continually being modified and new ones created. Along these lines, Bowker and Star (2000) have further developed the idea of boundary objects and proposed what they call *boundary infrastructures*. They speak of boundary infrastructures as "stable regimes of boundary objects" (313) and highlight how any working infrastructure serves multiple communities of practice simultaneously.

There have also been suggestions to expand the scope of analysis to include practices and processes of collaboration associated with multiple communities that are interacting to achieve a common set of objectives. The idea of practice has found much importance in social research recently, and a consideration of objects as integral aspects of practice is indeed useful. An analysis of boundary objects thus becomes an analysis of the use of these objects in particular practices rather than merely an examination of their properties (Levina and Vaast 2005). Groups of objects facilitate action in practices, carrying meanings and knowledge as enacted in the practice at a given time. This leads to collective change in practices and results in changes to the very objects that facilitated such changes. Sapsed and Salter (2004) also point to the importance of organizational factors in the way boundary objects function. They examine the limits of project management tools as boundary objects in work involving globally distributed project teams. They found that project management tools were particularly ineffective when lines of authority were ambiguous and when there were no opportunities for face-to-face interaction or when lines of authority were blurred. This linkage between practices and objects was also pointed out by Star and Griesemer (1989) who observed that changes in collecting and curating processes formed one part of the outcomes of the functioning of the museum as a boundary object. Thus changes in organizational practices are inherent in the creation and usage of boundary object. Therefore, focusing on arrays and sets of objects together with other dynamics of practice and organizational contexts seem to provide a richer picture of how individual objects function.

BOUNDARY ORGANIZATIONS

In the area of sociology of science, many researchers refer to *boundary organizations* as a class that requires special attention. They propose that boundary organizations help connect diverse social groups such as scientists and policy makers (Guston 2001). They "perform tasks that are useful to both sides and involve people from both communities in their work but play a distinctive role that would be difficult or impossible for organizations in either community to play" (Guston 2001, 403). The work of nonprofits in enhancing responsible environmental and social practices by collaborating with firms and activists has been documented (Hoffman and Ventresca 2002). Various arrangements such as technology centers have helped in collaboration between academia and commercial establishments (Stern 2004, Murray and O'Mahony 2007).

Further work about boundary organizations has found their effectiveness outside the domain of science studies. O'Mahoney and Bechky (2008) explore the unlikely collaboration between commercial firms and software developers in open-source software development. They found that open-source software developers and firms engaged in commercial software development collaborate in interesting ways to achieve their varied objectives and that such collaborations are facilitated by the creation of boundary organizations.

> Boundary organizations can enable challengers and defenders to substantively collaborate by building a bridge between divergent worlds that allows collaborators to preserve their competing interests. Boundary organizations make collaboration possible by enrolling actors on the basis of their convergent interests. (O'Mahoney and Bechky 2008, 426)

Boundary organizations help leverage converging interests between various communities, groups, units, and firms involved in the collaborative enterprise. They do so by requiring modifications in practices concerning governance forms, membership, ownership, and control of production, but without total surrender of the divergent interests by parties involved. Thus they serve as enduring bridges across organizational domains.

However, given the flexibility of the concept of "objects" it seems possible that the concept of boundary organizations could be treated as a particular case of the more inclusive concept of boundary objects. This seems all the more reasonable given that many explorations, including the original work of Star and Griesemer (1989), focused on organizations. However, some argue that there is usefulness in retaining the distinctiveness of these two concepts. Often, there is lack of a clear-cut answer in the approaches adopted by many authors. For example, although Guston (2001) asserts that "entire organizations can serve as boundary objects" (400) an analytical separation is maintained when it is asserted that boundary organizations can "provide the opportunity and sometimes the incentives for the creation and use of boundary objects" (400). O'Mahoneyand Bechky (2008) seem to maintain a useful distinction between the concepts when they explain their approach:

> Like boundary objects, boundary organizations can accommodate the varying interests of parties by providing a mechanism that reinforces convergent interests while allowing divergent ones to persist. Unlike boundary objects, however, the concept of boundary organizations allows us to focus on the organizational mechanisms and processes that enable collaboration. Rather than objects that are highly transportable . . . and "weakly structured" when used in different locations . . . boundary organizations are more durable structures that encourage parties to isolate and organize around their convergent interests. Though they are stable, boundary organizations share the interpretive flexibility of boundary objects, enabling parties' divergent interests to coexist, as

they seek collaboration while pursuing mutual goals. (O'Mahoney and Bechky 2008, 428)

Given the discussion above, it still seems possible to achieve this by retaining the concept of boundary objects and focusing on different issues in particular explorations. However, as we shall see below, this inclusiveness of the concept has also led to problems.

NOT A BOUNDARY OBJECT

It is evident from above that the concept of boundary objects has been an extremely useful tool in understanding cross-boundary interactions. However, the concept seems to have been too widely used in an indiscriminate way. To the critic, every object can be treated as a boundary object because objects by their very nature are viewed and used differently by different communities while retaining certain commonalities. This is all the more the case with everyday physical objects. For example, a telephone or a computer can very well be used for divergent or even opposing purposes and yet retain the commonality that is easily identifiable across locations.

Certainly, such a broad interpretation of boundary objects is likely to be of less help in serious inquiry. This has prompted one of the originators of the concept to clarify what cannot be treated as a boundary object (Star 2010). Star outlines three features that are likely to characterize a useful employment of the concept. The first is the best-recognized quality of interpretive flexibility. Varied interpretations of the object and associated usages are often highlighted as an important characteristic of boundary objects. The second relates to "material and organizational structure of different types of boundary objects" (Star 2010, 602). Boundary objects arise organically due to the information needs and work requirements of different communities of practice that collaborate. Thus the structure of the object is invariably influenced by dynamics of practices that drive them. The incorporation of these dynamics in the researcher's analysis is thus necessary to treat an object as boundary object in its true sense. The third aspect that again is often ignored concerns the boundary object's scale and scope. The concept should be useful at the chosen level of scale that is suitable for the purpose of the examination. The practices that are involved in the evolution and use of a boundary object invariably determine the most useful scale and the limits of scope that is appropriate for the research.

Star summarizes the core qualities of boundary objects as follows:

- The object . . . resides between social worlds (or communities of practice) where it is ill structured.
- When necessary, the object is worked on by local groups who maintain its vaguer identity as a common object, while making it more

specific, more tailored to local use within a social world, and therefore useful for work that is NOT interdisciplinary.

- Groups that are cooperating without consensus tack back-and-forth between both forms of the object. (2010, 604–605)

Often these characteristics of boundary objects, especially the last, are not explored sufficiently in works that use the concept for analysis. Taken together, these guidelines enable the researcher to resist the temptation to label objects as boundary objects indiscriminately without consideration for their structures or processes, within and between practices at a scale and scope deemed most useful for the object of inquiry.

CONCLUSION

Often the incorporation of boundary objects is treated as a solution for problematic situations where collaboration is not forthcoming. However, it is well known that we cannot firmly expect certain types of objects to result in certain anticipated types of action and subsequent results. As seen above, affordances and constraints result not just from structural properties of objects but from a host of other factors.

Lee (2007) has questioned the assumption that all objects that travel across communities of practice are indeed boundary objects and establishes that objects can be used to separate and push boundaries as much as to connect. Swan et al. (2007, 1826) assert that "objects are not uniformly positive in the production of knowledge." Shared objects can often inhibit sharing of tacit knowledge across teams. In fact, they might serve to reinforce boundaries and authority patterns (Levina and Vaast 2006; Vaast and Levina 2006). Boland and Tenkasi (1995) point to dynamics of power that can influence the ways in which boundary objects are used. Barrett and Oborn (2010) found that boundary objects, when used during transitions involving redistribution of power, may indeed inhibit knowledge sharing in some cases. The popularity of boundary objects as an analytic device thus should not blind us to diverse ways in which objects are used by and between communities.

"The role of material artifacts in practice is incredibly important to collaborative work and is far too complex to be defined by a single concept, however compelling" (Lee 2007, 314). However, often boundary objects have been treated as a simple undifferentiated explanation for collaborative situations (Nicolini, Mengis, and Swan 2012). To avoid this trap, a deeper consideration of the assumptions that we employ when approaching the object of inquiry might be useful for the researcher. The achievement of "cooperative work in the absence of consensus" (Star 2010, 604) is still fascinating for many researchers, and the concept of boundary objects has formed a highly popular pioneering effort in this direction.

REFERENCES

Barrett, M., and E. Oborn. 2010. "Boundary Object Use in Cross-Cultural Software Development Teams." *Human Relations* 63 (8): 1199–1221.

Bechky, B. A. 2003a. "Sharing Meaning Across Occupational Communities: The Transformation of Understanding on a Production Floor." *Organization Science* 14 (3): 312–330.

Bechky, Beth A. 2003b. "Object Lessons: Workplace Artifacts as Representations of Occupational Jurisdiction." *American Journal of Sociology* 109 (3): 720–752.

Bijker, W. E., T. P. Hughes, and P. J. Pinch. 1987. *The Social Construction of Technological Systems*. Cambridge, MA: MIT Press.

Bødker, S. 1998. "Understanding Representation in Design." *Human-Computer Interaction* 13 (2): 107–125.

Boland, R. J., Jr., and R. V. Tenkasi. 1995. "Perspective Making and Perspective Taking in Communities of Knowing." *Organization Science* 6 (4): 350–372.

Bowker, G., and S. L. Star. 1994. "Knowledge and Information in International Information Management: Problems of Classification and Coding. In *Information Acumen: The Understanding and Use of Knowledge in Modern Business*, edited by L. Bud-Frierman, 187–213. London: Routledge.

Bowker, G., and S. L. Star. 2000. *Sorting Things Out: Classification and Its Consequence*. Cambridge, MA: MIT Press.

Bowker, G. C., S. Timmermans, and S. L. Star. 1995. "Infrastructure and Organisational Transformation: Classifying Nurses' Work in Information Technology and Changes. In *Organisational Work*, edited by W. Orlikowski, G. Walsham, M. R. Jones, and J. Degross, 344–369. London: Chapman & Hall.

Briers, M., and W. F. Chua. 2001. "The Role of Actor-Networks and Boundary Objects in Management Accounting Change: A field Study of an Implementation of Activity-Based Costing." *Accounting, Organizations and Society* 26: 237–269.

Brown, J. S., and P. Duguid. 1994. "Borderline Issues: Social and Material Aspects of Design." *Human-Computer Interaction*, 9 (1): 3–36.

Carlile, P. R. 2002. "A Pragmatic View of Knowledge and Boundaries: Boundary Objects in New Product Development." *Organization Science* 13 (4): 442–55.

Carlile, P. R. 2004. "Transferring, Translating, and Transforming: An Integrative Framework for Managing Knowledge across Boundaries." *Organization Science* 15 (5): 555–68.

D'Adderio, L. 2004. *Inside the Virtual Product: How Organizations Create Knowledge through Software*. Cheltenham: Edward Elgar.

Eckert, C., and J. Boujut. 2003. "The Role of Objects in Design Co-Operation: Communication through Physical or Virtual Objects." *Computer Supported Cooperative Work* 12 (2): 145–151.

Engeström, Y. 2000. "Comment on Blackler et al. Activity Theory and the Social Construction of Knowledge: A Story of Four Umpires." *Organization* 7 (2): 301–310.

Engeström, Y., R. Engeström, and M. Kärkkäinen. 1995. "Polycontextuality and Boundary Crossing in Expert Cognition: Learning and Problem Solving in Complex Work Activities." *Learning and Instruction* 5: 319–336.

Engeström, Y., and F. Blackler. 2005. "Special Issue: On the Life of the Object." *Organization* 12 (3): 307–330.

Fujimura, J.H. 1992. "Crafting Science: Standardized Packages, Boundary Objects, and Translation." In *Science as Practice and Culture*, edited by A. Pickering. Chicago, IL: University of Chicago Press.

Garrety, K., and R. Badham. 2000. "The Politics of Socio-Technical Intervention: An Interactionist View." *Technology Analysis and Strategic Management* 12: 103–18.

Guston, D.H. 2001. "Boundary Organizations in Environmental Policy and Science: An Introduction." *Science, Technology and Human Values* 26 (4): 399–408.

Henderson, K. 1991. "Flexible Sketches and Inflexible Data Bases: Visual Communication Conscription Devices, and Boundary Objects in Design Engineering." *Science, Technology and Human Values* 16 (4): 448–473.

Henderson, K. 1999. *On Line and on Paper: Visual Representations, Visual Culture, and Computer Graphics in Design Engineering*. Cambridge, MA: MIT Press.

Hoffman, A.J., and M. Ventresca. 2002. *Organizations, Policy, and the Natural Environment: Institutional and Strategic Perspectives*. Palo Alto, CA: Stanford University Press.

Karsten, H., K. Lyytinen, M. Hurskainen, and T. Koskelainen. 2001. "Crossing Boundaries and Conscripting Participation: Representing and Integrating Knowledge in a Paper Machinery Project." *European Journal of Information Systems* 10: 89–98.

Knorr Cetina, K. 1997. "Sociality with Objects: Social Relations in Postsocial Knowledge Societies." *Theory, Culture and Society* 14 (4): 1–30.

Latour, B. 1987. *Science in Action: How to Follow Scientists and Engineers through Society*. Cambridge, MA: Harvard University Press.

Latour, B. 1992. "Technology Is Society Made Durable." In *A sociology of Monsters. Essays on Power, Technology and Domination*, edited by J. Law, 103–131. London: Routledge.

Lave, J., and E. Wenger. 1991. *Situated Learning: Legitimate Peripheral Participation*. Cambridge, MA: Cambridge University Press.

Law, J., and V. Singleton. 2005. "Object Lessons." *Organization* 12: 331–355.

Lee, C.P. 2007. "Boundary Negotiating Artifacts: Unbinding the Routine of Boundary Objects and Embracing Chaos in Collaborative Work." *Computer Supported Cooperative Work* 16 (3): 307–339.

Levina, N, and E. Vaast. 2005. "The Emergence of Boundary Spanning Competence in Practice: Implications for Implementation and Use of Information Systems." *MIS Quarterly* 29 (2): 335–63.

Levina, N., and E. Vaast. 2006. "Turning a Community into a Market: A Practice Perspective on IT Use in Boundary-Spanning. *Journal of Management Information Systems* 22 (4): 13–38.

Murray, F., and S. O'Mahony. 2007. "Exploring the Foundations of Cumulative Innovation: Implications for Organization Science." *Organization Science* 18: 1006–1021.

Nicolini, D., J. Mengis, and J. Swan. 2012. "Understanding the Role of Objects in Cross-Disciplinary Collaboration." *Organization Science* 23(3): 612–629.

O'Mahoney, S., and B.A. Bechky. 2008. "Boundary Organizations: Enabling Collaboration among Unexpected Allies." *Administrative Science Quarterly* 53: 422–459.

Orlikowski, W. 2007. "Sociomaterial Practices: Exploring Technology at Work." *Organization Studies* 28 (9): 1435–1448.

Pawlowski, S. D,. and D. Robey. 2004. "Bridging User Organisations: Knowledge Brokering and the Work of Information Technology Professionals." *MIS Quarterly* 28 (4): 645–72.

Prasad, P. 1993. "Symbolic Processes in the Implementation of Technological Change: A Symbolic Interactionist Study of Work Computerization." *Academy of Management Journal* 36: 1400–30.

Sapsed, J., and A. Salter. 2004. "Postcards from the Edge: Local Communities, Global Programs and Boundary Objects." *Organization Studies* 25 (9): 1515–1534.

Star, S. L., and K. Ruhleder. 1996. "Steps toward an Ecology of Infrastructure: Design and Access for Large Information Spaces." *Information Systems Research* 7 (1): 111–134.

Star, S. L., and J. Griesemer, J. 1989. "Institutional Ecology, 'Translations,' and Coherence: Amateurs and Professionals in Berkeley's Museum of Vertebrate Zoology, 1907–1939." *Social Studies of Science* 19 (3): 387–420.

Star, S. L. 1999. "The Ethnography of Infrastructure." *American Behavioural Scientist* 43 (3): 377–391.

Star, S. L. 2000. "Infrastructure and Ethnographic Practice." *Scandinavian Journal of Information Systems* 14 (2): 107–122.

Star, S. L. 2010. "This Is Not a Boundary Object." *Science Technology Human Values* 35 (5): 601–617.

Stern, S. 2004. *Biological Resource Centers: Knowledge Hubs for the Life Sciences.* Washington, DC: Brookings Institution.

Subrahmanian, E., Monarch, I., Konda, S., Granger, H., Milliken, R., Westerberg, A., and The N-Dim Group (2003). Boundary Objects and Prototypes at the Interfaces of Engineering Design. *Computer Supported Cooperative Work* 12(2): 185–203.

Swan, J., M. Bresnen, S. Newell, and M. Robertson. 2007. "The Object of Knowledge: The Role of Objects in Biomedical Innovation." *Human Relations* 60 (12): 1809–1837.

Turner, W., G. Bowker, L. Gasser, and M. Zackland. 2006. "Information Infrastructures for Distributed Collective Practices." *Computer Supported Cooperative Work* 15: 93–110.

Vaast, E., and N. Levina. 2006. "Multiple Faces of Codification: Organizational Redesign in an IT Organization." *Organization Science* 17 (2): 190–201.

Wastell, D. G. 1999. "Learning Dysfunctions in Information Systems Development: Overcoming the Social Defenses with Transitional Objects." *MIS Quarterly* 23 (4): 581–600.

Wenger, E. 1998. *Communities of Practice: Learning, Meaning and Identity.* Cambridge, UK: Cambridge University Press.

Wenger, E. 2000. "Communities of Practice and Social Learning Systems." *Organization* 7 (2): 225–256.

Yakura, E. K. 2002. "Charting Time: Timelines as Temporal Boundary Objects." *Academy of Management Journal* 45 (5): 956–970.

Zeiss, R., and P. Groenewegen. 2009. "Engaging Boundary Objects in OMS and STS? Exploring the Subtleties of Layered Engagement." *Organization* 16 (1): 81–100.

3 From Individual to Collective Boundary-Spanning

Knowledge Outcomes from Recombinative Actions

Preeta M. Banerjee and Rafael A. Corredoira

INTRODUCTION

Research on boundary-spanning has found that the individual brain is capable of amazing things, like making connections that gave rise to Darwin's theory of evolution and the creation of Virgin Atlantic Airlines (Johansson 2006). Yet the most interesting inventions occur collectively, across groups of individuals, such as at the technology or industry level (Dosi 1982). Invention is a unique solution to a practical problem, a solution that can be the outcome of recombination involving spanning knowledge boundaries. As Schumpeter (1934) describes, recombination can be finding novel combinations of old ideas or having new eyes but not new things, as well as novel combinations of novel ideas, where the former is recombination of near knowledge and the latter of far knowledge. In particular, we characterize knowledge recombination as a form of boundary-spanning or *bridging* of two previously unrelated technology spaces to come up with a knowledge outcome (A+B = C). For example, as Diamond (1999) describes, James Watt designed his steam engine to pump water from mines, but it soon was supplying power to cotton mills, then (with much greater profit) propelling locomotives and boats. As elaborated in a long literature, knowledge can often be used over and over without losing its value (Arrow 1971), and collective action propels technologies to evolve in number (depth) and variety (breadth). While the literature has studied boundary-spanning at macro levels, i.e., spanning across group of individuals, organizations, and regions, we claim that studying the knowledge recombination process and performance outcomes is justified since this process is the building block underlying the phenomenon captured at macro levels of theorizing and analysis. In this sense, we address the micro-foundations driving effect of macro-level boundary-spanning on invention.

These processes have very different outcomes at different levels of action: within the individual, across individuals, and across groups of individuals. Being management innovation scholars interested in technology evolution, we focus on the collective action of inventors. When knowledge is created across individuals, there needs to be a social network (typically within a firm, although lately external social networks have been more common with outsourcing). When knowledge is created across groups of individuals (or across firms), there is an element of collective knowledge, or what has been referred to as a knowledge network. By discussing boundary-spanning's impact on technology evolution across a knowledge network, this chapter highlights the importance of distinguishing that collective knowledge indeed has higher-level properties than individual knowledge, and does not simply reflect the composition of underlying individual knowledge.

In what follows, this chapter focuses on intrinsic characteristics of the invention process and how those characteristics affect the utilization of prior knowledge and the resulting inventions. In particular, we study the effect of boundary-spanning of collective knowledge. We do this by analyzing a knowledge network of patents from the semiconductor industry. Patents have been used as indicators of technological knowledge flows since seminal papers by Scherer (1982, 1984). More recently, patents are seen as building on and extending knowledge contained in cited patents to examine knowledge networks (Nerkar and Paruchuri 2005). Thus, new knowledge created by recombining existing knowledge (Fleming 2001; Henderson and Cockburn 1994; Kogut and Zander 1992) builds new nodes of the knowledge network. Unlike related diversification for firms, where more benefits accrue from combining similar areas (Rumelt 1974; Varadarajan and Ramanujam 1987), it seems that patents that create new knowledge by recombining unrelated areas can have a higher number of citations and can spur generality of the knowledge network. The type of recombination in a patent can determine whether the patent receives a greater sheer number of citations (cites) and whether the patent enables diversity in citations (generality). The semiconductor industry is a particularly appropriate setting for this study because of the semiconductor firms' heavy reliance on patents to protect their intellectual capital (Almeida and Kogut 1997; Cohen, Nelson, and Walsh 2000).

This chapter offers two main contributions by investigating how patents that connect unrelated knowledge domains impact the rate and type of technological progress, or subsequent invention, in the semiconductor industry. First, we look at the outcome of collective boundary-spanning—at the technical knowledge network, not the individual or social network. To understand technological progress in the semiconductor industry, we expand knowledge networks from the firm level (Nerkar et al. 2005) to the industry level. Second, we find the impact of boundary-spanning, as a type of knowledge recombination, on technology evolution. Although combining either related or unrelated knowledge can create new inventions, there are different consequences of each type of exploration to the technological community. We analyze a universe of 8,913 patents that were granted to 144 semiconductor firms. We find that a patent that cites classes not cited together before in its main class receives a larger number of citations and has higher generality. On the other hand, when a patent cites classes that have not been cited by patents in its main class, it receives fewer citations, but its generality is not different from patents that do not.

KNOWLEDGE RECOMBINATION THROUGH BOUNDARY-SPANNING

While invention can be of many types, we focus on that which results from the recombination of knowledge, or the grouping of existing concepts, principles, and factors (Schumpeter 1934; Nelson and Winter 1982). As researchers of knowledge recombination have delineated, there are multiple ways to recombine knowledge, including using knowledge that is near and far in different spaces-geographic, social, technological, commercial, etc. (Banerjee 2008; Dannells 2007; Rosenkopf and Almeida 2003; Benner and Tushman 2003), where the former can be categorized as exploitation and the later as exploration (March 1991). The actual action of recombination also can be done directly by actors at different levels, namely within individuals or across individuals at the firm level, or indirectly through the use of knowledge brokers or mediators (e.g., consultants). For the purposes of this chapter, we focus on knowledge recombination in the form of boundary-spanning (i.e. A+B = C) where the focus is on the technological space. In other words, we study how the collectivity shares a knowledge base that is understood from a shared cognitive map that organizes the principles, components of the technology, and outcomes achievable by their combinations (i.e., a knowledge network). We then hypothesize how the discovery of solutions to technical problems (in our case, patents) is bounded by the cognitive limitations of the individuals manipulating the space (through the search) in a way that drives near or far boundary-spanning knowledge recombination and, thus, technological evolution depth (number of citations) and breadth (generality).

From the Individual to the Collective

There is a gap in the boundary-spanning literature that necessitates moving from the individual to collective action. Collective action differs from individual action, as division of labor is constrained by the availability of people with relevant human capital (Smith 1776) and by the coordination costs inherent in team production (Becker and Murphy 1992). While it may be desirable for a pin factory to employ only specialists and reap the benefits of labor division, firms may not desire to pursue this strategy because of the requirements of knowledge and the need for collaborative knowledge work (Garud and Karnøe, 2003). This is particularly true in invention, where knowledge has been found to be situated and contextual (Tyre and Von

Hippel 1997). Managing knowledge boundaries is critical to successful technology invention (Dougherty 1992). Although there are returns to a firm for utilizing specialists (even for workers with identical skill endowments [Rosen 1983]), the costs of coordinating a team increase with the degree of team member specialization. In other words, invention is a distributed process (Garud and Karnoe 2003), where project success requires integration across individuals.

Additionally, at the collective level, higher-level properties happen to differentiate knowledge—properties that we call emergent. The term *emergent* was utilized by Brodbeck (1958) to refer to higher-order phenomena, group behavior in the context of her discussion that are "not derivable from the laws including whatever composition laws there are, about individual behavior." Thus, we argue that collective knowledge boundary-spanning results in breakthrough invention or influential inventions for one main reason: group-level selection (Sober 1984).

Group-level selection (Sober 1984) indicates that knowledge can become fixed or spread in a population because of the benefits it bestows at the group level; thus there cannot be attribution to the individual. For example, in organizational systems, even if individual actions are independent of one another, market forces operate on aggregate entities called firms. On the other hand, relying on individual capability or nonemergent knowledge can be considered a summary statistic of underlying, independent attributes. In this case, knowledge is a function of derivable interaction effects among underlying elements of the system. This type of recombination can be broken into different components for analysis—reverse engineering. In contrast to well-defined composition effects, some knowledge may not be derivable from a set of independent underlying attributes. Invention is often more complex than an assumption of independence or reductionism suggests. The consequences of a given action may depend on other choices at the same time or potentially even more complex actions and choices at earlier and subsequent time periods. Actions are often inextricably intertwined. In other words, reductionism—the strategy of seeking full knowledge of a system by analysis or "reduction" of a system to its parts, followed by study of the parts—is insufficient in understanding invention that arises from emergence, collective action. Thus, emergence harkens back to the old adage that a whole is more than the sum of its parts.

This is not to say that reductionism is not necessary, that looking at individual boundary-spanning is not fundamental. On the contrary, reductionism yields information about the properties of the subcomponents or parts that are consistent with emergent properties of the system (i.e., collective knowledge and technology evolution). Thus, there is nothing mysterious about emergence. However, reductionism will not allow for prediction of the emergence or full understanding and modeling of it.

Interactions between Knowledge Itself and between Knowledge and the Collective

From a conceptual point of view, even very small additions or changes to the knowledge base utilized to generate an invention can have qualitative differences in the outcome. Examples of small differences at the micro level resulting in outstanding differences at the macro level are abundant; for instance, in biology, humans and chimpanzees share about 95 percent of their DNA, and that 5 percent difference makes the difference between man and monkey (Britten 2002). Fleming and Sorenson (2001) have shown that the technological space can be modeled as a complex adaptive system. The key implication is that how a new combination of components will perform as a system cannot be estimated from knowing the performance of each component in isolation; it is an emergent outcome. The emergent property of a complex adaptive system is a function of the interconnectivity of the components that constitute the system. Steels explains:

> A component has a particular functionality but this is not recognizable as a subfunction of the global functionality. Instead a component implements a behaviour whose side effect contributes to the global functionality . . . Each behaviour has a side effect and the sum of the side effects gives the desired functionality. (Steels 1991, 454)

The recombinatory view of technological invention provides a framework that highlights some of the challenges to which inventors are exposed in the process. Due to the interconnectivity of the components, the functionality of a combination cannot be estimated *ex ante* by linear addition of each component effect. The functionality becomes an effect of the component in the presence of the other components. As inventors become more familiar with how components interact with each other, information available through the accumulation of "experiments" reflected in each patent, they develop a cognitive model that helps to guide their experimentation to combinations with higher probability of success (Schilling et al. 2003). The lack of linearity of the aggregation of components' effects to achieve the desired functionality for an invention (in our case, codified in a new patent) demands experimentation. The contribution of each component depends on its interaction with the environment (in other words, on how each and all components influence the contribution of every single component to the functionality of the combination) (Holland 1998). As a result, through superstitious learning (Barley 1988; Levitt and March 1988), inventors construct cognitive models utilizing analogies (Collins and Gentner 1987) that help them to guide the inventive process.

Knowledge networks that utilize patents capture this collective boundary-spanning, as each patent has more than one inventor. In addition, patents are cited by other patents, where a group of inventors in a patent is different from the other inventors in the patent they cite. Thus through an emergent process, the underlying technology is developed, i.e., technology evolution. We look at semiconductor technology and the evolution of technical inventions.

EFFECTS OF BOUNDARY-SPANNING ON TECHNOLOGY EVOLUTION

As mentioned previously, boundary-spanning (Tushman and Scanlan 1981), or the recoding of information between two diverse units, can be of technology knowledge. Thus, this type of knowledge boundary-spanning can result in technology invention, embodied in a patent. A boundary-spanning patent is the outcome of collective action that must convert knowledge into a second semantic space while retaining the meanings held in the first. Boundary-spanning when building a knowledge network can be thought of as filling a structural hole. Many advantages can be derived when a firm fills a structural hole (Ahuja 2000)—likewise benefits accrue when a patent fills a gap between two knowledge areas. Namely, filling the structural hole creates depth of technology evolution (or a greater number of citations) as well as breadth of technology evolution (or "generality") (Hall, Jaffe, and Trajtenberg 2001; Henderson, Jaffe, and Trajtenberg 1998; Jaffe, Fogarty, and Banks 1997).

Boundary-spanning contributes to invention's ability to serve multiple functions in a variety of industries. Unlike non-boundary-spanning inventions, firm inventions that explore new application domain knowledge change the technology from specialist to generalist (Adner and Levinthal 2001; Levinthal 1998). In other words, boundary-spanning patents create 1) an opportunity for the selection environment to continue in the technology's future development (increased depth/citations); and 2) new technology streams; they are likely to be applied on a broader range of knowledge areas (increased breadth/generality).

In particular, generality measures the amount of diversity that a focal invention has on subsequent invention in a variety of application domains (Hall et al. 2001; Henderson et al. 1998; Jaffe et al. 1997). With generality there is an increase in the pervasiveness of use (Bresnahan and Trajtenberg 1995), the utilization of a technology as an input by a wide and ever expanding range of sectors in the economy (Helpman and Trajtenberg 1996). The value of pervasiveness of use to the knowledge network is described by Rosenberg (1963). Rosenberg identified that inventions in tools and techniques used in, for example, bicycle production made them available for numerous new uses, most importantly automobile manufacturing. As such, these inventions possess an extensive range of use and are "enabling technologies," opening up new opportunities rather than offering complete, final solutions (Lipsey, Bekar, and Carlaw 1998).

However, while boundary-spanning inventions open new areas of research or spur invention activity in existing areas, there are costs. First, relying on exploitation (non-boundary-spanning) appears to reduce the need for re-sources. For example, searching recently created knowledge reduces search costs (Katila 2002) and also conserves cognitive capabilities (Cyert and March 1963). Thus, exploitation is "genetically conservative" (Adner and Levinthal 2000), meaning that there is no introduction of ideas that have not been cog-nitively understood prior. A second benefit to leveraging existing technology is lower risk. By lower risk, we mean that the quality of existing knowledge is said to be more reliable (March, Sproull, and Tamuz 1991). Exploitation is more likely to lead to successful rewards (Cyert and March 1963). Organi-zational memory of firms is embodied in the routines of the firm, and these routines represent the capability of the firm (Nelson and Winter 1982). These routines help firms maintain continuity and build competence (March 1991). Through exploitation, firms use embedded routines that decrease the chance of errors and increase the chance of successful recombination and successful invention (Katila 2002). For example, firms that build on recent knowledge are frequently better able to predict the nature of technological advances and, by investing in an area early, the firm increases the chances of being part of future developments (Cohen and Levinthal 1989; McGrath 1999). Second, exploitation appears to increase potential for competitive advantage (Katila 2002). Unlike external (collective) capabilities that are accessible to all firms (Mansfield 1988), internal (individual) capabilities are proprietary and not widely accessible. Individual capability thereby forms the basis for sustain-able competitive advantage.

Yet, by involving collective capabilities, the firm can integrate develop-ments both inside and outside of the firm. Exploration at the industry level could be exploitation at the firm level (a firm that hires an inventor with expertise in a novel area). Exploitation at firm level can also be leveraged by adding some exploration (that allows using the existing resource in new ways, by a small modification or the addition of exploratory knowledge for the firm). Exploration for the firm may just be exploitation for the industry (the firm starts using something novel for the firm, but well known and widely applied by the industry). The firm searches for solutions in the neigh-borhood of its current expertise of knowledge (Stuart and Podolny 1996). However, exploitation can avoid many of the disadvantages of local search, such as competency traps (Levitt and March 1988) and core rigidities (Leonard-Barton 2007) by incorporating feedback from the environment (Katil 2002). While results of past innovative searches become natural starting points for new innovative searches, firms do not have to rely solely on their own estab-lished knowledge to determine what is important and useful.

In addition, by bridging areas of knowledge that have not been put together before, boundary-spanning of near knowledge also becomes a foundation for a new technological stream and are is likely to be cited by any other patent that engage in this line of research. By addressing the different boundaries around the knowledge and lowering the barri-ers to entry, boundary-spanning of far knowledge creates an opportunity for an increased number of citations. As in the case of near knowledge, boundary-spanning of far knowledge becomes the first building block of a new technology stream, increasing its likelihood of being cited by patents following it. On the other hand, in the process of spanning to completely new areas, a boundary-spanning patent may be moved into a technological position too far away from the class knowledge base for those working on that base to pick up this new stream. This might reduce the number of patents following suit into the new area. Which of the two phenomena dominates is a question for empirical testing.

Hypothesis 1 (H1): Boundary-spanning results in a higher number of citations received.

Hypothesis 2 (H2): Boundary-spanning results in greater generality.

Is All Boundary-Spanning the Same?

In building knowledge networks, a firm's R&D activity is closely related to its previous R&D activity, e.g., local search (Helfat 1994; March and Simon 1958; Nelson and Winter 1982; Rosenkopf and Nerkar 2001). Thus, the firm searches for solutions in the neighborhood of its current expertise of knowledge (Stuart and Podolny 1996). Among the disadvantages of local search are competency traps (Levitt and March 1988) and core rigidities (Leonard-Barton 2007). Local search involves capturing value of existing R&D and technology, supply chain, manufacturing, sales and marketing, and distribution activities. The industry becomes efficient at crossing the same bridges that have already been built. There are best practices around capabilities and technology that can be shared from one firm to another. It is hard to overcome local search. Often there are costs of creating separate entities within a firm, or separate firms to pursue new knowledge combinations (Bower and Christensen 1995).

In high-tech industries, like semiconductors, boundaries around knowledge exist and are difficult to cross. In general, startups, which are abundant in this industry, are small, with few employees and limited resources, and they tend to focus in one area. Few firms are large enough to have significant presence across knowledge areas. This creates an industry where knowledge is fragmented and distributed across firms, making it difficult to identify connections to unrelated areas. Extant research has shown the importance of interfirm learning mechanisms such as alliances and employee mobility in overcoming these obstacles (Almeida, Dokko, and Rosenkopf 2003; Corredoira and Rosenkopf 2010; Song, Almeida, and Wu 2003) This implies that the further away the underlying technology is from where the patent draws from, the more difficult it is for those working in the same technological area to perceive and understand the opportunities. While, by definition, boundary-spanning of near knowledge is grounded on the knowledge that is part of the technological area, and only creates a novel connection between knowledge bases, boundary-spanning of far knowledge draws on uncharted technological spaces for the knowledge base where it is located. For these reasons we expect the size of the effect on number of citations received to be larger for near than far boundary-spanning patents.

On the other hand, boundary-spanning of far knowledge brings together knowledge that has not been utilized previously by the technological area. This is more likely to generate a new technological stream than boundary-spanning of near knowledge, which only creates a novel connection between knowledge areas that might have already been explored by the technological area. For these reasons, when boundary-spanning recombines knowledge that is proximate to the industry's knowledge, inventors are more efficient and inventions are easier to introduce to the market; hence firms are more likely to understand and support the inventors' efforts. Therefore, we expect inventions spanning into near knowledge to be utilized more often—to have a larger impact—than those spanning into far knowledge. On the other hand, the spanning of far knowledge introduces novelty and should open the invention for application in novel areas, embedding it with breakthrough characteristics and larger generality. Spanning of near knowledge does not; therefore, they should have less generality than far spanning inventions.

> Hypothesis 3 (H3): Boundary-spanning of near knowledge has more impact than boundary-spanning of far knowledge.
> Hypothesis 4 (H4): Boundary-spanning of near knowledge has less generality than boundary-spanning of far knowledge.

METHODOLOGY

Sample

Our data was obtained from National Bureau of Economic Research (NBER) and National University of Singapore (NUS) U.S. patent datasets that contain the information on patent records from the United States Patent and Trademark Office (USPTO). We include information about patents from 1967 to 2004, inclusive, and derive our measures as described below. We run our models on all the patents that were granted in semiconductor classes to 144 firms identified as semiconductor firms. The list of semiconductor firms was built from information available from ICE and Dataquest, two private databases specializing in the semiconductor industry.

Our unit of observation is a patent. Our dataset is built from all the patents granted during the period 1990–1994, which includes 12,372 patents in the NBER dataset semiconductor category. For those patents we measured generality and number of citations of the patent, identified recombinant and boundary-spanning inventions, and recorded the assignee as described below. We derive our measures for dependent variables (*impact*—citations received—and *adjusted generality*—diversity of areas on which the patent can be used, from citations received between 1995–2004), as well as independent variables (*NEAR spanner*—pioneering combination of familiar knowledge bases—and *FAR spanner*—pioneering utilization of knowledge bases, from citations of prior art between 1967–1989) and control variables for assignee and granting year.

Variables

Dependent Variables

Adjusted generality: In order to capture the diversity of areas on which the patent can be used, we utilize Generality (G), a measure originally utilized by Jaffe, Fogarty, and Banks (1997) and Henderson, Jaffe, and Trajtenberg (1998), which measures the diversity of citations for a single patent, based on the three-digit U.S. patent classes of the patent's forward citations. The original measure is adjusted following Hall, Jaffe, and Trajtenberg (2001) to correct bias. Adjusted Generality (γ) is defined by:

$$\gamma_i = \frac{N_i}{N_i - 1}\left(1 - \sum_{j}^{N_i} s_{ij}^{2}\right)$$

3.1

where s_{ij} denotes the percentage of patent forward citations to the patent i that belong to patent class j, and N_i is the number of forward patent citations for the patent i. To generate these variables we collected the patents that cited the focal patents in our dataset during the ten-year window starting the year after the granting of the patent. We recorded how many patents cited the focal patent from each primary class and used this information to calculate the focal patent Generality and Adjusted Generality.

Number of citations received (Cites): To capture the number of citations of the patent we utilize the count of forward citations the patent received. The number of citations received by a patent is an indication of how important the patent has been for the technological development (Hall et al. 2001). The OTAF report noted:

> If a single document is cited in numerous patents, the technology revealed in that document is apparently involved in many developmental efforts. Thus, the number of times a patent document is cited may be a measure of its technological significance. (1976, 167)

Independent Variables

The procedure we utilized to identify near spanners versus far spanners was by utilizing those classes that were cited by semiconductor patents between 1990 and 1994 and were not cited during 1980 and 1989.

NEAR Spanner is a dichotomous variable that takes a value of 1 when the patent cites at least two patents with different main classes identified as bridged classes, and zero otherwise. *FAR Spanner* is a dichotomous variable that takes a value of 1 when the patent cites another patent with a main class identified as spanned, and zero otherwise. *Firm* is a categorical variable that identifies each one of the 144 firms in our list of semiconductor firms. *Year* is a categorical variable that captures temporal differences over the period 1990–1994.

Data Description

From NBER and NUS U.S. patents databases, we collected patent number, main class, application and issuing year, and citations for all the patents granted in the NBER semiconductor category from 1980 to 1989. This resulted in a total of 9,157 patents. We also collected main class for all the patents granted after 1964 cited by those 9,157 patents (which includes 95% of the citations made). This resulted in 16,841 cited patents for which we have main class of a total of 17,781 cited patents by the set of 9,157 patents. The same was done for the patents granted from 1990 to 1994. It resulted in a total of 12,372 patents that cited 27,224 patents with granting date later than 1964 (which included 92% of the 29,882 citations made). As described in the next section, of those 12,372 patents, our models were run on the 8,913 granted to firms in our sample.

Table 3.1 presents descriptive statistics and correlation matrix. Our dataset has the 8,913 patents in the semiconductor category granted to the 144 firms in our sample between 1990 and 1994. Of those patents, 611 are NEAR spanner patents and 307 are FAR spanner patents (see Table 3.2). Since firms have the tendency to explore in areas proximate to their current position (Cyert and March 1963; Nelson et al. 1982), these numbers of *NEAR Spanner* and *FAR Spanner* are consistent with our expectations, as FAR spanner patents should be less frequent since they involve exploring into areas that are more distant than NEAR spanner patents.

Models

We create two sets of models to test our hypotheses about *Cites* and generality. Number of citations is a count of citations received by the focal patent over different time periods. An estimation of a Poisson model indicates that our data suffers from overdispersion. This is congruent with the standard deviations being larger than the dependent variable mean (see Table 3.1). In addition, our dataset violates the assumption of independence across observations. The number of citations of the patents could also be the result of effects stemming from assignee's unobserved characteristics. For these reasons, we estimate negative binomial regressions with fixed effects on the firm for which the focal patent was granted (PROC GENMOD, SAS v 9.1).

Table 3.1 Descriptive Statistics and Correlation Matrix

	Mean	Standard Error	Cites (1 to 5)	Cites (6 to 10)	Cites (1 to 10)	Adjusted Generality	Near Spanner	Far Spanner	Near Spanner *Far Spanner
Cites (1 to 5)	8.84	10.75	1						
Cites (6 to 10)	5.93	9.69	0.65	1					
Cites(1 to 10)	14.77	18.5	0.92	0.9	1				
Adjusted Generality	0.52	0.26	0.07	0.11	0.1	1			
Near Spanner	0.07	0.25	0.03	0.03	0.04	0.09	1		
Far Spanner	0.03	0.18	0.01	0	0.01	0.05	0.54	1	
Near Spanner* FAR Spanner	0.03	0.16	0.01	0.01	0.01	0.05	0.62	0.89	1
Number of Observations		8913							

Table 3.2 Frequency of Near and Far Boundary-Spanning Patents

	Non-Near Spanner	Near Spanner	Total
Non-Far Spanner	8239	367	8606
Far Spanner	63	244	307
Total	8302	611	8913

These models included only the patents granted to firms in our sample.[1] Generality is a censored variable (range 0 to 1). For this reason we estimate a generalized Tobit regression (PROC QLIM, SAS v9.1). As with the case of *Cites*, and because of the independence assumption violation, we estimate a model with fixed effects on the semiconductor firm to which the focal patent was granted. The fixed effect estimation controls unobserved heterogeneity and corrects spuriousness (Allison 1999). The correlations between the independent variables are high (see Table 3.1) but Collins, variance inflation factor, and tolerance tests (SAS v.9.1) confirm that the data do not have multicollinearity problems.

Model Specification

For *Cites*, our full models for semiconductor firms' patents take the form:

$$IMPACT_{ki} = \beta_0 + \beta_1 Near\ Spanner_i + \beta_2 Far\ Spanner_i + \beta_3 Near\ Spanner * Far\ Spanner_i + \gamma_i + Firm_i + \varepsilon_i \qquad 3.2$$

Where $IMPACT_{ki}$ is number of citations for patent i calculated for time windows 1 to 5, 6 to 10, and 1 to 10 years for patent i; and ε_i is a log-gamma distributed error.

For Generality, our full models for semiconductor firms' patents take the following form:

$$y_{ki}^* = \beta_0 + \beta_1 Near\ Spanner_i + \beta_2 Far\ Spanner_i +$$
$$\beta_3 Near\ Spanner * Far\ Spanner_i + \gamma_i + Firm_i + \varepsilon_i \qquad 3.3$$

$$Generality_{ki} = \begin{cases} 1 & \text{if} & y_i^* \geq 1 \\ y_i^* & \text{if} & 0 < y_i^* < 1 \\ 0 & \text{if} & y_i^* \leq 0 \end{cases} \qquad 3.4$$

Where $Generality_{ki}$ is adjusted generality for patent i; ; and $\varepsilon_i \sim i.i.d.\ N(0, s^2)$. For both models, $Near\ Spanner_i$, $Far\ Spanner_i$, and $Near\ Spanner * Far\ Spanner_i$ are the values for the variables and their interaction for patent i; $Firm_i$ is a vector of dummy variables that capture firm's unobserved fixed effects; γ_i is a vector of dummy variables capturing year effects; β_0—β_3 are coefficients to be estimated.

Results and Discussion

In a spirit of full disclosure, we report results for reduced and full models for the three measures for *Impact* (1 to 5, 6 to 10, and 1 to 10 years after granting), and for *Adjusted Generality*. However, in this section we will focus our attention to models NB5 for *Impact* (see Table 3.3) and GT1 for *Adjusted Generality* (see Table 3.4). The 1- to 10-year window for *Impact* is consistent with the window utilized to measure *Generality*. We also report the preferred model (†) based on a likelihood ratio test[2] between nested models.

The negative binomial model for *Impact* provides partial support to Hypothesis 1: *Near Spanner* is positive and significant (See Table 3.3, Model NB5, coefficient = 0.098, p-value<0.05); however, *Far Spanner* is negative and significant. Generalized Tobit models for *Adjusted Generality* provide partial support for Hypothesis 2: *Near Spanner* is positive and significant (see Table 3.4, Model GT1, coefficient = 0.083, p-value <0.01); however, *Far Spanner* is not significant. Hypothesis 3 is supported: *Near Spanner* is significantly larger than *Far Spanner* (see Table 3.5, Model NB5, p-value <0.05); while hypothesis 4 is not supported: *Near Spanner* is significantly larger than *Far Spanner* (see Table 3.5, Model GT2, p-value <0.01). Comparisons for models based on *Impact* for the first and second lustrum show that most of the effect for *Impact* occurs in the second half of the decade.

As expected, the empirical results support the argument of at least one type of knowledge boundary-spanning resulting in inventions with more *Impact* and *Generality*. For boundary-spanning recombinations reaching

Table 3.3 Negative Binomial Regressions Estimates for Impact

	Semiconductor Industry[1]					
	Model NB1	Model NB2	Model NB3	Model NB4	Model NB5	Model NB6
Dependent variable	*Impact (1to5)*	*Impact (1to5)[†]*	*Impact (6to10)[†]*	*Impact (6to10)*	*Impact (1to10)[†]*	*Impact (1to10)*
Intercept	2.01*** (0.302)	2.168*** (0.305)	1.658** (0.813)	1.816** (0.827)	2.633*** (0.624)	2.786*** (0.634)
Near Spanner	0.060*** (0.016)	0.080*** (0.017)	0172*** (0.06)	0.196*** (0.064)	0.098** (0.045)	0.122** (0.048)
Far Spanner	−0.040* (0.023)	0.099** (0.043)	−0.246*** (0.083)	−0.111 (0.155)	−0.125** (0.061)	0.005 (0.114)
*Near Spanner *Far Spanner*		−0.188*** (0.051)		−0.194 (0.185)		−0.189 (0.136)
-Log Likelihood	101225	101232	70241	70242	274766	274767
Number of Obse	8913	8913	8913	8913	8913	8913
LR GOF test		0.00		0.29		0.16

*p-value< 0.10 ** p-value< 0.05 *** p-value< 0.01
[1]Negative Binomial Regression with controls for assignee and issuing year (not reported)
[†]Preferred model according to Likelihood Ratio test.

Table 3.4 Generalized Tobit Regression Estimates for Generality

	Semiconductor Industry	
	Model GT1	Model GT2
Dependent variable	Adjusted Generality[†]	Adjusted Generality[†]
Intercept	0.548** (0.214)	0.610*** (0.217)
Near Spanner	0.083*** (0.016)	0.093*** (0.017)
Far Spanner	0.010 (0.021)	0.063 (0.039)
Near Spanner Far Spanner*		−0.076 (0.047)
-Log Likelihood	3485	3484
Number of Observations	8913	8913
LR GOF test		0.10

*p-value < 0.10 ** p-value <0.05 *** p-value <0.01
[1]Generalized Tobit Regression (censored dependent variable, upper boundary = 1 and lower boundary = 0) with controls for assignee and issuing year (not reported)
[†]Preferred model according to Likelihood Ratio test.

Table 3.5   Z-test for *Near Spanner* > *Far Spanner*

Dependent variable Impact		Estimate (Near Spanner – Far Spanner)	Std Error (Near Spanner – Far Spanner)	p-value
Model NB1	Cites(1 to 5)	0.100	0.028	0.000
Model NB2	Cites(1 to 5)[†]	–0.019	0.046	0.681
Model NB3	Cites(6 to 10)[†]	0.412	0.102	0.000
Model NB4	Cites(6 to 10)	0.306	0.168	0.068
Model NB5	Cites(1 to 10)[†]	0.218	0.076	0.004
Model NB6	Cites(1 to 10)	0.117	0.124	0.344
Dependent variable Adjusted Generality				
Model GT1	Adjusted Generality[†]	0.073	0.026	0.006
Model GT2	Adjusted Generality	0.030	0.043	0.481

[†]Indicates the preferred model according to the LogLikelihood Ratio test.

closer knowledge bases the effects are as hypothesized. However, results appear to not support the positive effect of *Far Spanner*. A couple of reasons could be driving these results, while *Far Spanner* might still have the expected effect on inventions. First, our window of observation for capturing impact of the invention may be too short for technology to be able to incorporate the *Far Spanner* into technological solutions. Second, and in part suggested by results in model NB2, *Far Spanner* has a positive effect on $Impact_{(1\ to5)}$. The interaction term appears to be the one driving the overall effect of *Far Spanner* into the negative side. Therefore, it may be too much novelty (by combining *Far* and *Near Spanner* in the same solution) that is causing the negative sign for *Far Spanner*.

Conclusion

This chapter focuses on one type of recombinative action—boundary-spanning—and moves beyond individual to collective boundary-spanning. Collective boundary-spanning is important to understanding technology evolution. Thus, we highlight the importance of studying how the collective performs and not just the individual inventor. Looking at how an inventor performs is not enough to understand the technological evolution—to study technology evolution we need to look at the technological space—inventor collectivity as a system. Thus instead of individual patents and individual inventors, we investigate the knowledge network that encompasses the entire semiconductor industry.

We find that knowledge recombination in the form of boundary-spanning drives technological evolution depth (number of citations) and breadth (generality). In particular, we find that boundary-spanning resulting in knowledge combinations that are more proximate (near) have the most depth and generality of application. These effects did not materialize for spanning distant (far) knowledge. The purpose of this chapter is to take a first step by empirically testing how inventions that utilize knowledge from areas never utilized before or that combine knowledge from areas that have never been utilized together in previous inventions impact technology evolution in terms of number of citations and generality.

Thus, this chapter contributes to the literature of knowledge networks by empirically testing how boundary-spanning affects differently the evolution of technology. Using a conceptualization of knowledge as a space that can be mapped by means of patents, Patent main class and citations made and received are utilized to generate the knowledge space. Main class becomes the indicator of knowledge base, patents with the same main class are assumed to utilize similar knowledge. Citations to patents show the utilization of knowledge in the main class of the cited patent (backward citations) and the impact the patent has on the evolution of technology (forward citations). Results show that the way in what a patent connects knowledge areas has a distinct effect on its future application in different knowledge areas and on its ability to create new research streams, measured as forward citations.

The study also contributes to the innovation literature by identifying that not all boundary-spanning is the same. We found that near and far boundary-spanning have separate and distinct effects on number of citations and generality in a relatively short period of time. Future research should explore whether these effects extend over time. Perhaps the most important puzzle created by this study is whether, despite the non-significant results, boundary-spanning inventions are important beyond the number of citations and generality in defining the technological evolution. We may be facing the case of inventions for which we are not able to capture their relevance or which have 'long shot' characteristics; in other words, a few hit the 'jackpot' but on average, boundary-spanning inventions do not perform better than other patents regarding number of citations and generality. It is the distribution of outcomes that is of particular importance when trying to understand firm's decisions based on behavioral theories of decision making and the 'price' of engaging in this type of invention. Future research can better identify how different types of collective knowledge boundary-spanning result in breakthrough invention or influential inventions, or inventions that open new areas of research or spur invention activity in existing areas.

Due to the interconnectivity of the knowledge bases, which according to Sorenson and Fleming (2001) is significant, the potential for the invention to have emergent properties that cannot have been fully derived from prior experience is significant. The introduction of the novel knowledge base into the combination has the potential to reduce the fidelity of industry inventors' cognitive maps, which were developed from the experience accumulated in the industry knowledge base, resulting in a poor representation of the actual interaction effects. In other words, there are two levels of uncertainty: 1) how the novel knowledge will contribute to the solution in the presence of the familiar knowledge, and 2) how the familiar knowledge utilized will contribute in the presence of the novel and familiar knowledge. While spanning inventions have very high potential for becoming breakthrough, the limitations that industry inventors will face to understand the full potential of a far spanner patent is likely to limit or at least slow down the utilization of this type of patent in future recombination.

This chapter defines the type of invention at the industry level. We assess how different types of invention affect the technological evolution of the whole industry. A valuable area of research is the study of how the type of invention affects the technological evolution of a firm. In order to study this, future research should address how technological inventions, defined from a firm and industry perspectives, affect a firm's technological evolution and performance. It should answer questions such as: Do firms that engage in recombinant invention expand into different technological areas? Do inventions that are boundary-spanning for a firm lead to higher generality applications at the firm and industry level? What happens when an invention is boundary-spanning for the firm but not for the industry? Does it have a different number of citations?

While within this chapter empirics are based on a restrictive definition of technology, the idea that this model is based on applies to the broader definition of technology espoused by W. Brian Arthur (2009). Thus, the findings apply to any solution of a specific problem based on existing technologies, principles, and earthly constraints. As such, organizations are a technological solution that combines human capital, financial capital, and technology based on managerial cognition, and principles that allow for the delivery of products or services in a manner that solves a social need. We are addressing the microfoundations of observable phenomena that provide an explanation of why boundary-spanning of different types has an impact in, for example, invention, creativity, or performance. It is the incorporation of novel knowledge that is reached through the spanning, which can be achieve by many means, e.g., a person, an organizational tie, or even cross training, that opens new opportunities to solve existing problems that can be related to invention, performance, or efficiency.

Thus these concepts of collective boundary-spanning and knowledge recombination can expand into other areas. For example, one could think about a market system, where the marketing managers act as inventors selecting combinations of products, markets, and distribution channels. Knowledge boundary-spanning would involve recombinations that utilize products, markets, or distribution channels never utilized before. In thinking about a human resources (HR) department, similarly, there would be a search for combinations of policies, employee characteristics, and organizational structures for a solution that satisfies the need of a certain business.

Collective knowledge boundary-spanning involves structures, employees, and policies that have not been utilized before in that industry as part of the combination and organizational design. In both cases, the marketing and HR managers would be making decisions about what to include in the combination in order to find solutions to their marketing and organizational problems.

NOTES

1. Assignee codes in NBER and NUS databases identify unique firms; however, unfortunately, it is common, but unknown, when a firm is identified by only one assignee number. For this reason, we restricted our fixed effect analysis to those firms in our list of semiconductor firms for which the assignee numbers of each firm we know.
2. The likelihood ratio test statistic—$ABS(2logL.modelA–2logLmodelB)$—has approximately a χ^2 distribution with *d.f.* equal to the difference in the number of parameters between reduced and full models. The null hypothesis of this test is that the reduced model is equivalent to the full model. The full model is preferred over the reduced one when *p*-value is less than 0.05.

REFERENCES

Adner, Ron, and Daniel Levinthal. "Technology speciation and the path of emerging technologies." In G. Day and P. Schoemaker (Eds.), *Wharton on Emerging Technologies*. New York: John Wiley and Sons, 2000: 57–75.

Adner, Ron, and Daniel Levinthal. "Demand heterogeneity and technology evolution: Implications for product and process innovation." *Management Science* 47, no. 5 (2001): 611–628.

Ahuja, Gautam. "The duality of collaboration: Inducements and opportunities in the formation of interfirm linkages." *Strategic Management Journal* 21, no. 3 (2000): 317–343.

Almeida, Paul, Gina Dokko, and Lori Rosenkopf. "Startup size and the mechanisms of external learning: Increasing opportunity and decreasing ability?" *Research Policy* 32, no. 2 (2003): 301–315.

Almeida, Paul, and Bruce Kogut. "The exploration of technological diversity and geographic localization in innovation: Start-up firms in the semiconductor industry." *Small Business Economics* 9, no. 1 (1997): 21–31.

Arrow, K. J. *Essays in the Theory of Risk Bearing.* Chicago: Markham, 1971.

Arthur, W. Brian. *The Nature of Technology: What It Is and How It Evolves.* New York: Simon and Schuster, 2009.

Banerjee, P.M. "Leveraging existing technology: The role of alliances in cross-application." *Strategic Management Review* 2, no. 1 (2008): 1–22.

Barley, Stephen R. "Technology, power and the social organization of work: Toward a pragmatic theory of skilling and deskilling." In Nancy DiTomaso, Samuel B. Bacharach (Eds.), *Research in the Sociology Organizations*, vol. 6, pp. 33–80. Greenwich, CT: JAI Press, 1988.

Becker, Gary S., and Kevin M. Murphy. "The division of labor, coordination costs, and knowledge." *The Quarterly Journal of Economics* 107, no. 4 (1992): 1137–1160.

Benner, Mary J., and Michael L. Tushman. "Exploitation, exploration, and process management: The productivity dilemma revisited." *The Academy of Management Review* 28, no. 2 (2003): 238–256.

Bresnahan, Timothy F., and Manuel Trajtenberg. "General purpose technologies 'Engines of growth'?" *Journal of Econometrics* 65, no. 1 (1995): 83–108.

Britten, Roy J. "Divergence between samples of chimpanzee and human DNA sequences is 5%, counting indels." *Proceedings of the National Academy of Sciences* 99, no. 21 (2002): 13633–13635.

Brodbeck, May. "Methodological individualisms: Definition and reduction." *Philosophy of Science* 25, no. 1 (1958): 1–22.

Bower, Joseph L., and Clayton M. Christensen. "Disruptive technologies: Catching the wave." *Harvard Business Review* 73, no. 1 (1995): 43–53.

Cohen, Wesley M., and Daniel A. Levinthal. "Innovation and learning: The two faces of R & D." *The Economic Journal* 99, no. 397 (1989): 569–596.

Cohen, Wesley M., Richard R. Nelson, and John P. Walsh. "Protecting their intellectual assets: Appropriability conditions and why US manufacturing firms patent (or not)." *National Bureau of Economic Research*, No. w7552. 2000.

Collins, A., and D. Gentner. "How people construct mental models." In N. Quinn and D. Holland (Eds.), *Cultural Models in Language and Thought*, 243–265. New York: Cambridge University Press, 1987.

Corredoira, Rafael A., and Lori Rosenkopf. "Should auld acquaintance be forgot? The reverse transfer of knowledge through mobility ties." *Strategic Management Journal* 31, no. 2 (2010): 159–181.

Cyert, Richard M., and James G. March. *A Behavioral Theory of the Firm*. Englewood Cliffs, NJ: Prentice-Hall, 1963.

Danneels, Erwin. "The process of technological competence leveraging." *Strategic Management Journal* 28, no. 5 (2007): 511–533.

Diamond, J. *Guns, Germs, and Steel: The Fates of Human Societies*. New York: W.W. Norton & Company, 1999.

Dosi, G. "Technological paradigms and technological trajectories: A suggested interpretation of the determinants and directions of technical change." *Research Policy* 11, no. 3 (1982): 147–162.

Dougherty, Deborah. "Interpretive barriers to successful product innovation in large firms." *Organization Science* 3, no. 2 (1992): 179–202.

Fleming, L. "Recombinant uncertainty in technological search." *Management Science* 47, no. 1 (2001): 117–132.

Fleming, Lee, and Olav Sorenson. "Technology as a complex adaptive system: Evidence from patent data." *Research Policy* 30, no. 7 (2001): 1019–1039.

Garud, Raghu, and Peter Karnøe. "Bricolage versus breakthrough: distributed and embedded agency in technology entrepreneurship." *Research Policy* 32, no. 2 (2003): 277–300.

Hall, Bronwyn H., Adam B. Jaffe, and Manuel Trajtenberg. "The NBER patent citation data file: Lessons, insights and methodological tools." *National Bureau of Economic Research*, No. w8498. 2001.

Helfat, Constance E. "Evolutionary trajectories in petroleum firm R&D." *Management Science* 40, no. 12 (1994): 1720–1747.

Helpman, Elhanan, and Manuel Trajtenberg. "Diffusion of general purpose technologies." *National Bureau of Economic Research*, No. w5773. 1996.

Henderson, Rebecca, and Iain Cockburn. "Measuring competence? Exploring firm effects in pharmaceutical research." *Strategic Management Journal* 15, no. S1 (2006): 63–84.

Henderson, Rebecca, Adam B. Jaffe, and Manuel Trajtenberg. "Universities as a source of commercial technology: A detailed analysis of university patenting, 1965–1988." *Review of Economics and Statistics* 80, no. 1 (1998): 119–127.

Holland, J.B. "EPISTACY: A SAS program for detecting two locus epistatic interactions using genetic marker information." *Journal of Heredity* 89 (1998): 374–375

Jaffe, Adam B., Michael S. Fogarty, and Bruce A. Banks. "Evidence from patents and patent citations on the impact of NASA and other federal labs on commercial innovation." *National Bureau of Economic Research*, No. w6044. 1997.

Johansson, F. *The Medici Effect: Breakthrough Insights at the Intersection of Ideas, Concepts, and Cultures*. Cambridge, MA: Harvard Business School Press, 2006.

Katila, Riitta. "New product search over time: Past ideas in their prime?" *Academy of Management Journal* 45, no. 5 (2002): 995–1010.

Kogut, B., and U. Zander. "Knowledge of the firm, combinative capabilities and the replication of technology." *Organization Science* 3 (1992): 383–387.

Leonard-Barton, Dorothy. "Core capabilities and core rigidities: A paradox in managing new product development." *Strategic Management Journal* 13, no. S1 (2007): 111–125.

Levinthal, Daniel A. "The slow pace of rapid technological change: gradualism and punctuation in technological change." *Industrial and Corporate Change* 7, no. 2 (1998): 217–247.

Levitt, Barbara, and James G. March. "Organizational learning." *Annual Review of Sociology* 14 (1988): 319–340.

Lipsey, Richard G., Cliff Bekar, and Kenneth Carlaw. "What requires explanation." *General Purpose Technologies and Economic Growth* 2 (1998): 15–54.

Mansfield, Edwin. "Industrial R&D in Japan and the United States: A comparative study." *American Economic Review* 78, no. 2 (1988): 223–228.

March, James G. "Exploration and exploitation in organizational learning." *Organization Science* 2, no. 1 (1991): 71–87.

March, James G., and Herbert Alexander Simon. *Organizations*. New York: John Wiley & Sons, 1958.

March, James G., Lee S. Sproull, and Michal Tamuz. "Learning from samples of one or fewer." *Organization Science* 2, no. 1 (1991): 1–13.

McGrath, Rita Gunther. "Falling forward: Real options reasoning and entrepreneurial failure." *Academy of Management Review* 24, no. 1 (1999): 13–30.

Nelson, Richard R., and Sidney G. Winter. *An Evolutionary Theory of Economic Change*. Cambridge, MA: Belknap Press, 1982.

Nerkar, A., and Srikanth Paruchuri. "Evolution of R&D capabilities: The role of knowledge networks within a firm." *Management Science* 51, no. 5 (2005): 771–785.

Rosen, Sherwin. "Specialization and human capital." *Journal of Labor Economics* (1983): 43–49.

Rosenberg, Nathan. "Technological change in the machine tool industry, 1840-1910." The Journal of Economic History 23.4 (1963): 414-443.Rosenkopf, Lori, and Paul Almeida. "Overcoming local search through alliances and mobility." *Management Science* 49, no. 6 (2003): 751–766.

Rosenkopf, Lori, and Atul Nerkar. "Beyond local search: boundary-spanning, exploration, and impact in the optical disk industry." *Strategic Management Journal* 22, no. 4 (2001): 287–306.

Rumelt, R. *Strategy, Structure and Economic Performance*. Boston, MA: Harvard Business School Press, 1974.

Schilling, Melissa A., Patricia Vidal, Robert E. Ployhart, and Alexandre Marangoni. "Learning by doing something else: Variation, relatedness, and the learning curve." *Management Science* 49, no. 1 (2003): 39–56.

Schumpeter, J. *The Theory of Economic Development: An Inquiry into Profits, Capital, Credit, Interest, and the Business Cycle*. New York: Oxford University Press, 1934.

Smith, Adam. *The Wealth of Nations*. (London, 1776).

Sober, E. *The Nature of Selection: Evolutionary Theory in Philosophical Focus*. Cambridge, MA: M1T Press, 1984.

Song, Jaeyong, Paul Almeida, and Geraldine Wu. "Learning-by-hiring: when is mobility more likely to facilitate interfirm knowledge transfer?" *Management Science* 49, no. 4 (2003): 351–365.

Steels, L. "Towards a theory of emergent functionality." In J.-A. Meyer and S. W.

Wilson (Eds.), *From Animals to Animats: Proceedings of the First International Conference*

on Simulation of Adaptive Behavior, 451–461. Cambridge, MA: MIT Press, 1991.

Stuart, Toby E., and Joel M. Podolny. "Local search and the evolution of technological capabilities." *Strategic Management Journal* 17, no. S1 (1996): 21–38.

Tushman, Michael L., and Thomas J. Scanlan. "Boundary spanning individuals: Their role in information transfer and their antecedents." *Academy of Management Journal* 24, no. 2 (1981): 289–305.

Tyre, Marcie J., and Eric Von Hippel. "The situated nature of adaptive learning in organizations." *Organization Science* 8, no. 1 (1997): 71–83.

Varadarajan, P.R., and Vasudevan Ramanujam. "Diversification and performance: A reexamination using a new two-dimensional conceptualization of diversity in firms." *Academy of Management Journal* 30, no. 2 (1987): 380–393.

PART II
Groups and Teams

4 Framing Wicked Problems in Enterprise-Systems Innovation Project Groups

Susan Gasson

INTRODUCTION

Organizations are increasingly focusing on the design of organizational information systems that incorporate both business process and information technology (IT) change, to achieve alignment between business and IT objectives. These information systems (IS) span functional boundaries and business units, requiring many different disciplinary, organizational, and political interests to be negotiated and multiple, diverse ways of working to be reconciled. Organizational IS design, especially when this spans functional or business unit boundaries, conceptualizes and implements changes to the organization and practices of work, as well as technological change. IS managers thus need to balance the need for actionable, objective definitions of IT-related change with a need for radical, boundary-spanning inquiry into what needs to change (Engeström, Engeström, and Kärkkäinen 1995; Liu, Sun, and Bennett 2002). In the organizational and MIS literature, we have an increasing awareness of the emergent nature of IT-systems definition and its embeddedness within wider processes of organizational problem solving and business-process change. The term *information system* is used here to mean an integrated social system of organizational actors, using information to perform purposeful activity, who may or may not use computer-based technology to facilitate their work and to provide information (Silva and Hirschheim 2007). Following the use of the term in other fields, such as architecture, product design, or graphic design, the term *design* is viewed here as the complete process of conceptualizing, developing, refining, and evaluating an artifact-related solution to a problem, rather than as a single stage of the IT systems development life cycle (Lawson, 2000). Increasingly, the critical processes of boundary-spanning design take place "upstream" of the development life cycle waterfall model. Organizational change and problem-solving projects drive business process change and provide "early requirements" for IT systems development. This form of design involves emergent knowledge processes, for which goals emerge during the process of design (Markus et al., 2002). As I will argue below, it involves a dialectic between the processes of inquiry and processes of closure, whereas the typical IS design method focuses exclusively on closure.

Contemporary business enterprises are knowledge-intensive firms, which are composed of multiple communities of practice, each of which employs highly specialized technologies and knowledge domains. These groups span multiple organizational boundaries: administrative, geographical, functional, and product-line related. In engineering companies, for example, winning a new contract involves collaboration between accountants, marketing, product design, engineering, production, customer support, and corporate planning strategists (Gasson 2006). This means that knowledge about what needs to change, to produce effective processes, is difficult to share. Enterprise change involves the design of emergent knowledge processes, through which technology and organization are mutually constituted and explored (Markus, Majchrzak, and Gasser 2002). Successful collaboration in such groups must integrate or reconcile many different ways of interpreting, representing, defining, and resolving problems, which are situated in the various contexts of work spanned by the group of enterprise design participants.

This chapter deals with how members of enterprise-level project groups tasked with organizational and IT-related change collaborate and share knowledge to achieve mutually satisfying outcomes. Change management groups are typically referred to as "business process reengineering project groups" or "enterprise systems taskforces." They recruit senior middle managers from multiple business areas and functions, to redesign business processes and to define the IT systems changes required to support new ways of working. I employ a sensemaking view (Weick 1995) of organizational design project groups, focusing on the processes that various participants use to make sense of and interpret organizational phenomena, to understand how change occurs in the business enterprise.

COMPETING MODELS OF DESIGN AND CHANGE PROCESSES

Structured Design (Hierarchical Decomposition of Requirements)

The dominant process model underlying both organizational and technological design is Simon's (1973) normative model of ill-structured problem solving. In this model, a designed solution results from the analysis of a consensus problem definition and a set of goals for its resolution. *These goals derive from structures inherent in the situation* (Simon 1988, 1996). Because human beings cannot cope sufficiently with complexity, analysts unconsciously bound and select the set of variables, constraints, and goals that they consider as relevant to the design problem, to produce a "satisficing" solution. A set of consensual goals for change is agreed, then the analyst engages in a process of problem structuring and decompositional means-end analysis—a "gap analysis" of requirements for change achieved through a comparison of relevant elements of the current situation

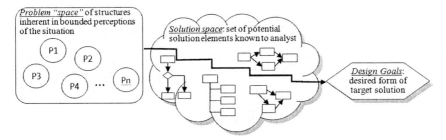

Figure 4.1 A Traditional Model of the IS Design Process (Adapted from descriptions in Simon, 1973; Simon, 1996)

(the problem space), with the desired situation (the design goals). A solution space, consisting of alternative (often partial) solution elements known to the analyst, is structured around a hierarchical decomposition of the structures inherent in the problem space[1]. This process is shown in Figure 4.1.

This structured analysis model of problem solving underlies most views of organizational change today. The model underpins the waterfall model (analysis based on hierarchical decomposition), which is still used to manage the majority of IS design and development projects (Barry and Lang 2003). The most significant problem with this model is that it assumes that the structure of the problem space is given, i.e., *inherent in the situation*. The stopping point for design from this perspective is thus when a set of solution criteria based on this problem structure—the design or change goals—are satisfied.

The inappropriateness of applying a goal-directed model to complex organizational change situations appears to have escaped attention (Checkland and Holwell 1998). Organizational change problems are wicked problems (Rittel and Webber 1973). These have no definable stopping point, as wicked problems are systems of interacting, subjectively defined problems that resist disentangling or definition. So the problem structure and goals for change are subject to interpretation and negotiation, reflecting many different points of view (Dorst 2006). In addition, the inability of a normative (rational) model to scale up to collaborative processes at the enterprise level appears to have escaped attention. One person's benefit is another person's problem. Structured decomposition may be appropriate for the design of a technology artifact, whose role and purpose is well understood. But the paradigm of means-end analysis embedded in goal-directed design grants certain problem-definitions an objective existence, privileging these over other interpretations. We need alternative models that cater to the emergent nature of organizational goals, problem definitions, and solutions.

Opportunistic Design

In contrast, we have a more organizationally situated literature that reflects goals as evolving, as groups of design participants and other stakeholders interact. Following from Mintzberg's model of strategic planning (Mintzberg and Waters 1985) and Suchman's concept of situated action (Suchman 1987, 2007) the organizational change literature provides us with an alternative view of goals and change planning. In this literature, goals most frequently reflect *post hoc* reasoning about the meanings and problem structures perceived in the situation after change has been implemented (Lave 1988, Nardi 1995). Actors engaged in boundary-spanning change projects redefine the problem periodically, based on reflective, experiential learning. This changes both the design goals and the locus of change. Organizational problems are situated within a specific social context and culture which require knowledge that is local, often implicit, and embedded in locally originated work practices and assumptions (Brown and Duguid 1992; Lave and Wenger 1991). Goals emerge through reflective interactions with the social context of the problem and through designer-stakeholder dialogue (Boland and Tenkasi 1995; Carlile 2002; Markus et al. 2002). Designers are "thrown" into a situation where local actors understand and assume problem elements, solution constraints, and criteria for a solution that are embedded in the experience of the organization and its evolving goals. They must engage with local practices and meanings, to acquire an understanding of the generic subjectivity (taken-for-granted understanding) that is shared by other design participants and stakeholders with whom they interact (Weick 2004). It is with this understanding that we seek an alternative model of the design process—one that fits with the reframing of problems and solution search that appears to underlie emergent knowledge processes.

Empirical evidence from studies of the early stages of software design suggests that experienced designers appear to be "opportunistic" in their use of contextual information to identify problem-structures, based on partial solutions taken from their experience of similar problems (Ball and Ormerod 1995, Guindon 1990). Design problems appear to be defined around available solutions—designers extrapolate solutions from previously encountered problems, incorporating implied requirements into the framing of new solutions. If there are no solutions available for a design problem, as currently defined, *the problem may be redefined to fit available solutions* (Dorst and Dijkhuis 1995; Turner 1987). The lack of a "structured" approach does not mean that design lacks a systematic process. From the evidence presented, the answer appears to lie in a model that parallels the "garbage can" theory of problem solving, which presents organizational change as a complex interaction between four independent streams of events: "a collection of choices looking for problems, issues and feelings looking for decision situations in which they might be aired, solutions looking for issues to which they might be the answer, and decision makers looking for work" (Cohen, March, and Olsen 1972, 2). Perhaps designers do not analyze the problem space at all, but just identify plausible solution fragments and collectively fit these to an evolving problem-space bricolage?

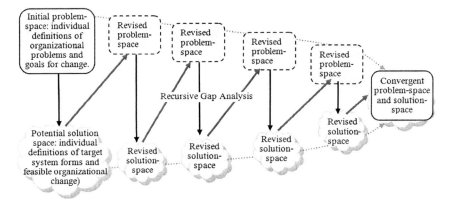

Figure 4.2   Design as a Convergence Between Problem Space and Solution Space

Convergent Design

Halfway between the ordered universe of structured decomposition and the opportunistic anarchy of bricolage lies the convergent design model, shown in Figure 4.2. This model, originated from studies of early software program design, views design as the coevolution of a problem space and a solution space (Maher and Poon 1996; Poon and Maher 1997; Maher and Tang 2003). A similar process of convergence has been observed in think-aloud protocol studies of creative product design (Dorst and Cross 2001).

A convergence model seems to provide a convincing explanation for the lack of an ordered decomposition strategy in "opportunistic" design analysis. But if we wish to apply this model to group processes, we face the issue of scalability—a process model derived from studies of individual cognition may be overly simplistic for group collaboration, especially when this involves stakeholders from multiple backgrounds and functional disciplines. A collective evolution of the design solution space is explored by Bergman, King, and Lyytinen (2002), who distinguish between the solution space as it exists now (i.e., the ecology of functional requirements that solves current perceptions of the problem structure) and a potential, future solution structure that results from analyst deliberation. But this perspective treats the problem space as negotiated rather than evolutionary: it does not deal with the evolution of *perceived* problem structures discussed in the previous section. Experienced analysts are subjective in their definition of the problem space and actively recognize learning outcomes as they proceed with a design. Individuals develop a richer understanding of the problem space as they proceed with a design; this process is multiplied in group design, and so disagreements and breakdowns in group consensus occur, during which the group must reassess what they know and consider what new information they can assemble between them (Gasson 2006; Gasson 2007). The next section presents an epistemological lens—how group processes of framing take place—to allow us to explore what model we might adopt if we account for the multiplicity of perspectives that present themselves in boundary-spanning groups.

BOUNDARY-SPANNING COLLABORATION AS ORGANIZATIONAL SENSEMAKING

Three Levels of Socially Situated Cognition

The creative processes underlying joint sensemaking "emerge from a process of negotiating multiple and potentially competing interests between different communities or groups within the organization" (Drazin, Glynn, and Kazanjian 1999, 286). A stable (accepted and incorporated) design does not need to be based on the establishment of common understandings but rather on the intersection between different positions and perspectives (McLaughlin et al. 1999). This involves the elicitation and sharing of organizational knowledge about the meaning of work practices across multiple organizational and domain boundaries (Carlile 2002, 2004). The meanings that we attribute to business processes and technology are defined by reference to culturally situated *frames* or mental models: the adoption of specific frames of reference, which derive from our experiential learning, our membership of specific interest groups or communities of professional practice, and our organizational affiliations (Goffman 1974; McLoughlin, Badham, and Couchman 2000).

We need to employ multiple levels of analysis in any exploration of sensemaking processes, in order to reflect the complexity of real-world innovation and to account for interaction effects between levels (Drazin, Glynn, and Kazanjian 1999). Weick (1995) defines four levels of sensemaking in organizations:

1. An intrasubjective (cognitive) level, which represents an individual, internal view of organizational reality;
2. An intersubjective level, which represents tacitly shared frames of reference that are constructed through joint participation in shared work practices;
3. A generically subjective (collective) level, which represents a commonly accepted (consensus) view of organizational reality; and
4. An extra-subjective, cultural environment, which provides a well of background knowledge from the extraneous environment that enables or constrains meanings.

I employ the first three distinctions here, categorizing three levels of sociocognitive framing: (i) the individual level of cognitive framing, (ii) the group level, which defines joint frames, and (iii) the organizational level, which reconciles distributed frames across knowledge domain boundaries. A socio-cognitive analysis would exclude the extraneous level, as this provides a generalization of social reality that is far distant from individual and group framing (Cecez-Kecmanovic and Jerram 2002).

Individual Framing and Organizational Learning

The internal, cognitive structures that guide human perceptions and their interpretation of reality are variously referred to as interpretive schemas (Bartlett 1932; Neisser 1976), personal constructs (Kelly 1955), cognitive scripts (Schank and Abelson 1977), or mental models (Gentner and Stevens 1983; Johnson-Laird 1983). These belief structures, or frames of reference, permit individuals to make sense of phenomena or events in terms of their own, individual interpretation of reality (Goffman 1974). They make sense of events and determine how to act as a consequence of an automatic "ordering" of reality, which we refer to as sensemaking (Weick 1995). A frame analysis examines how individuals and groups place a communication or interpret an event within a relevant context and interpret its meaning. Frames may be analyzed by means of discourse analysis (Tannen 1993; Ensink and Sauer 2003). By examining language terms, constructs, and metaphors, it is possible to understand how various people take a position on, or interpret the subject of, discussion in different ways. A specific frame embodies a set of expectations that constrain action and the scope of change: this tends to lead to "automatic" or unquestioned action or a resistance to change (Tannen 1986; Goffman 1974; Winograd and Flores 1986). To change a situation, we need to break frame: making explicit and questioning the dominant frame that stakeholders in that situation inhabit, causing them to reframe the situation (Goffman 1974; Tannen 1986). Design reframing may be triggered by cognitive breakdowns (Winograd and Flores 1986). Heidegger (1962) argued that objects and their properties are not part of an objective reality, but become apparent only in the event of breaking down, in which they change from "ready-to-hand" (used automatically) to "present-at-hand" (requiring reflection). Breakdowns can be used constructively in design: a breakdown is "a situation of non-obviousness" (Winograd and Flores 1986, 65). The breakdown uncovers an aspect of the design task and is a source of learning. For example, IS analysts appear to define a system according to implicit assumptions that are not questioned or realized until they conflict with explicit user requirements, during user interactions (Malhotra et al. 1980; Urquhart 2001). So a breakdown may be the mechanism by which an individual breaks out of or adapts an existing design frame to include new evidence.

To examine what triggers a breakdown, we employ the concept of cognitive dissonance. When there is a discord between incompatible belief structures, for example when an individual's assumptions of how a process works are inconsistent with how the individual is rewarded for performing that process, the individual experiences cognitive dissonance (Festinger 1957).

People avoid exposure to information that is likely to increase dissonance and are more likely to change their attitudes and beliefs to accommodate behaviors to which they have already committed than to change their behavior (Festinger 1957). Members of socially cohesive groups appear to experience dissonance reduction that brings about a commitment to new methods and ideas, even when these conflict with previously held beliefs (Nelson and Cooprider 1996). So one would expect group members to display increasing individual commitment to group perspectives, as social disparity is reduced.

Shared Framing and Group Consensus

When people habitually work together to achieve common aims—for example, the production of corporate accounts or the design of new products—we term this type of group a community of practice. Members of a community of practice tend to develop systems of shared values, belief structures, culture, and norms that govern how group members behave, interact, and communicate. These shared understandings provide a framework for action that allows group members to take shortcuts in communication and decision making—they implicitly know "how we do things here" without the need for debate or agreement (Lave and Wenger 1991). This results in shared frames that encompass not just how work is done, but why, defining shared rationale, and by whom, defining role allocations within the group (Brown and Duguid 1991). Shared frames represent a negotiated order that permits group members to operate cohesively, wasting less effort in resolving individual differences (Walsh, Henderson, and Deighton 1988). The critical issue for enterprise innovation is that each member of a boundary-spanning group belongs to a different community of practice. A typical enterprise systems design group might include accountants, product design engineers, production managers, marketing representatives, human resource managers, and information systems professionals. Each of those individuals will prioritize frames of reference that are salient to their own functional community of practice and may not understand the frames of other participants in the group. The result is a set of frames that intersect sufficiently for group members to discuss problems and solutions with some degree of commonality, but which provide only a small degree of shared understanding, as shown in Figure 4.3. This is why accusations of political game-playing are so common in boundary-spanning groups. Various individuals simply do not understand that they use the same words differently than members of other functional groups, or that they perceive the basis for their joint agreement differently, based on the scope and logic that derive from frames commonly employed within their own community of practice (Gasson 2005).

It is important to distinguish between intersubjectively shared group frames and consensus, as consensus depends on joint framing, which is distributed

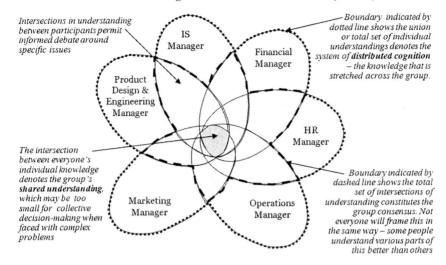

Figure 4.3   Intersections of Understanding and Knowledge in Boundary-Spanning Groups

across the total set of intersections of understanding in Figure 4.3, rather than shared framing. Individuals in boundary-spanning change projects build these intersections of understanding through argumentation and debate, during which they negotiate shared interpretations of phenomena and "scripts" for how to act in various circumstances (Rittel 1972).

Organizational Framing and Generic Subjectivity

At the organizational or boundary-spanning level of analysis, we cannot assume cognitively shared understanding just because group members share a similar organizational culture (Krauss and Fussell 1991; Miranda and Saunders 2003). As we saw above, shared understanding depends on a history of developing shared practices, frames, and values. Boundary-spanning collaborations rely upon consensus, which does not require the shared belief structures required for intersubjectivity. Instead, consensus accommodates the perspectives of others when these do not entirely conflict with one's own. As Fiol comments, "Meaning . . . encompasses multiple dimensions. Consensus may develop around one dimension of meaning and not around another." (Fiol 1994, 404–405).

Consensus-building is emergent and multidimensional. The knowledge required for complex change is often distributed across many different people, and it is difficult to predict what knowledge will be required for specific areas of change (Markus, Majchrzak, and Gasser 2002; Fiol 1994). In boundary-spanning groups, members of multiple communities of practice *negotiate* a set of common belief structures—a framework for action that allows them to interpret reality consistently and to act effectively as a group (Walsh, Henderson, and Deighton 1988). To achieve this, boundary-spanning groups must engage in both "perspective taking," the ability to reflect upon and reframe the familiar to open up new insights and under-standings, and "perspective making," the ability to evolve joint language, methods, theories, and values, and a framing rationale for change (Boland and Tenkasi 1995). But to engage in either of these mechanisms, we need ways of communicating our perspectives to others.

Repeated engagement in boundary-spanning group work processes pro-duces a system of distributed cognition, where understanding is *stretched across*, rather than shared between, collaborating individuals from different functional groups (Lave 1988). Boundary-spanning groups develop shared work practices that are mediated via a web of well-defined functional roles. These systems of interlocking routines allow boundary-spanning groups to negotiate the intersections of individual understanding that result—and re-quire divergent framing perspectives to be reconciled only when this is nec-essary for the coordination of joint work processes or outcomes (Boland, Tenkasi, and Te'eni 1994; Hollan, Hutchins, and Kirsh 2002; Star 1989). The interlocking work processes and routines engaged in by members of boundary-spanning groups produce a form of generic subjectivity that al-lows group members to interpret organizational events and phenomena in the same way (Weick 1995). These "generic frames" leverage the intersec-tions of understanding built over time to provide a common language for collaboration, reducing misunderstandings and conflict, even in enterprise-spanning, problem-solving, and design groups.

Punctuated Equilibrium in Boundary-Spanning Framing

Given that boundary-spanning groups do appear to develop a common language for collaboration over time, it is odd that organizational prob-lem-solving and IS design groups often appear to follow a process of "punc-tuated equilibrium." This term is derived from studies of evolution, where biological adaptation is associated with short, rapid disruptions to long pe-riods of equilibrium during which the form remains stable. The concept has been applied to the evolution of organizations, explaining why firms period-ically restructure or reorganize their technology infrastructure (Sabherwal, Hirschheim, and Goles 2001; Silva and Hirschheim 2007).

There is some evidence that relatively stable, generic frames in boundary-spanning groups are punctuated by disruptions that cause the group to com-pletely redefine their problem and as a consequence, rethink their solution. Gersick studied a number of project groups, from MBA student groups in-volved in three-month course projects to organizational groups involved in four- to six-month change initiatives. She hypothesized that reframing is driven by group perceptions of time constraints, observing that there is always a major redefinition of the problem structure midway through the project

duration (Gersick 1991, 1988, 1989). A similar type of punctuated or inter-
rupted process has been observed in user-analyst system requirements definition (Newman and Robey 1992) and in larger-scale studies of heterogeneous
IS requirements analysis (Bergman, King, and Lyytinen, 2002). But these studies focus on relatively heterogeneous groups and do not delve into the detail of
how or why disruptions occur. To investigate this issue in boundary-spanning
collaboration groups, we need an analytical lens that explores not only the
evolution of problem and solution spaces over time, but also the catalysts
that drive an evolving design consensus across design participants and stakeholders from multiple knowledge domains. The following sections explore
the processes underlying enterprise-spanning business process and information system design through the examination of a longitudinal case study.

CASE STUDY: THE UNIVERSITY STRATEGIC ENTERPRISE SYSTEM

Organizational Context

This case study explores the framing processes of a group of strategic senior
managers engaged in the definition of financial and enterprise systems in a
U.S. university (not the author's own institution), over a period of two years.
Representatives from various areas of university operations were involved,
as shown in Table 4.1. The Taskforce was assembled by the director of information services and the university registrar, in response to a perception
that the university's enterprise systems (ES) were inadequate for financial
management and reporting. The university employed an ES that was used
by many similar institutions, but which had not been fully implemented due
to political considerations. Several functional groups, in particular human
resources, were suspicious of the introduction of an overarching administration system, viewing this as an attempt to impose control over their group
culture and practices.

The issue facing the Taskforce at the start of the study was how to manage the introduction of new degree programs. Taskforce members raised
the issue that strategic planning was influenced too much by opportunities
offered by community interest groups and international non-government
organizations (NGOs). From the perspective of the information services
group, this was a strategic management issue: new programs were an-
nounced before the various administrative groups had time to evaluate the
implications or prepare for program administration. The university registrar
and the manager of admissions complained that students were often recruited to programs for which no classroom location, instructor, or facilities
were available. The dean of finance saw this as an admissions management
issue: students were recruited at the last minute, in order to ensure the program's financial viability, so there was a high degree of uncertainty about

Table 4.1 Taskforce participants

Regular Attendees:

Director of Information Services	Executive Director of Student Accounts	University Registrar
Dean of Academic Affairs	Director, Office of Stud. Accounts	Associate Registrar
Dean of Finance & Operations	Director of Financial Aid	Financial Systems Manager
Coordinator of Special Projects	Manager, Admissions & Student Services	Senior Systems Analyst
Director of Marketing (or delegate)		

Ad Hoc Attendees:

University President	Executive Dean (Academic Programs)	Program Administrators
Academic Deans & Administrators	Program Sponsors (External Community Organizations & NGOs)	Academic Committee Chairs

class sizes. The director of information services argued that many programs included textbooks and computers in their tuition costs and there was insufficient time for these to be ordered. Financial aid group members often found that degree eligibility requirements (e.g., the number of instruction weeks in a specific academic year) were not being met—even though recruiters had promised students that they would be eligible for financial aid.

EPISODES OF ENTERPRISE SYSTEM FRAMING

Episode 1: Exploring New Program Procedures

The Taskforce met frequently to explore the timeline for new programs and to determine the arrangements that needed to be made at various points, including changes to Enterprise System configuration. The *Process Timeline* provided a consensus frame for the group—both in terms of its role as a negotiation object and also in terms of its ability to embody a boundary-spanning framework for action. This framework provided a sufficiently abstract "script" for the problematized business process (the introduction of new degree programs) that members of the various groups involved could agree to this without it conflicting with individual perspectives of how the process would be conducted. In particular the Timeline, shown in Figure 4.4, aligned the interests of various groups in coordinating boundary-spanning arrangements.

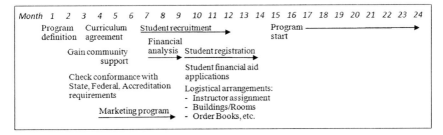

Figure 4.4   New Program Process Timeline

On the surface, the Timeline—and its embedded formalized procedures—appeared uncontentious. Taskforce members clearly recognized the need for coordination and control across a wide range of related functional groups and were willing to accommodate some changes to their processes in return for the quid-pro-quo of their information needs being met (i.e., obtaining sufficient warning of student numbers and details to do their job). But the ways in which detailed information needs were framed diverged greatly between group representatives. The information services group saw the key issue as one of coordinating transient information about student and program arrangements that the Enterprise System could not cope with—for example ordering printed course materials and booking rooms for classes in advance of formalized registration. The university registrar framed the issue as one of ensuring that students were registered in time for the degree start. The financial aid group framed the key issue as one of processing and validating financial aid applications prior to registration. The university financial controller's office framed the issue as ensuring that the new program was economically viable in advance of its start. Each of these frames led to a variety of ad hoc, informal arrangements that allowed groups to coordinate operations, but bypassed the formal information system. A shared spreadsheet of student status allowed the financial controller's office to anticipate class size, student services to order printed materials in advance of formal registration, information services to reserve rooms, and the financial aid office to check student applications. But none of these information sources could be trusted—the spreadsheet version used by various groups often disagreed and a whole host of informal coordinating processes were required to make this process work, in addition to the formal processes agreed upon by the Taskforce.

Disruption to the fragile consensus around a standardized Process Timeline frame arose when feedback from various faculty committees and external stakeholders led to a realization by the Systems Taskforce that the attempt at standardization had failed. A Taskforce workshop was held, to explore the problems faced in new program introduction. The information services director attempted to generate procedure flowcharts that reflected the "big picture" of program administration across all affected groups.

This failed, as each member group framed the issues very differently. Each group framed a number of special cases—many disagreements arose around which should be accepted as legitimate and which not. The aggregated set complicated the flowchart to the point at which the wider group agreed it to be unusable as a shared representation of procedures.

Episode 2: Framing Coordination Issues

Conflicts arising from the breakdown of the standardized Process Timeline frame were resolved in the next Taskforce meeting, when members brainstormed how to address major differences between academic program formats. They agreed that the solution to resolving differences should lie in *standardizing the format of new academic programs.* Taskforce members identified four different types of program calendar: Semester Programs, Certificate Programs, Quarter Programs, and Ad Hoc Programs. A new University Calendar, shown in Figure 4.5, was standardized around these program formats. Start-date ranges for each type of program were defined and program introduction requirements were formalized in terms of the lead time required for the various program types within each category. The student accounts and financial aid groups were especially active in this episode, leading discussions about standardization needs and explaining their information requirements in great detail.

When the standardized calendar was introduced, it appeared to have an immediate effect. Operations to coordinate work between groups were simplified, student aid issues were reduced, and the longer planning lead times were felt to have led to higher quality across various academic programs. But as the administrative year proceeded, there appeared to be an increasing number of exceptions to these program formats—formalized for historical program continuity, or to meet the needs of specific community groups.

The *disruption* to the program format standardization frame occurred because of an increasing frustration across the global network of coordinated

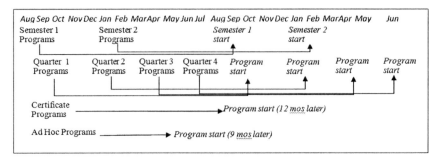

Figure 4.5 A Process Calendar for Four Standard Program Formats

groups and stakeholders, reflected in some quite heated exchanges in Task-force meetings. There was also increasing dissatisfaction from strategic planners. Both the executive committee and the university president were pushing for an expansion of the university's strategic plan, to take advantage of opportunities offered by private funding agencies and expand outreach to underserved areas of the U.S. This led to a tension between the regulating influence of the "standardized" program formats and the way in which new program requirements were framed as fulfilling the university mission—even when they did not conform to a standardized format. There were rising tensions around how this could be accommodated.

Episode 3: Invisible Expansion of the Problem Boundary

After a series of disagreements in Taskforce meetings, the constraints of four standardized program formats were rejected. New programs were created that did not accord with these formats and that had shorter lead times than required for effective planning. The various groups represented on the Taskforce agreed that they would *implement contingency procedures to deal with exceptions*. In adopting these, the Taskforce approved an expansion of the regular scope of activity with activities that lay outside of their normal business process boundary. These contingency procedures, were viewed as short-term "interfaces" and were largely taken over by information services and the registrar's office, expanding the scope of both groups.

The implications of this expanding, implicit information system boundary were slow to be realized. The increasing complexity of operations was obscured by the information services group, who developed short-term workarounds for each group. They made phone calls to warn student services that action was required, provided interim calculations of student numbers to the registrar's office, and fed student data to the financial aid office for aid application processing and to the financial controller's office for planning purposes. In effect the information services group became a de facto coordination system, operationalizing the implicit frames of various Taskforce members to bypass the formal Enterprise System and business processes based on the standardized calendar. When the group mapped out the systems used to support enterprise decisions, shown in Figure 4.6, they appeared genuinely shocked.

Disruption to the contingency frame occurred as the complexity of the "workaround systems"—as these came to be called—introduced a sense of urgency into Taskforce group meetings. It became clear that the Taskforce needed a way to enforce the use of the formal Enterprise System, as no one had a clear picture of what was happening with the new programs—whether they were financially viable, whether they met the course-credit and calendar requirements that would enable students to obtain financial aid (a key criterion for open-access programs), and whether these programs were

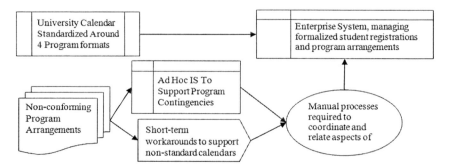

Figure 4.6   Process Workarounds Resulting from Enterprise System Inadequacies

even fulfilling local community objectives. Many disagreements centered on how to obtain a "big-picture view" and how to regain control of program planning. It was clear that consensus had broken down, as members of each functional group blamed the others for "allowing so many workarounds to creep into the system."

Episode 4: Exploring the Breakdown of Planning

Matters came to a head when external program accreditation was threatened, because the new programs did not conform to the credit or delivery requirements agreed with the national accreditation board. The threat to accreditation refined the minds of everyone, not least members of the Systems Taskforce. When the group mapped out planning procedures for new programs, they were shocked to discover how much more complex these had grown since the institution of the standardized program calendars. It proved impossible for the Taskforce to model these procedures—there were so many special cases that the director of information services observed that they were modeling "a calendar per academic program." The variety of academic programs was reviewed and the Taskforce agreed to abandon the calendar approach to evaluating programs, as this produced a false sense of security. Instead, they adopted a *standardized form of program cost structure* as their consensus solution. This was represented as shown in Figure 4.7.

The program cost structure embodied a key concern of Taskforce members—that programs were being expanded without any analysis of the cost implications—and provided a script for coordinated action. An analysis of indirect program costs was performed by each group involved— Taskforce members appeared shocked to discover the cost implications of program expansion. Various Taskforce members volunteered to discuss cost implications with individual Deans, with strategic managers, and with other stakeholders. The Taskforce worked on analyzing the costs of a failure to standardize the university calendar in detail. The "informal cost structure" form presented a new coordinating object for the group. They were

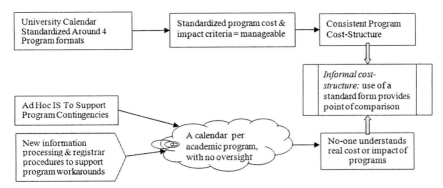

Figure 4.7 Role of "Informal Cost-Structure" Form in Reconciling Programs

continually surprised by the totals reported, as various Taskforce members volunteered to investigate the costs of time and resources spent on ad hoc program workarounds. These totals made a huge impression on strategic managers—the university president instructed the Taskforce to "take control of the situation." But it was clear that the key problem lay with the president and other executive decision makers, who disowned responsibility for their continued initiation of nonconforming, ad hoc programs. The Taskforce group debated how to manage this, but could reach no conclusion.

Disruption to the cost-reconciliation frame came with the news that accreditation was threatened by the failure of recent academic programs to meet accreditation requirements. The lack of conformity with calendar credit requirements, national evaluation, and quality criteria had led to pressure from a major undergraduate program accreditation board. There were several heated meetings, as Taskforce members debated how to manage the situation and who should take responsibility for change. In the end, the university registrar took control of the situation and met with the president to discuss how to manage the situation.

Episode 5: Aligning a Standardized Calendar with Senior Management Interests

The Taskforce received instructions from the executive board to explore what needed to happen for the university to *standardize around a single program calendar*. Taskforce members now realized the need to develop a universal set of procedures that would formalize coordination across the various groups involved in program administration, as shown in Figure 4.8.

The external crisis allowed them each group involved to resurrect problem-formalization frames that had been rejected by other groups during Episode 2—for example, the financial aid office insisted that a formal coordination framework should include twelve weeks' notice of individual student registrations prior to start of the academic program year. Eventually, the Systems

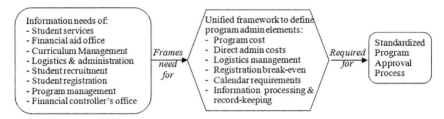

Figure 4.8   Strategic Planning Frame Indicates Need for Effective Coordination Framework

Taskforce standardized around a single academic calendar, with two program variations (semester and quarter) and a uniform start week for all programs. This allowed programs to conform to both accreditation and financial aid requirements without further checking. A set of standardized procedures and templates was created for new programs and courses, without conformance to which programs would not be approved. It was the "would not be approved" frame that provided the unifying script embedded in this framework.

Disruption to the strategic planning and coordination frame came about when the introduction of the standardized program approval framework caused problems. Recruiters felt that they were being cheated of the opportunity to recruit late students, and some compromise had to be made to keep this group on board. Executive decision makers had to be monitored carefully and reminded of the implications of abandoning the standardized calendar and procedures—whenever they attempted to do so, under pressure from community organizations to provide open-access programs. There were ongoing tensions between the needs of accreditation conformance and the way in which the university mission, to provide open access to education, was framed. In the end, these were resolved by the information services director, whose group had devised the workarounds that had previously caused so many problems. He (and other information services group members) appeared mortified by the realization that they were to blame for enabling the escalating costs of program nonconformance. The information services group developed an informal cost estimation system (a detailed spreadsheet) that reflected the true costs of introducing a new academic program, based on the cost estimates generated during Episode 5. Each time a new program was planned, the cost estimation spreadsheet was used to reflect the true costs of introduction. This reduced the nonconformance of new programs to the standardized calendar formats to almost nil. By disrupting the *strategic mission* frame ("open access requires responsive, ad hoc program creation") with an adapted version of the cost-reconciliation frame used in Episode 4, they were able to introduce a collective breakdown that made the group realize that they genuinely needed to formalize their "standardized program approval" procedures by means of changes to the Enterprise System—which was why the Taskforce had been assembled.

Episode 6: Implementing Enterprise System Changes

Predictable conformance to the four program formats for a standardized calendar and procedures allowed changes to be defined to the Enterprise System, so that this could implement the contingency planning functions that the information services group had been supporting with the ad hoc IS, shown in Figures 4.6 and 4.7. Once the information services group reframed the problem to demonstrate that various nonconformities could be defined with short-term system codes for legacy program completion, Enterprise System limitations were no longer a constraint. It appeared that the main barrier to coordination had simply been an unwillingness to invest IT development time and resources without some expectation of stability in the way that the new system was framed across groups.

As shown in Figure 4.9, the Taskforce rapidly defined a vision of change that would enable the Enterprise System both to track formal program planning and administration and to manage the informal practices required for program planning and student recruitment to work. For example, it was now possible to track student status before their registration was completed and at times when they were registered for a program but not yet registered for specific courses. This allowed planning to take place for facilities and logistics much earlier, ensuring a higher quality of delivery with fewer problems. The external accreditation board was presented with the new planning process and appeared satisfied that the university's programs were stable and well managed. Student satisfaction also increased, as financial aid application was simplified and became more certain. Not least, the cost structure of programs was reduced drastically, providing major benefits to the university and allowing it to fulfill its mission more effectively.

Summary of Case Study: The Wicked Problem-Solving Process

In this study, the Financial Systems Taskforce group defined the financial information system to register students for courses and evaluate their eligibility for financial aid at the start of the problem-solving process. They

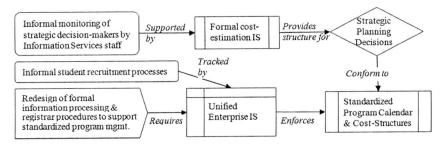

Figure 4.9 Framing Enterprise-Spanning Coordination as Combination of Informal and Formal Procedures

all agreed what this would mean, in terms of providing a framework for action that defined coordination procedures across groups. So the financial information system provided a unifying vision of the solution structure that allowed various stakeholders to frame subcomponents related to their individual sphere of operations. As the Enterprise System definition and implementation proceeded, however, shortcomings in the unifying vision were exposed. These were dealt with by a series of episodes in which Taskforce members appeared unwilling to face conflict in challenging the consensus solution, punctuated by rapid disruptions during which some external trigger forced them to adapt their consensus problem frame.

In each episode, short-term accommodations were implemented to deal with deficiencies of the solution in practice until external pressures indicated that the unifying vision was no longer adequate to provide a solution. At this point, a collective breakdown occurred, where debates around the unifying vision introduced more complexity in order to encompass the evolving, more complicated frames of individual group members (who introduced lessons learned from the failure of the previous frame). The result of each breakdown in equilibrium was not a more detailed model of the solution, but an abstraction that encompassed a wider range of individual member frames. The implications of this are explored below.

CASE STUDY SYNTHESIS OF BOUNDARY-SPANNING GROUP PROCESSES

Punctuated Equilibrium Around Unifying Visions of the Problem Space

The Enterprise System design project described above proceeded as a series of episodes, punctuated by rapid disruptions to group alignment around a dominant consensus frame. Shared understanding across disciplinary or work-group domain boundaries in each episode appears to have been coordinated around a representation of the target Enterprise System that allowed group members from diverse backgrounds to understand the high-level solution structure in the same way. This mechanism reflects the "primary generator" concept identified by Darke in her study of architectural design, where a material exemplar provided a conceptual metaphor for the designed solution, around which they could construct a shared vision of design requirements. For example, designing around a ranch-house concept allowed architects to envisage the house in a consistent way as they partitioned the work between team members that is required to design the frame for the house, the placement, the dimensions and style of doors and windows, the supply of utilities, the interior partitions and decorations, and so on. The "primary generator" provides a unifying solution frame that allows everyone to envision the solution in the same way, in order to distribute work on the basis of a shared understanding (Darke 1979). So we can understand the primary generator in terms of a meta-level solution structure that allows group members to apply an internally consistent set of criteria to the evaluation of solution elements that will change this structure.

It was observed that representations of the Enterprise System structure and its accompanying business processes did not change very much throughout the course of the project—if anything, this appeared to act as a constraint on change, as the IT systems group did not wish to implement software changes until they had confirmed that these would apply for the long term. So while the primary generator vision provided a meta-level frame—a shared perception of the Enterprise System solution structure—around which suggested design changes could be evaluated, it did not appear to evolve the solution space (the range of alternative design possibilities) available to the group. It would appear that the complex nature of the wicked problems faced by design group members precluded joint exploration of a single solution space. Instead, each group member appeared to explore a different solution space. Where these intersected, it was possible to build alliances that evolved the design, as external triggers for change required a replacement to the consensus problem frame—what I will call the unifying vision. So our process of punctuated equilibrium appears to revolve around a consensus problem space, rather than the solution space suggested by studies of individual design processes. Each unifying vision represented a deep appreciation of salient aspects of the problem structure (the organizational situation), which were relevant to how the group framed the rationale for change at that point. At the end of each design episode the unifying vision evolved, to be replaced by a more complex representation that incorporated salient aspects of the situation not dealt with by the previous consensus frame. This process of incremental design framing allowed the group to collaborate around a satisficing understanding of the problem, while deferring a shared understanding of the detailed solution to that time when the unifying vision broke down.

In this form of punctuated equilibrium, disruptions to shared understanding occurred on a regular basis in this case study, rather than at the halfway point proposed by Gersick (1988). This may perhaps be explained by the complex nature of this change initiative, compared to the relatively structured tasks faced by Gersick's (1988, 1989) problem-solving groups. As complexity is typical of enterprise-level codesign initiatives, the pattern of repeated disruptions appears more convincing, reflecting wicked problem structures that are appreciated in more detail as the group's distributed understanding of the situation evolves.

It has been noted that both problem and solution definitions emerge through interactions with the social context of inquiry, which includes other design participants, stakeholders, and users, as well as artifacts, documents, norms, goals, and local work practices (Boland, Tenkasi, and Te'eni 1994). This produces "surprising" information, which leads to the reframing of the design problem in unpredictable ways (Dorst and Cross 2001). In her synthesis of punctuated equilibrium studies, Gersick discusses the changes to group perceptions of what she calls "deep structure." But in common with most treatments of design or problem-solving processes, she treats the notion of deep structure as a frame that encompasses the solution space:

> Deep structure is a network of fundamental, interdependent "choices": of the basic configuration into which a system's units are organized, and the activities that maintain both this configuration and the system's resource exchange with the environment. Deep structure in human systems is largely implicit. (Gersick 1991, 15)

In contrast, the deep structures represented by this group were of the problem space. Each episode of design was accompanied by a graphical representation of the problem structure faced by the organization or design group—a unifying vision of the organizational situation rather than a model of the designed solution. Once a unifying vision was proposed to the group, it was accepted simply because one or more individuals could provide an analogy that enabled group members to visualize the relationship between organizational elements that comprised their current understanding of the wicked problems that they faced. This pattern represents problem-solving and design processes in prior studies of groups attempting wicked problem resolution (Gasson 2006, 2007, 2011, 2012).

Collective Breakdowns and Distributed Understanding

Each episode of design was terminated by a fairly rapid and disruptive period of conflict, which was only resolved when it was demonstrated to the group that the previous unifying vision had broken down. It was noticeable that the Taskforce attempted to avoid conflict, going to great lengths to avoid confrontations that would reveal divisions in the ways that details of the problem or solution space was framed by individuals. The transcripts of group meetings are littered with phrases like "let's agree to disagree on that issue" or "we need to put that one aside for another time." But when faced with external pressure to agree on detailed requirements for change, the Taskforce group experienced a collective breakdown, similar to the individual breakdowns discussed by Heidegger (1962) and observed by Winograd and Flores to be central to individual design progress (Winograd and Flores 1986). The collective breakdown forced the group as a whole to understand that their conceptual model of the problem was inadequate—and to reconceptualize how they framed organizational "reality" as a consequence.

As the design proceeded, the degree of shared understanding across the group did not appear to increase much, if at all, because the complexity of the organizational problem was too great for one person to understand. However, as individuals collaborated in framing joint design goals and solutions, the intersections of understanding between individuals appeared to increase—which meant that they developed joint (if not collective) ways of framing design issues with other individuals. This manifested itself by means of alliances between Taskforce members as the change initiative progressed—in contrast with early episodes where hardly anyone could agree about what the critical change issues were. Alliances between two or more members of the Taskforce seemed to be effective in exerting pressure on recalcitrant stakeholders who did not buy into the prevailing consensus, such as executive managers who ignored constraints in initiating new academic programs, or representatives of various functional groups who did not completely agree with the salient consensus frame. The result was that individual problem frames appeared to be aligned around the salient consensus frame for a substantial portion of each episode of design.

Increasing intersections of understanding also seemed to lead to higher levels of trust between Taskforce members. People deferred to each other's expertise more frequently in later episodes of the change initiative and would often suggest that one of their Taskforce colleagues "run with the idea," rather than debating every change in detail as they had in early episodes. This is especially interesting as typically, models of group cognition posit that groups depend on social cohesion to achieve shared understanding (Cannon-Bowers and Salas 2001). But similar indications are also emerging from studies of social interdependence in education (Johnson and Johnson 2009). It appears that distributed cognition relies upon the development of sufficient trust between individuals to enable effective problem partitioning in the implementation of a designed solution. Of course, trust building itself depends on the establishment of those intersections of understanding that support distributed knowledge in boundary-spanning groups. It seems that partial alliances around shared cognition are more feasible than collective understanding, in boundary-spanning groups faced with wicked problems.

Three Levels of Framing in Boundary-Spanning Groups

The resulting process appears to involve the coevolution of a designer's problem frame and the set of partial solutions available to them, until these merge to provide a target system design. But the process observed is more complex than the coevolution model shown in Figure 4.2, which is suggested by studies of individual design processes (Dorst and Cross 2001, Maher and Poon 1996, Poon and Maher 1997, Maher and Tang 2003). The model in Figure 4.10 shows interactions between three levels of design framing observed in this study.

At the highest level of framing, we have an evolving primary generator vision of the enterprise system solution space. This provides a consensus abstraction around which the group can frame design goals. It is replaced periodically, to provide the conceptual basis for a new, shared understanding as the problem structure evolves. The primary generator reflects an abstraction of the solution space, as understood by the group as a whole. The design group defined the solution for their financial planning problems as a

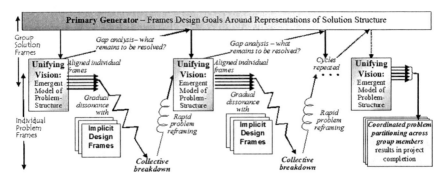

Figure 4.10   Multilevel Goals and Spaces In Design

standardized calendar, then standardized program formats, then as a set of contingencies for workarounds, and so on. None of these were particularly radical, in terms of changes to the Enterprise System, and none appeared to affect overall framing of the solution space, except in very small details.

The second level of framing is defined by a series of unifying visions of the group problem frame, each of which is developed and built on the previous one. In the case study presented here, each unifying vision represented consensus around the organizational and process structures that were most salient to the current focus of the design problem space. These did evolve in each episode, to incorporate aspects of the problem situation that reflected new issues of concern, while retaining previous structures. The design group defined the problem space around a process timeline, then explored the implications of four standard program formats for the process timeline, then explored process workarounds resulting from Enterprise System inadequacies, and so on. So each unifying vision was more complicated and encompassing than the previous one, to reflect group learning about the wicked problem situation. While the primary generator reflected a relatively homogeneous and slow-to-evolve solution space, the unifying vision reflected an emergent and progressively-more-complex problem space.

The third level represents the implicit design frames held by individuals: fragments of design goal definitions, beliefs about the nature and structure of the problem situation, and ideas that provide partial design solutions. In each episode, a unifying vision of the problem structure initially provided a consensus frame around which individual design frames could be aligned. But as each episode progressed, the unifying vision proved inadequate when compared with the implicit frames—encompassing design goals, problems, and partial solutions—held by individual group members. Group members' attempt to reconcile consensus frames with their implicit frames led to increasing levels of cognitive dissonance—the feeling of discomfort that results from attempting to hold two or more conflicting cognitions (ideas, beliefs, or values) simultaneously (Festinger 1957). There would be a rapid period of conflict, as individuals attempted to resolve their cognitive dissonance by reframing the details of the design solution. Taskforce group members were observed to be very accommodating in absorbing obvious differences between their own problem frames and those of other group members in order to avoid explicit conflict. It appeared that learning was seen as an explicit objective of the process at the individual level, and this only resulted in severe dissonance when an *external pressure*, such as the need to report to influential decision makers, or the external threat of losing accreditation, needed to be resolved. When this occurred, a collective breakdown would result. Each breakdown introduced a conceptual vacuum that led to a rapid, collective search for a substitute unifying vision, through a brainstorming process that developed ideas and integrated individuals' concerns into a more complex, richer unifying vision. A new unifying vision would only be acceptable to the group if it was accompanied by a visual problem-structure model that encompassed the concerns that individuals were trying to resolve, at an abstract level. The group would continue its debate and search for a unifying vision until one or more group members were able to conceptualize the problem-situation visually, in a way that satisfied the majority of individual concerns.

Negotiations, Bridging, and Breakdowns in Boundary-Spanning Design

So how did an accommodation take place between members of various established communities of practice (stakeholder groups) across the organization? Members of multiple communities of practice *negotiated* a set of common belief structures—a framework for action that allowed them to interpret reality consistently and to act effectively as a group (Walsh, Henderson, and Deighton 1988). The boundary-spanning group observed here engaged in both "perspective taking," the ability to reflect upon and renarrativize the familiar to open up new insights and understandings, and "perspective making," the ability to evolve a joint language, methods, theories, and values, and a framing rationale for change (Boland and Tenkasi 1995). Most design methods focus on perspective making—the representation of designed solutions, in terms of changes to business processes and IT systems. But this study has indicated the critical role played by perspective taking—the definition of a joint problem space around which the group can negotiate the rationale for change.

To engage in boundary-spanning consensus building, the group needs ways of communicating their perspectives to others. They achieve this by constructing a visual representation of the *problem structure*—a unifying vision—that can act as a straw man in negotiations between groups. This causes implicit assumptional frames to surface, so that they can be examined and subject to debate. Winograd and Flores (1986) argue that the use of specific boundary objects, such as design-solution representations, may trigger a *breakdown* in individual understanding, allowing the designer to reflect and learn about the context of the design. This study indicates that representations of the problem structure are the key boundary object required for effective design in boundary-spanning groups.

> Boundary objects are objects that are both plastic enough to adapt to local needs and constraints of the several parties employing them, yet robust enough to maintain a common identity across sites. They are weakly structured in common use, and become strongly structured in individual-site use. (Star 1989, 46)

An effective boundary-spanning problem representation must therefore be sufficiently vague (weakly structured) to mobilize consensus around the rationale for change, but specific enough (strongly structured) when applied to individual cases. As group understanding of the organizational situation evolves, this specificity is tested in more detail and its unifying power is lost. This leads to disruptions in the consensus and replacement with a more sophisticated boundary object that can maintain a "common identity" across a wider range of circumstances.

   Most studies of design groups simply assume that individual understanding—how the design problem and solution are framed—scale up to group design. But group relations change when conditions and deliverables change. Organizations faced with dynamic conditions must develop interdependence mechanisms: coordinating their activities across diverse group boundaries, developing trust mechanisms, and coming to rely on a social network of collaborators who view the organization very differently from themselves. An Enterprise System design group necessarily deals with wicked problems that span the organization. It involves representatives from diverse workgroups, disciplines, and functions. Its processes will involve conflict simply because group members need to negotiate a diversity of organizational problem frames, the existence of which they are unaware. This will result in repeated breakdowns in joint group sensemaking (Weick 1995). Early in the group's existence, negotiating trust relationships may require methods that do not directly challenge individual assumptions and frameworks of interpretation. But over time, trust between boundary-spanning group members appears to result from the ways in which collective breakdowns are negotiated, bridged, and reconciled. With sufficient trust comes the ability to engage in problem partitioning, the process by which various aspects of the problem are delegated to individual group members for their resolution. The stopping point for boundary-spanning groups is not reached when the group achieves shared understanding of the problem or its solution, as this is not feasible for the wicked problems faced by boundary-spanning groups. Instead, the stopping point appears to depend on a boundary-spanning group building sufficient levels of interpersonal trust for problem partitioning to take place. Trust is achieved by means of joint participation in collective learning, as the boundary-spanning group becomes a community of practice (Lave 1991). The implication is that, instead of the solution-oriented problem closure that is typically emphasized by design methods, we need to develop methods that emphasize joint participation in collective learning about the organizational problem situation.

CONCLUSIONS

This chapter examined the ways in which boundary-spanning groups engaged in Enterprise Systems change negotiate collective understanding. The design of organizational information systems provides a good example of a wicked problem, as systems of technology are embedded in an organizational context and procedures that must also change, requiring negotiation around a diverse set of perspectives (Rittel 1972). Enterprise Systems change projects involve participants from many different business areas and functions, who are required to engage with substantive issues of organizational and IT-related change over a long period of time, with repeated disruptions to group consensus. Because of this, participants share very little understanding of their "common goals." They assemble a jigsaw puzzle of process elements, based on ways of framing the situation that at best are poorly understood by participants from other functions or workgroups, and at worst are viewed by others as political game-playing. It is against this background that we need to find alternative methods for managing organizational change and design.

The case study discussed above reveals the significance of problem representations to achieving shared understanding. Taskforce members tested their individual solution frames against a shared representation of the problem structure—not the designed solution. Boundary-spanning design, in the form of collaborative organizational inquiry, appears to proceed via a set of episodes that were coordinated around unifying visions of the problem structure. To be useful in coordinating group inquiry, a unifying vision needs to act as a boundary object against which individual frames can be tested. It must be defined at a sufficiently abstract level that it does not conflict with individual problem frames (based on local workgroup practices, conventions, and norms), but have sufficient unifying power to maintain a common identity to which the whole group can relate. It must also act as a "negotiation object" in that it must be capable of adaption as group understanding evolves. Each disruption in group consensus leads to the unifying vision being replaced with a new problem-structure representation, which encompasses a wider set of concerns while also integrating issues of previous concern. Each unifying vision does not replace the prior vision—it complicates it.

I presented a multilevel, punctuated equilibrium model of boundary-spanning design in Figure 4.10. This model has critical implications for theory and practice in the management of boundary-spanning design and problem-solving groups. Unlike much of the work on distributed cognition (e.g., Stahl 2000; Zhang and Norman 1994; Hollan, Hutchins, and Kirsh 2002), this chapter argues that boundary-spanning group work does not result in a collective (cognitively shared) model of outcomes, nor does it result in designed artifacts that embody joint knowledge frameworks. Instead, the knowledge frameworks underlying design depend on social networks of distributed understanding—an understanding which resides firmly in the heads of individuals. Rather than depending on social cohesion to achieve joint understanding, it appears that distributed cognition relies upon the development of sufficient trust between individuals to enable effective problem partitioning in the implementation of a designed solution. Trust building enables the group to reach a natural stopping point, where the labor of implementing enterprise-spanning business process and IT systems change can be divided among those group members who are most familiar with each area of change. As Weick argues, the contemporary, corporate focus on achieving short-term goals tends to impede enterprise-spanning collaboration, simply because it focuses on organizational control at the expense of adaptation:

> Control drives out innovation, organization becomes synonymous with control and generic subjectivity becomes sealed off from any chance for reframing, learning and comprehension of that which seems incomprehensible. (Weick 1995, 73).

NOTE

1. The concepts of *problem space* and *solution space* derive from the psychology of programming and design literature. Initially, the problem-space concept was proposed as part of an algebraic representation of external problem structures that existed independently of the analyst (Newell and Simon 1972). More recently, the concepts have been used more fluidly, to denote a mental model or conceptual "space" of potential design problems or solutions that underlie the selection of specific design attributes (Dorst and Cross 2001). The concept is developed further by Bergman, King, and Lyytinen (2002) to distinguish between the solution space as it exists now (i.e., the ecology of functional requirements that solves current perceptions of the problem structure) and a target solution space (the set of solution elements that are implemented in the target system).

REFERENCES

Ball, L. J., and T. C. Ormerod. 1995. "Structured and opportunistic processing in design: A critical discussion." *Int. Journal of Human-Computer Interaction* no. 43 (1):131–151.

Barry, C., and M. Lang. 2003. "A comparison of 'traditional' and multimedia information systems development practices." *Information and Software Technology* no. 45 (4):217–227.

Bartlett, F. 1932. *Remembering: A Study in Experimental and Social Psychology.* London, UK: Cambridge University Press.

Bergman, M., J. King, and K. Lyytinen. 2002. "Large scale requirements analysis revisited: The need for understanding the political ecology of requirements engineering." *Requirements Engineering Journal* no. 7:152–171.

Boland, R. J. and R. V. Tenkasi. 1995. "perspective making and perspective taking in communities of knowing." *Organization Science* no. 6 (4):350–372.

Boland, R. J., R. V. Tenkasi, and D. Te'eni. 1994. "designing information technology to support distributed cognition." *Organization Science* no. 5 (3):456–475.

Brown, J. S., and P. Duguid. 1991. "Organizational learning and communities of practice: toward a unified view of working, learning, and innovation." *Organization Science* no. 2 (1):40–57.

Brown, J. S., and P. Duguid. 1992. "Enacting design for the workplace." In *Usability: Turning Technologies Into Tools*, edited by P. S. Adler and T. A. Winograd, 164–197. New York, NY: ACM Press.

Cannon-Bowers, J., and E. Salas. 2001. "Reflections on shared cognition." *Journal of Organizational Behavior* no. 22:195–202.

Carlile, P. R. 2002. "A Pragmatic view of knowledge and boundaries." *Organization Science* no. 13 (4):442–455.

Carlile, P. R. 2004. "Transferring, translating, and transforming: An integrative framework for managing knowledge across boundaries." *Organization Science* no. 15(5): 555–568.

Cecez-Kecmanovic, D., and C. Jerram. 2002. "A sensemaking model of knowledge management in organisations." Paper read at European Conference on Information Systems (ECIS 2002).

Checkland, P., and S. Holwell. 1998. *Information, Systems and Information Systems: Making Sense of the Field.* Chichester, UK: John Wiley & Sons.

Cohen, M. D., J. G. March, and J. P. Olsen. 1972. "A garbage-can model of organizational choice." *Administrative Science Quarterly* no. 17:1–25.

Darke, J. 1979. "The primary generator and the design process." *Design Studies* no. 1 (1) 36–44. Reprinted in *Developments in Design Methodology*, 1984, edited by N. Cross, 175–188. Chichester, UK: J. Wiley & Sons.

Dorst, C. H. 2006. "Design problems and design paradoxes." *Design Issues* no. 22 (3):4–17.

Dorst, C. H., and N. G. Cross. 2001. "Creativity in the design process: Co-evolution of problem–solution." *Design Studies* no. 22 (5):425–437.

Dorst, Kees, and Judith Dijkhuis. 1995. "Comparing paradigms for describing design activity." *Design Studies* no. 16 (2):261.

Drazin, R., M. A. Glynn, and R. K. Kazanjian. 1999. "Multilevel theorizing about creativity in organizations: A sensemaking perspective." *Academy of Management Review* no. 24 (2):286–307.

Engeström, Yrjo, Ritva Engeström, and Merja Kärkkäinen. 1995. "Polycontextuality and boundary crossing in expert cognition: Learning and problem solving in complex work activities." *Learning and Instruction* no. 5 (4):319–336.

Ensink, T., and C. Sauer. 2003. *Framing And Perspectivising In Discourse, Pragmatics & Beyond New Series 111.* Groningen, Germany: University of Groningen.

Festinger, L. 1957. *A Theory of Cognitive Dissonance.* Stanford, CA: Stanford University Press.

Fiol, C. M. 1994. "Consensus, diversity and learning in organizations." *Organization Science* no. 5 (3):403–420.

Gasson, S. 2006. "A genealogical study of boundary-spanning IS design." *European Journal of Information Systems* no. 15 (1):26–41.

Gasson, S. 2007. "Progress and breakdowns in early requirements definition for boundary-spanning information systems." Paper read at ICIS '07, Dec. 9–12, 2007, at Montréal, Québec, Canada.

Gasson, S. 2011. "The Role of Negotiation Objects in Managing Meaning across E-Collaboration Systems," in L. Toombs (ed.), Proceedings of Academy of Management Annual Meeting: OCIS Division, San Antonio, TX: Academy of Management. http://program.aomonline.org/2011/reportsaspnet/Proceedings.aspx.

Gasson, S. 2012. "The Sociomateriality of Boundary-Spanning Enterprise IS Design," in M-H. Huang, G. Piccoli, and V. Sambamurthy (eds.), Proceedings of the International Conference on Information Systems, ICIS 2012, Orlando, FL: AIS Electronic Library (AISeL). http://aisel.aisnet.org/icis2012/proceedings/SocialImpacts/8/.

Gasson, S. 2005. "The dynamics of sensemaking, knowledge and expertise in collaborative, boundary-spanning design." *Journal of Computer-Mediated Communication (JCMC)* no. 10 (4): Article 14, http://jcmc.indiana.edu/vol10/issue4/gasson.html.

Gentner, D., and A. L. Stevens. 1983. *Mental Models*. Hillsdale NJ: Erlbaum.

Gersick, C.J.G. 1988. "Time and transition in work teams: toward a new model of group development." *Academy of Management Journal* no. 31 (1):9–41.

Gersick, C.J.G. 1989. "Marking time: Predictable transitions in task groups." *Academy of Management Journal* no. 32 (2):274–309.

Gersick, C.J.G. 1991. "Revolutionary change theories: A multilevel exploration of the punctuated equilibrium paradigm." *Academy of Management Review* no. 16 (1):10–36.

Goffman, E. 1974. *Frame Analysis*. New York, NY: Harper and Row.

Guindon, R. 1990. "Designing the design process: Exploiting opportunistic thoughts." *Human-Computer Interaction* no. 5 (2/3):305–344.

Heidegger, M. 1962. *Being and Time*. New York, NY: Harper & Row.

Hollan, James, Edwin Hutchins, and David Kirsh. 2002. "Distributed cognition: Toward a new foundation for human-computer interaction research." *ACM Transactions on Computer-Human Interaction (TOCHI)* no. 7 (2):174–196.

Johnson-Laird, P. N. 1983. *Mental Models: Towards a Cognitive Science of Language, Inference, and Consciousness*. Cambridge, MA: Harvard University Press.

Johnson, D. W., and R. T. Johnson. 2009. "An educational psychology success story: Social interdependence theory and cooperative learning." *Educational Researcher* no. 38 (5):365–379.

Kelly, G. A. 1955. *The Psychology Of Personal Constructs*. New York, NY: W.W. Norton.

Krauss, R.M., and S.R. Fussell. 1991. "Constructing shared communicative environments." In *Perspectives on Socially Shared Cognition*, edited by L.B. Resnick, J.M. Levine and S.D. Teasley, 172–200. Washington, DC: American Psychological Association.

Lave, J. 1988. *Cognition in Practice: Mind Mathematics and Culture in Everyday Life*. Cambridge UK: Cambridge University Press.

Lave, J. 1991. "Situating learning in communities of practice." In *Perspectives on Socially Shared Cognition*, edited by L. B. Resnick, J. M. Levine, and S. D. Teasley, 63–82. Washington, DC: American Psychological Association.

Lave, J., and E. Wenger. 1991. *Situated Learning: Legitimate Peripheral Participation*. Cambridge, UK: Cambridge University Press.

Liu, Kecheng, Lily Sun, and Keith Bennett. 2002. "Co-design of business and IT systems—introduction by guest editors." *J. of Information Systems Frontiers* no. 4 (3):251–256.

Maher, M. L., and J. Poon. 1996. "Modelling design exploration as co-evolution." *Microcomputers in Civil Engineering* no. 11 (3):195–210.

Maher, M. L., and H.-H. Tang. 2003. "Co-evolution as a computational and cognitive model of design " *Research in Engineering Design* no. 14 (1):47–64.

Malhotra, A., J. Thomas, J. Carroll, and L. Miller. 1980. "Cognitive processes in design." *International Journal of Man-Machine Studies* no. 12:119–140.

Markus, M. L., A. Majchrzak, and L. Gasser. 2002. "A design theory for systems that support emergent knowledge processes." *MIS Quarterly* no. 26 (3):179–212.

McLaughlin, J., P. Rosen, D. Skinner, and J. Webster. 1999. *Valuing Technology: Organisations, Culture and Change*. London: Routledge.

McLoughlin, I., R. Badham, and P. Couchman. 2000. "Rethinking political process in technological change: Socio-technical configurations and frames." *Technology Analysis & Strategic Management* no. 12 (1):17–37.

Mintzberg, H., and J. H. Waters. 1985. "Of strategies deliberate and emergent." *Strategic Management Journal* no. 6 (3):257–72.

Miranda, S. M., and C. S. Saunders. 2003. "The social construction of meaning: an alternative perspective on information sharing." *Information Systems Research* no. 14 (1):87–106.

Nardi, B. 1995. *Context and Consciousness: Activity Theory and Human-Computer Interaction*. Cambridge, MA: MIT Press.

Neisser, U. 1976. *Cognition and Reality*. San Francisco, CA: W.H. Freeman.

Nelson, Kay M., and Jay G. Cooprider. 1996. "The contribution of shared knowledge to IS group performance." *MIS Quarterly* no. 20 (4):409.

Newell, A., and H. A. Simon. 1972. *Human Problem-Solving.*, Englewood Cliffs, NJ: Prentice Hall.

Poon, J., and M. L. Maher. 1997. "Co-evolution and emergence in design." *Artificial Intelligence in Engineering* no. 11 (3):319–327.

Rittel, H.W.J. 1972. "Second generation design methods." In *Design Methods Group 5th Anniversary Report: 5–10*. DMG Occasional Paper 1. Reprinted in *Developments in Design Methodology*, 1984, edited by N. Cross, 317–327. Chichester, UK: J. Wiley & Sons.

Rittel, H.W.J., and M. M. Webber. 1973. "Dilemmas in a general theory of planning." *Policy Sciences* no. 4:155–169.

Sabherwal, Rajiv, Rudy Hirschheim, and Tim Goles. 2001. "The dynamics of alignment: Insights from a punctuated equilibrium model." *Organization Science* no. 12 (2):179–197.

Schank, R. C., and R. P. Abelson. 1977. *Scripts, Plans, Goals, and Understanding: An Inquiry into Human Knowledge Structures*. Hillsdale, NJ: Lawrence Erlbaum Associates.

Silva, Leiser, and Rudy Hirschheim. 2007. "Fighting against windmills: Strategic information systems and organizational deep structures." *MIS Quarterly* no. 31 (2):327–354.

Simon, H. A. 1973. "The structure of ill-structured problems." *Artificial Intelligence* no. 4:145–180.

Simon, H. A. 1988. "Scientific discovery as problem solving; Peano lecture." In *Economics Bounded Rationality and the Cognitive Revolution Edward Elgar Publishing Limited Aldershot UK*, edited by M. Egidi and R. Marris, 102–119. Published in this form 1992.

Simon, H. A. 1996. *The Sciences of the Artificial*. 3rd. ed.. (1st edition 1969). Cambridge, MA: MIT Press

Stahl, G. 2000. "A model of collaborative knowledge-building." In Proceedings of Fourth International Conference of the Learning Sciences (ICLS 2000), Ann Arbor, MI, 70–77.

Star, S. L. 1989. "The structure of ill-structured solutions: Boundary objects and heterogeneous distributed problem solving." In *Distributed Artificial Intelligence, Vol. II.*, edited by L. Gasser and M. N. Huhns, 37–54. San Mateo, CA: Morgan Kaufmann. Original edition, Proceedings of the 8th AAAI Workshop on Distributed Artificial Intelligence, Department of Computer Science, University of Southern California, 1988.

Suchman, L. 1987. *Plans and Situated Action*. Cambridge, MA: Cambridge University Press.

Suchman, L. 2007. *Human–Machine Reconfigurations: Plans and Situated Actions*. Cambridge, UK: Cambridge University Press.

Tannen, D. 1986. *That's Not What I Meant! How Conversational Style Makes or Breaks Relationships*. New York, NY: Ballantine Books.

Tannen, D. 1993. "What's in a frame?" In *Framing in Discourse*, edited by D. Tannen. Oxford, UK: Oxford University Press, 137–181.

Turner, J. A. 1987. "Understanding the elements of systems design." In *Critical Issues in Information Systems Research*, edited by R. J. Boland and R. A. Hirschheim, 97–111. New York, NY: Wiley.

Urquhart, C. 2001. "Analysts and clients in organisational contexts: a conversational perspective." *The Journal of Strategic Information Systems* no. 10 (3):243–262.

Walsh, J. P., C. M. Henderson, and J. Deighton. 1988. "Negotiated belief structures and decision performance: An empirical investigation." *Organizational Behavior and Human Decision Processes* no. 42 (2):194–216.

Weick, K. E. 1995. *Sensemaking In Organizations*. Thousand Oaks, CA: Sage.

Weick, K. E. 2004. "Designing for Throwness." In *Managing as Designing*, edited by R Boland, J. Collopy, and F. Collopy, 74–78. Stanford, CA: Stanford University Press.

Winograd, T., and F. Flores. 1986. *Understanding Computers and Cognition*. Norwood, NJ: Ablex Corporation.

Zhang, J., and D. A. Norman. 1994. "Representations in distributed cognitive tasks." *Cognitive Science* no. 18 (87–122).

5 Toward a Conceptualization of Inter-Team Boundary Activities
Identifying Intra- and Inter-Team Contextual Facilitators

Anit Somech and Anat Drach-Zahavy

The emergence of team-based organizations requires shifting the focus from an intra-team to an inter-team perspective so as to understand organizational functioning (Drach-Zahavy and Somech 2010). Teams need other teams for input essential to their functioning, because they cannot generate all the required resources independently. Consequently, teams must engage in boundary activities to protect, preserve, and/or acquire such resources (van Knippenberg 2003). Team boundary activities refer to those processes necessary for a team to be able to carry out the task at hand, activities which are directed toward external agents in the team's focal environment (Drach-Zahavy and Somech 2010; Yan and Louis 1999). Although in the past three decades a great deal of theoretical and empirical work has emerged within boundary activity research (Ancona and Caldwell 1998; Choi 2002; Faraj and Yan 2009; Joshi, Pandey, and Han 2009; Marrone 2010; Yan and Louis 1999), the structure of the concept and its antecedents are not fully understood for three main reasons: First, although the literature has grasped the boundary activity phenomenon in the context of teams, it has focused on how specific members of the team communicate with external agencies for promoting team functioning (e.g., Johnson and Chang 2000) without considering how the team as a unit operates toward its boundary. Second, the common approach in the literature has been to refer to all boundary activities as unified "external activities," overlooking the inherent differences among them (e.g., Choi 2002). Moreover, this approach focuses exclusively on external activities as contrasting sharply with internal activities (Ancona and Caldwell 1998; Choi 2002; Howell and Shea 2006; Marrone 2010).

Only recently have several scholars posited convincing arguments for why internal activities might also be classified as boundary activities (Drach-Zahavy and Somech 2010; Faraj and Yan 2009; Yan and Louis 1999). According to these scholars, internal activity is the manifestation of a team's inherent propensity to distinguish itself from its environment by establishing its own workspace, work time, task structure, operational rules, and goals (Choi 2002); namely, internal activity sharpens the team boundary from within. This perspective, which views internal and external team activities as being synergistic rather than supplementary, suggests a more holistic view of boundary activities (Faraj and Yan 2009). Finally, most research on boundary activities has tended to examine its consequences for the team (e.g., Ancona and Caldwell 1998), leaving the study of boundary activity antecedents lagging behind (Drach-Zahavy and Somech 2010).

To fill these voids, the aim of this chapter is threefold: First, to conceptualize a team-level perspective on boundary activities. Second, to introduce a typology for inter-team boundary activities, referring to four mutually exclusive activities in which a team engages to manage its boundaries: *scouting*, *coordinating*, *buffering*, and *bringing up borders*. The third aim, based on the social identity theory (Ashforth and Mael 1989; Brewer 1996, 2000; Hogg 2000), is to develop a model identifying contextual antecedents of inter-team boundary activities. These include team functional heterogeneity, team boundedness, inter-team task and goal interdependence, and organizational environment. The chapter concludes by considering the challenges to both research and practice implied by the proposed model for organizational effectiveness.

TEAM BOUNDARY ACTIVITIES

Team Boundary Activities: A Historical Overview

Teams do not operate in a vacuum; they function in a context of interdependent relationships with other organizational teams (van Knippenberg 2003). Organizational teams might, for instance, be interdependent for their task performance. These teams need other teams to provide them with necessary information, products, or services. They also rely on other teams to take their interests into account and resolve potential conflicts of interest in a constructive manner. This interdependence requires teams to coordinate their efforts and attempt to accommodate not only their own but also the other team's needs (van Knippenberg 2003).

The scarce research on work units as open systems and on associated boundary issues can be at least partially attributed to the fact that work teams have for the most part, and until quite recently, been located within traditional organizational structures. These hierarchical structures, whether functional or multidivisional in form, have protected or insulated teams from exposure to the external environments (Yan and Louis 1999) by appointing a specific organizational liaison role or departments to be accountable for boundary activities. These liaisons are held responsible for executing the boundary activities across the boundaries of the team and the organization to other constituencies both inside and outside the organization (Elkins and Keller 2003). Accordingly, most research has concentrated on spanning roles as an important means through which ideas and information are transferred to and from the organization's boundaries. Other researchers have investigated the roles assigned to individuals who act as boundary spanners to the organization. While the benefits of individual-level boundary-spanning to the organization as a whole have been established, scholars do not fully understand this concept at the team level (Golden and Veiga 2005).

The seminal work of Ancona and Caldwell (1992a, 1992b) has extended boundary activities research to the team level of analysis. In their establishment of an external perspective, Ancona and Caldwell link boundary-spanning to differences in team effectiveness. As suggested by Ancona and Caldwell (1992a), teams that engage in boundary-spanning are perceived as being more effective and as being more likely to achieve team goals. Their results indicate that teams develop distinctive strategies toward their organizational environment; some specialize in particular external activities, some remain isolated from the external environment, and others engage in multiple external activities. Over time, teams engaging in multiple external activities are the most effective ones.

Ancona and Caldwell (1992a), building on the earlier works of Allen (1977), Katz and Tushman (1979), and Malone (1987), classified a team's externally focused activities into four major types: (1) *Ambassadorial activities*—teams taking on this set of activities protect their team from outside pressure, persuade others to support the team, and lobby for resources. Ambassadorial activities provide access to the power structure of the organization as members promote the team, secure resources, and protect the team from excessive interference. (2) *Task coordinator activities* represent interactions aimed at coordinating technical or design issues, obtaining feedback on team activities, and coordinating and negotiating with outsiders. Task coordinator activities provide access to the workflow structure; they are aimed at managing horizontal interdependence. Through coordination, negotiation, and feedback, these activities allow for a tighter coupling with other organizational teams, often filling many of the gaps left by formal integrating systems. (3) *Scout activities* describe behaviors that involve general scanning for ideas and information about the competition, the market, and/or the technology. These activities include many aspects of mapping, information gathering, and scanning activities. Scouting activities provide access to the information structure; they are aimed at adding to the group's expertise. These activities allow the group to update its information base, providing new ideas about technologies and markets. (4) *Guard activities* represent actions aimed at avoiding the release of information. These activities differ from the other three aspects in that they do not represent initiatives toward the organizational environment, but rather internal activities designed to safeguard vital information from the environment.

Based on the above typology, Ancona and Caldwell (1992a) found that ambassadorial and task coordinating activities were found to be positively correlated to managers' rating of performance among forty-five new product teams. Excessive scouting on the teams' part was negatively correlated to these outcomes. In a related study, Ancona and Caldwell (1992b) found external communication (measured simply as a frequency variable) to be positively associated with managers' ratings. Similarly, Keller (2001) found a positive association between external communication and managers' assessments among ninety-eight R&D teams.

Yan and Louis (1999) introduced a different approach to the concept of boundary activities, which was later elaborated by other scholars (Drach-Zahavy and Somech 2010; Faraj and Yan 2009). These authors suggest that teams might engage in boundary activities not only for managing interactions across teams but also to delineate and maintain boundaries. Team boundary activities, therefore, include acquisition of resources and information and management of relationships with external stakeholders, while also protecting team resources from competing with external demands. Furthermore, teams have to maintain internal boundaries in order to cultivate the sustained commitment of their members to their common task (Druskat and Wheeler 2003). Hence, a team's essential mission is to create boundaries that are sufficiently porous to allow resources and information in, yet sufficiently resistant to prevent any doubt as to who belongs to the team and whether these members are accountable for the team's collective outputs (Faraj and Yan 2009). In line with this thinking, as mentioned, we define a team's boundary activities as those processes necessary for a team to be able to carry out the task at hand, which are directed toward external agents in the team's focal environment, so as to obtain resources and promote and protect itself (Drach-Zahavy and Somech 2010; Yan and Louis 1999). In so doing, boundaries may be crossed between the team and its organization, between teams within the same organization, and between the team and its external environment. The present study focuses on the interrelations between teams within the same organization.

Team Boundary Activities: A Multidimensional Construct

Reviewing the literature to date has revealed that the common approach for understanding boundary activities was generally characterized by a sweeping consideration of external activities as conduits for attaining social capital, thus contributing to team effectiveness, while ignoring its potential costs. Moreover, most research lacks a systematic consideration of boundary activities in terms of the targets of activities or of "whom the team is interacting with" (e.g., Bartel 2001; Choi 2002). For example, Ancona and Caldwell (1992a) distinguished a team's lateral interactions with teams on the same hierarchical level from a team's vertical interactions, for instance, with top management teams. Therefore, only by considering valence, targets, and the specific types of boundary activities can we accurately gauge the contribution of these activities to the organization. To this end, we present our three-dimensional typology referring to type, target, and valence of boundary activities.

Type of boundary activities. Based on a holistic approach, which emphasizes the explicit external versus internal perspective, namely that boundary activities should refer to all the activities in which teams engage to manage their boundaries, we propose a typology composed of four types (Drach-Zahavy and Somech 2010): *scouting, coordinating, buffering* and *bringing up borders*.

1. *Scouting activities* refer to actions undertaken by a focal team to reach out into its environment for acquisition of important resources and support (Faraj and Yan 2009). These activities describe behaviors and actions, such as scanning for ideas, seeking support, and accessing information and other resources. These activities encompass many aspects of mapping, information gathering, and scanning, all aimed at enhancing the team's capability (Amedore and Knoff 1993; Ancona and Caldwell 1992, 1998; Druskat and Wheeler 2003; Yan and Louis 1999).

2. *Coordinating activities* represent processes aimed at attaining team interdependence via coordination, collaboration, negotiation, and feedback. These activities, which promote working in greater harmony with other teams within the organization, often fill many of the gaps produced by formal integrating systems (Ancona and Caldwell 1992).

3. *Buffering activities* are team processes aimed at insulating the system from unwanted exposure to the environment. An entity buffers itself to protect against disturbances and uncertainties, to prevent negative input caused by undesired access to the team boundaries, and to keep valuable resources from leaking into the external environment (Faraj and Yan 2009; Scott 1992; Yan and Louis 1999).

4. *Bringing up borders activities* are team processes aimed at enlisting members' attachment and energies and focusing them on accomplishing the common task. These activities involve creating a coherent unit for team members, despite the diversity of their backgrounds. Consequently, the boundaries that emerge between the team and its environment tend to be quite natural (Druskat and Wheeler 2003; Yan and Louis 1999).

Target of boundary activities. In the conceptualization of the target dimension in our typology, we borrow from networking research and suggest that teams might cross lateral/vertical boundaries within the organization (Oh, Labianca, and Chung 2006). *Lateral* boundary activities refer to activities targeted at teams on compatible hierarchical levels within the organization; *vertical* boundary activities refer to activities targeted at teams typically on different hierarchical levels of the organization (Joshi 2006). Here we extend previous boundary activities research, which referred to targets mainly in the discussion of the spanning boundary activity. That research differentiated between vertical boundary activity, which is ambassadorial, and lateral boundary activity, or scouting (Ancona and Caldwell

1992a; Janssens and Brett 1997). In our typology the four types of boundary activities can further be typified according to "whom the team is talking to," namely targets of the boundary activity. For example, a production team might close its boundaries and buffer information from leaking to a top management team, but allow access to the same information for a marketing team, within the organization.

Valence of boundary activities. Valence refers to the emotional orientations people hold with respect to outcomes. Boundary activities literature has typically viewed a team's engagement with those activities as containing positive valence for the team (Ancona and Caldwell 1998). Nevertheless, all encounters of boundary activities may have positive or negative valence, depending on the foci of interest: the team or the organization. For example, involvement in buffering may have positive valence for the team when it succeeds in preventing negative information from leaking out of its boundaries; it may have negative valence for the organization when it prevents the opportunity for organizational learning, thus affecting overall organizational performance. As this performance is our focus here, we further typify the valence of engaging in the four boundary activities for the organizational outcomes: positive or negative valence.

TOWARD A THEORETICAL MODEL: CONTEXTUAL ANTECEDENTS OF INTER-TEAM BOUNDARY ACTIVITIES

The above review has shown that boundary activities have the potential to contribute to team and organizational effectiveness. Therefore, a major challenge for theoreticians and practitioners is how to organize teams in ways that encourage them to engage in the full range of boundary activities. Here, we develop a model identifying contextual antecedents of inter-team boundary activities from a multilevel perspective. These include: at the team level, team functional heterogeneity and team boundedness; at the organizational level, inter-team task and goal interdependence, and organizational environment.

The social identity approach guides the fundamental framing of the model. According to this perspective team-level identities are often prevalent in members' interactions within the organization due to physical proximity, interpersonal similarity, etc. (Ashforth and Mael 1989). Increasing the salience of team identity over organizational identity establishes team favoritism and positive distinctiveness between the in group and the out group, thus engendering out-group biases. However, to claim that the social identity approach assumes that inter-team relations are always competitive or that it denies the role of compatibility of team interests with organizational interests is misleading (Kramer 1991). The theory identifies a number of important contingencies for mitigating in-group favoring and out-group derogating attitudes and behavior (Bartel 2001; Hogg and Terry 2000; van

Knippenberg 2003). Therefore, structural variables can reduce and/or increase the salience of an individual's primary team membership over the salience of his or her membership in the organization, which in turn determine the extent to which team members will engage in certain inter-team boundaries activities.

Team Functional Heterogeneity

Team composition, which is the configuration of members' attributes in a team (Levine and Moreland 1990), was found to be a crucial resource that has an impact on team processes and outcomes (for review, Hulsheger et al. 2009). In the present model, we refer to team heterogeneity, and specifically to functional heterogeneity, which is defined as "the diversity of organizational roles embodied in the team" (Jackson 1992, 353). A team will be characterized as possessing increased functional heterogeneity if different professionals are grouped together as a multidisciplinary team. Most research on teams' functional heterogeneity has demonstrated the benefits of more heterogeneous teams in terms of creativity, quality decision making, and innovativeness (e.g., Ancona and Caldwell 1992; Somech 2006), but also several drawbacks, such as lower levels of cohesiveness, commitment, and member satisfaction as compared with more homogeneous teams (e.g., Tsui, Egan, and O'Reilly 1992). However, as mentioned, the challenge of organizational teams is to manage intra- as well as inter-team relations.

A functional heterogeneous team elicits communication with individuals from outside the team and is associated with higher levels of information exchanged, which provide the team with broader informational resources and knowledge (Drach-Zahavy and Somech 2010). Diversity in members' experience, expertise, and previous membership can promote a team's connections to external actors, an asset that is not available to homogeneous teams (Arrow and McGrath 1995). Therefore, heterogeneous teams are more likely to have contacts of greater number and diversity outside the group boundary, which eventually will lead them to engage more in scouting and coordinating activities (Choi 2002).

This logic is in congruence with the social identity approach. Homogeneous teams create perceptual boundaries and team favoritism that distinguish them from others in the external environment (Joshi and Jackson 2003). Conversely, in heterogeneous teams members perceive themselves and their peer team members less as an in group, with the effect that team favoritism based on team belongingness is less salient (Joshi 2006; Joshi and Jackson 2003). These members have a limited sense of belonging to their team due to their diverse disciplines, origins, positions, and roles. Therefore, members in functional heterogeneous teams might feel the urge to connect with members from other teams that speak the same professional jargon. This tendency may result in investing more time and energy in activities aimed outside the team boundary, namely, in scouting and coordinating activities (Choi 2002). In contrast, functional homogeneous teams will probably invest their energy and efforts in tightening boundaries through systematic monitoring and regulation of the inner system; namely, in bringing up borders and buffering activities. Initial support for these arguments can be found in the study of Halyla (2010), who examined R&D teams. The results indicated positive relationships between team functional heterogeneity and scouting and coordinating activities in contrast to negative relationships with buffering and bringing up borders. Similarly, Drach-Zahavy (2011), who investigated inter-organizational teams, found a positive link between functional heterogeneity and scouting and coordinating activities.

> *Proposition 1. There is a stronger positive relationship between team functional heterogeneity and scouting and coordinating activities than between functional heterogeneity and buffering and bringing up borders.*

Team Boundedness

Team boundedness refers to the multiple modes by which members can be involved in the team and consists of three features. The first is *full or partial cycle membership* on the team: Does the team consist of the same members for the team's full life cycle, or do members serve only for part of it? The second is *full or part-time assignment to the team*: Do members work exclusively on the team's tasks or do they have other responsibilities and roles in the organization? The third feature is *core or peripheral membership* on the team: Are some members assigned to "core" positions and others to more "peripheral" positions (Ancona and Caldwell 1998)? At one extreme—high boundedness—a team's boundaries may be stretched to include all relevant actors in a continuous mode of structuring, which is stable across the life cycle of the team. That would require all team members to be equally active throughout, to interact continuously, to invest equal amounts of time, and to contribute actively to the team's assignments from start to finish. At the other extreme—low boundedness—a team may be designed more flexibly, with parties recruited to fill specific tasks only as needed and/or at certain stages. Thus, they would be required to invest different amounts of time and exhibit different saliency in the team, depending on their potential contribution (Ancona and Caldwell 1998).

Most research on teams has typically advocated team boundedness as a preferred mode of structuring (Armbruster et al.1999; Butterfoss et al. 1998; Green 2000; Kegler et al. 1998). True, boundedness carries notable advantages for team building, commitment, and synergism (e.g., Green 2000; Naidoo and Wills 2000). However, due to the team's elevated need to engage in boundary activities, team boundedness may also impose certain limitations that have often been ignored in previous research. In line with the social identity theory (Reynolds, Turner, and Haslam 2000), team boundedness tends to strengthen attitudes of team favoritism and out-group biases. Hence, members of bounded teams are more likely to form in-group relationships with other team members rather than with other teams in their focal environment. In contrast, less bounded teams create more permeable boundaries, dampening out-group derogating attitudes; hence, team members are encouraged to engage in scouting and coordinating activities (Ancona and Caldwell 1998; Drach-Zahavy and Baron-Epel 2006). Initial support for our arguments can be found in the study of Drach-Zahavy (2011), who found negative relationships between boundedness and scouting and coordinating activities among inter-organizational teams.

> *Proposition 2. There is a negative relationship between team boundedness and scouting and coordinating activities, and a positive relationship with buffering and bringing up borders.*

Inter-Team Task and Goal Interdependence

Inter-team goal interdependence refers to the degree to which teams believe that their team is assigned team goals or is provided with team feedback that is aligned with the organization's goals. Inter-team task interdependence refers to the extent to which a team believes it is dependent on other teams in the organization to carry out its tasks and perform effectively (Hülsheger, Anderson, and Salgado 2009). Several authors (e.g., Victor and Blackburn 1998) have argued that these two structural features are independent dimensions of social interdependence and that their effects on team and organizational effectiveness strongly depend on how they are combined. We follow this approach and propose that the combination of inter-team task and goal interdependence can predict the salient boundary activities that the team will engage in. Overall, in line with the social identity theory, we suggest that incongruent cues of task and goal interdependence (i.e., low-high and high-low) contribute to uncertainty about how to behave and what to expect from the physical and social environment within which the team acts (Hogg and Terry 2000). Because team members are motivated by the need to reduce subjective uncertainty, incongruence cues increase the tendency of team members to maintain their positive social identity through team favoritism and out-group biases. In comparison, congruent cues of task and goal interdependence (i.e., low-low and high-high) reduce subjective uncertainty, thereby limiting derogatory attitudes to others.

Low inter-team task interdependence and low inter-team goal interdependence. For teams working under congruent conditions of low inter-team task and low inter-team goal interdependence, little interaction among teams is required, and teams can pursue their own interests with little potential for conflict with other teams (Weick 1976). Under these conditions, team members are more likely to maintain team favoritism, but not at the price of projecting out-group biases onto their counterpart teams (Gaertner and Dovidio 2000). The focal team serves as the reference group, while the counterpart teams are not regarded as such (William and Hickey 2005). We suggest that the combination of team favoritism and relatively few out-group biases impels team members to invest their efforts within the team, namely to engage in bringing up borders.

> *Proposition 3a. Low inter-team task and goal interdependence will be associated with more bringing up boundaries activities in comparison with buffering, scouting, and coordinating activities.*

Low inter-team task interdependence and high inter-team goal interdependence. Teams working under the combined conditions of low inter-team task interdependence and high inter-team goal interdependence encounter a typical social dilemma: i.e., working cooperatively with other teams to attain joint goals (high goal interdependence) might expose the team to exploitation efforts taken by their counterparts, due to the fact that the contribution of each team to the shared goal cannot be identified (low task interdependence). Moreover, the high goal interdependence signals organizational belongingness, whereas the low task interdependence signals team belongingness. Since team members have a fundamental need to feel confident about their team, other teams, and their place within the world, such a situation motivates behavior that reduces subjective uncertainty. For this reason, team members will attend to categorical information to validate their social identity (Hogg 2000; van der Vegt, van de Vliert, and Osterhof 2003). This formulation implies that under conditions of low task and high goal interdependence, team belongingness is more likely to be salient. Therefore, the team chooses a strategy of social loafing to benefit from the other teams' efforts (free riding) or to avoid becoming the "sucker team" (Erez and Somech 1996). Hence, we expect these teams to engage less in scouting and coordinating activities. Furthermore, because such teams perceive other teams as a potential threat to attaining their goals and fear the risk of exploitation, we expect them to engage more in buffering activities.

> *Proposition 3b. Low inter-team task interdependence and high inter-team goal interdependence will be associated with more buffering behaviors than bringing up, spanning, and coordinating activities.*

High inter-team task interdependence and low inter-team goal interdependence. In teams working under such incongruent conditions of high inter-team task interdependence and low inter-team goal interdependence, members of distinct teams have to interact and exchange information, resources, and material in order to perform their task; yet each team is rewarded relatively independently of the other teams. Again, according to the social identity theory, this uncertainty draws attention to the dissimilarity among teams and increases the salience of team identity over organizational identity (Hogg 2000). Moreover, research has shown that when organizational teams share scarce resources (high task interdependence), competitive strategies may be used to gain maximal resources and power. Naturally, conditions of low goal interdependence may favor disruptive tactics that can undermine the relationships (Schopler 1986). According to our model, engaging primarily in scouting boundaries might help teams to gain an advantage over other teams, to gather information and other resources, and to explore other teams' intentions and actions.

> *Proposition 3c. High inter-team task interdependence and low inter-team goal interdependence will be associated more with scouting behaviors than with bringing up, buffering, and coordinating activities.*

High inter-team task interdependence and high inter-team goal interdependence. Finally, teams working under congruent conditions of high task interdependence and high goal interdependence have to work together and need each other to achieve common organizational goals. Each team's contribution to the effectiveness of the organization is required; resources and communication exchange and coordination are encouraged because the more teams cooperate, the more they can contribute to the attainment of common organizational goals. Taking the social theory perspective, because members of such teams receive congruent information concerning inter-team task and goal interdependence, the degree of experienced uncertainty is relatively low. Team members see themselves as part of the organization rather than focusing on differences among teams. Consequently, they will tend to create boundaries of the organization as a whole, rather than boundaries around teams. In other words, these teams will embrace a cooperative orientation toward their counterparts. Hence, we expect these teams to engage less in bringing up borders and buffering activities. Furthermore, because such teams perceive other teams as potential partners for attaining their goals (high goal interdependence) we expect them to engage more in coordinating. Engaging primarily in coordinating boundaries might help teams to cooperate in order to achieve shared organizational goals.

> *Proposition 3d. High inter-team task interdependence and high inter-team goal interdependence will be associated more with coordinating activities than with buffering, scouting, and bringing up borders activities.*

Organizational Environment

Organizational environment consists of three components (Koka, Madhavan, and Prescott 2006): (1) *Environmental complexity* refers to the diversity of elements that must be dealt with by the organization. (2) *Dynamism* refers to the rate of variability, stability, and turbulence of the environment; and (3) *uncertainty* indicates the unpredictability of the environment and the extent to which it is possible (or impossible) to forecast its behavior in advance. Complex, dynamic, and uncertain environments are more difficult to work in because the performance challenges that arise are nonroutine and often require unique and system-wide responses within limited time periods (Dutton and Dukerich 1991). In the following, we refer to these as unfavorable environmental conditions, as compared with simpler, more stable, and more certain environments, which we label as favorable environmental conditions.

According to the social identity theory, the external organizational environment serves as an inter-team social comparative context, which has a powerful impact on inter-team organizational identity, and hence on attitudes and behaviors. Unfavorable organizational environmental conditions create social attraction and solidarity within an organization through organizational identification, which leads to favoritism toward the organization as a whole and develops positive distinctiveness with respect to the external environment (Hogg and Terry 2000). These challenging environmental conditions may lead teams to unite and experience the external environment as the out group. In comparison, teams working within more favorable organizational environmental conditions maintain intra-group identification and favor the team's interest over the interest of the "organization as a whole" (Gaertner and Dovidio 2000).

Therefore, we argue that in an unfavorable environment, teams will be urged to cooperate with their counterpart teams, namely, to engage in coordinating activities; whereas in more favorable organizational environmental conditions, teams will attempt to invest in their own team, namely, to engage in scouting, buffering, and bringing up borders.

> *Proposition 4: There is a positive relationship between an unfavorable organizational environment and coordinating activities versus a positive relationship between favorable organizational environmental and scouting, buffering, and bringing up borders activities.*

SUMMARY AND IMPLICATIONS

Our approach has implications for the study of organizational teams. First, we have integrated the previous literature and developed a comprehensive conceptualization of inter-team boundary activities consisting of three domains: types, target, and valence. Regarding the types of boundary activities, our typology takes on a more holistic approach, integrating external and internal activities. While internal activities tighten the team boundary from within, external activities loosen the team boundary by initiating interactions with counterpart teams. The target domain highlights the importance of considering "whom the team is interacting with," as different targets might determine the type of boundary activity the team engages in. Nevertheless, this quandary has not gained sufficient research attention among boundary activity scholars until now. The valence domain exemplifies the complex considerations involved in choosing the appropriate boundary activity. It raises such questions as: Is engaging in all types of boundary activities always warranted? Does engaging in buffering or spanning boundaries also carry positive valence for the organization as a whole? Are there possible tradeoffs between the valence for the team and the organization? How does engaging in the four boundary activities affect different team and organizational outcomes such as effectiveness, efficiency, and innovation? Future theory and research are needed to understand the dynamics among these three dimensions. Only by considering the specific types, valence, and targets of boundary activities can we accurately gauge the nature and contribution of these activities to the organizational context.

Furthermore, our approach raises a potential dilemma for teams and their parent organizations concerning possible tradeoffs among the various boundary activities. For example, Gersick (1988) suggests that teams may deal with internal and external demands sequentially, first acting on initial information from the environment in isolation and then emerging to obtain further feedback and information from outsiders. Nevertheless, teams might encounter tradeoffs in pursuing these four activities. Most of the previous research suggests that external activities interfere with the development of effective internal operations, and vice versa. Teams can be under-bounded—having many external ties but an inability to coalesce and motivate members to pull together their external knowledge, or over-bounded—having high internal loyalty and a complex set of internal dynamics but an inability to reach out to the external world (Alderfer 1976). Future research might refer to questions such as what the interrelationships among the four boundary activities are, and how they affect one another.

Second, this chapter adopts a multilevel perspective for boundary activities by opening the inquiry to a host of antecedents embedded in the team, organizational, and environmental levels. Based on the social identity theory, we derived specific propositions concerning the four possible antecedents of boundary activities: functional heterogeneity, team boundedness, inter-team task and goal interdependence, and organizational environment. The specified antecedents here are only examples of the influences that context variables might have on the team's engagement in a specific boundary activity. Future research should extend the inquiry to other antecedents, embedded in different levels of the team context. For example, most inter-team relations research has been developed from a Western perspective and has paid less attention to the impact of diverse national cultures (Golden and Veiga 2005).

Third, the focus of this chapter was on identifying the antecedents of boundary activities. Of course, each boundary activity might have a distinctive impact on team and organizational effectiveness. Reviewing the literature reveals that because the primary focus was on the team, authors (e.g., Ancona and Caldwell 1992a) used the team as the focal unit for understanding its process and its outcomes. This perspective relies on an unspoken assumption that team effectiveness should be clearly aligned to the organization's overall effectiveness. However, effectiveness at the team level may be unrelated to, and may even conflict with, effectiveness at the organizational level (Cohen and Bailey 1997; Yan and Louis 1999). For example, a project team may be successful in achieving its goals, but not be successful in contributing to the organization's success because it wastes resources or hurts other efforts with which it is interdependent. Consequently, this "duel" between teams within the same organization raises doubts concerning organizational effectiveness, or concerning possible tradeoff relationships between the team and its organization's effectiveness. Future studies should specify the terms under which organizational effectiveness is in fact the combination of its teams' effectiveness, and those under which a possible productivity loss might occur. Further research should examine how engagement in a certain boundary activity affects both team and organizational effectiveness. With respect to the social identity perspective, team identification and organizational identification have generally been regarded as being in opposition, such that the more salient one form of identity is in a given context, the less likely (and feasible) is the emergence of the other. This raises the question of whether these two cognitive systems may be orthogonal rather than bipolar, thus allowing the possibility that team and organizational identities may be simultaneously significant. This debate is congruent with the recent focus on a paradoxical approach to management, as opposed to an 'either/or' focus (Lewis et al. 2002; Somech 2006).

REFERENCES

Alderfer, C.P. 1976. "Boundary Relations and Organizational Diagnosis." In *Humanizing Organizational Behavior*, edited by M. Meltzer and F. Wickert, 142–175. Springfield, IL: Charles C. Thomas.

Allen, T.J. 1977. *Managing the Flow of Technology: Technology Transfer and the Dissemination of Technological Information Within the R & D Organization.* Cambridge, MA: MIT Press.

Amedore, G. H., and H. M. Knoff. 1993. "Boundary Spanning Activities and the Multidisciplinary Team Process: Characteristics Affecting School Psychological Consultation." *Journal of Educational and Psychological Consultation* 4: 343–356.

Ancona, D.G., and D.F. Caldwell. 1992a. "Bridging the Boundary-External Activity and Performance in Organizational Teams." *Administrative Science Quarterly* 37: 634–665.

———. 1992b. "Demography and Design: Predictors of New Product Team Performance." *Organization Science* 3: 321–341.

———. 1998. "Rethinking Coalition Composition from the Outside In." In *Research on Managing Groups' and Coalitions' Composition,* edited by D. H. Gruenfeld, 1: 21–37. Elsevier Science: JAI.

Armbruster, C., B. Gale, J. Brady, and N. Thompson. 1999. "Perceived Ownership in A Community Coalition." *Public Health Nursing 16:* 17–22.

Arrow, H., and J. E. McGrath. 1995. "Membership Dynamics in Groups at Work: A Theoretical Framework." In *Research in Organizational Behavior,* edited by B. M. Staw and L. L. Cummings, 17: 373–411. Greenwich, CT: JAI.

Ashforth, B. E., and F. Mael. 1989. "Social Identity Theory and the Organization." *Academy of Management Review 14:* 20–39.

Bartel, C. A. 2001. "Social Comparisons in Boundary-Spanning Work: Effects of Community Outreach on Members' Organizational Identity and Identification." *Administrative Science Quarterly 46:* 379–413.

Brewer, M. B. 1996. "When Contact Is Not Enough: Social Identity and Intergroup Cooperation." *International Journal of Intercultural Relations 20:* 291–304.

Brewer, M. B. 2000. "Social Identity Theory and Change in Intergroup Relations." In *Social Identity Processes,* edited by D. Capozza and R. Brown, 117–132. London: Sage.

Butterfoss, E. D., A. L. Morrow, J. Rosenthal, E. Dini, R. C. Crews, J. D. Webster, and P. Louis. 1998. "CINCH: An Urban Coalition for Empowerment and Action: Consortium for the Immunization of Norfolk's Children." *Health Education Behavior 25:* 212–225.

Choi, J. N. 2002. "External Activities and Team Effectiveness: Review and Theoretical Development." *Small Group Research 33:* 181–192.

Cohen, S. G., and D. E. Bailey. 1997. "What Makes Teams Work: Group Effectiveness Researchfrom the Shop Floor to the Executive Suite." *Journal of Management 23:* 239–290.

Drach-Zahavy, A. 2011. "Inter-Organizational Teams as Boundary Spanners: The Role of Team Diversity, Boundedness, and Extra-Team Links." *European Journal of Work and Organizational Psychology 20:* 89–118.

Drach-Zahavy, A., and O. Baron-Epel. (2006). "Health-Promotion Teams' Effectiveness: A Structural Perspective from Israel." *Health Promotion International 21:* 181–190.

Drach-Zahavy, A., and A. Somech. 2010. "From an Intra-Team to an Inter-Team Perspective of Effectiveness: The Role of Interdependence and Boundary Activities." *Small Group Research 41:* 143–174.

Druskat, V. U., and J. V. Wheeler. 2003. "Managing from the Boundary: The Effective Leadership of Self-Managing Work-Teams." *Academy of Management Journal 46:* 435–457.

Dutton, J. E., and J. M. Dukerich. 1991. "Keeping an Eye on the Mirror: Image and Identity in Organizational Adaptation." *Academy of Management Journal 34:* 517–554.

Elkins, T., and R. T. Keller. 2003. "Leadership in Research and Development Organizations: A Literature Review and Conceptual Framework." *The Leadership Quarterly 14:* 587–606.

Erez, M., and A. Somech. 1996. "Is Group Productivity Loss the Rule or the Exception? Effects of Culture and Group-Based Motivation." *Academy of Management Journal 39:* 1513–1537.

Faraj, S., and A. Yan. 2009. "Boundary Work in Knowledge Teams." *Journal of Applied Psychology* 94: 604–617.

Gaertner, S. L., and J. F. Dovidio. 2000. *Reducing Intergroup Bias: The Common Ingroup Identity Model*. New York: Psychology Press.

Gersick, C. J. G. 1988. "Time and Transition in Work Teams: Toward a New Model of Group Development." *Academy of Management Journal* 31: 9–41.

Golden, T. D., and J. F. Veiga. 2005. "Spanning Boundaries and Borders: Toward Understanding the Cultural Dimensions of Team Boundary Spanning." *Journal of Managerial Issues* 17: 178–193.

Green, J. 2000. "Working Together for Injury Reduction: A Study of Accident Alliances in South East England." *Health Education Journal* 59: 23–38.

Halyla, A. 2010. *The Influence of Structural Features on Teams Boundary Activities and Consequences on Team Effectiveness*. Israel: University of Haifa.

Hogg, M. A. 2000. "Social Identity and Social Comparison." In *Handbook of Social Comparison: Theory and Research*, edited by J. Suls and L. Wheeler, 401–421. New York: Kluwer Academic/Plenum.

Hogg, M. A., and D. J. Terry. 2000. "Social Identity and Self-Categorization Processes in Organizational Contexts." *Academy of Management Review* 25: 121–140.

Howell, J. M., and C. M. Shea. 2006. "Effects of Champion Behavior, Team Potency, and External Communication Activities on Predicting Team Performance." *Group Organization Management* 31: 180–211.

Hülsheger, U. R., N. Anderson, and J. F. Salgado. 2009. "Team-Level Predictors of Innovation at Work: A Comprehensive Meta-Analysis Spanning Three Decades of Research." *Journal of Applied Psychology* 94: 1128–1145.

Jackson, S. E. 1992. "The Consequences of Group Composition for the Interpersonal Dynamics of Strategic Issue Processing." *Advances in Strategic Management* 8: 345–382.

Janssens, M., and J. M. Brett. 1997. "Meaningful Participation in Transnational Teams." *European Journal of Work and Organizational Psychology* 6: 153–168.

Johnson, J. D., and H. Chang. (2000). "Internal and External Communication, Boundary Spanning, and Innovation Adoption: An Over-Time Comparison of Three Explanations of Internal and External Innovation Communication in a New Organizational Form." *Journal of Business Communication* 37: 238–263

Joshi, A. 2006. "The Influence of Organizational Demography on the External Networking Behavior of Teams." *Academy of Management Review* 31: 583–595.

Joshi, A., and S. E. Jackson. 2003. "Managing Workforce Diversity to Enhance Cooperation in Organizations." In *International Handbook of Organizational Teamwork and Cooperative Working*, edited by M. West, D. Tjosvold, and K.G. Smith, 277–294. Chichester, UK: Wiley.

Joshi, A., N. Pandey, and G. Han. 2009. "Bracketing Team Boundary Spanning: An Examination of Task-Based, Team-Level, and Contextual Antecedents." *Journal of Organizational Behavior* 30: 731–759.

Katz, R., and M. Tushman. 1979. "Communication Patterns, Project Performance and Task Characteristics: An Empirical Evaluation and Integration in an R & D Setting." *Organizational Behavior and Human Performance* 23: 139–162.

Kegler, M. C., A. Steckler, S. H. Malek, and K. McLeroy. 1998. "A Multiple Case Study of Implementation in 10 Local Project ASSIST Coalitions in North Carolina." *Health Education Research* 13: 225–238.

Keller, R. T. 2001. "Cross-Functional Project Groups in Research and New Product Development: Diversity, Communications, Job Stress, and Outcomes." *Academy of Management Journal* 44: 547–555.

Koka, B. R., R. Madhavan, and J. E. Prescott. 2006. "The Evaluation of Interfirm Networks: Environmental Effects on Patterns of Network Change." *The Academy of Management Review 31*: 721–737.

Kramer, R. 1991. "Intergroup Relations and Organizational Dilemmas. In *Research in Organizational Behavior*, edited by L. L. Cummings and B. M. Staw, 13: 191–228. Greenwich, CT: JAI.

Levine, J. M., and R. L. Moreland. 1990. "Progress in Small Group Research." *Annual Review of Psychology 41*: 585–634.

Lewis, M. W., M. A. Welsh, G. E. Dehler, and S. G. Green. 2002. "Product Development Tension: Exploring Contrasting Styles of Project Management." *Academy of Management Journal 45*: 546–564.

Malone, T. W. 1987. *Modeling Coordination in Organizations and Markets: Fulfilling the Promise of the New Organization*. Boston, MA: Harvard Business School Press.

Marrone, J. A. 2010. "Team Boundary Spanning: A Multilevel Review of Past Research and Proposals for the Future." *Journal of Management 36*: 911–940.

Naidoo, J., and J. Wills. 2000. "Partnerships for Health—Working Together." *Health Promotion Foundations for Practice,*. Edinburgh, UK: Bailliere Tindell.

Oh, H., G. Labianca, and M. Chung. 2006. "A Multilevel Model of Group Social Capital." *Academy of Management Review 31*: 569–582.

Reynolds, K. J., J. C. Turner, and S. A. Haslam. 2000. "When Are We Better Than Them and They Worse Than Us? A Closer Look at Social Discrimination in Positive and Negative Domains." *Journal of Personality and Social Psychology 78*: 64–80.

Schopler, J. H. 1986. "Inter-Organizational Groups: Origins, Structure and Outcomes." *Academy of Management Review 12*: 702–713.

Scott, W. R. 1992. *Organizations: Rational, Natural, and Open Systems* (3rd ed.). Englewood Cliffs, NJ: Prentice Hall.

Somech, A. 2006. "The Effects of Leadership Style and Team Process on Performance and Innovation in Functionally Heterogeneous Teams." *Journal of Management 32*: 132–157.

Tsui, A. S., T. D. Egan, and C. A. O'Reilly. 1992. "Being Different: Relational Demography and Organizational Attachment." *Administrative Science Quarterly 37*: 549–579.

van der Vegt, G., E. van de Vliert, and A. Osterhof. 2003. "Informational Dissimilarity and Organizational Citizenship Behavior: The Role of Intrateam Interdependence and Team Identification." *Academy of Management Journal 46*: 715–727.

van Knippenberg, D. V. 2003. "Intergroup Relations in Organizations." In *International Handbook of Organizational Teamwork and Cooperative Working*, edited by M. West, D. Tjosvold, and K. G. Smith, 381–400. Chichester, UK: Wiley.

Victor, B., and R. S. Blackburn. 1998. "Interdependence: An Alternative Conceptualization." *Academy of Management Review 12*: 486–498.

Weick, K. E. 1976. "Educational Organizations as Loosely Coupled Systems." *Administrative Science Quarterly 21*: 1–19.

William, T., and J. Hickey. 2005. *Society in Focus*. Boston, MA: Pearson.

Yan, A., and M. R. Louis. 1999. "The Migration of Organizational Functions to the Work Unit Level: Buffering, Spanning, and Bringing Up Boundaries." *Human Relations 52*: 25–47.

6 Difficulties in Organizing Boundary-Spanning Activities of Inter-Organizational Teams

Thomas Stephen Calvard

THE STATE OF THE RESEARCH

Inter-organizational teams engaged in boundary-spanning sit at the junction of three separate but converging areas of organizational research. These three areas are: inter-organizational relationships; effective team working; and finally, the structures, processes, and competencies supporting boundary-spanning activities themselves. In this chapter I summarize some of the key organizational contexts and issues where these three topics converge, backed up where appropriate by research and practice that speaks selectively to them.

By taking each of the three areas briefly in turn, I can present and elaborate on some key definitions. First, there are many key examples of business contexts and activities where inter-organizational relationships and collaboration are considered useful and necessary for achieving joint objectives. I define inter-organizational relationships broadly here as any cooperative relationship involving explicit awareness and management of plans, budgets, control mechanisms, processes, and resources that flow between organizations, creating interdependency of joint actions that affect the success of those organizations (Dekker 2004; Ring and Van de Ven 1994). These include strategic alliances (Kale and Singh 2009), business-to-business (B2B) links between supplier and customer companies (Stock 2006), multi-agency cross-sectoral partnerships working on complex policy and public service delivery issues (Williams 2002), product development involving multiple companies (Majchrzak et al. 2000), investor-board relations (Rao and Sivakumar 1999), auditor-client relations (Seabright, Levinthal, and Fichman 1992), public-private partnerships (PPPs) (Noble and Jones 2006), mergers and acquisitions, joint ventures, and outsourcing. This list can be expanded further still if we think about other stakeholder agendas that transcend the boundaries of a single organization, such as those of pressure groups, interest groups, professional associations, multi-institutional multidisciplinary research collaborations, and employee unions.

It is therefore no coincidence that some of the earliest organizational research on boundary-spanning started by acknowledging and trying to explain why organizations need to manage their boundaries with other organizations in their environment (Aldrich and Herker 1977). The theoretical arguments were based on viewing organizations from an open-systems and resource-dependent perspective; companies needed to engage boundaries with their environments for gaining power and control over important resources as inputs, to protect themselves from disruptive environmental forces, and to dispose of key outputs and risks (Drach-Zahavy 2011; Stock 2006). If we consider promises made between organizations, mutual expectations, and reciprocal interdependencies around information and resources for task completion, then social exchange theory is also relevant in explaining the dynamics of these relationships (Das and Teng 2002). Furthermore, multinational companies (MNCs) have become so large in the last twenty-five years that they can to some extent be legitimately considered as global inter-organizational networks, and thus social network theory can be used to understand uneven, differentiated power and communication distributions across subsidiary boundaries (Ghoshal and Bartlett 1990). In general, patterns of inter-organizational and stakeholder interaction can be said to have become more complex and differentiated over time, which is why boundary-spanning remains such an important concept for business structures and processes. Currently, research is attempting to keep pace with explaining the design and types of these emerging organizational forms, requiring the use of multiple institutional theories simultaneously (Greenwood and Miller 2010). In any case, there has been a general move away from modern bureaucratic hierarchical forms with differentiated tasks and functions toward overlapping postmodern systems with networking, collaboration, governance, and partnership occurring across the boundaries of single individual organizations (Williams 2002).

Second, in order to consider inter-organizational relationships that explicitly involve teams, there is also a need to connect with team effectiveness research. The vast majority of organizational team research has taken an input-process-outcome (IPO) approach (Mathieu et al. 2008). The teams are set up with inputs defining members, leadership, and boundaries with the environment. Team processes describe how members interact and relate to each other as they try to accomplish their tasks, which might conceivably include boundary-spanning activities. Outcomes are results and by-products of teamwork that are valued by stakeholders (Mathieu et al. 2008). Generally, IPO team effectiveness models do contain an external environment component, but this is typically focused on the context internal to a single organization, and not elaborated on much further.

Nevertheless, there has been some key work, a relatively small proportion of overall team research, looking more specifically at external and inter-team activity. In particular, Deborah Ancona's work has really explored and established the 'external perspective' on teams (e.g., Ancona 1990; Ancona and Caldwell 1992). Typically this research has focused on boundary-spanning between teams within a single organization, both vertically with senior management and horizontally with other functions or divisions, a common necessity for teams working in product development or in knowledge-intensive sectors. Some researchers have identified 'X-teams' as a specific type of team that takes a particularly fluid, open, and networked approach to achieving its objectives (Ancona, Bresman, and Kaeufer 2002; Hollenbeck, Beersma, and Schouten 2012). Five key characteristics that set them apart from other teams are: external activity, extensive ties, expandable structures, flexible membership, and internal mechanisms for execution (Ancona et al. 2002). They are not touted as a cure for all ills and require careful management, but have potential relevance for many industries trying to spread and extend working processes around innovation, sales, technology, and product development. Importantly, they can also in principle work across inter-organizational boundaries, in a consortium-type structure, to spur innovation across an entire industry. One example of this is the Vehicle Design Summit (VDS), where X-teams collaborated internationally on issues of design, funding, research, and technological development to build a two-hundred mile-per-gallon car (Ancona, Bresman, and Caldwell 2009).

Other researchers have also worked to advance this 'inter-team' or 'team of teams' perspective on teamwork. Richter and colleagues empirically developed and validated a survey measure of inter-team effectiveness in healthcare organizations across the UK (Richter, Scully, and West 2005). They confirmed that teams relate to other teams in terms of resource utilization/exchange, transaction costs where one team benefits more than another from an arrangement, and a relationship that varies in terms of its viability according to how teams carry out their commitments and responsibilities to each other over time (Richter et al. 2005). Teams can withdraw from other teams, free ride off their successes, compete, and cooperate (Drach-Zahavy and Somech 2010). The degree of overlap or separation depends on how interdependent their tasks and goals are, the overlapping diversity of each team's members, the attraction of each team's power, how collectivistic or individualistic the team's cultures are, and the need to 'club together' if environmental conditions are unfavorable (Drach-Zahavy and Somech 2010).

Despite the large structures involved, there is some more research that has begun to embrace the challenge of understanding multiple teams working in concert: an emerging subdiscipline of teamwork research focusing on multiteam systems (MTSs), where two or more teams work together interdependently to achieve a common distal goal, while simultaneously striving to achieve the proximal goals distinctive to their own single team (Mathieu, Marks, and Zaccaro 2001; Zaccaro, Marks, and DeChurch 2012). MTS boundaries may lie within an organization, across several, or both. Typical inter-organizational examples might involve emergency services (police, fire, ambulance) or military armed forces (army, navy, air force), as well as other forms of inter-organizational relationship described above. Teams have proximal goals (e.g., 'fight and put out a fire') while keeping oriented to a distal goal shared with other teams (e.g., 'make the community safe').

Overall, then, team research appears to have gradually evolved to some extent from understanding the effectiveness of single teams to understanding outward-facing teams, and further to understanding overlapping pairs and sets of team boundaries. But it is still fair to ask—what of teams that are specifically made up from entirely different organizations? The lack of research is perhaps partly because inter-organizational groups or teams sit at the intersection of macro (multiple organizations, industry and sector-level issues) and micro (group work, norms, team behaviors) phenomena. In theory and in practice, inter-organizational groups ironically sit at a challenging boundary. Here I adopt an early broad definition: "inter-organizational groups are composed of members representing parent organizations and community constituencies, who meet periodically to make decisions relevant to their common concerns, and whose behavior is regulated by a common set of expectations" (Schopler 1987, 703). Within this definition, inter-organizational groups will also vary in terms of how firmly mandatory or voluntary their agenda for participation is, and how strongly their internal task structure is shaped by other external, surrounding stakeholders or based more on relative autonomy to develop their own internal ways of working (Schopler 1987). Drach-Zahavy (2011) also highlights three key characteristics that make inter-organizational teams distinct from intra-organizational teams: inter-organizational teams have members that represent or act on behalf of various host or origin constituencies; are typically subject to more temporary ways of working under conditions with greater conflicting demands and pressure; and are typically expected to engage in even more boundary-spanning within a more complex web of external stakeholders that emanate from more than one organization.

Thus there is an ongoing challenge of trying to generalize from existing research on traditional teams to these new inter-organizational forms of team. We can also infer the increasing importance of boundary-spanning activity as most team researchers would agree that, in general terms, teams are gradually moving away from functional and even cross-functional forms toward more delayered, self-managing, empowered, virtual structures with dynamically changing membership and boundaries that can be more or less fluid and permeable (Tannenbaum et al. 2012; Wageman, Gardner, and Mortensen 2012). In some senses, the very idea of a team is being challenged by new inter-organizational conditions that make it less grounded and more fluid and network-like, and boundary-spanning represents one way of navigating and adapting to such new conditions.

The third and final aspect of research relevant to this chapter is therefore the study of boundary-spanning activities themselves. What do team boundary-spanners do and why? Much research has been concerned with this, although as above, the distinction between boundaries within a single organization and inter-organizational boundaries across multiple organizations is often not made. While there is some overlap in terms of the general external environment around a team, we should be cautious in assuming that the boundary-spanning activities involved are identical. One theme running throughout this chapter is the proposition that inter-organizational boundaries will heighten dilemmas, tensions, and opportunities more than those within one organization, because the perceived distances and differences involved across the boundaries are more acute. One organization with teams within it still has one overarching common umbrella, whereas it is reasonable to assume multiple organizations may require much more sophisticated, autonomous boundary work.

In spite of this, researchers have evolved a set of general verbs to describe the activities of team boundary-spanners. Seminal work started with longer lists of external activity verbs (e.g., informing, coordinating, translating, filtering, delivering, protecting) and empirically narrowed it down by classifying them into four key factors: ambassadorial activities that are often vertical and protect a team by persuading others to support it; task coordination activities that often involve horizontal communication discussing work and feedback with outsiders; scouting activities scanning for new ideas and information over boundaries; and guard activities that shield the team from outside influences (Ancona and Caldwell 1992). Generally, these activity categories have stood the test of time. In a recent review, guarding and ambassadorial activities were collapsed into a single 'representation' category of boundary-spanning to make three categories overall (Marrone 2010). In terms of the relationships, boundary-spanners are generally motivated to work with someone who has greater power, equal power, or is an expert in a particular area (Marrone 2010). The inter-organizational level of analysis can also be referred to as the 'network' level of analysis, and boundary-spanning activity is expected to bring widespread benefits at this level, including better strategic decision making, large-scale innovations, better reputation, learning, adaptation, and achievement of cross-organizational goals (Marrone 2010).

Other research on boundary-spanning activities tends to involve variations on the basic three or four themes above. Some research refers to 'buffering' in a similar sense to guarding, and also 'bringing up' or 'reinforcing' boundaries: working proactively on keeping the inside of the team boundary compelling and distinct, to keep insiders in as opposed to defensively keeping outsiders out (Cross, Yan, and Louis 2000; Faraj and Yan 2009). Regarding boundary-spanning leadership activity, a more generic term used is 'relating,' denoting a range of political, trust-building, and caring activities inside and outside a team (Druskat and Wheeler 2003). Drach-Zahavy (2011) also tried to measure 'empowering' activities involving delegation and participatory encouragement across boundaries, but found it played little role in shaping team effectiveness, perhaps because of similarities with elements of scouting and coordination.

A general definition of team boundary-spanning activity relevant for this chapter reads as follows: "activity that refers to team processes necessary for the task in hand that are directed to reach over the team's boundary and engage with external agents in the team's focal environment" (Drach-Zahavy 2011, 92–93). Of course, as has been noted, in the specific case of inter-organizational teams, boundary-spanning activity takes on a new complexity and importance, as it can refer to boundaries between the parties represented within the team, between the team itself and host organizations, or between the team itself and yet other organizations in its focal environment. In sum, the "intermingling of the objectives, values, resources, and strategies of all the parties involved is thus more salient in inter-organizational teams' boundary-spanning than in that of traditional teams" (Drach-Zahavy 2011, 93).

A key ongoing debate surrounding boundary-spanning activities is how external activities and internal activities should be somehow balanced, given that both sharpen the boundaries involved and keep them coherently defined in the minds of team members (Choi 2002; Drach-Zahavy and Somech 2010). The next section in this chapter therefore takes a closer look at how some of these boundary-spanning dilemmas, trade-offs, synergies, and balances might need to be considered in particular inter-organizational contexts or situations.

INTER-ORGANIZATIONAL TEAM BOUNDARY-SPANNING DILEMMAS

As discussed above, the key boundaries seem to be threefold: the inter-organizational boundaries represented within the team between its members; the boundary surrounding the entire inter-organizational team as a whole that separates it from its host organizations; and finally any additional inter-organizational boundaries entirely outside of the team's current representation that constitute relations with other relevant 'third-party' stakeholders (the ties or contacts defining this type of boundary might of course vary across subsets of team members or individuals).

The main issue here is in defining and being aware of where the boundaries actually lie: whether the team itself is a boundary, or there is a boundary within the team, or there are multiple intersecting boundaries within the team and surrounding it. Managers and team members need to ask: Where do the teams and organizations start and finish? The boundaries are continually socially constructed through various interactions and perceptions, as well as being shaped by external forces and changes (Heracleous 2004). There is a perceived need to move beyond 'hard' economic approaches that focus only on maximized efficiency, minimized transaction costs, and contracting across boundaries, to also include social, psychological, and political aspects of boundaries, whether they are overtly observed by all involved or not (Heracleous 2004). Boundaries can vary in terms of how mentally or psychologically abstract they are, how social they are, and how physical they are with regards to formal rules, membership, and environments (Hernes 2004).

Here, I also introduce the term *dilemma*, to reflect the difficult choices and tensions that are intrinsic to boundaries. With relevance for boundaries, social dilemmas reflect conflicts of interest and in particular weighing one's own personal allegiances and self-interested motives against acting and co-operating for the sake of the good of some greater collective (Kollock 1998). If boundary-spanners act too narrowly in terms of their own self-interest, it is likely to compromise their future activities in some way, and if they give themselves too heartily to one form of cooperation or another, they may also become too detached or partisan, so balancing and negotiating their loyalties is an ongoing dilemma, both in a team itself (Glance and Huberman 1994), and in learning to collaborate in multi-organizational projects (Leufkens and Noorderhaven 2011). Resolving these dilemmas can take considerable time: time spent on building demonstrations of trust, momentum, and forging common interests.

In inter-organizational teams, these dilemma-like choices appear to stem from the overall dilemma challenging the very fabric of any team: how external versus internal can or should the team aspire to be in terms of its structures, resources, activities, and general focus? Answers will vary depending on the context; some teams may need military precision for reliable internal coordination, while others may be highly diffuse and purposively open to their environments. A slightly unrealistic ideal might appear to be for a team to have a perfectly symmetrical, ambidextrous balance between its competing internal and external agendas, although this balance will be dynamically affected by, and dependent upon, other factors, including the team's strategy, accountability, uncertainties associated with other stakeholders in the environment, working developments over time, how esoteric its inside knowledge and practices are, clashes, synergies, and so on (Choi 2002). Research tends to suggest that some deliberate inbuilt loosening of inter-organizational teams is needed to facilitate effective ongoing boundary-spanning activity and keep their activities in balance; namely members with diverse knowledge, more flexible membership as and when needed, and further short-term extra-team links where outsiders can be briefly consulted when needed (Drach-Zahavy 2011). In short, the structure of the team is understood to be more loose, open, and agile by design. This again challenges traditional notions of cohesive, committed teams with strong, unified internality. Inter-organizational teams embody this internal-external dilemma and seem to question the very idea of where boundaries should lie, in some contexts diffusing teams until they become more like virtual networks (Cummings and Pletcher, 2011; Hernes 2004; O'Leary and Cummings 2007). Furthermore, teams often have to fit their internal and external work together, particularly to ensure learning; one study in pharmaceutical teams found that teams can get distracted and suffer poorer performance if they neglect their internal learning in favor of external learning from experts and competitors (Bresman 2010). Thus teams need to clarify, explore, and learn about their internal issues in order to be able to transfer in and apply equivalent external advice and knowledge to their task and context effectively, bringing it from the outside in, and over the boundaries. Thus as a result, the internal and external become synergistically intertwined, perhaps the ideal to be aspired to after all.

Despite management commentaries that organizations and careers are becoming 'boundaryless,' these claims can appear overstated or unclear, and the more plausible reality appears to be that boundaries are intrinsic to most, if not all, working configurations, with equal potential to provide structure (order, distinctions, and thresholds), innovation, or great conflict and blurred confusion (Hernes 2004). In the following sections, I seek to summarize issues of inter-organizational team boundary-spanning by presenting—with some examples—four key dilemmas around: how to define the roles and relationships involved; how to manage the diversity of the parties involved; how to manage multiple social and personal identities; and how to lead inter-organizational inter-group structures.

Dilemma #1: Defining the Boundaries of Roles and Relationships

The first dilemma is particularly fundamental in terms of boundary-spanning activity in an inter-organizational team. Roles and relationships dilemmas refer to choices of: who should do the boundary-spanning within the team and outside the team, how much, with which partners, and why? This relates to carefully defining role relationship boundaries and what interdependencies they threaten or bring together, and how they can be crossed and merged appropriately. This further involves trying to choose the right boundaries to span, between the right people, and in the right ways; to ensure mutually beneficial, trusting relationships that serve higher objectives, while avoiding exclusion, disengagement, unfairness, or even exploitation in boundary relationships. Inter-organizational teams will involve difficult choices about how boundary-spanners represent their host organization and their partner organizations, and dividing tasks accordingly.

One potential way to resolve this dilemma is for host organizations to provide their boundary-spanning team members with role autonomy: freedom to balance diverse expectations and devise appropriate actions and behaviors that encourage trust-building with diverse others (Perrone, Zaheer, and McEvily 2003). Research has shown that trust is enhanced between boundary-spanning buyers and suppliers if they have greater role autonomy in terms of: freedom from ties to internal functions in their host organization, freedoms afforded them via greater tenure with their host organization, and autonomy derived from a clan culture in their host organization that allows them to express the company values flexibly through behaviors and relations of their choosing (Perrone et al. 2003). Role autonomy relates closely to other similar organizational concepts, including job crafting, role expansion, and psychological contracts (Grant and Hofmann 2011; Wrzesniewski and Dutton 2001; Yan, Zhu, and Hall 2002), that allow organizations to help their boundary-spanners 'fly the nest' and explore building relationships and working reciprocally with diverse other stakeholders in appropriately tailored ways. Considering these role autonomy issues helps to identify the individuals best placed to be boundary-spanning team members and to foster further relationships with other representatives outside the organization. In B2B inter-organizational supply chain teams, role autonomy and supervisory support have been shown to enable boundary-spanners to pursue roles of environmental stewardship, and contribute to broader social and corporate responsibility issues away from the narrower economic interests of their host organizations (De Ruyter, De Jong, and Wetzels 2009). Also relevant is careful consideration of a 'large enough' team size and an overall shared understanding of how the boundary-spanning divisions of labor will be supportively balanced, to avoid individuals experiencing role overload (Marrone, Tesluk, and Carson 2007). Neglecting team size and balanced roles threatens the confident viability of the inter-organizational team if members need to abandon aspects of boundary-spanning and retreat to their host organizations as a result of role conflict and competing demands.

For inter-organizational projects to work, the boundary-spanners need to quickly become socially embedded into their new team environments, sometimes within short time frames, building roles and relationships that reduce the uncertainty of losing out in terms of progress, productivity, power, or voice (Jones and Lichtenstein 2008). This all means freedom and space for boundary-spanners to make promises, draw up contracts, synchronize, familiarize, and allow new cultures and procedures to develop. Boundary-spanning roles and relationships are concerned with 'boundary work,' understanding the distinctions between relevant people and groups; and 'practice work,' shaping shared routines within the inter-organizational teams (Zietsma and Lawrence 2010). For boundary-spanning teams to successfully effect change and new connections in an institutional field of multiple organizations, this involves explicitly recognizing that their roles and relationships will sometimes be concerned with redefining, detaching from, and disrupting the boundaries and practices associated with more traditional roles and relationships.

In the private sector, this may need to be done very quickly; research on interactive Internet marketing projects shows that boundary-spanners quickly set up a transparent technologically supported 'trading zone' of visible, legible knowledge sharing between their communities and organizations. Although not without some jurisdictional conflicts and process losses, overall this does allow quick, adaptable learning and coordination in a postbureaucratic nonhierarchical fashion, delivering solutions to clients on time (Kellogg, Orlikowski, and Yates 2006). One example from a more public sector context is that of the coastal forestry industry in British Columbia, Canada, which used group boundary-spanning roles and relationships from the mid-1980s into the twenty-first century to carefully update forest harvesting practices and redraw more inclusive boundaries around participatory decision making, requiring lengthy processes of challenging and respecting inter-organizational relationships across a series of projects (Zietsma and Lawrence 2010).

Other illustrative examples of boundary-spanning roles and relationships of inter-organizational teams in the public eye include International Red Cross crisis response teams working across national and organizational boundaries in countries like Syria to engage with local organizations (Syrian Arab Red Crescent) (Itv News 2012), expansive film production teams, and large-scale projects with elements of design, construction, and architecture (Jones and Lichtenstein 2008). Typically the teams' roles and relationships are designed to get at locations and innovations that would be difficult to reach via more traditional organizational structures and processes. The National Health Service (NHS) in the UK uses inter-organizational teams at public sector-SME boundaries to efficiently design, develop, and adopt medical devices (NHS Supply Chain 2012). The World Bank has an Enterprise Outreach Team (EOT) for reaching out to the private sector to encourage participation in world economic development activity, supported further by a Private Sector Liaison Officers (PSLO) Network of roles and relationships that autonomously foster trade and investment with the backing of the World Bank's products and services (The World Bank 2011).

Dilemma #2: Managing Boundaries Created by Diversity

Moving on from the structure and design of role relationships, the second dilemma concerns the diverse composition of the inter-organizational team. Differences are a core feature of boundaries. The dilemma here lies in trying to avoid choosing between a team where differences are starkly insurmountable, unworkable, impermeable, or incomprehensible, or at the other extreme, a team that proves too homogeneous to innovate, in which the boundaries become nonexistent or negligible in their capacity to distinguish beneficial differences.

A few key issues can be managed here to minimize this tension and optimize boundary-spanning operations. In general, greater diversity in information and functional expertise of team members can enhance the positive links between boundary-spanning and team performance by keeping the team open to a greater range of outside perspectives (Drach-Zahavy 2011; Marrone 2010), and is often part of the reason an inter-organizational team might be formed and composed in the first place. However, excessively strong 'fault lines,' where the team splits cleanly into mutually exclusive subgroups with multiple diversity characteristics in common, can threaten the team's cohesion and performance, particularly for more overt, noninformational differences like race and gender (Thatcher and Patel 2011). Inter-organizational teams are already vulnerable for 'us versus them' splits if they are composed of people with strong existing organizational allegiances.

Boundary spanners need to be vigilant for these diversity pressure points. For example, if the team is composed of members from two organizations, with two ethnic subgroups present due to each organization being based in a different country, this internal boundary should be openly addressed to ensure adequate team integration. This can be done by: communicating an explicit 'hybrid' team culture where unique, team-specific ways of informally managing diversity are developed over time (Earley and Mosakowski 2000), reinforcing positive beliefs in diversity by explaining how it can directly facilitate team performance (Homan et al. 2007), and emphasizing the diversity of experiences held by individual team members (i.e., countries worked in, languages spoken, functions/organizations/sectors worked in, social network ties) to dilute the starkness of fault lines and show diversity's 'cross-cutting' areas of partial overlap (Bunderson and Sutcliffe 2002). Finally, besides working through demographic and functional differences, issues of power and status composition can be considered to resolve diversity dilemmas. Research on inter-organizational change implementation teams in the U.S. public-school sector found some evidence that having a diversity of authority positions in a team can facilitate team learning by keeping roles stable and democratically representing boundaries with different status groups (Higgins, Weiner, and Young 2012). Similarly, team effectiveness is maximized when 'inter-organizationality' is also maximized; that is, the diverse organizations involved are reflected by equal compositions in the team and power over decision making is equally distributed across these subgroups (Stock 2006).

Practical examples reveal the challenges of team diversity where inter-organizational boundaries are involved. Although not strictly a team, the UK's Coalition Government of Conservative and Liberal Democrat politicians shows how an inter-party alliance can be threatened and put on the verge of collapse by a deep representational fault line, with some arguing that by joining the Coalition, the Democrats have ultimately 'assimilated' themselves with the more powerful Conservatives, ceding their status, diversity, and independent subgroup identity, losing the support of voters and stakeholders at their boundaries (Rawnsley 2012; Wintour and Clark 2012). A more positive example is the Ohio Aerospace Institute of research, which stresses care in bringing together diverse experts from interdisciplinary fields, track records at reaching difficult consensus on past projects, openness to team-building with clear team types and roles, and partnership experiences with industry, government, and academia (Ohio Aerospace Institute 2012). Team BFK, a joint venture between three of the world's tunneling, civil engineering, and construction companies, positively emphasizes the diverse boundaries of its team projects through its Web site, communicating community responsibilities, a history of proven delivery with effective diverse team performances around the world, and representative space and information on sister companies and key organizations involved (Team BFK 2012).

Dilemma #3: Managing Multiple Identity Boundaries

Moving on from diverse team composition and internal splitting is the partly related dilemma of which personal and social identity issues to emphasize in an inter-organizational team. These issues revolve around the subjective psychological perceptions of oneness and inclusion that make an inter-organizational team a positively distinctive collective. The resolution lies in ensuring identification without it threatening to usurp or competitively threaten other personal and social identities that team members may hold. How does a team of boundary-spanners maintain overarching cohesion of identity, while also juggling other crucial personal, organizational, and relational sources of identity with external stakeholders?

There are several hints from identity theory and research about how to try to resolve this dilemma of privileging one identity over others. Models of optimal distinctiveness in identity argue that individuals strive for self-definitions that are distinctive and included at the same time (Brewer 1991). Thus in order to feel fully effective and committed to their work, inter-organizational team members need to feel simultaneously part of the team while retaining distinctive identities associated with their organizations of origin and other stakeholders at various boundaries. This premise is confirmed by research showing that the most productive boundary-spanning teams are those that retain a strong 'dual identity'; identifying strongly with both the team and the wider organization simultaneously (Richter et al. 2006).

While working in inter-organizational teams, boundary-spanners may therefore wish to express multiple identities. The expression of these identities can be supported through careful and systematic inter-group contact between boundary-spanners and the organizational environments associated with other team members, auditing relevant identities and linking them to the development of a set of organically evolving, inclusive goals for the team (Haslam, Eggins, and Reynolds 2003). As a result of a careful set of identity-focused meetings, rotations, and discussions across the inter-organizational boundaries the team represents in its individuals and/or subgroups, it can then blend the subjectively important elements into an inspirational team identity that faithfully captures the distinctive personal and social resources of the team (Dutton, Roberts, and Bednar 2010). This process may also involve the inter-organizational team drawing favorable comparisons between itself and competitors or other stakeholders playing different roles on the other side of boundaries, to boost self-esteem, identification with the appropriate foci, and effective coordination (Bartel 2001).

In practicing inter-organizational teams, wrestling with the expression of boundary-spanners' valued array of identities and the potential conflicts involved present dilemmas needing to be openly addressed. MITRE is a not-for-profit research organization that assists the U.S. government by working collaboratively across time zones and organizations on issues of aviation safety, frequently using social media and multiday workshops to build collaboration around awareness of diverse identities and activities (Drury 2009; Power 2012). Similar example contexts include those of teams at the Lakehurst Naval Air Warfare Centre working across defense agency boundaries (Bury 2008), the Software Engineering Institute at Carnegie Mellon University developing secure IT systems across organizations (CERT Software Engineering Institute, Carnegie Mellon University 2012), and London Council's local government association managing public services and community projects across organizations (LondonCouncils 2012). All these groupings direct efforts at careful negotiation and recognition of identities in terms of 'tribes,' language, terminology, overarching goals, and subsidiary conflicts, flows, and jurisdictions. Mapping inter-organizational boundaries means mapping identities and building them explicitly into a systemic architecture of goals and culture, forming crucial backdrops for the focal boundary-spanning project teams of the moment.

Dilemma #4: Who Should Lead Across Boundaries and How

The final dilemma proposed here for inter-organizational teams is based around leadership; there are difficult choices to be made around who should best represent the team's interests and how distant or close to various boundaries the leader or leaders (if leadership is shared or distributed) should be in their approach. Does boundary-spanning require leadership at all, and if so, what particular kinds of activities and approaches are most appropriate?

One key leadership task for resolving these dilemmas lies in actively and successfully constructing a shared inter-group relational identity, where the inter-organizational boundaries and relations become an explicit part of the team's identity (Hogg, van Knippenberg, and Rast 2012). To achieve this, the leader may well need to be an embodied prototype of these inter-organizational identity links. Therefore, if available, any team members who have significant experience working for or with the multiple organizations involved might be suitable leadership candidates. Furthermore, the leader is likely to be most effective if he or she: engages organizations and stakeholders relevant to the team's objectives via multiple boundary-spanning activities; can be open and transparent about the complementary strengths and weaknesses of each organization; can clarify the differential roles and status of each organization (which may be unequal or hierarchical); can form a leadership coalition with other leaders who can best represent the various groups within the inter-organizational team; and has a track record of relevant inter-organizational successes or technical contributions for team members to identify with (Druskat and Wheeler 2003; Fleming and Waguespack 2007; Hogg et al. 2012).

If a team sits at the intersection of three or more organizations, it can take on network characteristics that require a leadership focused around devising influential rules for designating activities and relationships, more akin to 'governance' or 'orchestration' than visionary leadership per se, given the power of key players and large organizations that are often involved (Müller-Seitz 2012). Overall there may be several leadership roles to be played by different team members or shared informally to some degree, including knowledge exchange, developmental review, establishing trust, formulating a joint vision, and governance structuring (Müller-Seitz 2012). Those occupying central positions in internal and external friendship networks will already have reputations and make natural choices for these leadership roles (Mehra et al. 2006a). In terms of social capital, a leader is often a 'broker' who connects otherwise disconnected parties, especially in terms of physically present interactions with them, although not all boundary-spanners are brokers by definition (Fleming and Waguespack 2007). In terms of supporting followers, leaders will also need to try to ensure smooth participative systems by shielding team members from inter-organizational bureaucracy, spotting emerging alliances, guiding adaptation to changes induced by key boundary events, and facilitating trusting, collaborative knowledge sharing (Connelly 2007).

Overall, the most effective leader or leaders will need to divide attention between the internal environment and the external environment, between the team itself and the network surrounding it (Marrone 2010). These are often described as difficult 'in-group/out-group leadership trade-offs' faced by inter-group leaders, with success inside one boundary coming at the expense of failure outside (Pittinsky and Simon 2007). Leaders therefore need to work on switching between the two foci, managing contact time with various parties, developing a team vision that is popular but specific, allocating resources to inside versus outside issues, and challenging negative attitudes toward important boundaries (Pittinsky and Simon 2007).

To the extent that these leaders are trying to balance activities positively and coherently across internal and external boundaries, it is a very challenging role to play in any inter-organizational team, and practical examples reflect that. The UK Health Foundation awards funding to cross-sector working project teams set up to improve the quality of health-care initiatives, and emphasizes that leaders need highly positive attitudes, change management skills, the ability to develop networks, and a focus that zooms in on stakeholders, building from the bottom up toward high-level visions (The Health Foundation 2012). In pharmaceutical contract research organizations (CROs), leaders have to manage statisticians, contractors, and medical monitors to bring drugs through trial to high-quality, cost-efficient, and timely specifications. Effective leaders are those who make all partnership information as explicit as possible, proactively map out problems and pressure points, hold weekly meetings, develop distinctive metrics for success early, and carefully sequester some time for team building (Zuckerman and Higgins 2002). At its most difficult, effective inter-organizational leadership may mean taking bold actions to cut across boundaries and transcend them by adhering to a higher-level objective or stakeholder. New Jersey Governor Chris Christie chose to praise Obama while working with the president on handling relief efforts after Hurricane Sandy. Despite drawing harsh criticism from many in the Republican Party for embracing the political opposition so literally and symbolically, his approval ratings jumped across the board as a trusted leader doing right by the citizens (Forbes Leadership 2012). At the other extreme, interdisciplinary cross-organizational research collaborations such as the Emotion Regulation of Others and Self (EROS), a project group of five universities across the UK, may prefer to use network language and downplay the relative leadership of the principal investigator, instead locating them within a 'central node' while maintaining some level of democratically distributed leadership across other nodes of geographical location and subject matter expertise (EROS 2012). Clearly, effective leadership approaches do depend on the structure, scope, and contextual patterning of the inter-organizational boundaries involved, as well as how they best serve the interests of the various individual and collective agendas.

PRACTICAL INTERVENTIONS FOR INDIVIDUALS AND WORKPLACES

Attempting to directly address the four interrelated dilemmas of this chapter has practical implications for managers or team leaders, boundary-spanners, inter-organizational team members in general, HR, and other stakeholders working around an inter-organizational team in a particular work context. Here I discuss three key practical agendas for supporting inter-organizational boundary-spanning teams, particularly in terms of reconciling the overall dilemmas of external versus internal focus and striving for narrower individual or team interests versus wider coordination benefits.

First, practitioners need to experiment with new building blocks, designs, and structures to ensure that inter-organizational teams function effectively. This might mean treating the boundary-spanners as a multiteam system (MTS) of subunits from the two or more component organizations and implementing practices such as: setting smaller proximal subunit goals that feed into superordinate shared goals for the MTS as a whole, monitoring information flows in and out of the MTS and across subunits, establishing forums or protocols whereby the MTS can integrate the more disparate boundary-spanning activities of its subunits, and formulating a synchronizing communication strategy so that the inter-organizational team members can work interdependently as needed, around their other duties (Zaccaro et al. 2012). Similarly, employing the practical design of an X-team may mean having a clearly defined, tiered role structure for full-time, part-time, and one-time contributing members with varying levels of boundary-spanning responsibility, or some similar design that differentiates those doing work at the core of the team and those emanating away from it. This will help to minimize issues of role overload, inefficient redundant working, and role conflict. Overall, the X-team needs to be carefully staffed, built, and supported around a multilayered externally oriented design, with a rich information infrastructure, precise resource allocations, and explicit decision-making rules that can be updated transparently for learning and adaptation purposes (Ancona et al. 2002).

Put differently, the inter-organizational team needs to set up a 'trading zone' where the work of the team is visibly represented, assembled across boundaries, and allows some open revision atop the robust foundation of a specified coordination structure (Kellogg et al. 2006). This trading zone may take the form of a Web-based intranet platform, a novel physical location, or some other symbolic work design that captures the inter-organizational business context in question. Governance patterns of control and reward should be firmly aligned with the positive reasons why the organizations have partnered together to ensure swift trust and avoid coordination concerns (Dekker 2004).

A second area of practical intervention following from the initial structure or design is to define and measure the inter-organizational boundary work, based on the argument that 'what gets measured gets done.' To ensure coherence, the boundary-spanning project will need to recognize the milestones and successes of both the team unit and key individual contributors, as well as being able to clearly inform outside organizations and other outlying constituents of its work. This means wrestling with the cause-and-effect mechanisms of the inter-organizational team's work and the impacts of effective boundary-spanning behaviors on the bottom line, in terms of innovative product or service delivery, mutually beneficial negotiation outcomes, and successful changes at the industry or sector level.

As well as defining outcomes, there is also the need to practically define and measure the boundaries themselves. This means measurement in terms of cataloguing or listing them, prioritizing them, ordering them temporally, and characterizing them in various ways (e.g., permeability, communication technology or virtuality, symbolic significance, tightness of interdependence) (Hernes 2004). The boundaries between team members with different organizational backgrounds and other stakeholders may also have connotations of hierarchy, market exchange, affiliation, regulation, or conflict informing their definition (Alexander 1998). Although at first glance conducting boundary audits or maps might seem rather managerial or bureaucratic, it seems reasonable to assume that if the analysis is participative and inclusive, it can be part of an effective practical intervention for the team. At the very least it should serve to raise awareness around multiple boundaries and an acceptance of the language of boundary-spanning and what it means in a particular business context.

At the team-member level, there is also the issue of measuring boundary-spanning activity itself. Job analyses, competency frameworks, and job descriptions can be used to specify boundary-spanning activities and divisions of labor, particularly if there are multiple leadership roles. Ideally, these analyses should be realistic about what boundary-spanning individuals can achieve alone and make some clear distinctions about internal versus external activity, as well as common problems, constraints, and critical incidents where performance can be extremely strong or extremely poor. Research into the profile of the inter-organizational boundary-spanner has revealed a formidable list of communicatory, political, networking, and accountability-based competencies (Williams 2002). Nevertheless, these competencies can also be used to drive further practical interventions, such as training needs analyses for developing more effective boundary-spanners in the future. If the team is working on a particularly high-level industry-based or societal issue, then the concept of stewardship may help to define and evaluate boundary-spanning roles in practice, in terms of standards of accountability to stakeholders and transcending self-interest to improve social contexts larger than that of an individual organization (De Ruyter et al. 2009).

The inter-organizational relationships themselves can be defined and evaluated within teams by following best practice around strategic alliances (Kale and Singh 2009). These team activities might include keeping records of boundary meetings and transactions, broadcasting cross-boundary successes, and managing an ongoing portfolio of boundary-spanning work activities.

A final practical issue highlighted here concerns team process interventions to manage potential boundary-spanning dilemma issues as they arise, often on a one-off basis. Team leaders and members may need to call sudden meetings to address issues of roles, diversity, identity, and leadership, and should be vigilant in anticipating and flagging such issues so that boundaries can be patched up, recast, destroyed, or explored. This may include issues of change within the team; member attrition and replacement, for example. The selection and development of leaders and team members might best be guided by considering their locations in key social and organizational networks, with a team agenda being set that connects to these networks from day one (Ancona et al. 2009). Addressing team composition and process may mean making dynamic use of diversity or talent management practices and trying to ensure some power symmetry, position representation, and reflection on fault-line rifts that may cause damage if left unchecked. Given that alliances, teams, and inter-organizational boundaries involve so many tensions, in practice such teams might best explicitly adopt a dialectical approach, where tensions are quickly identified and rebalanced when necessary, over the project and life cycles of the team. These tensions include expansion-contraction, vigilance-trust, design-emergence, and so on (de Rond and Bouchikhi 2004). Other dilemma management interventions may involve enhancing role autonomy of team members to maintain trust with stakeholders, backing up or even pulling back team members to avoid excessive negative spillover from boundaries into their role (Ramarajan et al. 2010), and invoking institutional or regulatory rhetoric to reinforce team identity and leadership across boundaries (Marchington and Vincent 2004). For larger teams, another way to cut through the complexity would be to encourage boundary-spanners to work in pairs or dyads, perhaps using an 'opposite number' system across organizations where appropriate, providing a sense of balance, and minimizing extreme problems of individual isolation or collective bias (Brickson 2000).

In sum, these initiatives are likely to help ensure the sustained viability of an inter-organizational team to complete its work assignations (Bell and Marentette 2011), and to treat the structure like an organization or complex system in its own right, existing in a dynamic landscape where the appropriate attractor and receptor points of contact on boundaries can be configured and connected most effectively (Arrow, McGrath, and Berdahl 2000).

A FUTURE RESEARCH AGENDA: ISSUES OF ONGOING IMPORTANCE

In concluding this chapter, I will outline four key issues for enabling future research to describe and explain important boundary-spanning issues in inter-organizational teams.

First, although this chapter does not propose a formal conceptual model, it does highlight four dilemmas around role relationships, diversity management, identity work, and leadership. The dilemmas are interrelated under an overall dilemma which concerns how boundary-spanners choose to manage their resources, striving to react to conditions internal and external to an inter-organizational team. Future research therefore might continue to try to explore how these dilemmas operate in field settings, testing key constructs as antecedents, boundary conditions, mechanisms, and outcomes in empirical frameworks. Particularly relevant variables might include the boundary-spanning activities themselves, patterns of team agreement or aggregation on role, identity, or leadership-based constructs (DeRue et al. 2010), and types of inter-organizational team diversity (Harrison and Klein 2007). Studies could choose to focus on a single dilemma in detail, or more broadly investigate how conditions associated with the four dilemmas act in combination: offsetting, compensating, or mutually reinforcing one another. Currently, researchers are still striving to home in on the basic and optimal conditions needed to fulfill the notion of an effective contemporary work team (Hackman 2012). Similarly, understanding the basic groundwork or ingredients that fundamentally affect whether boundary-spanning in inter-organizational teams will thrive or fail, and in what areas, may be more fruitful than merely testing a laundry list of causal factors.

Second, future research needs to address issues of business context and generalizability (Johns 2006). Researchers need to try to specify their inter-organizational contexts clearly and establish which intra-organizational and intra-team processes generalize to inter-organizational and inter-team contexts and phenomena, and which do not. Much team boundary-spanning research literature appears to implicitly assume the context of a single organization, and yet the same findings and propositions may not apply to mergers, strategic alliances, public service delivery, supply chains, and other forms of boundary-spanning across organizations that vary in formality and openness. Researchers need to try to be clear on what type of inter-organizational coordination is occurring, and reflect on how inter-organizational contextual conditions stretch and distort traditionally grounded team structures in dynamic ways as they extend over boundaries. Resolving dilemmas may be easier or more difficult, depending on the context and how it affects the conditions described in this chapter. Research using quasi-experimental field designs where possible, or multiple case studies, may help to shed light on how contextual variables affect the competencies, activities, and practices aimed at addressing boundary-spanning conflicts of interest and securing formal and informal cooperation (Smith, Carroll, and Ashford 1995). For example, relational HRM practices are often tailored to reinforce cross-boundary working more flexibly than control or commitment systems (Mossholder, Richardson, and Settoon 2011).

Third, future researchers need to expose and embrace the methodological and analytical challenges of researching inter-organizational team boundaries. Boundaries can and should be measured in terms of many types and characteristics. In an inter-organizational context, boundary characteristics need to be controlled for and tested in interaction with one another using multiple sources of data, to separate the perceived from the more objective formal aspects, and to properly understand whether outcomes are a result of organizational, functional, temporal, or geographical boundaries, or some combination of these factors and others (Espinosa et al. 2003). In addition, researchers will likely need to adopt multilevel approaches to test models and theories surrounding boundary-spanning. Although this chapter does not formally specify a multilevel model, several exist already (Marrone et al. 2007; Marrone 2010), and the dilemmas discussed imply that shared team-level characteristics such as diversity compositions and leadership strategies can interact in a top-down fashion with individual-level characteristics such as role and identity perceptions to shape outcomes for boundary-spanners. The inter-organizational level of analysis is particularly challenging in scope and complexity, and may require novel or contrasting analytic mindsets and techniques to capture the effects of these far-reaching boundaries. Boundary analyses may benefit from the use of more than one analytic technique on the same data in a single study (Zyphur 2009). For example, structural equation models can link the predictors and outcomes of dilemmas, whereas social network analyses, cognitive mapping, and latent class analyses might be better equipped for charting various boundaries, subgroups, and their interconnections.

Social network analyses may be particularly useful for identifying boundary role and relationship patterns precisely in terms of inter-organizational ties. A rigorous snowball or stratified sampling strategy is also crucial for capturing data from all relevant boundaries and from various sides and tiered distances. Sociometric network analyses can shed light on which inter-organizational team member configurations resolve team dilemmas to maximize performance, such as distributed leadership arrangements, for example (Mehra et al. 2006b). Researchers may need to juxtapose team-level analyses alongside network analyses to fully understand the structural dilemmas that inter-organizational boundary-spanning presents, particularly as it has been argued that network forms are becoming more prominent in Western societies generally (Raab and Kenis 2009). Such methodological and analytical pluralism will ensure that the who, what, why, when, and where questions of inter-organizational boundary-spanning are adequately addressed.

A final agenda for future research in this area is continuing to develop and consolidate the educative list or repertoire of potentially relevant theories, including approaches based on complex open systems, social exchanges, role theory, structural contingencies, structuration, social identity, sense-making, and properties of boundaries themselves. One area I perceive to be in particular need of theory building is examining some of the deviant, counterproductive, darker, more dysfunctional aspects of inter-organizational boundary-spanning activities, including spying, poaching talent, contract breach or violation, theft, deception or duplicity, and aggression. Boundary-spanners often have ambiguous roles and are particularly vulnerable to some of the pressures to engage in deviant activity, even inadvertently so (Litzky, Eddleston, and Kidder 2006). Much research on boundary-spanning has remained relatively silent or vaguely positive on the implicit theoretical value and necessity of boundary-spanning itself, and I would therefore encourage future research to begin to more explicitly discuss the conflicts of interest, paradoxes, dilemmas, and dialectics of boundary-spanning across organizations (Smith and Lewis 2011). This chapter, and indeed much of this volume, is intended to provide helpful steps in this direction.

CONCLUSION

In this chapter I have examined the current state of research in three key areas: inter-organizational relationships, effective team working, and boundary-spanning activities. I then investigated inter-organizational team boundary-spanning contexts, with examples, at the intersection of these three areas by conceptualizing them in terms of social dilemmas. Specifically, I broke down the higher-order dilemmas of internal vs. external team activity and narrower self-interest vs. wider cooperative endeavor into four more manageable dilemmas concerning roles and relationships, diversity representation, valued social or personal identities, and leadership practice. I have also discussed the implications of these dilemmas for those practicing and researching within inter-organizational boundary-spanning team contexts. Just as these various complex cooperative structures can allow for organic and liberating achievements of ambitious business aims across boundaries, they can also prove challenging in stretching traditional notions of organizational structure, governance, and resources. In this chapter I have attempted to specify and address these challenges more closely than previous work, so that inter-organizational boundary-spanning teams can be engaged with more proactively, systematically, and effectively as they become more commonplace work arrangements.

REFERENCES

Aldrich, Howard, and Diane Herker. 1977. "Boundary Spanning Roles and Organization Structure." *Academy of Management Review* 2:217–230.

Alexander, E. R. 1998. "A Structuration Theory of Inter-Organizational Coordination: Cases in Environmental Management." *International Journal of Organizational Analysis* 6:334–354. Accessed December 23, 2012. doi: 10.1108/eb028890.

Ancona, Deborah Gladstein. 1990. "Outward Bound: Strategies for Team Survival in an Organization." *Academy of Management Journal* 33:334–365.

Ancona, Deborah Gladstein, Henrik Bresman, and David F. Caldwell. 2009. "The X Factor: Six Steps to Leading High-Performing X-Teams." *Organizational Dynamics* 38:217–224. Accessed November 27, 2012. doi:10.1016/j.orgdyn.2009.04.003.

Ancona, Deborah Gladstein, Henrik Bresman, and Katrin Kaeufer. 2002. "The Comparative Advantage of X-Teams." *MIT Sloan Management Review* 43:33–39.

Ancona, Deborah Gladstein, and David F. Caldwell. 1992. "Bridging the Boundary: External Activity and Performance in Organizational Teams." *Administrative Science Quarterly* 37:634–665.

Bell, Suzanne T., and Brian J. Marentette. 2011. "Team Viability for Long-Term and Ongoing Organizational Teams." *Organizational Psychology Review* 1:275–292. Accessed December 23, 2012. doi:10.1177/2041386611405876.

Bresman, Henrik. 2010. "External Learning Activities and Team Performance: A Multimethod Field Study." *Organization Science* 21:81–96. Accessed November 28, 2012. doi:10.1287/orsc.1080.0413.

Brewer, Marilynn B. 1991. "The Social Self: On Being the Same and Different at the Same Time." *Personality and Social Psychology Bulletin* 17:475–482. Accessed November 30, 2012. doi:10.1177/0146167291175001.

Brickson, Shelley. 2000. "The Impact of Identity Orientation on Individual and Organizational Outcomes in Demographically Diverse Settings." *Academy of Management Review* 25:82–101.

Bunderson, J. Stuart, and Kathleen M. Sutcliffe. 2002. "Comparing Alternative Conceptualizations of Functional Diversity in Management Teams: Process and Performance Effects." *Academy of Management Journal* 45:875–893.

Bury, Greg. 2008. "Hail to the Chief: GIS Challenges of Cross-Organizational Teams." Naval Air Engineering Station, Lakehurst, NJ. Accessed November 30, 2012. http://proceedings.esri.com/library/userconf/feduc08/papers/chief.pdf.

CERT Software Engineering Institute, Carnegie Mellon University. 2012. "Cross-Organizational Team (X-Team): Mission, Goals, Objectives and Composition." Accessed November 30, 2012. http://www.cert.org/governance/ges-xteam.html.

Choi, Jin Nam. 2002. "External Activities and Team Effectiveness: Review and Theoretical Development." *Small Group Research 33*:181–208. Accessed November 27, 2012. doi:10.1177/104649640203300202.

Connelly, David R. 2007. "Leadership in the Collaborative Inter-Organizational Domain." *International Journal of Public Administration 30*:1231–1262. Accessed December 15, 2012. doi:10.1080/01900690701230150.

Cross, Robert L., Aimin Yan, and Meryl Reis Louis. 2000. "Boundary Activities in 'Boundaryless' Organizations: A Case Study of a Transformation to a Team-Based Structure." *Human Relations 53*:841–868. Accessed November 27, 2012. doi:10.1177/0018726700536004.

Cummings, Jonathon, and Carol Pletcher. 2011. "Why Project Networks Beat Project Teams." *MIT Sloan Management Review 52*:75–80.

Das, T.K., and Bing-Sheng Teng. 2002. "Alliance Constellations: A Social Exchange Perspective." *Academy of Management Review 27*:445–456. Accessed November 26, 2012. doi:10.5465/AMR.2002.7389937.

Dekker, Henri C. 2004. "Control of Inter-Organizational Relationships: Evidence on Appropriation Concerns and Coordination Requirements." *Accounting, Organizations and Society 29*:27–49. Accessed November 26, 2012. doi:10.1016/S0361-3682(02)00056-9.

De Rond, Mark, and Hamid Bouchikhi. 2004. "On the Dialectics of Strategic Alliances." *Organization Science 15*:56–69. Accessed December 23, 2012. doi:10.1287/orsc.1030.0037.

DeRue, D. Scott, John Hollenbeck, Dan Ilgen, and Deborah Feltz. 2010. "Efficacy Dispersion in Teams: Moving Beyond Agreement and Aggregation." *Personnel Psychology 63*:1–40. Accessed December 23, 2012. doi:10.1111/j.1744-6570.2009.01161.x.

De Ruyter, Ko, Ad de Jong, and Martin Wetzels. 2009. "Antecedents and Consequences of Environmental Stewardship in Boundary-Spanning B2B Teams." *Journal of the Academy of Marketing Science 37*:470–487. Accessed November 27, 2012. doi:10.1007/s11747-009-0138-0.

Drach-Zahavy, Anat. 2011. Inter-Organizational Teams as Boundary Spanners: The Role of Team Diversity, Boundedness, and Extrateam Links." *European Journal of Work and Organizational Psychology 20*:89–118. Accessed November 26, 2012. doi: 10.1080/13594320903115936.

Drach-Zahavy, Anat, and Anit Somech. 2010. "From an Intrateam to an Interteam Perspective of Effectiveness: The Role of Interdependence and Boundary Activities." *Small Group Research 41*:143–174. Accessed November 27, 2012. doi:10.1177/1046496409356479.

Drury, Jill L. 2009. "A Survey of Time-Sensitive, Cross-Organizational Team Collaboration Research for Application to Aviation Crisis Management." Accessed November 29, 2012. http://www.mitre.org/work/tech_papers/tech_papers_09/09_2190/.

Druskat, Vanessa Urch, and Jane V. Wheeler. 2003. "Managing From the Boundary: The Effective Leadership of Self-Managing Work Teams." *Academy of Management Journal 46*:435–457.

Dutton, Jane E., Laura Morgan Roberts, and Jeffrey Bednar. 2010. "Pathways for Positive Identity Construction at Work: Four Types of Positive Identity and the Building of Social Resources." *Academy of Management Review 35*:265–293.

Earley, P. Christpher, and Elaine Mosakowski. 2000. "Creating Hybrid Team Cultures: An Empirical Test of Transnational Team Functioning." *Academy of Management Journal* 43:26–49.

EROS. 2012. "Emotion Regulation of Others and Self." Accessed December 5, 2012. http://www.erosresearch.org/.

Espinosa, J. Alberto, Jonathon N. Cummings, Jeanne M. Wilson, and Brandi M. Pearce. 2003. "Team Boundary Issues Across Multiple Global Firms." *Journal of Management Information Systems* 19:157–190.

Faraj, Samer, and Aimin Yan. 2009. "Boundary Work in Knowledge Teams." *Journal of Applied Psychology* 94:604–617. Accessed November 27, 2012. doi:10.1037/a0014367.

Fleming, Lee, and David M. Waguespack. 2007. "Brokerage, Boundary Spanning and Leadership in Open Innovation Communities." *Organization Science* 18:165–180. Accessed December 15, 2012. doi:10.1287/orsc.1060.0242.

Forbes Leadership. 2012. "Three Reasons Christie's Falling out With the GOP Made him a More Trusted Leader." Accessed December 22, 2012. http://www.forbes.com/sites/forbesleadershipforum/2012/12/21/three-reasons-christies-falling-out-with-the-gop-made-him-a-more-trusted-leader/.

Ghoshal, Sumantra, and Christopher A. Bartlett. 1990. "The Multinational Corporation as an Inter-Organizational Network." *Academy of Management Review* 15:603–625.

Glance, Natalie S., and Bernardo A. Huberman. 1994. "The Dynamics of Social Dilemmas." *Scientific American* March:76–81.

Grant, Adam M., and David A. Hofmann. 2011. "Role Expansion as a Persuasion Process: The Interpersonal Influence Dynamics of Role Redefinition." *Organizational Psychology Review* 1:9–31. Accessed November 27, 2012. doi:10.1177/2041386610377228.

Greenwood, Royston, and Danny Miller. 2010. "Tackling Design Anew: Getting Back to the Heart of Organizational Theory." *Academy of Management Perspectives* 24:78–88. Accessed November 26, 2012. doi:10.5465/AMP.2010.55206386.

Hackman, J. Richard. 2012. "From Causes to Conditions in Group Research." *Journal of Organizational Behavior* 33:428–444. Accessed December 23, 2012. doi:10.1002/job.1774.

Harrison, David A., and Katherine J. Klein. 2007. "What's the Difference? Diversity Constructs as Separation, Variety or Disparity in Organizations." *Academy of Management Review* 32:1199–1228. Accessed December 23, 2012. doi:10.5465/AMR.2007.26586096.

Haslam, S. Alexander, Rachael A. Eggins, and Katherine J. Reynolds. 2003. "The ASPIRe Model: Actualizing Social and Personal Identity Resources to Enhance Organizational Outcomes." *Journal of Occupational and Organizational Psychology* 76:83–113. Accessed December 1, 2012. doi:10.1348/096317903321208907.

Heracleous, Loizos. 2004. "Boundaries in the Study of Organization." *Human Relations* 57:95–103. Accessed November 28, 2012. doi:10.1177/0018726704042716.

Hernes, Tor. 2004. "Studying Composite Boundaries: A Framework of Analysis." *Human Relations* 57:9–29. Accessed November 28, 2012. doi: 10.1177/0018726704042712.

Higgins, Monica C., Jennie Weiner, and Lissa Young. 2012. "Implementation Teams: A new Lever for Organizational Change." *Journal of Organizational Behavior* 33:366–388. Accessed November 29, 2012. doi:10.1002/job.1773.

Hogg, Michael A., Daan van Knippenberg, and David E. Rast III. 2012. "Intergroup Leadership in Organizations: Leading Across Group and Organizational Boundaries." *Academy of Management Review* 37:232–255. Accessed December 10, 2012. doi:10.5465/amr.2010.0221.

Hollenbeck, John R., Bianca Beersma, and Maartja E. Schouten. 2012. "Beyond Team Types and Taxonomies: A Dimensional Scaling Conceptualization for Team Description. *Academy of Management Review* 37:82–106. Accessed November 27, 2012. doi:10.5465/amr.2010.0181.

Homan, Astrid C., Daan van Knippenberg, Gerben A. Van Kleef, and Carsten K. W. De Dreu. 2007. "Bridging Faultlines by Valuing Diversity: Diversity Beliefs, Information Elaboration and Performance in Diverse Work Groups." *Journal of Applied Psychology* 92:1189–1199. Accessed November 29, 2012. doi:10.1037/0021–9010.92.5.1189.

Itv News. 2012. "Red Cross: Organization Needs 'Safe and Unhindered Access.'" Accessed December 15, 2012.http://www.itv.com/news/update/2012–06–28/red-cross-organisation-needs-safe-and-unhindered-access/.

Johns, Gary. 2006. "The Essential Impact of Context on Organizational Behavior." *Academy of Management Review* 31:386–408. Accessed December 23, 2012. doi:10.5465/AMR.2006.20208687.

Jones, Candace, and Benyamin B. Lichtenstein. 2008. "Temporary Inter-Organizational Projects: How Temporal and Social Embeddedness Enhance Coordination and Manage Uncertainty." In *The Oxford Handbook of Inter-Organizational Relations*, edited by Steve Cropper, Mark Ebers, Chris Huxham and Peter S. Ring, 231–255. New York: Oxford University Press.

Kale, Prashant, and Harbir Singh. 2009. "Managing Strategic Alliances: What Do We Know now, and Where Do We Go from Here?" *Academy of Management Perspectives* 23:45–62. Accessed November 26, 2012. doi:10.5465/AMP.2009.43479263.

Kellogg, Katherine C., Wanda J. Orlikowski, and Joanne Yates. 2006. "Life in the Trading Zone: Structuring Coordination Across Boundaries in Postbureaucratic Organizations." *Organization Science* 17:22–44. Accessed November 27, 2012. doi:10.1287/orsc.1050.0157.

Kollock, Peter. 1998. "Social Dilemmas: The Anatomy of Cooperation." *Annual Review of Sociology* 24:183–214.

Leufkens, Aukje S., and Niels G. Noorderhaven. 2011. "Learning to Collaborate in Multi-Organizational Projects." *International Journal of Project Management* 29:432–441. Accessed November 28, 2012. doi:http://dx.doi.org/10.1016/j.ijproman.2011.01.004.

Litzky, Barrie E., Kimberley A. Eddleston, and Deborah L. Kidder. 2006. "The Good, the Bad and the Misguided: How Managers Inadvertently Encourage Deviant Behaviors." *Academy of Management Perspectives* 20:91–103. Accessed December 23, 2012. doi: 10.5465/AMP.2006.19873411.

LondonCouncils. 2012. "Cross-Organizational Working." Accessed November 30, 2012. http://www.londoncouncils.gov.uk/policylobbying/crime/crossworking/.

Majchrzak, Ann, Ronald E. Rice, Arvind Malhotra, Nelson King, and Sulin Ba. 2000. "Technology Adaptation: The Case of a Computer-Supported Inter-Organizational Virtual Team." *MIS Quarterly* 24:569–600. Accessed November 26, 2012. doi:10.2307/3250948.

Marchington, Mick, and Steven Vincent. 2004. "Analysing the Influence of Institutional, Organizational and Interpersonal Forces in Shaping Inter-Organizational

Relations." *Journal of Management Studies* 41:1029–1056. Accessed December 23, 2012. doi:10.1111/j.1467–6486.2004.00465.x.

Marrone, Jennifer A. 2010. "Team Boundary Spanning: A Multilevel Review of Past Research and Proposals for the Future." *Journal of Management* 36:911–940. Accessed November 27, 2012. doi:10.1177/0149206309353945.

Marrone, Jennifer A., Paul E. Tesluk, and Jay B. Carson. 2007. "A Multilevel Investigation of Antecedents and Consequences of Team Member Boundary-Spanning Behavior." *Academy of Management Journal* 50:1423–1439. Accessed November 27, 2012. doi:10.5465/AMJ.2007.28225967.

Mathieu, John, Michelle A. Marks, and Stephen J. Zaccaro. 2001. "Multiteam Systems." In *International Handbook of Work and Organizational Psychology*, edited by Neil Anderson, Deniz S. Ones, Handan Kepir Sinangil, and Chockalingham Viswesvaran, 289–313. London: Sage.

Mathieu, John M., Travis Maynard, Tammy Rapp, and Lucy Gilson. 2008. "Team Effectiveness 1997–2007: A Review of Recent Advancements and a Glimpse into the Future." *Journal of Management* 34:410–476. Accessed November 27, 2012. doi:10.1177/0149206308316061.

Mehra, Ajay, Andrea L. Dixon, Daniel J. Brass, and Bruce Robertson. 2006a. " The Social Network Ties of Group Leaders: Implications for Group Performance and Leader Reputation." *Organization Science* 17:64–79. Accessed December 10, 2012. doi:10.1287/orsc.1050.0158.

Mehra, Ajay, Brett R. Smith, Andrea L. Dixon, and Bruce Robertson. 2006. "Distributed Leadership in Teams: The Network of Leadership Perceptions and Team Performance." *Leadership Quarterly* 17:232–245. Accessed December 23, 2012. doi:10.1016/j.leaqua.2006.02.003.

Mossholder, Kevin W., Hettie A. Richardson, and Randall P. Settoon. 2011. "Human Resource Systems and Helping in Organizations: A Relational Perspective." *Academy of Management Review* 36:33–52. Accessed December 23, 2012.

Müller-Seitz, Gordon. 2012. "Leadership in Inter-Organizational Networks: A Literature Review and Suggestions for Future Research." *International Journal of Management Reviews* 14:428–443. Accessed December 10, 2012. doi:10.1111/j.1468–2370.2011.00324.x.

NHS Supply Chain. 2012. "Case Studies." Accessed December 15, 2012. http://www.supplychain.nhs.uk/product-news/publications/case-studies/.

Noble, Gary, and Robert Jones. 2006. "The Role of Boundary-Spanning Managers in the Establishment of Public-Private Partnerships." *Public Administration* 84:891–917. Accessed November 26, 2012. doi: 10.1111/j.1467–9299.2006.00617.x.

Ohio Aerospace Institute. 2012. "Research and Technology: Multi-Organizational Teams." Accessed December 2, 2012. http://www.oai.org/research/teams/index.html.

O'Leary, Michael B., and Jonathon N. Cummings. 2007. "The Spatial, Temporal, and Configurational Characteristics of Geographic Dispersion in Teams." *MIS Quarterly* 31:433–452.

Perrone, Vincenzo, Akbar Zaheer, and Bill McEvily. 2003. "Free to be Trusted? Organizational Constraints on Trust in Boundary Spanners." *Organization Science* 14:422–439. Accessed November 28, 2012. doi:10.1287/orsc.14.4.422.17487.

Pittinsky, Todd L., and Stefanie Simon. 2007. "Intergroup Leadership." *Leadership Quarterly* 18:586–605. Accessed December 15, 2012. doi:10.1016/j.leaqua.2007.09.005.

Power, Brad. 2012. "Get Your Team to Work Across Organizational Boundaries." HBR Blog Network, April 9. Accessed November 30, 2012. http://blogs.hbr.org/cs/2012/04/building_a_team_across_organiz.html.

Raab, Jörg, and Patrick Kenis. 2009. "Heading Toward a Society of Networks: Empirical Developments and Theoretical Challenges." *Journal of Management Inquiry* 18:198–210. Accessed December 23, 2012. doi:10.1177/1056492609337493.

Ramarajan, Lakshmi, Katerina Bezrukova, Karen A. Jehn, and Martin Euwema. 2011. "From the Outside In: The Negative Spillover Effects of Boundary Spanners' Relations with Members of Other Organizations." *Journal of Organizational Behavior* 32:886–905. Accessed December 23, 2012. doi: 10.1002/job.723.

Rao, Hayagreeva, and Kumar Sivakumar. 1999. "Institutional Sources of Boundary-Spanning Structures: The Establishment of Investor Relations in the Fortune 500 Industrials." *Organization Science* 10:27–42. Accessed November 26, 2012. doi: 10.1287/orsc.10.1.27.

Rawnsley, Andrew. 2012. "The Lib Dems Aren't Going to Rescue Themselves by Being Timid." *The Observer*, September 23. Accessed December 2, 2012. http://www.guardian.co.uk/commentisfree/2012/sep/23/andrew-rawnsley-future-for-lib-dems.

Richter, Andreas W., Judy Scully, and Michael A. West. 2005. "Intergroup Conflict and Intergroup Effectiveness in Organizations: Theory and Scale Development." *European Journal of Work and Organizational Psychology* 14:177–203. Accessed November 26, 2012. doi:10.1080/13594320444000263.

Richter, Andreas W., Michael A. West, Rolf van Dick, and Jeremy F. Dawson. 2006. "Boundary Spanners' Identification, Intergroup Contact, and Effective Intergroup Relations." *Academy of Management Journal* 49:1252–1269. Accessed November 30, 2012. doi:10.5465/AMJ.2006.23478720.

Ring, Peter S., and Andrew H. Van de Ven. 1994. "Developmental Processes of Cooperative Inter-Organizational Relationships." *Academy of Management Review* 19:90–118.

Seabright, Mark A., Daniel A. Levinthal, and Mark Fichman. "Role of Individual Attachments in the Dissolution of Inter-Organizational Relationships." *Academy of Management Journal* 35:122–160. Accessed November 26, 2012. doi:10.2307/256475.

Schopler, Janice H. 1987. "Inter-Organizational Groups: Origins, Structure, and Outcomes." *Academy of Management Review* 12:702–713.

Smith, Ken G., Stephen J. Carroll and Susan J. Ashford. 1995. "Intra- and Inter-Organizational Cooperation: Toward a Research Agenda." *Academy of Management Journal* 38:7–23.

Smith, Wendy K., and Marianne W. Lewis. 2011. "Toward a Theory of Paradox: A Dynamic Equilibrium Model of Organizing." *Academy of Management Review* 36:381–403. Accessed December 23, 2012.

Stock, Ruth Maria. 2006. "Inter-Organizational Teams as Boundary Spanners Between Supplier and Customer Companies." *Journal of the Academy of Marketing Science* 34:588–599. Accessed November 26, 2012. doi:10.177/0092070306288765.

Tannenbaum, Scott I., John E. Mathieu, Eduardo Salas, and Debra Cohen. 2012. "Teams are Changing: Are Research and Practice Evolving Fast Enough?" *Industrial and Organizational Psychology* 5:2–24. Accessed November 27, 2012. doi:10.1111/j.1754-9434.2011.01396.x.

Team BFK. 2012. "BFK: Barn/Ferrovial/Kier." Accessed December 2, 2012. http://www.teambfk.co.uk/.

The Health Foundation. 2012. "Cross Sector Working to Support Large-Scale Change." Accessed December 3, 2012. http://www.health.org.uk/publications/cross-sector-working-to-support-large-scale-change/.

The World Bank. 2011. "Enterprise Outreach Services. PSLO Network: 137 PSLOs in 94 Countries." Accessed December 12, 2012. http://web.worldbank.org/WB-SITE/EXTERNAL/OPPORTUNITIES/ADVISORYSERVICES/EXTEOS/0,,menuPK:575141~pagePK:64168427~piPK:64168435~theSitePK:575135,00.html.

Thatcher, Sherry M. B., and Pankaj C. Patel. 2011. "Demographic Faultlines: A Meta-Analysis of the Literature." *Journal of Applied Psychology* 96:1119–1139. Accessed November 29, 2012. doi:10.1037/a0024167.

Wageman, Ruth, Heidi Gardner, and Mark Mortensen. 2012. "The Changing Ecology of Teams: New Directions for Teams Research." *Journal of Organizational Behavior* 33:301–315. Accessed November 27, 2012. doi:10.1002/job.1775.

Williams, Paul 2002. "The Competent Boundary Spanner." Public Administration 80:103–124. Accessed November 26, 2012. doi:10.1111/1467–9299.00296.

Wintour, Patrick, and Tom Clark. 2012. "Coalition Government Will Not Survive Until 2015 Election, Voters Predict." *The Guardian*, August 12. Accessed December 2, 2012. http://www.guardian.co.uk/politics/2012/aug/12/coalition-government-brink-collapse-voters.

Wrzesniewski, Amy, and Jane E. Dutton. 2001. "Crafting a Job: Revisioning Employees as Active Crafters of Their Work." *Academy of Management Review* 26:179–201.

Yan, Aimin, Guorong Zhu, and Douglas T. Hall. 2002. "International Assignments for Career Building: A Model of Agency Relationships and Psychological Contracts." *Academy of Management Review* 27:373–391. Accessed November 26, 2012. doi:10.5465/AMR.2002.7389910.

Zaccaro, Stephen J., Michelle A. Marks, and Leslie A. DeChurch, eds. 2012. *Multiteam Systems: An Organization Form for Dynamic and Complex Environments.* New York: Routledge.

Arrow, Holly, Jennifer L. Berdahl, and Joseph E. McGrath. 2000. *Small Groups as Complex Systems: Formation, Coordination, Development and Adaptation.* Thousand Oaks, CA: Sage.

Zietsma, Charlene, and Thomas B. Lawrence. 2010. "Institutional Work in the Transformation of an Organizational Field: The Interplay of Boundary Work and Practice Work." *Administrative Science Quarterly* 55:189–221. Accessed November 27, 2012. doi:10.2189/asqu.2010.55.2.189.

Zuckerman, David S., and Michael B. Higgins. 2002. "Optimizing Cross-Organizational Team Performance and Management." Accessed December 3, 2012. http://www.pharmtech.com/pharmtech/data/articlestandard/pharmtech/222002/20449/article.pdf.

Zyphur, Michael J. 2009. "When Mindsets Collide: Switching Analytical Mindsets to Advance Organization Science." *Academy of Management Review* 34:677–688.

7 Boundary-Spanning to Address Indigenous Disadvantage in Australia

Fiona Buick

INTRODUCTION

Working across boundaries has been argued to be necessary for the effective resolution of wicked problems: intractable problems that are complex and multifaceted. Recognition of the cross-cutting nature of such problems led to the trend toward joined-up working in countries such as Australia, Canada, New Zealand, and the United Kingdom during the late twentieth and early twenty-first centuries. The effective enactment of joined-up working requires the ability of public servants to work across boundaries; thus a critical competency is boundary-spanning. This chapter discusses the boundary-spanning roles undertaken by inter-organizational groups in the Australian Public Service (APS) to address Indigenous disadvantage. In doing so, it draws on a case study incorporating two integrated service delivery sites that comprised officials from multiple APS organizations who worked across organizational, jurisdictional, and sectoral boundaries on a daily basis.

THE TREND TOWARD JOINED-UP WORKING IN THE TWENTIETH AND TWENTY-FIRST CENTURIES

Many contemporary problems facing governments globally are highly complex and multifaceted. Problems such as social exclusion, homelessness, alcohol and drug abuse, crime, poverty, and health and indigenous disadvantage are becoming increasingly prevalent (Bogdanor 2005; Christensen and Lægreid 2007b; Jackson and Stainsby 2000; Keast, Mandell, Brown, and Woolcock 2004; Williams 2002). These "wicked problems" (Rittel and Webber 1973) present a challenge for society because of uncertainty or disagreement regarding the definition of the problem itself, its causes, and/or what the solution should look like (Bogdanor 2005; Kettl 2006; Rittel and Webber 1973). Due to their intractable and uncertain nature, wicked problems pose long-term, cross-cutting, and interconnected puzzles (Kettl 2006). Therefore, to effectively address them requires holistic thinking and a commitment to the building of inter-organizational capacity in order to develop complex and interdependent responses (Kettl 2006; Williams 2002).

Such approaches include those involving working across boundaries, or joined-up working.

During the late twentieth century and early twenty-first century, the trend toward joined-up working was most evident in the Anglo-Saxon countries, such as Australia, Canada, New Zealand (NZ), and the United Kingdom (UK) (Christensen and Lægreid 2007a; Pollitt 2003). The trend is called "joined-up government" (JUG) in the UK (Ling 2002; Pollitt 2003); "horizontal government" in Canada (Edwards 2002; Halligan 2007); and "whole-of-government" (WG) in Australia and NZ (Gregory 2006; Halligan 2007)[1].

While the terminology, solutions, methods, and intensity of joined-up working has varied across countries, the main premises of the concept are similar; they are all concerned with public sector organizations working across boundaries. These boundaries are intra-organizational (within an organization), inter-organizational (across organizations at the same level of government), inter-governmental (across the different levels of government), and inter-sectoral (relations with nongovernment actors such as the private, public, and voluntary sectors) (Cowell and Martin 2003; Ling 2002; Matheson 2000).

Terms such as *coordination, cooperation, coherence, integration,* and *collaboration* are often used interchangeably to describe the phenomena of working across boundaries (see, for example, Management Advisory Committee 2004; National Audit Office 2001). One approach to conceptualizing working across boundaries is to depict joined-up working along a continuum (see Figure 7.1).

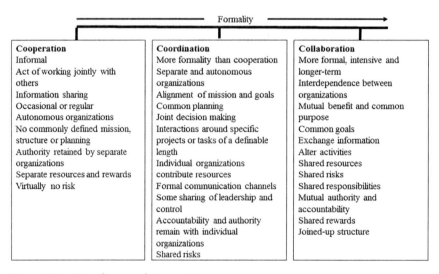

Figure 7.1 Joined-up working continuum
Source: Agrnoff (2006), Himmelman (2002), Keast, Brown and Mandell (2007) and Mattessich and Monsey (1992)

The continuum shows that joined-up working may be synonymous with cooperation, coordination, and collaboration, yet these terms are not necessarily synonymous with one another. They represent different degrees and levels of joining up. Joined-up working ranges from informal and short-term cooperation among individuals and/or organizations to more formalized intermittent and short-term arrangements comprising coordination and, finally, to collaboration, which is the most formalized and longest-term mode of joining up, consisting of shared resources, risks, and joint structures (Agranoff 2006; Himmelman 2002; Keast, Brown, and Mandell 2007; Mattessich and Monsey 1992).

In this chapter, the primary focus is the intermediate point of the continuum, coordination, which has been described as a "typical boundary-spanning activity" (Askim et al., 2009, 1008).

BOUNDARY-SPANNING AND JOINED-UP WORKING

Williams (2002) argues that the effectiveness and success of joined-up endeavors largely relies on the people involved in the process and their ability to apply collaborative skills and mind sets to the improvement and/or resolution of complex problems. In order to solve complex problems, public servants require the ability to engage in joined-up working both within and outside of their organizations; this often involves groups with different and competing interests (Broussine 2003).

A critical competency that underpins the success of joined-up working is boundary-spanning (Lodge and Gill 2011; Painter 2011). Boundary-spanners connect areas within an organization or with similar networks outside of the organization (Cross and Parker 2004). They act as a mediator between environmental influences and organizations (Leifer and Huber 1977), enabling organizations to adapt to environmental contingencies and cope with environmental constraints (Aldrich and Herker 1977). The boundary-spanning function is particularly important in heterogeneous and dynamic environments where constraints and contingencies are greater (Thompson 1967).

Boundary spanners play a central role in intergroup relations (Friedman and Podolny 1992); they are the "key agents" managing within inter-organizational domains (Williams 2002, 103). These individuals are strongly linked to their colleagues and have extensive links outside their subunit (Tushman and Scanlan 1981a, 1981b). Through providing these critical links, boundary spanners enable their organization to integrate with elements in its environment (Aldrich and Herker 1977). Therefore, they play a crucial role in organizations as the ability of an organization to interact effectively with its external environment has been argued to be a "condition of organization survival" (Adams 1983, 1175).

Boundary spanners are primarily concerned with the transfer of data and information across organizational boundaries (Broussine 2003). They facilitate the sharing of expertise by linking two or more groups of people separated by location, hierarchy, or function (Cross and Parker 2004). Because of their position, they are an important mechanism by which subunits are linked to external sources of information (Tushman and Scanlan 1981a). Information from external sources comes into an organization through boundary roles, with boundary spanners interpreting, filtering, and channeling information to ensure the organization has the appropriate information to take action, while also protecting it from information overload (Aldrich and Herker 1977).

Boundary spanners are identifiable through the tasks they undertake and competencies they demonstrate. Ranade and Hudson (2003), for example, outlined the myriad of tasks faced by boundary spanners, differentiating them from those of conventional line management functions. These tasks include: managing across and upward, rather than downward; influencing and motivating others over whom they have little control; creating and assembling resources owned by others; building trust between partners with different interests, perspectives, and organizational imperatives; achieving tangible outcomes, to keep members committed to the partnership while moving the wider agenda forward; and maintaining relationships and communication networks across organizations at a variety of levels. Similarly, Williams (2002) identified a number of boundary-spanning skills, abilities, experience, and personal characteristics that are crucial for effective joined-up working. These include building sustainable relationships, managing through influencing and negotiation, managing complexity and interdependencies, and managing roles, accountabilities, and motivations.

This chapter discusses the boundary-spanning roles undertaken by inter-organizational groups in the Australian Public Service (APS) to address Indigenous disadvantage. In doing so, it draws on a case study incorporating two regional integrated service delivery sites—Indigenous Coordination Centres (ICCs). In these sites, officials established ways of operating that mirror the critical boundary-spanning competencies and tasks identified by Williams (2002) and Ranade and Hudson (2003) in order to broker solutions to address Indigenous disadvantage, a wicked problem identified by the Australian Government.

AUSTRALIAN CASE STUDY: INDIGENOUS
COORDINATION CENTRES

The Indigenous Coordination Centres (ICCs) were established in 2004 as a part of the Australian Government's "bold experiment" with joined-up working to address Indigenous disadvantage (Shergold 2004). Indigenous Australians consistently score lower on measures such as life expectancy, infant mortality, educational attendance and attainment, literacy and numeracy skills, health, employment, and income, than do non-Indigenous Australians. Moreover, they are at more risk of adverse living conditions and homelessness than non-Indigenous Australians (Australian Institute of Health and Welfare 2011; Steering Committee for the Review of Government Service Provision 2011). Because of its intractable nature, the Australian Government has labeled Indigenous disadvantage a "wicked problem" (Australian Public Service Commission 2007, 2).

As part of the joined-up arrangements for Indigenous affairs, 30 ICCs were established in urban, regional, and remote locations[2] to work with Indigenous communities to determine their local needs and priorities (KPMG 2007). They represented a form of coordination, the intermediate level of joined-up working on the joined-up continuum (see Figure 7.1). The aim was to provide an integrated service delivery site or "one-stop-shop" for Indigenous communities (O'Flynn, Buick, Blackman, and Halligan 2011, 247), with local programs aligned to present a joined-up citizen interface arrangement and coordinated approach to Indigenous issues. In line with definitions of coordination set out by Keast, Brown, and Mandell (2007) and Mattessich and Monsey (1992), they comprised representatives from multiple organizations operating in a co-location model, with the key organizations responsible for Indigenous programs, such as education, employment, community services, legal aid, and health, to be represented on-site (Shergold 2004). The organizations functioned relatively independently of one another with authority and accountability for organizational outputs remaining with individual organizations.

This chapter focuses on two regional ICCs that were located in central business areas of regions outside of the capital cities (referred to as Redvale and Waytown ICCs). These ICCs were responsible for the delivery of customized Indigenous-specific programs and coordination of mainstream programs for Indigenous communities; special provision was also made for coordinating intensive place-based intervention strategies for communities identified as being in crisis (ANAO 2007). Because little empirical research has been undertaken in ICCs, this study utilized a case study research design to understand and explore the phenomenon under examination *in situ* (Merriam 1988; Stake 2000; Yin 2003). Twenty-four semistructured interviews and one focus group discussion were conducted with twenty-eight participants between April 2009 and June 2010. Nonparticipant observation of joined-up meetings was also utilized to complement interview and focus group data.

Boundary-Spanning in Regional Indigenous Coordination Centres

In the Redvale and Waytown ICCs, their core purpose was to serve Indigenous communities on behalf of the Australian Government to ensure community members' basic needs were adequately met and they had the same access to resources and opportunities as the non-Indigenous population. The regional ICCs represent the use of boundary spanners in "normal" boundary-spanning roles (Aldrich and Herker 1977); all members were employed in full-time boundary-spanning positions devoted to acting as the "linking pin" (Organ 1971, 73) between organizations and their environment. Because of their proximity to Indigenous communities, these roles were critical for organizations understanding the complex and multidimensional nature of Indigenous disadvantage. The ICCs reflect what Thompson (1967) referred to as segmented clusters that that were developed to deal with and adapt to a heterogeneous environment.

Members of the Redvale and Waytown ICCs played critical boundary-spanning roles as they facilitated their home organizations' understanding of the needs of Indigenous communities and where linkages with other organizations resided. To do so, ICC members interacted with three main groups: their line organization supervisors and upper management, their subordinates (when relevant), and the various contact people in their external environment, mirroring the groups proposed by Russ, Galang, and Ferris (1998). In the regional ICCs, the various contact people in their external environment included the members of the ICCs who represented four different organizations, representatives of state/territory government organizations, local government organizations, non-government organizations (NGOs), and Indigenous community members.

In the following section, boundary-spanning competencies and tasks outlined by Williams (2002) and Ranade and Hudson (2003) will be used to describe how ICC members performed these boundary-spanning functions to address Indigenous disadvantage in Australia. These competencies and tasks are managing complexity and interdependencies; building sustainable relationships and networking; communication and information sharing; managing through influence and negotiation; and managing roles, accountabilities, and motivations.

Managing Complexity and Interdependencies

Working in an environment where boundary-spanning was essential to making progress in an area such as Indigenous affairs was highly complex and fraught with challenges. These challenges emerged from the intractable nature of Indigenous disadvantage, the majority of public sector organizations being dominantly focused on organizational programs and the limited timeframes for the delivery of programs; described as an environment that was "*hard and it's getting harder*" (middle manager, Redvale ICC).

The complex business of boundary-spanning, where officials are required to navigate disparate bodies of technical knowledge, professional expertise, and organizational cultures, demands an appreciation of connections and inter-relationships across boundaries (Williams 2002). In the regional ICCs, members gained an appreciation for the inter-relationships between these disparate bodies through learning over time how to navigate this complex terrain.

> There are lots of different demarcation [and] portfolio responsibilities, unclear direction, site barriers in that space. My view in relation to it is

you've got to navigate your way through those and find a solution . . . I think, you just basically work your way through it and you come to a conclusion that is productive long-term. (ICC manager, Redvale ICC)

Williams (2002) found that three main factors that contribute to the ability of boundary spanners to manage interdependencies: inter-organizational experience, transdisciplinary knowledge, and cognitive capability. In the Redvale and Waytown ICCs, all three factors were evident. Collectively, ICC members had decades of experience working with Indigenous communities and the public sector; *"people like [Mark] and [Trevor] and myself have worked in Indigenous Affairs probably for twenty years [so] you['ve] probably got a collective of sixty years' experience minimum"* (middle manager, Redvale ICC). Over this time, they obtained extensive inter-organizational experience, working with officials from multiple organizations across various areas in regional communities. Similar to Williams (2002), who found that the main source of understanding is acquired through accumulated 'on-the-job' inter-organizational experience, the ICC members' extensive knowledge and expertise largely derived from their decades of on-the-job experience. Moreover, it was their experience working in Indigenous communities that provided them with the "passport of legitimacy" (Williams 2002, 119) necessary to develop relationships with officials from other organizations and members of Indigenous communities.

Building Sustainable Relationships and Networking

A necessary part of joined-up working involves building and sustaining effective personal relationships (Williams 2002). An important task of boundary spanners is to maintain relationships and communication networks across organizations at a variety of levels (Ranade and Hudson 2003). In the Redvale and Waytown ICCs, members utilized relationships and networks to find solutions and to coordinate services for Indigenous communities.

Boundary spanners are strongly linked to their colleagues and have extensive and strong links outside their subunit, with linkages facilitated by formal and informal mechanisms, such as transfers and networking (Tushman and Scanlan 1981a). In these ICCs, particular attention was paid to informal networks as a means to access the knowledge of others, access diverse perspectives, understand the broader context and broker solutions to address community issues; reflecting Williams's (2002: 117) finding that networking is the predominant *"modus operandi* of choice" of boundary spanners. In the Redvale ICC, a middle manager used the metaphor of being a *"double adaptor,"* where they acted as a conduit that connected communities with different parts of government. In doing so, the middle manager would review issues community members raised and coordinate existing resources from across multiple organizations to meet these needs.

ICC members discussed the importance of building relationships with key people within and across organizations, jurisdictions, and communities, establishing clear informal and formal communication channels across boundaries to enable connections to these people. These relationships were important for understanding the work and priorities of other organizations and where complementarities existed in order to enhance effectiveness. This reflects Adams's (1983) argument that the effectiveness of boundary spanners relies on their ability to have knowledge of and sensitivity toward the preferences, needs, beliefs, attitudes, norms, and aspirations of the external organizations with which they are dealing.

This study found that the Redvale and Waytown ICCs routinely utilized networks and relationships for information sharing, for maintaining awareness of current events, and for coordinating resources to meet community needs. The development and maintenance of inter-organizational relationships within the ICCs was also particularly important to their ability to perform their roles.

Cross-Organizational Relationships within the Regional Indigenous Coordination Centres

The development of long-term professional relationships was essential to joining up in the Redvale and Waytown ICCs. Despite working for different organizations, members of both sites had a history of working together in Indigenous affairs. This was particularly apparent in the Redvale ICC, where senior ICC members and their staff had worked together for over a decade. The history of working together meant led to one middle manager declaring "*we've always worked together and cooperated and helped each other*" (middle manager, Redvale ICC). These long-term relationships formed the foundation for ICC members to work as a joined-up team and "*get solutions for communities*" (middle manager, Redvale ICC).

Over their history of working together, members of the Redvale and Waytown ICCs developed trusting cross-organizational relationships with one another that evolved and strengthened over time. Trust is the confidence people are "disposed to act benignly" (Alford 2004, 3) toward one another and the belief that their incentives are oriented toward cooperation with, and support of, others (Hardin 1992). It has been argued to be one of the most important factors in inter-organizational relations; it is the glue that holds a joined-up initiative together (Hopkins, Couture, and Moore 2001; Jackson and Stainsby 2000; Williams 2002). Thus, building trust between partners is a critical task for boundary spanners when building and sustaining relationships (Ranade and Hudson 2003; Williams 2002).

In the Redvale and Waytown ICCs, a platform of strong relationships and trust meant that members were comfortable expressing their divergent opinion and ideas, with healthy debates and discussions regarding approaches to working, problem identification and resolution encouraged.

This encouraged lateral, creative, and innovative thinking and operating as multiple possibilities were explored and considered as viable pursuits. Ultimately, this helped the ICCs to better service their communities as they were more likely to gain a broader understanding of the issues at hand and derive solutions that were based on well-considered ideas.

The cooperative nature of the relationships in the Redvale and Waytown ICCs can be partially explained through Adams's (1983) observation that expectations of repeated interactions between boundary spanners are more likely to result in conciliatory and cooperative behavior. Because of their long history working together and continued partnership, ICC members were predisposed to working cooperatively with one another and saw the mutual benefits of doing so. Trusting and cooperative relationships also established the platform for frequent communication and information sharing in the ICCs.

Communication and Information Sharing

Boundary spanners perform two roles: information processing and external representation. They filter and facilitate information flow from their organization to their environment (Aldrich and Herker 1977). In the Redvale and Waytown ICCs, members learned that rich communication enabled them to perform their organizational role effectively and feed information back to their organization; it also allowed them to deal with daily demands and challenges and work together as a cross-organizational team. ICC members communicated with one another on a daily basis, with open discussions taking place regarding all facets of work: "*we're always talking about the job and what we're doing and what you're up to*" (middle manager, Redvale ICC). Members professed that frequent and open, two-way communication and information sharing was critical for the internal working of the ICCs.

> Now you know that you're able to work better and come to a solution. Obviously we call it the "code of silence" because it doesn't go outside this office, and we certainly don't discuss it with anyone else. (middle manager, Redvale ICC)

There was a shared understanding that, in some occasions, information was otherwise deemed confidential and was not for wider distribution. This supports Williams's (2002) finding that trust entails a reciprocal risk-taking involving the giving and receiving information that is not widely accessible in the public domain. The willingness to share information was reinforced over time as members' encountered situations that could have had a different and negative outcome had they not worked together, communicated and shared information. It also equipped ICC members' with the information required to influence stakeholders outside of the ICCs.

Managing Through Influence and Negotiation

Boundary spanners influence and motivate partners where they lack direct line management authority and have little control over (Ranade and Hudson 2003; Williams 2002); these partners may also have fundamentally different interests and priorities (Adams 1983). In the Redvale and Waytown ICCs, a key mechanism for exercising such influence was through underpinning proposals, briefs and work with qualitative and quantitative data.

To obtain data, ICC members utilized relationships and networks from within the communities and surrounding areas. Members' networks and relationships with community members, officials from government and non-government organizations and service providers meant they were able to ascertain current issues and demographical information and gain an accurate representation of the community's needs and priorities. In doing so, ICC members demonstrated a critical competency of boundary spanners; the knowledge to bring together disparate areas of expertise (Lodge and Gill 2011). Through utilizing networks, ICC members were also able to influence and elicit the cooperation of stakeholders. This supports Manev and Stevenson's (2001) assertion that the level of influence exercised by boundary spanners beyond their hierarchical position and level has been linked to their involvement and centrality in external and internal networks.

Embedding proposals in data provided the evidence base required for facilitating inter-organizational, inter-governmental and inter-sectoral cooperation and coordination. The attainment of a clear understanding of the situation in communities, and the issues community members faced, provided a solid basis for interaction, a focal point for discussion and a common understanding of the issues involved. This common understanding provided a mechanism for influencing stakeholders and acquiring the resources necessary to deliver programs. This enabled ICC members to manage across boundaries and assemble resources owned by others, a necessary boundary-spanning task (Ranade and Hudson 2003). Through assembling resources owned by others, ICC members could overcome the issues associated with operating in a tight resource environment. This was most important because *"most of your service providers within a particular region will all have the cash. This is about coordinating it and focusing around a particular outcome so you don't need a lot of money"* (middle manager, Waytown ICC).

One participant in the Redvale ICC described influencing stakeholders over whom they had no authority over as *"river dancing,"* which involved liaising with officials in state and Commonwealth government organizations to sell the benefits and anticipated outcomes of proposed approaches, and influencing them through conveying the circumstances the community faced. Frequently this required a great deal of perseverance, as many of these officials were removed from day-to-day circumstances so therefore had different worldviews, pressures, and priorities influencing their decisions.

Consequently, proposals were not necessarily approved in the first instance, resulting in a great deal of background work being undertaken in preparation for when the opportunity arose. This prepared ICC members to be able to capitalize on opportunities, as projects were ready to be progressed when the timing was right, highlighting what Williams (2002: 119) referred to as "the value of opportunism."

Embedding proposals in evidence was crucial to the ability of the Redvale and Waytown ICCs to identify community needs and elicit the cooperation of stakeholders. In both regional ICCs, grounding proposals in evidence provided ICC members with the perceived legitimacy necessary to act as an "honest broker" (Williams 2002, 117) for both their organizations and the Indigenous communities. This legitimacy was particularly important when managing disparate accountabilities.

Managing Roles, Accountabilities, and Motivations

Boundary spanners have a deep awareness of, and appreciation for, the political and professional contexts they operate within. An area that particularly requires sound judgment is the management of multiple accountabilities, accountabilities of which may conflict as boundary spanners are simultaneously required to be both an organizational representative and that of a partner in a multi-organizational environment (Williams 2002). For both the Redvale and Waytown ICCs, carefully managing the accountability interface was a central component of their roles. The ICCs were established as inter-organizational coordination with representatives retaining strong vertical links to their home organization. They operated in an environment that demanded joined-up working, yet simultaneously required them to deliver on organizational and vertical performance targets.

These accountabilities meant that the role of ICC members consisted of a spectrum of activity ranging from satisfying vertical accountabilities, through delivering organizational programs, to satisfying horizontal accountabilities, through large-scale coordination. Because of members' proximity to, and interaction with, Indigenous communities, they saw themselves as directly accountable to community members; as they *"see them in the street and the shop every day and we have to interact with those people so you are held accountable 24/7"* (middle manager, Redvale ICC). Because of their proximity to communities, ICC members saw the interconnectedness of issues faced by Indigenous communities and how their ability to deliver organizational programs and satisfy organizational accountability demands relied on the resolution of issues in other areas. This meant that aiding others to achieve their objectives indirectly enabled ICC members to achieve the objectives of their home organization. Thus, a horizontal focus was prominent and necessary for effective service delivery; ICC members perceived their role holistically and as one beyond that of an organizational representative. This focus was accentuated through ICC members being geographically separated from their home organizations, as their prominent focus was the Indigenous communities. In the ICCs, their holistic focus meant they saw themselves as working for the Australian Government, rather than a particular organization. This mirrors Adams's (1983) claim that boundary spanners' distance from their organization and close proximity to the external environment and agents of outside organizations weakens their organizational bonds.

ICC members were also acutely aware of their responsibilities as public servants, however, and demonstrated a sound knowledge of the political and administrative context they operated within. Because the organizational (vertical) and joined-up (horizontal) accountabilities may conflict at times (Williams 2002), embedding approaches in evidence-based logic was essential for the careful management of the accountability interface and their ability to manage upward, a key task of boundary spanners (Ranade and Hudson 2003). This required the ICC members to have a good understanding of their responsibilities as public servants; *"there has to be a range of checks and balances in that . . . you need to understand the risk arrangements around what you do"* (ICC manager, Redvale ICC). It also meant they required a firm grasp of their political environment and an understanding of the accountability requirements they needed to address.

> If we're ever asked the question, "why are you doing something in this way," we need some evidence base to talk that through and support it . . . But also I can sit up with good conscience at a Senate Estimates Committee that says, "[Trevor] why did you spend $4.5 million?" In the pen trail I'll be able to say "well these are the reasons and this is the process we went through and this is the evidence supporting it and this is the codesign work we did." (ICC manager, Redvale ICC)

Embedding approaches in evidence was also important for ICC members to ensure that organizational, joined-up, and community needs were adequately met. Through embedding approaches in evidence, ICC members could increase the objectivity of decisions and address Adams's (1983) remark that conflict can potentially arise between achieving optimal outcomes and boundary spanners displaying their organizational loyalty. Through embedding approaches in evidence, ICC members could mitigate this conflict through demonstrating to their organizations that their interests were being served, while also satisfying joined-up interests.

CONCLUSION

Joined-up working has been heralded as the main mechanism for addressing wicked problems: problems that are intractable, complex, and multifaceted. Indigenous disadvantage is an example of a wicked problem that has defied the Australian Government for decades. In the mid-2000s, the Australian Government embarked upon a whole-of-government approach to addressing Indigenous disadvantage; this approach involved the establishment of Indigenous Coordination Centres (ICCs). Established as one-stop shops, the ICCs comprised representatives from multiple organizations that had responsibility for the coordination of services and programs to Indigenous communities.

This chapter discussed the effective boundary-spanning behaviors demonstrated by inter-organizational groups operating in a highly complex area. Using Williams's (2002) and Ranade and Hudson's (2003) boundary-spanning competencies and tasks as an analytical frame, these boundary-spanning behaviors were: managing complexity and interdependencies; building sustainable relationships and networking; communication and information sharing; managing through influence and negotiation; and managing roles, accountabilities, and motivations.

In the Redvale and Waytown ICCs, the success of joined-up working relied on the boundary-spanning abilities of their members, supporting the claim by Lodge and Gill (2011) and Painter (2011) that boundary-spanning is a critical competency for joined-up working. Joined-up success in the ICCs relied on the boundary spanners' ability to understand the political and administrative environments they operated within, balance diverse organizational interests and priorities and manage an accountability interface that incorporated both organizational and joined-up outcomes. It relied on the ability of members to establish relationships and networks to facilitate the access of Indigenous communities to the coordinated services they required, and establish trusting inter-organizational relationships within the ICCs in order to cope with day-to-day challenges. It highlights the importance of on-the-job experience as decades of experience enabled the boundary spanners to establish essential relationships and elicit the trust and legitimacy required to operate in Indigenous communities.

The findings of this study suggest that, when attempting to address wicked problems, organizations can facilitate boundary-spanning through appointing officials in full-time boundary-spanning positions. In the appointment of boundary spanners, recruitment should be targeted at officials with extensive knowledge of the relevant environment and experience working across boundaries in complex and ambiguous areas. This knowledge and experience should mean they are well-equipped to broker joined-up solutions while simultaneously addressing vertical accountability demands. These skills and experience are particularly important in areas where the environments are heterogeneous and require boundary spanners to work with multiple organizations and directly with stakeholders in order to perform highly complex roles. Boundary-spanning can be further facilitated through ensuring officials are loosely coupled with their home organizations, meaning they have sufficient autonomy to engage in boundary-spanning behaviors.

This study makes a contribution to the boundary-spanning literature through linking this concept to the ICC setting and explaining how the propensity toward boundary-spanning has enabled joined-up working in the area of Indigenous disadvantage. It highlights areas for future research that may be useful in exploring the concept of boundary-spanning further, particularly in these settings. Two areas in particular are addressed here. First, this study focused purely on the process of boundary-spanning utilizing qualitative research methods within the two ICC settings. Future research could adopt a mixed methods approach, incorporating surveying and interviewing stakeholders and Indigenous community members to explore the extent to which they consider the boundary spanners to be effective. Second, future research could also specifically focus on the boundary-spanning individuals to develop a boundary-spanning profile comprising key competencies required for effective boundary-spanning. Through further exploration of successful boundary spanners, both as an inter-organizational group and individuals, greater insight could be provided into the factors that enable "wicked problems" to be addressed.

NOTES

1. In this chapter, the more generic term 'joined-up working' will be used to discuss the working across boundaries in all variations and contexts.
2. As at January 2012, there were 29 ICCs across Australia (Department of Families Housing Community Services and Indigenous Affairs [FaHCSIA] 2011).

REFERENCES

Adams, J. Stacy. 1983. "The Structure and Dynamics of Behavior in Organizational Boundary Roles." In *Handbook of Industrial and Organizational Psychology*, edited by Marvin D. Dunnette, 1175–1199. Toronto: John Wiley and Sons.
Agranoff, Robert. 2006. "Inside Collaborative Networks: Ten Lessons for Public Managers." *Public Administration Review* 66(s1): 56–65. DOI: 10.1111/j.1540-6210.2006.00666.x.
Aldrich, Howard, and Diane Herker. 1977. "Boundary Spanning Roles and Organization Structure." *Academy of Management Review* April: 217–230. http://www.jstor.org/stable/257905.
Alford, John. 2004. "Building Trust in Partnerships Between Community Organisation and Government." *Paper prepared for the Changing the Way Government Works Seminar*, Melbourne, Australia: Institute of Public Administration Australia (IPAA). October 5.
Askim, Jostein, Tom Christensen, Anne Lise Fimreite, and Per Lægreid. 2009. "How to Carry Out Joined-up Government Reforms: Lessons from the 2001–2006 Norwegian Welfare Reform." *International Journal of Public Administration* 32(12): 1006–1025. DOI: http://dx.doi.org/10.1080/01900690903223888.
Australian Institute of Health and Welfare [AIHW] 2008. *The Health and Welfare of Australia's Aboriginal and Torres Strait Islander Peoples*. Cat. no. IHW 42. Canberra, Australia: Commonwealth of Australia.

Australian National Audit Office [ANAO] 2007. *Whole of Government Indigenous Service Delivery Arrangements.* Canberra, Australia: Commonwealth of Australia. Accessed July 20 2011, http://www.anao.gov.au/Publications/Audit-Reports/2007–2008/Whole-of-Government-Indigenous-Service-Delivery-Arrangements.

Australian Public Service Commission [APSC] 2007. *Tackling Wicked Problems: A Public Policy Perspective.* Canberra, Australia: Commonwealth of Australia. Accessed October 16 2012, http://www.apsc.gov.au/publications-and-media/archive/publications-archive/tackling-wicked-problems.

Bogdanor, Vernon. 2005. "Introduction." In *Joined-Up Government*, edited by Vernon Bogdanor, 1–18. Oxford: Oxford University Press.

Broussine, Mike. 2003. "Leading and Managing at the Boundary: Perspectives Created by Joined Up Working." *Local Government Studies* 29(3): 128–138. DOI: http://dx.doi.org/10.1080/03003930308559383

Christensen, Tom, and Per Lægreid. 2007a. "The Whole-of-Government Approach to Public Sector Reform." *Public Administration Review* 67(6): 1059–1066. DOI: 10.1111/j.1540–6210.2007.00797.x.

Christensen, Tom, and Per Lægreid. 2007b. "Introduction—Theoretical Approach and Research Questions." In *Transcending New Public Management: The Transformation of Public Sector Reforms*, edited by Tom Christensen and Per Lægreid, 1–16. Aldershot, Hampshire: Ashgate Publishing Ltd.

Cowell, Richard, and Steve Martin. 2003 "The Joy of Joining Up: Modes of Integrating the Local Government Modernisation Agenda." *Environment and Planning C: Government and Policy* 21(2): 159–179.

Cross, Rob, and Andrew Parker. 2004. *The Hidden Power of Social Networks: Understanding How Work Really Gets Done in Organizations.* Boston, MA: Harvard Business School Press.

Department of Families Housing Community Services and Indigenous Affairs [FaHCSIA]. 2011. *Indigenous Australians: Overview.* Accessed December 5 2011, http://www.fahcsia.gov.au/sa/indigenous/overview/Pages/default.aspx.

Edwards, Meredith. 2002. "Public Sector Governance—Future Issues for Australia." *Australian Journal of Public Administration* 61(2): 51–61. DOI: 10.1111/1467–8500.00272.

Friedman, Raymond A., and Joel Podolny. 1992. "Differentiation of Boundary Spanning Roles: Labor Negotiations and Implications for Role Conflict." *Administrative Science Quarterly* 37: 28–47. http://www.jstor.org/stable/2393532

Gregory, Robert. 2006. "Theoretical Faith and Practical Works: De-autonomizing and Joining-Up in the New Zealand State Sector." In *Autonomy and Regulation. Coping with Agencies in the Modern State*, edited by Tom Christensen and Per Lægreid, 137–161. Cheltenham: Edward Elgar.

Halligan, John. 2007. "Horizontal Coordination in Australian Government." *Journal for Comparative Government and European Policy* 5(2): 203–217.

Hardin, Russell. 1992. "The Street-Level Epistemology of Trust." *Analyse & Kritik* 14(2): 152–176. *http://www.analyse-und-kritik.net/1992-2/AK_Hardin_1992.pdf.*

Himmelman, Arthur T. 2002. *Collaboration for a Change: Definitions, Decision-making Models, Roles, and Collaboration Process Guide.* Minneapolis, MN: Himmelman Consulting.

Hopkins, Mark, Chantal Couture, and Elizabeth Moore. 2001. *Moving from the Heroic to the Everyday: Lessons Learned from Leading Horizontal Projects (CCMD Roundtable on the Management of Horizontal Initiatives)*, Ottawa: Canadian Centre for Management Development.

Jackson, Peter M., and Lynn Stainsby. 2000 "The Public Manager in 2010: Managing Public Sector Networked Organizations." *Public Money and Management* 20(1): 11–16. DOI: 10.1111/1467–9302.00196

Keast, Robyn, Kerry Brown, and Myrna Mandell. 2007. "Getting the Right Mix: Unpacking Integration Meanings and Strategies." *International Public Management Journal* 10(1): 9–33. DOI: 10.1080/10967490601185716.

Keast, Robyn, Myrna P. Mandell, Kerry Brown, and Geoffrey Woolcock. 2004. "Network Structures: Working Differently and Changing Expectations." *Public Administration Review* 64(3): 363–371. DOI: 10.1111/j.1540–6210.2004.00380.x.

Kettl, Donald F. 2006. "Managing Boundaries in American Administration: The Collaboration Imperative." *Public Administration Review* 66(s1): 10–19. DOI: 10.1111/j.1540–6210.2006.00662.x.

KPMG 2007, *Department of Families, Community Services and Indigenous Affairs evaluation of Indigenous Coordination Centres Final Report*. Australia: Department of Families Community Services and Indigenous Affairs. Accessed November 20 2008, http://www.fahcsia.gov.au/our-responsibilities/indigenous-australians/publications-articles/evaluation-research/evaluation-of-indigenous-coordination-centres.

Leifer, Richard, and George P. Huber. 1977. "Relations among Perceived Environmental Uncertainty, Organization Structure, and Boundary-Spanning Behavior." *Administrative Science Quarterly* 22(June): 235–247. http://www.jstor.org/stable/2391958.

Ling, T. 2002. "Delivering Joined-Up Government in the UK: Dimensions, Issues and Problems." *Public Administration* 80(4): 615–642. DOI: 10.1111/1467–9299.00321.

Lodge, Martin, and Derek Gill. 2011. "Toward a New Era of Administrative Reform? The Myth of Post-NPM in New Zealand." *Governance: An International Journal of Policy, Administration, and Institutions* 24(1): 141–166. DOI: 10.1111/j.1468–0491.2010.01508.x.

Management Advisory Committee [MAC]. 2004. *Connecting Government: Whole of Government Responses to Australia's Priority Challenges*. Canberra, Australia: Commonwealth of Australia.

Manev, Ivan M., and William B. Stevenson. 2001. "Balancing Ties: Boundary Spanning and Influence in the Organization's Extended Network of Communication." *The Journal of Business Communication* 38(2): 183–205. DOI: 10.1177/002194360103800203.

Matheson, Craig. 2000. "Formation in Australian Government: Vertical and Horizontal Axes." *Australian Journal of Public Administration* 59(2): 44–55. DOI: 10.1111/1467–8500.00150.

Mattessich, Paul W., and Barbara R. Monsey. 1992. *Collaboration: What Makes It Work. A Review of Research Literature on Factors Influencing Successful Collaboration*. St Paul, MN: Amherst H. Wilder Foundation.

Merriam, Sharan B. 1988. *Case Study Research in Education: A Qualitative Approach*. San Francisco: Jossey-Bass.

National Audit Office 2001. *Joining Up to Improve Public Services*. Report by the Comptroller and Auditor General (HC 383) Session 2001–2002, Victoria,

London. Accessed November 15 2008, http://www.nao.org.uk/publications/0102/joining_up_to_improve_public.aspx.

Organ, Dennis W. 1971. "Linking Pins between Organizations and Environment: Individuals Do the Interacting." *Business Horizons* 14: 73–80. DOI: 10.1016/0007–6813(71)90062–0.

Painter, Chris. 2011. "State, Markets and Society—Big Society Joins the Fray." *Public Money and Management* 31(1): 71–74. DOI: 10.1080/09540962.2011.545550.

Patton, Michael Quinn. 1990. *Qualitative Evaluation and Research Methods*. Newbury Park, CA: SAGE.

Pollitt, Christopher. 2003. "Joined-Up Government: A Survey." *Political Studies Review* 1(1): 34–49. DOI: 10.1111/1478–9299.00004.

Ranade, Wendy, and Bob Hudson. 2003. "Conceptual Issues in Inter-Agency Collaboration." *Local Government Studies* 29(3): 32–50. DOI: 10.1080/03003930308559378.

Rittel, Horst W. J., and Melvin M. Webber. 1973. "Dilemmas in a General Theory of Planning." *Policy Sciences* 4: 155–169.

Russ, Gail S., Maria Carmen Galang, and Gerald R. Ferris. 1998. "Power and Influence of the Human Resources Function through Boundary Spanning and Information Management." *Human Resources Management Review* 8(2): 125–148. DOI: 10.1016/S1053–4822(98)80001–6.

Shergold, Peter. 2004. "Connecting Government: Whole-of-Government Responses to Australia's Priority Challenges." *Canberra Bulletin of Public Administration* 112: 11–14.

Stake, Robert E. 2000. "Case Studies." In *Handbook of Qualitative Research* (2nd ed.), edited by Norman K. Denzin and Yvonna S. Lincoln, 435–454. Thousand Oaks, CA: SAGE.

Steering Committee for the Review of Government Service Provision. 2011. *Overcoming Indigenous Disadvantage: Key Indicators 2011 Report*. Melbourne, Australia: Commonwealth of Australia. Accessed November 30 2012, http://www.pc.gov.au/gsp/indigenous.

Thompson, James D. 1967. *Organizations in Action: Social Science Bases of Administrative Theory*. New York: McGraw-Hill.

Tushman, Michael L., and Thomas J. Scanlan. 1981a. "Characteristics and External Orientations of Boundary Spanning Individuals." *Academy of Management Journal* 24(1): 83–98. DOI: 10.2307/255825.

Tushman, Michael L., and Thomas J. Scanlan. 1981b. "Boundary Spanning Individuals: Their Role in Information Transfer and Their Antecedents." *Academy of Management Journal* 24(2): 289–305. DOI: 10.2307/255842.

Williams, Paul. 2002. "The Competent Boundary Spanner." *Public Administration* 80(1): 103–124. DOI: 10.1111/1467–9299.00296.

Yin, Robert K. 2003. *Case Study Research: Design and Methods* (3rd ed.). Beverly Hills, CA: SAGE.

8 Conspiring for the 'Common Good'
Collusion and Spanning Boundaries in Organizations

Janice Langan-Fox, Sharon Grant, and Vikas Anand

COLLUSION IN ORGANIZATIONS

'Collusion,' "a secret agreement between two or more parties for a fraudulent, illegal, or deceitful purpose, from the Latin *collūsiō* . . . to collude" (American Heritage Dictionary of the English Language 2006), is infamous, and can be found in descriptions at various times in history: during the Roman Empire at slave auctions when nobles colluded in price fixing to outbid the state (Hopkins 1981); in accounts of medieval guilds who secured rents for their members at the cost of outsiders (Dessí and Ogilvie 2004); and more recently in corporate financial scandals where organizational dealings resulted in significant investor losses. In the literature collusion has typically received a strong negative connotation and is associated with clandestine behaviors and especially *self-interest* (Li 2009; Zarkada-Fraser 2000). It involves deception, the manipulation of information, rule breaking, covert tactics, masked intentions, fraudulent secret understandings (Turner 1987), and most of all, *personal gain* (Hubbell, Chory-Assad, and Medved 2005). However, we argue that there is a positive side to collusion. Positive collusion involves behind-the-scenes, secret activities involving two or more parties who work to help, protect, and/or grow the organization, but these activities are nonetheless in contravention of established organizational norms and procedures and often require individuals to work across internal organizational boundaries—the vertical functional boundaries or the horizontal hierarchical boundaries.

Collusion and Boundary-Spanning

Those contemplating positive collusion will find that their enterprise would benefit from enlisting the collaboration of a boundary-spanner—a systems thinker who understands the specific needs and interests of the organization and whose greatest asset is their ability to move across and through, the formal and informal features of their organization. Boundary-spanners have a diverse knowledge base and draw on a wide range of expertise. Their greatest assets to positive collusion are that they are change agents; furthermore, they are flexible, mobile, multiskilled, and more than anything, connected and networked across a wide range of people in departments and units, both inside and outside the organization. The positive colluder could be a boundary-spanner themselves—but if they are not, they would want to recruit the expertise of one. And, it's not hard to find boundary-spanners in organizations; such individuals are well known—they become legend and folklore. Often, they are individuals that everyone wants to know, or would like to know and be seen to be with. Therefore, the boundary-spanner is a positive boon, perhaps a *necessary* accessory to the positive collusion enterprise.

Positive collusion has rarely been studied by organizational researchers. A better understanding of why, when, and where positive collusion happens in organizations is strategic to organizational development because it may be possible to structure and organize units so that collusion is less likely to occur. Or, when it does happen, it can be detected, and the reasons for it occurring can be identified, analyzed, and rectified. Depending on the circumstances, it may be either reprimanded or applauded.

In this article, we (a) introduce and develop the concept of positive collusion; (b) describe the characteristics of collusion (secrecy, circumvention of mandated practices, perceived beneficial objectives), (c) reveal its dynamics by illustrating two positive collusion types, vertical and horizontal, that require different forms of boundary-spanning, (d) describe the antecedents of positive collusion (trust, employee identification, organizational formalization), and (e) discuss the implications of collusion and suggest avenues for future research at the individual, group, and organizational level.

POSITIVE COLLUSION AND BOUNDARY-SPANNING IN ORGANIZATIONS

Organizations have been viewed as the agency through which individuals act in concert and achieve goals that they could not have attained acting alone. In order to carry out their regular business, organizations develop structures with a hierarchy and positions (Weber 1968). Each position is infused with authority and also associated with the goals that the holder of the position needs to pursue and the norms and behaviors that he or she should exhibit while achieving those objectives (March and Simon 1993). The hierarchies embodied in these positions constitute horizontal boundaries that represent informal rules for spanning and crossing. In addition, organizations develop specific procedures and routines that allow employees to carry out activities in a reliable, efficient, and coordinated manner (Cyert and March 1963; Nelson and Winter 1982). Apart from the official roles of procedures, groups of employees within the organization form communities that develop their own norms, cultures, and routines. Such norms often act as an informal organizational structure that complements the formal one and provides guidance to employees on appropriate behavior in key organizational situations (Thompson 1967).

Despite being a critical success factor for an organization, beginning in the 1970s, the term *boundary-spanning* has had an intermittent research history: there has been no systematic body of research that has evolved over time, as has happened with more familiar concepts, such as job satisfaction; in general then, the literature, being only thirty to forty years old, is somewhat spartan. Scholars on the topic of boundary-spanning have given attention to a range of variables including organizational structure, roles, networks, communication, teamwork, and decision making. With some exceptions, this literature has been North American.

There are many types of boundaries associated with an organization, for example, horizontal (function and expertise), vertical (status, hierarchy), geographic, demographic, and stakeholder. Boundaries are the defining characteristic of organizations, with functions crucial to the effectiveness and success of the organization, and forming the basis for strategic jobs at a senior level. Many management and leadership roles can be conceptualized as boundary-spanning and an important capability across all levels of leadership, but perhaps all individuals working in organizations have some aspect of boundary-spanning contained in their role because there has been a global increase in networked forms of organizational structures. Also, there is a parallel growing challenge for organizations to enhance their performance and stakeholder engagement through identifying and rewarding individuals and teams who can effectively perform boundary-spanning roles and who are able to operate across multiple internal and external boundaries, build relationships, identify threats and opportunities, and return insights back to the organization. The drive for innovation and creativity requires leaders to be more effective at spanning multiple boundaries, in cross-functional, cross-generational, and cross-country/region learning and coordination, which hopefully will lead to breakthrough insights. Boundary-spanning roles are part of competitive business practices and market developments, and have been at the heart of cutting-edge advances in space exploration and hand-held technology.

Typically, the concept of boundary-spanning has been concerned with how organizations can maximize talent in their workforces, how they can be competitive in a global market, and in general, is positively oriented. But, there is a dark side to boundary-spanning. Common in organizations these days, there is a greater level of job insecurity; a complex web of politics; and barriers associated with vested interests in the professions, unions, departments, and sometimes senior management. Such dynamics are often accompanied by imbalances of power, lack of meaningful engagement and communication, inability to think laterally, and an endemic lack of trust, which results in conflict, collusion, and sometimes hatred of those in boundary-spanning roles. Those 'sent to Coventry,' and those employed in contract and casual jobs, for whatever reason, are kept outside the box, and are not carried along by the boundary-spanning individual or team engaged in developing the goals of the organizations. Such individuals may find they need to develop a unique form of boundary-spanning *themselves*: trying to develop organizational ties and relationships to avoid being ostracized and disenfranchised from the organization; or, develop a boundary-spanning style where the internal aspect of their organizational relationship partially dissolves, and they develop boundary-spanning activities more concerned with external factors, whether that is collusion with colleagues in other organizations or closer involvements with family and outside interests. Such boundary-spanning is not in the typical form found in the literature, but of someone struggling to survive organizational change, ferment, and chaos.

As implied from the foregoing, while the defined roles, procedures, and routines are necessary for effective organizational functioning, they often become dysfunctional over time (see, e.g., Langan-Fox, Cooper, and Klimoski 2007). These dysfunctional mechanisms, however, may persist for long periods of time, often causing significant damage to the organization's viability. This excessive persistence of norms and procedures occurs for a variety of reasons. First, as March and Simon (1984) point out, individuals stop reacting to each other as sensitive individuals and interact more impersonally, as dictated by the norms associated with their roles. Thus, for instance, a worker may see the need to assist a manager but may not do so because such acts are forbidden by his or her union contract. Second, many activities, once institutionalized, are enacted mindlessly without significant thought about their propriety and utility—individuals enacting an outdated procedure may be unaware that their activities may be harming the organization (Ashforth and Anand 2003). Third, organizations may be hesitant to change procedures that are accepted industry practice because such activities confer the organization with legitimacy in the eyes of the stakeholders and key resource providers (Elsbach 1994). Finally, when an organization is underperforming, employees often fear adverse personal consequences for improper decisions or actions—at such times, sticking to existing procedure allows them to justify their decisions and actions if they were ever called to account.

The preceding arguments suggest a strong tendency within organizations to carry on 'business as usual' and avoid changing outdated procedures and roles. However, despite the ominous conclusion, successful organizations *do* make these changes, suggesting that there must be mechanisms in organizations which allow for questioning and alteration of embedded structures and routines (Adler and Borys 1996; Adler, Goldoftas, and Levine 1999; Raisch et al. 2009). We argue that one such mechanism involves the coming together of committed individuals who, despite bearing personal risk, cross one or more organizational boundaries and work together to go around existing procedures and norms in order to benefit their organizations. This is the bedrock on which positive collusion is based.

We define positive collusion as a secret alliance that is carried out by individuals or groups in an organization who implicitly or explicitly agree to circumvent mandated practices, norms, hierarchies/structures, or roles in order to achieve goals they believe are beneficial to the organization. While activities embodied in positive collusion may violate organizational procedures, or may deviate from norms traditionally assigned to organizational roles, they are not illegal. Although positive collusion could occur *between* organizations, in this article, we are referring only to the construct as it occurs *inside* (intra) organizations, or between organizational units within a single organization. We focus on collusion that is 'positive' and aspires to honorable goals. Although deception, covert tactics, and information manipulation are involved in the collusive arrangements, attaining goals for the common good is intended by the colluding parties. Self-interest is *not* a major motive in positive collusion even though colluders may sometimes incidentally benefit from the end result.

Characteristics of Positive Collusion

We propose that the following characteristics are common to positive collusion in organizations: (i) secret alliances, (ii) mandated practices, (iii) perceived beneficial objectives. The alliance between parties referred to in the above definition suggests that at least two people engage in the collusive activities—in many cases the individuals involved operate across key hierarchical or functional boundaries in this regard, the boundary-spanner is the perfect operative. In addition, as defined, positive collusion is secret and may comprise what Egan (1994) describes as the "shadow side of the organization"— the covert and the unmentionable. The extent of secrecy could vary on a continuum from high to low—in some cases, the collusion is so secret that few individuals other than the involved actors know about it. As in the case of all organizational secrets, there exist targeted outsiders from whom the collusive activity needs to remain hidden (Anand and Rosen 2008; Bok 1983). Such targeted outsiders may be individuals who advocate adherence to organizational procedures or members of a collective who enforce group norms. In the event that these outsiders were to discover the secret, the colluders bear risk of adverse personal consequences that could range from social or organizational sanctions to termination. Thus, since positive collusion is not aimed at furthering self-interest (at least not directly) and carries the risk of negative personal consequences, it is most likely carried out by individuals who are highly committed to the organization's success and are thus willing to risk personal negative consequences in order to further perceived organizational interests.

Positive collusion reflects actions that try to circumvent mandated practices and norms. Such practices and norms may be of two types. The first of these may be organizational mandates or procedures. Consider, for instance, the following scenario: a firm might have a policy specifying that products for international customers should not enter production until the receipt of a confirmed letter of credit (a bank document guaranteeing payment on shipment of the goods). However, letters of credit from developing countries could take several weeks to arrive and waiting long periods before manufacturing the goods could inordinately delay product shipments. To overcome this glitch in efficiency, a marketing department could use faxed confirmations about the issuance of a letter of credit as a basis for requesting production of the needed goods. The firm's finance and audit departments could enact collusion by overlooking this deviation from established practice based on the realization that strict compliance can be impractical and could lead to reduced customer satisfaction. In this case, the two involved departments have reached out across their boundaries and implicitly or explicitly agreed to circumvent organizational procedure to further organizational goals. Note that while this example seems to suggest that positive collusion is usually enacted to counter bureaucracy, that is not always the case. It is quite possible that positive collusion may be used to resist organizational change if the colluders believe that the change in question is harmful to the organization.

The second kind of norm is one which may exist in the culture of a subunit or class of employees (Sackman 1992; Schein 1996). For instance, scientists and engineers in an organization are sometimes at odds with administrators of high-technology firms about the extent to which key information needs to be shared with colleagues and even competitors or about the extent to which cost considerations should dilute the technological specifications of a product (Deeds, DeCarolis, and Coombs 1998; Leibiskind et al. 1996). In such situations, if a scientist were to collude with administrators, he would be crossing the informal boundaries of his professional community and going against the norms held sacred therein. Indeed, if discovered he may face significant social sanctions from his fellow scientists.

As pointed out, self-gain and self-interest are *not* defining characteristics of positive collusion and its goals. The objectives of collusion should benefit the organization as *perceived* by the colluders—however, they may or may not actually benefit the organization. Since positive collusion aims to benefit the organization as believed by the colluders, it leaves open the possibility that it may sometimes actually be harmful to the organization. For instance, there may exist situations where the colluding parties may have limited knowledge about the relevance and purpose of the practices they seek to subvert—in these situations, their actions are based on their 'local rationality' and may cause ultimate harm to the organization. Indeed in organizations such as the army, soldiers sometimes have limited knowledge about the reasons underlying the actions they have to perform. In such cases efforts may be made to train members to carry out orders without question—thus minimizing the likelihood of inadvertent harm through good intentions.

Note that in defining positive collusion we deliberately exclude illegal activities. Such activities may meet most major criteria for positive collusion, but to the extent they risk legal sanctions against the firm, they cannot be seen as meeting the 'perceived benefit' criteria and hence cannot be termed positive collusion.

An analysis of the literature reveals a number of constructs that share similarities with collusion: heedful interrelations, positive politics, pro-social rule breaking, and various forms of positive extra-role behavior. We summaries the similarities and differences between these constructs in Table 8.1 below.

Table 8.1. Comparison between positive collusion and related constructs

Construct / key characteristics	Definition	Secret alliance	Contravenes mandated practices	Beneficial to organization
Positive collusion	A secret alliance that is carried out by individuals or groups in an organization who implicitly or explicitly agree to circumvent mandated practices, norms, hierarchies/structures, or roles in order to achieve goals they believe are beneficial to the organization.	Yes	Yes	Yes
Heedful interrelations	Actors in the system construct their actions (contributions), understanding that the system consists of connected actions by themselves and others (representation) and interrelate their actions within the system (subordination) (Weick & Roberts 1993, 357).	No	No. Operates within organizationally prescribed routines.	Yes
Positive politics	Political behavior in organizations that is functional in the sense of getting things done or moving the organization beyond the status quo (Fedor et al. 2008).	Involves back-room maneuvering, but this may be enacted by individual workers rather than by dyads or groups of workers.	Positive politics involves deviating from informal rules governing behavior, while collusion involves deviating from formal rules governing behavior e.g., practices, hierarchies/roles.	No. Motivated by self-gain.
Pro-social rule breaking	Intentional violation of explicit organizational rules governing how employees are supposed to do their jobs with the intention Behavior that is intentional, discretionary	No. Pro-social rule breaking is an individual-level phenomenon	Yes	Yes. Employees engage in pro-social rule breaking because they

	of promoting the welfare of the organization or its stakeholders (Morrison 2006).	while collusion is a collective (dyadic or group-level) phenomenon, which may be enacted vertically or horizontally across the organization.	want to benefit the organization by exercising initiative and doing what they see as necessary to perform their jobs effectively, responsibly, or responsively.
Positive extra-role behavior (ERB)	(not explicitly expected or required), positively intended by the actor or positively perceived by the observer, and undertaken primarily to benefit someone or something other than oneself e.g., the organization (see Van Dyne, Cummings, and McLean Parks 1995). Van Dyne et al. (1995) distinguished between four general ERB types: affiliative/promotive e.g., organizational citizenship behavior, challenging/promotive, e.g., voice (speaking up with constructive suggestions for change), affiliative/prohibitive, e.g., stewardship behavior (intervening to protect less powerful employees), and challenging/prohibitive, e.g., whistle blowing or principled organizational dissent (a protest and/or effort to change the status quo based on conscientious objection to current policy or practice).	No. Overt rather than covert, and typically enacted by individual workers (no alliances required).	No. The obedience component of OCB is inconsistent with collusion, which involves circumventing organizational routines; OCB is not change-oriented or controversial. Voice is directed at encouraging or promoting change rather than actively implementing it. Stewardship behavior does not contravene prescribed roles/hierarchies. However, like principled organizational dissent, collusion is considered and planned, and involves having an innovative (and possibly better) idea of how things might be done.	Yes. Focus is on helping specific people in the organization (e.g., altruism, courtesy) or the organization itself (e.g., conscientiousness, obedience etc.). Note: OCB is concerned with the outcome of the behavior rather than its intent (the outcome of positive collusion may be negative even if the intent is positive).

Types of Positive Collusion

Based on the relationship between the colluding parties, we classify positive collusion into two distinct types: vertical collusion, which crosses hierarchical boundaries between (a) a manager and a subordinate, and (b) horizontal collusion, which crosses vertical boundaries that occurs between workers or units, e.g., departments. Vertical collusion is usually an explicit arrangement that is endorsed by management and can either be seen as a clever political strategy (because it can be used to make the manager look good), or as a form of 'conscious incompetence' (the manager is aware that there is a problem but is unable to resolve it single-handedly) (Buhler 1994; Hayes 1984). In vertical collusion, the colluder's assistance is actively sought by the manager; in contrast, horizontal collusion is covert collaboration and cooperation between workers or units who operate at a similar level within the organization. While vertical collusion often involves circumventing formal hierarchical structures and power relationships, horizontal collusion involves the coming together of interdependent units or workers who may or may not have formal hierarchical relationships. Unlike vertical collusion, horizontal collusion might emerge without management detection. The two types are described in detail below.

Vertical Collusion

In vertical collusion, the deviation from the norm is a deviation from prescribed hierarchies/structures or roles (more than procedures and practices); the manager is willing to share or defer responsibility for organizational problem solving to the subordinate colluder. Vertical collusion is used to offset the gap between management competence and the needs of the organization. It is most likely to occur when managers fear losing authority and control, or have already lost it. Such a situation can emerge when an organization and its staff are under duress, for instance during organizational change: old routines have been demolished, or change is being resisted by employees, but there is a prolonged delay in introducing and implementing new routines (Collinson and Wilson 2006). During such a period, an air of uncertainty, tension, and rudderless leadership can pervade the organization and employees may tighten the boundaries of their subgroups, which provide certainty and stability in an uncertain world (Lengnick-Hall and Beck 2005; Tajfel and Turner 1985), and vertical collusion can provide a way out. The subordinate colluder (usually one key power broker) may have the informal power to turn things around and be willing to work with management to manipulate organizational politics even though this may not be part of his or her traditional role. Of course, subordinate colluders must accept core organizational norms and values and, at the same time, modify peripheral norms and values (Howell and Higgins 1990). Whereas overt politicking on behalf of management is likely to damage an employee's credibility or legitimacy, covert politicking through collusion can be executed without the knowledge of others, avoiding damage to the colluder's power base.

The subordinate colluder's informal power may stem from collegial/referent power (respect), connection power (who they know), endorsed power (backing), expert power (knowledge), and/or information power (what they know) (Steensma and van Milligen 2003; Walker and Newcombe 2000) and is not an attribute of the colluder in isolation, but rather is embedded in his or her relationship to other workers (Mallalieu and Faure 1998). Thus, although formal power is a major source of influence, power is certainly not restricted to managers (Bennebroek Gravenhorst, and Boonstra 1998). In fact, the conventional organizational chart is virtually useless for understanding the distribution of power in organizations (Buhler 1994) and probably needs to be redrawn to reflect the reality: formal power transmitted *down* through the chain of command; informal power invisibly transmitted *up* the chain of command and 'superimposed' on the formal structure (Walker and Newcombe 2000). Indeed, in some firms, managers suffer from a 'power deficit' and subordinates enjoy surplus power due to informal power (Singh 1988).

The subordinate colluder's job can be seen as wavering between that of a back-room manager, a typical worker, and a double agent. For example, the first author once interviewed a driver ('Frank') working for a large business enterprise in the communications industry. Although the driver was essentially a shop floor worker with minimal education, he was approached by management to negotiate the smooth amalgamation of two opposing divisions of the business, which he did by manipulating the interface between management and opposing forces within the trade union.

The colluder is essentially an organizational chameleon, traversing the boundaries between managers and subordinates. The role is marginalized in that the subordinate does not clearly belong to any one group within the organization. In the broader literature, marginalized people have been described as isolated or segregated, existing on the fringe of society away from the mainstream (Bennett 1997). In this particular case however, we argue that marginality is advantageous.

In the case of the initiating manager, the risk is twofold—not only does he/she bear risk because of untimely disclosure to the rest of the workforce, he/she also bears risk because the colluder may refuse to go along with management plans, and could make public the manager's efforts to initiate such a collusion. Clearly, there needs to be a prior level of trust between the actors before one of them initiates an explicit collusion effort. Trust, then, is a key component of successful position collusion.

A good vertical collusion arrangement needs to be well-maintained, often by tacit reciprocity and exchange agreements, lest the two parties find themselves in conflict with each other over important issues affecting the organization. The manager's role is to maintain the subordinate colluder's trust by reciprocating with information and loyalty (Buhler 1994). In this mutually interdependent collusive relationship, sponsorship is given on the proviso that something will be provided in return (Buhler 1994; Kets de Vries 1999). Another important aspect of vertical collusion is coordination. While it is necessary for the manager and the colluder to construct their own understanding of the task and the organizational environment, it is probably even more important that they *collectively* share an understanding of the problem at hand. Thus, managers should ensure that collusive activity is meticulously planned and organized: the colluder should know what they are going to do, when they are going to do it, and what they are aiming to achieve. The manager would also need to monitor the colluder's activity. Thus, regular communication is important to prevent ambiguity. Since it is essential that the collusion contract be kept secret' the manager and subordinate colluder may need to adopt a mediated mode of communication (e.g., e-mail, cell phone) and/or communicate outside of normal working hours to avoid detection. Given the trickiness of vertical collusion, there is an onus on the manager to choose the right candidate for the job. Discretion should be a key factor in selecting colluders; they cannot be seen to be working with management as this may jeopardize their standing among peers, negating their informal power.

Horizontal Collusion

Horizontal collusion is used to offset the gap between system effectiveness and the needs of the organization. It may occur between interacting and interdependent employees when existing practices are seen to be insufficient or redundant in some way. Horizontal collusion can occur within units (intra-unit horizontal collusion) or between units (inter-unit horizontal collusion), for example, a marketing and a finance department. Horizontal collusion between units goes beyond individual workers and involves crossing formal organizational boundaries. It may involve two or more units, possibly in different locations within the organization. Instead of *formally* changing existing systems, procedures, or routines embedded in organizations, workers or units may collude to override these practices, thereby getting the job done more efficiently. It is different from vertical collusion in that there is no clear demarcation of rank or official status among the parties involved. Horizontal collusion may occur because workers or units believe that it would take too long to implement new practices through official channels or that management is incapable of constructing and implementing new practices. Furthermore, there may exist a view among workers or units that, despite rhetoric to the contrary, management prefers not to know about the circumvention of practices and/or the development of new ones, because they would rather be seen to initiate new practices themselves or be able to claim plausible deniability.

Horizontal collusion is based on workers accepting and reacting to explicit or implicit cues that are at odds with established practices from another interdependent entity within the organization. This type of collusion can be best explained in terms of Nelson and Winter's (1982) view of complex organizations, in which key organizational activities are represented as a collection of routines whereby the output of one routine is the cue for the commencement of another routine. Consider the example described earlier where the marketing and finance departments worked with faxed copies of letters of credits instead of real documents. Such a procedure was most likely to occur when two key employees crossed across departmental boundaries and agreed to the nonstandard procedure. Once the practice has been implemented, and a nonoriginal document is received (the normal cue for the finance/accounting department), the monitoring individual approves action without red-flagging the procedural deviation.

The two kinds of collusion represent two very different dynamics and hence need to be differentiated. Vertical collusion occurs when individuals at different levels in the organizational hierarchy go against the behavioral norms associated with the role and the hierarchy, while in horizontal collusion, the colluders usually act against a prescribed procedure that is mandated or monitored within the organization—the colluding parties are likely to be from different organizational departments but can also be from within the same department. Given these differences in the two forms of collusion, they are often independent of each other—the existence of one form may or may not be accompanied by the existence of the other. Additionally, as we describe in the next section, their antecedents also tend to be different.

ANTECEDENTS TO POSITIVE COLLUSION

We now explore the factors that may increase or decrease the likelihood of positive collusion occurring in an organization. In selecting the antecedent factors of positive collusion, we focus on three that suggest themselves based on the characteristics of collusion: trust levels within the organization, employees' identification with the organization, and the level of formalization/bureaucracy within the organization.

Trust Levels within the Organization

Since positive collusion involves secret actions with risk involved for the enactors, it is much more likely to occur when such activities are likely to remain secret. Such secrets, in turn, are likely to be more prevalent in organizations and groups when (a) there is a high level of interpersonal trust among members (especially between members who are separated by formal or informal boundaries) that allows them to share private information with select insiders, (b) when there exist strong social norms that inhibit secret holders from sharing the information that they are privy to, or (c) when the organization is willing to use legal methods such as noncompete or nondisclosure agreements to keep the contents of a secret confined to the selected insiders (Bok 1983; Hannah 2007; Keane 2008; Liebeskend 1997; Rodriguez and Ryave 1992). Both social control and organizational contracts are likely to be relatively less relevant with respect to collusion. For instance, to a large extent social controls cannot be used to keep collusive activity secret because the colluders (especially positive colluders) are usually acting against these norms. Similarly, since the collusive activity needs to be hidden from the organization itself, the question of a formal NDA does not arise. Thus the primary mechanism through which collusive activity is kept hidden is through the efforts of the colluders themselves. This suggests that the prevalence of interpersonal trust is a key for the presence of high levels of positive collusion. In the absence of such trust, an individual may not initiate collusion for fear that she may be exposed by the other party.

Mayer, Davis, and Schoorman (1995, 712) define trust as "the willingness of a party to be vulnerable to the actions of another party based on the expectation that the other will perform a particular action important to the trustor, irrespective of the ability to monitor or control that other party." The trust required for collusion involves not breaking the confidence of the colluder, and acting to fulfill their part of the bargain. Trust is composed of two distinct components: (a) the colluder must believe in the good intentions of the other parties, and (b) the colluder must also believe in the ability and competence of the other parties to deliver on their part of the deal (Jeffries and Reed 2000). Both forms of trust are essential.

Trust may play out in very different ways with respect to vertical and horizontal collusion. In vertical collusion, the collusive action essentially involves two individuals—the boss and the subordinate. If the two of them trust each other they are likely to collude and this is, to some extent, independent of the overall level of trust within the organization. Indeed the very need for a collusive arrangement may arise because both the subordinate and boss do not trust the others in the organization to interpret their actions correctly. Thus vertical collusion often requires a high level of bilateral trust between the colluders but is likely to be independent of the overall trust levels in the organization.

In the case of horizontal collusion however, colluders may be from different organizational subunits—unlike in the case of the boss subordinate relationship described above, the colluders may not have enough of a history or working together to have high levels of trust in each other. Additionally, more than one individual in each subunit may be aware of the collusive activity. For instance, in our earlier example of collusion, the collusion was likely known to various people who worked on export transactions. Many of the people who knew about the operation may not have had a strong relationship with the original colluders. So, the initial collusion was initiated with the belief that the people in the different subunits would go along with and not expose the collusion. The colluders were thus likely to initiate the collusion only if they had a fairly high degree of trust in their coworkers.

Consequently, horizontal collusion is much more likely in organizations where the average trust levels among employees are high.

Employee Identification

Another key characteristic of positive collusion is that it is enacted by individuals who risk their standing in the organization or peer-community in order to benefit the organization. This suggests that the colluding employees are especially committed to the organization and feel that the organization's success is very important and meaningful to them. Employees may display such attitudes when they strongly identify with the organization. Employee identification occurs when there exists a strong 'cognitive linking' between the definition of the organization and the definition of self (Dutton, Dukerich, and Harquail 1994, 242), and when employees derive a large part of who they are from their membership in an organization (Tajfel and Turner 1985). Within an organization, individuals may strongly identify with the organization or with a subunit, or may even develop a relational identification with specific individuals, such as their immediate coworkers or boss (Dukerich, Golden, and Shortell 2002; Riketta 2005; Sluss and Ashforth 2008). For the sake of parsimony, we are currently focusing only on organizational and subunit identification, even though we agree with Sluss and Ashforth's (2008) argument that an employee's identification with a lower level organizational unit (such as a manager) affects identification with other components of the organization.

Vertical collusion occurs across hierarchical boundaries. For the most part, hierarchical relationships exist within a subunit or department, and rarely cross subunit boundaries. Thus subgroup identification is likely to come into play: When employees strongly identify with a subunit, they are likely to exhibit "intragroup cohesion, cooperation, and altruism, and positive evaluations of the group . . . It is also to be expected that identification would be associated with loyalty to, and pride in, the group and its activities." (Ashforth and Mael 1989, 26). The loyalty and pride felt for their subunits, coupled with perceptions of a shared destiny, makes it likely that an individual may be willing to undertake risks to remedy perceived problems in the subunit. While the motives are altruistic, individuals will be especially motivated to engage in acts such as positive vertical collusion, because workers with high levels of subunit identification are likely to perceive the unit's success as their personal success (Ashforth and Mael 1996; Tajfel and Turner 1985). In the absence of subunit identification, employees will see less synergy between subunit and personal outcomes—while the subunit or organization may benefit from the collusive actions, the individuals per se are unlikely to benefit from such outcomes. Indeed, while having no significant stake in the subunit's benefit, the employees are likely to be conscious of the negative personal consequences that may result from their collusive acts.

The impact of subunit identification on horizontal collusion is likely to be mixed. As far as intra-unit horizontal collusion is concerned, for the same reasons stated above, individuals will be motivated to engage in it—colluders are likely to view the benefit to the subunit as their personal benefit. However, *inter-unit* horizontal collusion is likely to be negatively influenced by *subunit* identification. When employees identify with the subunit instead of the organization, they tend to mistrust 'outsiders' while developing an 'us versus them' mentality (Ashforth and Anand 2003; Ashforth and Mael 1996). Strong subunit identification can even increase inter-group rivalry as group members enhance their own identity by enhancing their group's prestige often at the expense of other groups (Hogg and Terry 2000). For instance, an auditing or accounting department may enhance perceptions of its own effectiveness by highlighting errors and procedural violations that occur in other departments. Thus employees who strongly identify with their subunits are less likely to engage in inter-unit horizontal collusion because they view other departments as rivals and they may risk incurring the wrath of their own unit employees if they are known to have colluded with another department.

Organizational identification, as opposed to subunit identification, is likely to play a much stronger role with respect to horizontal collusion. When employees identify with the organization as a whole they feel personally threatened by the likelihood of organizational failure, and also exhibit increased cohesion and cooperation within the organization (Ashforth and Mael 1989). Consequently, when they encounter an organizational procedure that affects the future performance of the firm they may see it as a personal threat, motivating them to circumvent that procedure and risk organizational or social sanctions by defying established rules and procedures for the benefit of the firm (and for their personal identity). The increased cohesion fostered by identification increases the likelihood that they would more easily find partners who would share their beliefs in the need for horizontal collusion (Ashforth and Mael 1996; Elsbach 1999). Such partners could exist within a subunit or across it and thus organizational identification is likely to increase all forms of positive collusion. On the other hand, when employees do not identify with the organization, they shift their attention to personal benefit—consequently they are likely to avoid collusive activity since it could bring about adverse personal consequences and the likely positive organizational outcomes are not very personally meaningful for them.

Organizational Formalization and Organizational Change

Positive collusion requires effort against existing norms and procedures. This presupposes the existence of such norms in the firm—obviously positive collusion is unnecessary in organizations with a culture that encourages and empowers employees to change their work procedures and systems without resorting to lengthy bureaucratic procedures. This suggests that positive collusion is much more likely to occur in complex, mechanistic organizations where procedures cannot be easily changed through normal efforts.

Today's organizations differ in terms of the extent to which they formalize the work of their employees through routines and procedures (Adler and Borys 1996; Adler et al. 1999). Citing the work of Marsden, Cook, and Knoke (1984), Adler and Borys (1996, 61) pointed out that "surveys show that the vast majority of employees work in establishments with extensive formal procedures: over 74 percent have written job descriptions, and 80 percent have rules and procedures manuals." Such formalized rules, which are characteristics of organizational bureaucracies, have both enabling and coercive features. To the extent that such rules and procedures reduce uncertainty for employees, give them better focus on their key priorities, and better master their tasks, they can be considered enabling. To the extent that such procedures are designed to ensure compliance with organizational norms, they are coercive. Regardless of whether the formal rules are coercive or enabling, their existence at times creates occasions where observing a formal rule may lead to poor performance—creating a need for collusion.

However, we believe that whether or not employees cater to a need for collusion depends on the characteristics of the formal rules in the organization. When the rules formalize relatively routine activities and enable employees to work with reduced stress, the formalization is seen as an enabling factor and employees are likely to be comfortable making one time exceptions in order to collude (Damanpour 1991; Reay, Golden-Biddle, and Germann 2006). However, as the extent of formalization increases and begins to cover large aspects of organizational life the bureaucracy is likely to be perceived as stifling and coercive (Rousseau 1978).

We could argue that a less likely scenario for collusion would occur in low levels of formalization, i.e., when job autonomy is high, since employees have the ability to change what they do in the absence of established procedures (Lawler 1986; 1992). In such instances, the very nature of the organizational structure eliminates the need for positive collusion. Consequently, as the level of formalization within the firm increases, there are greater challenges in changing established customs and practices—collusion thus becomes necessary.

When formalization reaches very high levels, however, even though there is a greater need for collusion, the organization is likely to be viewed as extremely coercive with very little flexibility for action. Employees are likely to be less satisfied, less attached to the organization, and less likely to take risks in trying innovative activities that may be questioned because they do not adhere to organizational rules. Hence, collusive activities could possibly decline. This would suggest an inverted U-shaped relationship between formalization levels and positive collusion. Initially, as the degree of formalization increases, there is increased positive collusion, but then it starts to decline.

The primary reason for a negative relationship between formalization and collusion at high levels of formalization is the reduced expectancy of success. However, it is possible that organization, whose employees strongly identify with the organization continue to focus on positive collusion despite low success expectancy because they equate personal success with organizational success. Given the higher perceived stake they have, such individuals may persist even in the face of low expectancy of success. Consequently, the relationship between formalization and collusion is likely to be moderated by employee identification: the positive relationship is likely to persist even at high levels of formalization.

IMPLICATIONS AND DIRECTIONS FOR FUTURE RESEARCH

Collusion in organizations has had a long and murky past, associated as it has been with fraud, scandal, corruption, and personal gain. In this article, a different type of construct, positive collusion, has been proposed, which involves employees engaged in activities that have good intent and aspired beneficial outcomes. It's vital that organizational and management researchers are cognizant of this important phenomenon given its impact on employees and firms. Positive collusion happens when dysfunction emerges in organizations and solutions need to be found by employees because supervisors and management (or the established organizational routines) are unable or unwilling to remedy the situation. To ignore dysfunction, from the perspective of positive colluders, is to ignore the damage being done to jobs, people, and the organization. As a result, positive collusion occurs quietly, unobtrusively, and effectively bypasses rules and procedures which limit productivity and efficiency. To this extent, management scholars and practitioners need to be armed with requisite knowledge and skill about the potential for positive collusion in cases of organizational dysfunction, and for diagnostic purposes—in providing remedies, in addressing adverse trends, rectifying mistakes, and in bringing about well-being.

We have illustrated how and why positive collusion happens in an organization and provided a definition which should help toward its theoretical development. To this end, we have elaborated dynamics of the construct—its characteristics (secret alliances, mandated practices, perceived beneficial objectives), its types (horizontal and vertical), its relationship to other variables (heedful interrelations, positive politics, pro-social rule breaking, positive extra-role behaviors), and its predictors (employee identification, trust, and organizational formalization).

Descriptions of construct elements help build toward an understanding of positive collusion, however further work needs to be conducted in order to take the construct forward, to illustrate its potential for impacting organizations, and to provide a platform for theoretical and empirical development. Variables recommended for this future work include factors at the individual, group, and organizational level.

A number of motives help explain why individuals and groups would be willing to engage in positive collusion. Previously, identification with the company was one variable thought to predict positive collusion. However there are several others that are possible. An employee's willingness to collude may stem from altruistic or egoistic motives (Peloza and Hassay 2006). Altruistic motives for positive collusion could include company pride or a 'warm glow' effect (e.g., a feeling associated with pro-social behavior that is motivating in itself, i.e., a high) or because of benefit obtained through status achieved from peers (Peloza and Hassay 2006). Achievement motives could be associated with positive collusion which can provide opportunities for influencing the organization without having the required formal credentials necessary for management. Becoming a colluder may be the 'next best thing.' Internal locus of control, the feeling that events and circumstances are controlled from within, is important to employees who feel they have little control in work environment. Thus, when job autonomy is low, it's possible that positive collusion might be more likely. Through positive collusion, ordinary workers may be able to fulfill an underlying desire for power or success (Cobb 1986; Winter 1992). Blue collar workers in particular may prefer to influence the organization in subtle, informal ways (Bussel 1997; Ramaswamy and Schiphorst 2000). For blue collar workers, positive collusion could be 'management by the back door.' Positive collusion might be able to make up for a lack of job enjoyment or job satisfaction. Positive collusion may contribute much needed satisfaction in a stagnant reward system. Schein (1979, 291–292) suggested that engaging in covert organizational activities may be energizing and gratifying for workers; "deception and intrigue add interest to the otherwise routine environment."

The colluder's ability to leverage informal power effectively is likely to depend on his or her proficiencies. Employees may be willing to engage in collusion, but without the right social, political, tactical and influencing skills, they are unlikely to succeed (Douglas and Gardner 2004; Farmer et al. 1997; Farrell and Petersen 1982; Feldman 1988; Kipnis, Schmidt, and Wilkinson 1980).

Key brokers in positive collusion are significant actors such as the supervisor—a key to any successful collusion (Bensman and Gerver 1963). Significant actors have a strong controlling influence in the organization, bridging the gap between management and the shop floor. Supervisors are at the center of organizational plans and activities and usually have a complete knowledge of what is happening in the organization. Indeed it could be argued that collusion could not occur without the artfulness, knowledge, and cooperation of the supervisor—who might need to supervise the collusion. In the case of an inadequate supervisor, positive collusion would need to be highly secret in order to circumvent practices and procedures which typically require supervisor sign-off.

Opportunities exist when organizational structures are 'open' to collusion. Earlier, we referred to the importance of organizational formalization and how it can influence collusive activities. However, employee empowerment training programs introduced in the 1970s (Langan-Fox et al. 2002) could provide individuals and groups with an active orientation where "an individual wishes and feels able to shape his or her work role and context" (Spreitzer 1995, 1444; Spreitzer, De Janasz, and Quinn 1999). So, collusion might be found where empowered employees exist.

Organizational change potentially leads to collusion, initiated in response to leadership transitions, market competition, organizational introspection, or technological advancement (Worley and Lawler 2006). When implemented in a top-down manner, change can significantly increase ambiguity and uncertainty amongst employees (Feldman, 1988); senior management may be focused on big picture change at the expense of day-to-day functioning. Employees need to get their usual tasks completed, yet it may not be apparent how this can or should be done, contributing to a high-stress environment that is detrimental to both the individual and the organization (Grandey 2000; Manz et al. 2008). Organizations going through a change process are likely to see a greater incidence of positive collusion for a variety of reasons, including a lag between the termination of old practices and the implementation of new ones; lack of faith in management's ability to steer through organizational change (rudderless leadership); and greater potential for intra- and inter-group conflict with different stakeholders striving to protect their interests (Feldman 1988). Thus, organizational change is likely to be an antecedent to vertical collusion. Given that practices are already in a state of flux during change, employees (or units) may perceive less risk in deviating from existing practices: positive collusion can be camouflaged, slipping under the radar with less threat of detection.

In the first instance, positive collusion could be proposed by one or two individuals. To be successful on a broad scale, collusive activities need to envelope the supervisor, followed by groups. Eventually, positive collusion can become institutionalized, that is, procedures become routinely circumvented (e.g., Bensmen and Gerver 1963) and there is an expansion of the collusive activities so that they become imperceptibly embedded and institutionalized. As a consequence, positive collusion can become part of the organizational culture (Schein 1990). This could lead to both positive and negative outcomes.

Positive consequences range from better designed organizations to carefully trained and competent managers. At the individual level, there are potentially negative outcomes. Positive collusion may not be the easier option for individuals, and could require effort, conscientiousness, and diligence. Furthermore, personal conflict and occupational stress can arise as a consequence of secrecy, deception, contravention of rules, and so on. Finally, when collusion becomes institutionalized, the culture may become one that has scant regard for existing rules and procedures—this disregard may even extend to effective safeguards such as those instituted to prevent against fraud and unethical behaviors. There may be thus a very fine line between positive collusion and negative collusion, and it is quite possible that what was initially positive collusion may revert to something closer to the classically held notions of collusion. This remains a very important direction for future research.

REFERENCES

Adler, Paul S., and Bryan Borys. 1996. "Two types of bureaucracy: Enabling and coercive." *Administrative Science Quarterly* no. 41 (1):61–89.

Adler, Paul S., Barbara Goldoftas, and David I. Levine. 1999. "Flexibility versus efficiency? A case study of model changeovers in the Toyota Production System." *Organization Science* no. 10 (1):43–68.

American Heritage Dictionary of the English Language (2006). (4th ed.). Boston, MA: Houghton Mifflin.

Anand, Vikas, and Christopher C. Rosen. 2008. *The ethics of organizational secrets.* Journal of Management Inquiry. 17: 102-106.

Ashforth, Blake E., and Vikas Anand. 2003. "The normalization of corruption in organizations." In *Research in organizational behavior: An annual series of analytical essays and critical reviews. Volume 25*, edited by Roderick M. Kramer and Barry M. Staw, 1–52. Amsterdam; London and New York: Elsevier, JAI.

Ashforth, Blake E., and Fred Mael. 1989. "Social identity theory and the organization." *Academy of Management Review* no. 14 (1):20–39. doi: 10.5465/AMR.1989.4278999.

Ashforth, Blake E., and Fred A. Mael. 1996. "Organizational identity and strategy as a context for the individual." In *The embeddedness of strategy*, edited by Joel A. C. Baum and Jane E. Dutton, 19–64. Advances in Strategic Management, vol. 13. Greenwich, CT: JAI.

Bennett, Janet M. 1997. "Culture marginality." In *Education for intercultural experience*, edited by Michael Paige, 1–27. Yermouth, ME: International Press.

Bensman, Joseph, and Gerver Israel. 1963. "Crime and punishment in the factory: The function of deviancy in maintaining the social system." *American Sociological Review* no. 28 (4):588–598.

Bok, Sissela 1983. *On the ethics of concealment and revelation.* New York: Pantheon Books.

Boonstra, Jaap J., and Kilian M. Bennebroek Gravenhorst. 1998. "The use of influence tactics in constructive change processes." *European Journal of Work & Organizational Psychology* no. 7 (2):179–196. doi: 10.1080/135943298398862.

Buhler, Patricia. 1994. "Navigating the waters of organizational politics." *Supervision* no. 55 (9):24.

Bussel, Robert. 1997. "'Business without a boss': The Columbia Conserve Company and Workers' Control, 1917–1943." *Business History Review* no. 71 (3):417–443. doi: http://www.hbs.edu/bhr/.

Cobb, Anthony T. 1986. "Informal influence in the formal organization: Psychological and situational correlates." *Group & Organization Studies* no. 11 (3):229–253.

Collinson, Simon, and David C. Wilson. 2006. "Inertia in Japanese organizations: Knowledge management routines and failure to innovate." *Organization Studies* no. 27 (9):1359–1387. doi: 10.1177/0170840606067248.

Cyert, Richard M., and James G. March 1963. *A behavioral theory of the firm.* Englewood Cliffs, NJ: Prentice Hall.

Damanpour, Fariborz. 1991. "Organizational innovation: A meta-analysis of effects of determinants and moderators." *Academy of Management Journal* no. 34 (3):555–590. doi: 10.2307/256406.

Deeds, David L., Dona DeCarolis, and Joseph E. Coombs. 1998. "Firm-specific resources and wealth creation in high-technology ventures: Evidence from newly public biotechnology firms." *Entrepreneurship: Theory & Practice* no. 22 (3):55.

Dessi, Roberta, and Sheilagh Ogilvie. 2004. *The political economy of merchant guilds: Commitment or collusion?* Cambridge Working Papers in Economics, University of Cambridge.

Douglas, Ceasar, and William L. Gardner. 2004. "Transition to self-directed work teams: Implications of transition time and self-monitoring for managers' use of influence tactics." *Journal of Organizational Behavior* no. 25 (1):47–65. doi: 10.1002/job.244.

Dukerich, Janet M., Brian R. Golden, and Stephen M. Shortell. 2002. "Beauty is in the eye of the beholder: The impact of organizational identification, identity, and image on the cooperative behaviors of physicians." *Administrative Science Quarterly* no. 47 (3):507–533.

Dutton, Jane E., Janet M. Dukerich, and Celia V. Harquail. 1994. "Organizational images and member identification." *Administrative Science Quarterly* no. 39 (2):239–263.

Egan, Gerard. 1994. *Working the shadow side: A guide to positive behind-the-scenes management.* San Francisco: Jossey-Bass.

Elsbach, Kimberly D. 1994. "Managing organizational legitimacy in the California cattle industry: The construction and effectiveness of verbal accounts." *Administrative Science Quarterly* no. 39(1): 57–88.

Elsbach, Kimberly D. 1999. "An expanded model of organizational identification." In *Research in organizational behavior: An annual series of analytical essays and critical reviews,* vol. 21, edited by Robert I. Sutton and Barry M. Staw, 163–200. Stamford, CT: JAI.

Farmer, Steven M., John M. Maslyn, Donald B. Fedor, and Jodi S. Goodman. 1997. "Putting upward influence strategies in context." *Journal of Organizational Behavior* no. 18 (1):17–42. doi: 10.1002/(SICI)1099–1379(199701)18:1<17:: AID-JOB785>3.0.CO;2–9.

Farrell, Dan, and James C. Petersen. 1982. "Patterns of political behavior in organization." *Academy of Management Review* no. 7 (3):403–412. doi: 10.5465/AMR.1982.4285337.

Fedor, Donald, John Maslyn, Steven Farmer, and Kenneth Bettenhausen. 2008. "The contribution of positive politics to the prediction of employee reactions." *Journal of Applied Social Psychology* no. 38 (1):76–96. doi: 10.1111/j.1559–1816.2008.00297.x.

Feldman, Steven P. 1988. "Secrecy, information, and politics: An essay on organizational decision making." *Human Relations* no. 41 (1):73–90. doi: 10.1177/001872678804100105.

Grandey, Alicia A. 2000. "Emotion regulation in the workplace: A new way to conceptualize emotional labor." *Journal of Occupational Health Psychology* no. 5 (1):95–110.

Hannah, David R. 2007. "An examination of the factors that influence whether newcomers protect or share secrets of their former employers." *Journal of Management Studies* no. 44 (4):465–487. doi: 10.1111/j.1467–6486.2007.00694.x.

Hayes, John. 1984. "The politically competent manager." *Journal of General Management* no. 10 (1):24–33.

Hogg, Michael A., and Deborah J. Terry. 2000. "Social identity and self-categorization processes in organizational contexts." *Academy of Management Review* no. 25 (1):121–140. doi: 10.5465/AMR.2000.2791606.

Hopkins, Keith. 1981. *Conquerors and slaves.* New York: Cambridge University Press.

Howell, Jane M., and Christopher A. Higgins. 1990. "Champions of technological innovation." *Administrative Science Quarterly* no. 35 (2):317–341.

Hubbell, Anne P., Rebecca M. Chory-Assad, and Caryn E. Medved. 2005. "A new approach to the study of deception in organizations." *North American Journal of Psychology* no. 7 (2):171–180.

Jeffries, Frank L., and Richard Reed. 2000. "Trust and adaptation in relational contracting." *Academy of Management Review* no. 25 (4):873–882. doi: 10.5465/AMR.2000.3707747.

Keane, Carl. 2008. "Don't ask, don't tell: Secrets—their use and abuse in organizations." *Journal of Management Inquiry* no. 17 (2):107–110.

Kets de Vries, Manfred F. R. 1999. "What's playing in the organizational theater? Collusive relationships in management." *Human Relations* no. 52 (6):745–773. doi: 10.1177/001872679905200604.

Kipnis, David, Stuart M. Schmidt, and Ian Wilkinson. 1980. "Intraorganizational influence tactics: Explorations in getting one's way." *Journal of Applied Psychology* no. 65(4):440–452. doi: 10.1037/0021–9010.65.4.440.

Langan-Fox, Janice, Sharon Code, Rachel Gray, and Kim Langfield-Smith. 2002. "Supporting employee participation: Attitudes and perceptions in trainees, employees and teams." *Group Processes & Intergroup Relations* no. 5 (1):53–82. doi: 10.1177/1368430202005001807.

Langan-Fox, Janice, Cary Cooper, and Richard Klimoski 2007. *Research Companion to the Dysfunctional Workplace.* Glos, UK: Elgar Publishing.

Lawler, Edward E. 1986. *High-Involvement Management.* San Francisco: Jossey-Bass.

Lawler, Edward E. 1992. *The Ultimate Advantage.* San Francisco: Jossey-Bass.

Lengnick-Hall, Cynthia A., and Tammy E. Beck. 2005. "Adaptive fit versus robust transformation: How organizations respond to environmental change." *Journal of Management* no. 31 (5):738–757. doi: 10.1177/0149206305279367.

Li, Peter Ping. 2009. "The duality of crony corruption in economic transition: Toward an integrated framework." *Journal of Business Ethics* no. 85 (1):41–55.

Liebeskind, Julia Porter. 1997. "Keeping organizational secrets: Protective institutional mechanisms and their costs." *Industrial and Corporate Change* no. 6 (3):623–663. doi: http://icc.oxfordjournals.org.

Mallalieu, Lynnea, and Corinne Faure. 1998. "Toward an understanding of the choice of influence tactics: The impact of power." *Advances in Consumer Research* no. 25 (1):407–414.

Manz, Charles C., Vikas Anand, Mahendra Joshi, and Karen P. Manz. 2008. "Emerging paradoxes in executive leadership: A theoretical interpretation of the tensions between corruption and virtuous values." *The Leadership Quarterly* no. 19 (3):385–392. doi: 10.1016/j.leaqua.2008.03.009.

March, James G., and Herbert A. Simon. 1984. *"The dysfunctions of bureaucracy."* In *Organization theory,* edited by Derek S. Pugh, 28–39. *New York:* Penguin.

March, James G., and Herbert A. Simon. 1993. *Organizations.* Cambridge, MA: Blackwell.

Mayer, Roger C., James H. Davis, and F. David Schoorman. 1995. "An integrative model of organizational trust." *Academy of Management Review* no. 20(3):709–734.

Morrison, Elizabeth W. 2006. "Doing the job well: An investigation of pro-social rule breaking." *Journal of Management* no. 32 (1):5–28. doi: 10.1177/0149206305 277790.

Nelson, Richard R., and Sidney G. Winter 1982. *An evolutionary theory of economic change.* Cambridge, MA: Belknap Press.

Peloza, John, and Derek Hassay. 2006. "Intra-organizational volunteerism: Good soldiers, good deeds and good politics." *Journal of Business Ethics* no. 64 (4):357–379. doi: 10.1007/s10551–005–5496-z.

Raisch, Sebastian, Julian Birkinshaw, Gilbert Probst, and Michael L. Tushman. 2009. "Organizational ambidexterity: Balancing exploitation and exploration for sustained performance." *Organization Science* no. 20 (4):685–695. doi: 10.1287/orsc.1090.0428.

Ramaswamy, E. A., and F. B. Schiphorst. 2000. "Human resource management, trade unions and empowerment: Two cases from India." *International Journal of Human Resource Management* no. 11 (4):664–680. doi: 10.1080/09585190050075051.

Reay, Trish, Karen Golden-Biddle, and Kathy Germann. 2006. "Legitimizing a new role: Small wins and microprocesses of change." *Academy of Management Journal* no. 49 (5):977–998. doi: 10.5465/AMJ.2006.22798178.

Richter, Andreas W., Michael A. West, Rolf van Dick, Jeremy F. Dawson. 2006. "Boundary spanners' identification, intergroup contact, and effective intergroup relations." *Academy of Management Journal* no. 49 (6):1252–1269. doi: 10.5465/AMJ.2006.23478720.

Riketta, Michael. 2005. "Organizational identification: A meta-analysis." *Journal of Vocational Behavior* no. 66 (2):358–384.

Rodriguez, Noelie, and Alan L. Ryave. 1992. "The structural organization and micropolitics of everyday secret telling interactions." *Qualitative Sociology* no. 15 (3):297.

Rousseau, Denise M. 1978. "Characteristics of departments, positions, and individuals: Contexts for attitudes and behavior." *Administrative Science Quarterly* no. 23 (4):521–540.

Sackmann, Sonja A. 1992. "Culture and subcultures: An analysis of organizational knowledge." *Administrative Science Quarterly* no. 37 (1):140–161.

Schein, Edgar H. 1990. "Organizational culture." *American Psychologist* no. 45 (2):109–119. doi: 10.1037/0003–066X.45.2.109.

Schein, Edgar H. 1996. "Three cultures of management: The key to organizational learning." *Sloan Management Review* no. 38 (1):9–20.

Schein, Virginia E. 1979. "Examining an illusion: The role of deceptive behaviors in organizations." *Human Relations* no. 32 (4):287–295.

Singh, Chandra B. 1988. "Behavioral strategies for influencing immediate supervisors." *Psychologia: An International Journal of Psychology in the Orient* no. 31:34–41.

Sluss, David M., and Blake E. Ashforth. 2008. "How relational and organizational identification converge: Processes and conditions." *Organization Science* no. 19 (6):807–823. doi: 10.1287/orsc.1070.0349.

Spreitzer, Gretchen M. 1995. "Psychological, empowerment in the workplace: Dimensions, measurement and validation." *Academy of Management Journal* no. 38 (5):1442–1465. doi: 10.2307/256865.

Spreitzer, Gretchen M., Suzanne C. De Janasz, and Robert E. Quinn. 1999. "Empowered to lead: The role of psychological empowerment in leadership." *Journal of Organizational Behavior* no. 20 (4):511–526. doi: 10.1002/(SICI)1099–1379(199907)20:4<511::AID-JOB900>3.0.CO;2-L.

Steensma, Herman, and Femke van Milligen. 2003. "Bases of power, procedural justice and outcomes of mergers: The push and pull factors of influence tactics." *Journal of Collective Negotiations in the Public Sector* no. 30 (2):113–134.

Tajfel, Henri, and John C. Turner. 1985. "The social identity theory of intergroup behaviour" in *Psychology of Intergroup Relations* (2nd ed.), edited by Stephen Worchel and William G. Austin. Chicago: Nelson Hall.

Thompson, James D. 1967. *Organizations in action.* New York: McGraw-Hill.

Turner, George W. 1987. *The Australian concise Oxford dictionary of current English.* Melbourne: Oxford University Press.

Van Dyne, Lin, Larry L. Cummings, and Judi McLean Parks. 1995. "Extra-role behaviors: In pursuit of construct and definitional clarity (a bridge over muddied waters)." *Research in Organizational Behavior* no. 17: 215–285.

Walker, Anthony, and Robert Newcombe. 2000. "The positive use of power on a major construction project." *Construction Management & Economics* no. 18 (1):37–44. doi: 10.1080/014461900370933.

Weber, Max 1968. *Economy and Society.* Berkeley, CA: University of California Press.

Weick, Karl E. and Karlene H. Roberts. 1993. "Collective mind in organizations: Heedful interrelating on flight decks." *Administrative Science Quarterly* no. 38 (3):357–381.

Winter, David G. 1992. "Power motivation revisited." In *Motivation and personality: Handbook of thematic content analysis.*, edited by Charles P. Smith, John W. Atkinson, David C. McClelland, and Joseph Veroff, 301–310. New York: Cambridge University Press.

Worley, Christopher G., and Edward E. Lawler Iii. 2006. "Designing organizations that are built to change." *MIT Sloan Management Review* no. 48 (1):19–23.

Zarkada-Fraser, Anna. 2000. "A classification of factors influencing participating in collusive tendering agreements." *Journal of Business Ethics* no. 23 (3):269–282.

Part III

Management

9 The Complexities of School Leadership

Many Boundaries to Cross

Philip Riley

There are no objective grounds to determine which goals and practices in education are 'best' or 'important.' Hence, it is a rather ambiguous endeavor to decide whether or not a leader models best practice and important organizational values. (Kelchtermans and Piot 2013)

With remarkably few exceptions, leaders are conventionally constructed as causal agents of work outcomes. (Gronn 2003, 278)

INTRODUCTION

There is a vast literature on changing work practices and expectations of the school principal. These changes have been significant and rapid, occurring in one generation following a long period of stability. The aim of this chapter is to provide an overview of the complexity of issues facing current school principals/leaders, whether long-standing or newly added to the role description. It will be argued that these might better be conceived as a series of boundary-spanning rather than leadership challenges, as principals traverse the micro-political world of the school, and increasingly the meso-, exo-, and macro-systems that contain it (Brofenbrenner, 1977). The major human influencers in these systems are also included. The human costs and consequences of multiple boundary-spanning are outlined at the end of the chapter. The taxonomy lists detail about important boundaries and/or the degree of influence it has on principals.

Boundaries imply lines and edges. However, in education many boundaries are actually arbitrary midpoints on a continuum. For example, the boundary between a behaviorist and humanistic approach to education is arguable: it contains multiple separation points. While I outline the boundaries as a point of contact between two objects or ideas, in reality the distinction is often not nearly that simple. Table 9.1 lists the boundaries that are discussed either briefly or more substantially in the chapter. The list is neither exhaustive nor exclusive, and the boundaries are often not discrete. Many overlap. They are separated here for discussion purposes to go some way toward outlining the complexity of the modern-day school leaders' workplace environment. In terms of boundary-spanning, the chapter focuses on the boundaries between expectations and realities, conscious and unconscious processes, and the visible and invisible stakeholders who make up the human dynamic in schools.

Changes in Expectations

The changes in expectations about how principals operate pervades all stakeholders; from children beginning school through to governments' increasing accountability requirements. The person who takes up the role is also imagined differently now: from the slightly mysterious and remote *Man in the Principal's Office* (Wolcott 1973) to a networked, multiskilled, titular head of an organization whose boundaries are much more difficult to define than previously and whose gatekeeping role between those boundaries has become crucial to the smooth operation of the school (Kelchtermans and Piot 2013).

Table 9.1　An incomplete taxonomy of school-induced boundaries spanned by principals in carrying out their work role

Boundaries	
Changes in expectations	Global vs. local
Changes in power and influence	Universal vs. individual
Changes in language	Tradition vs. modernity
Instruction: the new fundamentalism	Long- and short-term considerations
The heroic leader	Competition and concern for equality of opportunity
The influencers: outside and inside, visible, and invisible	Extraordinary expansion of knowledge and human beings capacity to assimilate it
Stakeholder boundaries	Spiritual and material
Outcome boundaries	Contrived collegiality in times of intense competition
Head, heart, and hand	Public vs. private education
Historical boundaries	Concentrated and distributed approaches of school leadership
Micro politics and emotional regulation	Learning vs. instruction
Passion, anxiety, and resistance to change	Evidence-based practice vs. policy-led evidence seeking
Leadership vs. management	Telling vs. listening

Changes in Power and Influence

The title "principal" implies much more power, authority, and autonomy than it usually delivers to incumbents. While there is some power and authority associated with the title, the daily reality is often far from powerful or even autonomous as an organizational head. Where the position does have some real power is in the psyche of stakeholders, who need the principal to be the secure base of the organization (Riley 2011; Purkiss and Rossi 2007; Bibby 2010; Gallant and Riley 2013).

Changes in Language

A change in thinking about the role of principals has been reflected in language. While the members of a school organization may still use the term *principal* or *head master/mistress*, which implies first among equals, in the academy and central educational bureaucracies, this nomenclature has been largely replaced *with school leader*. The term *leader* remains a synonym for *principal* (Oxford University Press), but the change from one to the other implies a division of labor and qualitative differences between leaders and followers. This has been noted by a number of leadership scholars (Popper 2012; Gronn 1999; Kerr and Jermier 1978). Principals under this definition become qualitatively different to teachers, despite the fact that many continue to teach some of the time. This subtle form of dualistic thinking, the idea that the principal should be thinking like a teacher, *or* like a leader, is rarely helpful in the daily running of a school, and the false dichotomy assumes the two are disconnected. Worse, the language change encourages a similar kind of thinking in teachers, parents, and students. Binary oppositional thinking is never useful in nuanced leadership situations, particularly if there is anxiety involved for either side of the divide.

Changes to the language of leadership in schools has necessitated new language to account for the actual work that has always taken place. The terms *distributed leadership* and *leadership teams* have attempted to bridge the leader-follower gap created by the change in language from *principal* to *school leader*. The bridge is built by introducing leadership teams to distribute leadership tasks. This increasingly common school scenario attempts to position the principal as first among equals in the leadership team. He or she distributes tasks and responsibilities through consultation with the leadership team. However, this conceptualization positions teachers who are outside of the leadership team, and therefore still qualitatively different from those who are within it, as *student learning leaders*. This is a rather confused position and reflects a universal dilemma that education systems struggle with: role clarity.

Two eminently readable scholars have cogently argued these dilemmas under provocative titles. In the first, Egan (2002), whose *Getting It Wrong from the Beginning* carefully outlined the competing commitments of education systems that doom it to failure on one objective whenever another succeeds. For example, on the one hand education systems such as schools, regions, states, or nations encourage intellectual risk taking as a desired outcome, but also demand conformity and no rocking of the administrative boat. When push comes to shove it is order that is deemed more important than the intellectual risk taking. These kinds of competing commitments create tensions within organizations (Kegan and Lahey 2001) that often cause great trauma and can produce toxic work environments.

In the second example of a universal dilemma in education, Gronn (2003) asks a very important question with regard to schools in *Leadership: Who Needs It?* He argues that the myth of the heroic school leader, leaving his or her stamp on a school, has made the job of administering and managing schools more difficult. Without denying that there is a role for a leader in schools, determining what that person should do is very difficult. In fact it is the many leader substitutes (Kerr and Jermier 1978) who carry out most of the important tasks. Gronn (2003) suggests that the school would not function without leader substitutes, but they might easily function without "leaders." Most principals are managers, not leaders, who should be concerned with the small picture of education. To pretend otherwise, he argues, is to make the important tasks they do more difficult to carry out. Gronn is swimming upstream against a powerful force, but his argument is well documented. He delineates six boundaries, although he does not call them boundaries but "matters of particular concern," that needed to be addressed:

> First, the relationship between leadership and management; second, the connection between leadership and power; third, whether there are explanatory substitutes for leadership; fourth, the typical assumptions we make about the division of leadership labour; fifth, the problems generated by the prevailing cult of leader 'exceptionality'; and sixth, the consequences, intended and unintended, of the recent emergence of leadership design prototypes. (Gronn 2003, 269)

These matters of concern can be thought of as higher-order boundaries in multidimensional space. They are traversed theoretically by scholars of leadership and practically by the practitioners who are the focus of this chapter, although in light of Gronn's (2003) argument about leadership redundancy, I use the term "leader" with some trepidation and the reader is warned to approach it with some caution also.

School Leadership in Review

In a review of school leadership research, Leithwood and Day (2007) identified four broad categories of responsibility school leaders are expected to be competent in carrying out. Three are relatively easy to describe as leadership roles: setting visions or directions for the future; developing the talents of the people within the organization, which is taken to mean the long-term development of teachers so that they are better able to develop the talents of their students over time; and being a change agent within the organization. Taken together they represent another form of competing commitments. Under this model, the principal as change agent should be the one who is least happy with the organizational stance and current outcomes. Principal/leaders are at their best when driven to find new ways to improve the school even when it appears to be functioning smoothly. Each conception of leader identified by Leithwood and Day has a vast literature. The categories are relatively generic to many organizations, apart from the fourth, which is much more specific to schools: principal as instructional leader. The language associated with this category is very interesting. Teaching, learning, and pedagogy have been subsumed by a simplistic term: instruction. This return to contrived simplicity, or fundamentalism, creates a difficult boundary between reality and the way reality is perceived and communicated to stakeholder groups.

Instruction: The New Fundamentalism

Many societies deal with complexity by moving toward fundamentalism, or reflexive denial, as in the case of climate change skepticism. Educational fundamentalism, promoted by new right managerialists who seem to occupy most of the powerful positions in education bureaucracies, is *instruction*. In their neoliberal, neoconservative utopia, learning depends only on the quality of instruction. Learners are not active or even responsible for learning. They are simply the clay molded by the instructor, who is shaping the future with the right content, delivered in the right place, at the right tempo. This produces the right learning. This conception of learning is easy to measure with standardized tests and erroneously labeled "objective" assessments of the quality of instruction: independent of student variables, needs, or innate talents, cohort effects, socioeconomic status, and a host of other important factors, including pet ownership (Berliner 2012).

Most English-speaking countries have effectively returned to the three Rs as the only real "measure" of a "good" education. This kind of over-simplification of the complexity of education is a significant source of stress for school principals (Riley 2012) and is a boundary that is very difficult to span when dealing with bureaucrats who show little if any understanding of the complexity of a real education for real people. While not to deny the importance of the three Rs, elevating "the basics" to high stakes breaks both Campbell's (1976) two pessimistic social science laws:

> The more any quantitative social indicator is used for social decision-making, the more subject it will be to corruption pressures and the more

apt it will be to distort and corrupt the social processes it is intended to monitor. (Campbell 1976, 49)

Campbell goes on,

> Achievement tests may well be valuable indicators of general school achievement under conditions of normal teaching aimed at general competence. But when test scores become the goal of the teaching process, they both lose their value as indicators of educational status and distort the educational process in undesirable ways. . . . Achievement tests are, in fact, highly corruptible indicators. (Campbell 1976, 51–2)

Principals find this boundary between governmental demands for simplistic information and accountability measures with the need to provide sufficiently simple information to communicate their real resourcing, HR, and other logistical needs very difficult to span. Students become peripheral in the debate. They simply respond to instruction. They do not construct their own learning by engaging with others, the environment, or from their own curiosity, and learning is a checklist of content to be covered as efficiently, and therefore cheaply, as possible. The school leader who can achieve this outcome for a school is a hero; the teacher who can move the "lower average student to upper average" is also a hero. The temptation to game the system to appear heroic becomes increasingly hard to resist (Nichols and Berliner 2007).

The myth of the hero leader or hero teacher is easy to understand, has wide and deep roots in Western culture, and provides a permanent supply of individuals to blame when the hoped for outcome is not achieved. These are just some of the reasons why education takes pride of place in the "impossible professions." More than ever before, boundary-spanning has become the prerequisite for survival as leader of the diverse population of strange bedfellows that a school represents. It too is an impossible task, when the boundaries are arbitrary.

The principal spans the impossible boundary between narcissistic administrators, consumed by the myth of their own qualities as exceptional leaders and the reality of the school inhabitants. The administrator positions him or herself as the exceptional change agent, and the principal as "ordinary functionary" who must carry out the tasks set by the exceptional leader, "highlighting the presumed superiority of leaders, the idea of exceptionalism serves to residualize nonleaders as 'followers' and to infantilize them, sheep-like, within a culture of dependency" (Gronn 2003, 282). The danger in this is that it encourages principals to also become consumed by the same myth, then transfer the process to the school, where they picture themselves as heroic and everyone else as ordinary functionaries. A difficulty with boundary-spanning is that one can get caught on one side or the other.

The Impossible Profession

Freud (Freud et al. 1953)[1] identified pedagogy, governance, and psychoanalysis as the impossible professions. His reasoning was that the results of each are always unsatisfying because the ideal outcome can never be realized. If the reader is not convinced of this proposition by the evidence presented so far, it can easily be confirmed by asking a range of people a simple question: "What is the outcome of a good education?" If the profession of pedagogy/education is impossible, imagine trying to lead it!

The Influencers: Outside and Inside, Visible, and Invisible

Part of the impossibility of the profession is the multiple boundaries that must be spanned by education workers in schools, but particularly by school principals, who also have to deal with external stakeholders who are both visible and invisible, such as public service bureaucrats, including: regional supervisors, curriculum, logistical, legal, welfare, and social inclusion specialists, to name just a few. For example, the power of examination boards to influence how the teaching practices and learning opportunities are conducted in schools should not be underestimated, but this influence is difficult to map completely, as it interacts with so many other variables by the time it is operationalized in classrooms.

Two other groups of outside influencers on schools who create boundaries that principals have to span are: employer associations, who are quick to outline their needs when the economic levers shift; and politicians, who can have a great deal of influence through policy and accountability settings. However, neither group spends much time in schools attempting to understand what goes on and what may have changed from the time they were students. This highlights a difficult boundary span for principals: the outsider who thinks he or she understands how schools work through having once been a student and is therefore able to offer expert advice. A good example of this in the policy area has been the closer examination of calls for the adoption of evidence-based practice.

The administrative calls for evidence-based practice on the surface seem reasonable, but discredit the profession, as they are based on an assumption that leaders and teachers are not already doing so. Boden and Epstein (2006) found that the push for evidence-based practice from administration is often a pseudonym for policy-driven evidence seeking, used to discredit independent research, which challenges the current orthodoxy. The "right outcome" is achieved by commissioning the production of evidence that is likely to support the philosophical rather than empirical policy position, such as the introduction of performance pay to improve the quality of leadership in schools.

Influencers, such as those listed above, who rarely cross the school boundary, need to be made aware of the planning, operational, and logistical requirements that keep any school functioning. This is an important job of the principal. What is right for one school may not be completely right for another. Getting this message across, spanning the communication boundary, can be a difficult task for the principal, who is just one of a long line of other principals all competing for the same, often dwindling, resources while appearing and/or choosing to work collegiately on pedagogical issues with their colleagues. These outside influencers' impact are set against the three internal stakeholder influencer groups; teachers, including ancillary staff such as cleaners; parents; and students under more stressful conditions than they might be otherwise. This boundary is a very difficult one for principals to span.

Unions represent influencers who are both inside and outside the school boundary. Their influence varies with context. Some schools are heavily unionized and industrial issues are often aggregated around blue-collar issues such as working hours, numbers, and duration of weekly meetings. Other jurisdictions have unions that are more concerned with issues such as input into professional standard for teachers and the elevation of educators to a recognizable profession. Yet other schools have no union involvement other than complying with laws that unions have had input into drafting.

Unsustainable Leadership

The personal costs associated with those working in an impossible profession are high. These will be examined in more detail below. Many jurisdictions of the world are facing serious difficulties in attracting enough good people to maintain the current numbers of school leaders. The sting in the tail of distributed leadership may be that aspirants who get close enough to the top see these human costs first-hand and decide not to take the final leadership step. This has serious implications for the sustainability of education systems. For example, in Australia the Principals' Australia Institute estimates that up to 70 percent of current school principals will reach retirement age in the next five years. Concurrently the application rate for genuine replacements has fallen by approximately the same figure (Riley 2012). Similar stories have been reported in other countries (Gronn 2003). Surprisingly, perhaps, very little research has directly addressed the human cost of being an effective school leader.

Yet More Boundaries to Be Spanned

A taxonomy of boundaries not already mentioned that need to be spanned by school principals to ensure the smooth functioning of a school shows the difficulties associated with the role. This list is by no means exhaustive and different schools will have unique blends that must be addressed by school leaders if they are to succeed in the role; and sometimes when they are not going to succeed. Each is briefly mentioned.

Stakeholder boundaries. Who is the client: parents, children, teachers, examination boards, governments?

Outcome boundaries. The boundary between learning, good teaching, smooth running of the daily operation, coping with untoward incidents, keeping the supervisors/regions happy.

The boundary between *head, heart, and hand.* Roland Barth (2001) is probably one of the best-known advocates of the necessary pedagogical balance between these elements of a successful interrogation of the environment for learning by learners.

Historical boundaries. Schools are caught in habits that are hundreds of years old (Sizer 1984). These create boundaries between then and now, stability and change, and become invisible. They disappear into "the way we do things around here."

Micro-politics and emotional regulation have become more widely written about remain in relation to education (Kelchtermans 2005). For principals this means dealing with difficult parents and teachers (Riley and Langan-Fox 2013). There is a growing literature on teacher misbehavior (see Romi et al. 2011 for a review). The human costs associated with this kind of boundary-spanning teacher support versus performance management, in a system where hiring and firing is often not a real option, causes many principals high levels of stress.

The boundary between *passion, anxiety, and resistance to change.* From a psychodynamic perspective, organizational change threatens individual connections to organizations (Diamond 1986). So change creates psychological resistance. The motivation to resist is largely unconscious. If questioned, individuals may not be able to clearly articulate the threat they feel. This makes attempts to rationally discuss the issues difficult and frustrating, often leaving everyone feeling ignored. This is a difficult boundary for a principal or any change agent to span. Diamond (1986) argues that this is a psychological threat to both self-esteem and self-confidence. For many teachers, the initial motivation to join the profession can create a vulnerability to change processes (Riley 2011). This has begun to be studied more recently by taking an emotional rather than cognitive perspective, and some interesting results are beginning to surface (Mayseless and Popper 2007; Popper and Mayseless 2003; Riley 2009; Gallant and Riley 2013).

Yet other boundaries were conceived as tensions by the UNESCO taskforce charged with reporting on the state of education at the end of the twentieth century and looking forward to the twenty-first. The task force identified seven key tensions that might be better reconceived as boundaries to be spanned: *global and local; universal and the individual; tradition and modernity; long- and short-term considerations; competition and concern for equality of opportunity; extraordinary expansion of knowledge and human beings' capacity to assimilate it;* and the tension between the *spiritual and the material* (Delores et al. 1998).

Further boundaries consist of bridging *contrived collegiality in times of intense competition; public versus private education;* and the stalemate between "*concentrated and distributed approaches of school leadership*" (Kelchtermans and Piot 2013).

SUMMARY: IF SCHOOL IS THE SOLUTION, WHAT IS THE PROBLEM?

Increasingly principals have to be networkers and hustlers who straddle the gap between school needs and school resources with ingenuity, pleading, manipulation, and transactional interactions with the private sector who want "bang for their buck." Governments are looking to privatize education. Charter schools, public-private partnerships, and their equivalents are becoming common. In some sectors the public entity does not own or have control of the buildings in which the school operates. This relieves the principal's burden of ongoing maintenance but introduces a pedagogical restraint in that no modifications can be made to any building without the approval of the private owner of that building. When an alteration to a learning space that will aid pedagogy is suggested, it may be refused by the owner of the building as an unnecessary cost to a perfectly sound building rather than embraced as an investment in the learning futures of the children. This is a new external boundary within the footprint of the school boundary.

Part of the difficulty in writing about schools is the problem of perception versus reality. Many schools would be readily recognized as fitting the criteria for a complex organization: 100+ staff, 1,500+ students, multiple-million-dollar annual budgets, complex stakeholder networks, and a large geographical footprint. The leader of such an organization clearly has multiple tasks and responsibilities. These schools also contain many substitutes, whose work may or may not go unnoticed, that keep the organization functioning. However, there are many schools that are very small. At the extreme the "leader" may also be the only teacher in the organization, yet with all of the responsibilities, and few human support mechanisms available to the head of a large school. These are clearly two very different roles that are lumped together under the catchall "school leader." The term *leader* creates the binary *leader-follower*, which in these situations is misleading. It is interesting to note that the dichotomy of the leader-follower is not reflected in leadership descriptors, "authority, power, influence, persuasion, manipulation, coercion and force," which are all continuous (Gronn 2003, 275).

One of the major difficulties all school leaders and systems seem to be facing at present is the seemingly unchallenged assumption that uniformity equals quality. This is an example of the policy-led evidence seeking outlined above (Boden and Epstein 2006). As a field, education researchers can be slow to pick up on new thinking from outside domains. Thirty years ago, Ritzer (1983) warned about the MacDonaldization of society. Today schools are becoming MacDonaldized in ever increasing numbers, a move embraced by neoliberal managerialists who see this as progress. It is interesting to note that while education systems in the West are becoming increasingly prescriptive and uniformly rigid, the Chinese, once known for their rigid adherence to the Confucian model, are encouraging more diversity, creativity, and innovation.

Leadership as Boundary-Spanning

Boundary-spanning may actually be a better term than school leadership. The redundancy of leadership has been well argued (see e.g., Gronn 2003) and the case for collective effort and substitution is also well documented (see e.g., the special issue of *Leadership Quarterly 10*[1]). However, for all of the talk about the redundancy of leadership, the conceptualization exists very strongly as a taken-for-granted conceptualization of organizational functioning failure and success. So, is there something in the idea of leadership (school leadership in particular) that is important to distinguish? Perhaps it is the idea that leaders do not act in a vacuum, which is so pervasive that it is unchallenged. However, in many schools the leader does act in a vacuum for all intents and purposes. The key is autonomy. It is difficult enough to ride the boundaries outlined above. Having little say over which boundaries are most important, due to inherent restraints in any particular school context, creates irresolvable tensions within the organization that can create long-term toxicity in schools as workplaces and learning places. To examine this proposition the role of perceived autonomy by 2,050 school principals drawn from the Government, Catholic, and Independent school systems who participated in the 2011 Australian Principal Health and Wellbeing Survey[2] is examined in the following section.

Autonomy

Two subscales for autonomy were computed using ten items from the survey (see Table 9.2). Each subscale consisted of five items with good internal consistency. The first was the level of autonomy in managing staff, while the second related to the general running of the school. Table 9.3 displays the correlations between autonomy and offensive behavior subscales experienced by principals during the last twelve months, and perceived reactions to the stresses. These scores were all derived from the Copenhagen Psychosocial Coping Scale (Pejtersen et al. 2010). Table 9.4 displays personal correlates of stressful work and workplaces.

It is interesting to note the very small correlations between support from colleagues and all other subscales. One could assume that support from

Table 9.2 Principal autonomy subscales showing items and Cronbach's alpha coefficients

Subscale Items	α
Autonomy_Staff	.872
Leading the development of teaching and learning	
Managing teaching staff	
Providing strategic focus and direction to colleagues	
Managing other staff	
Managing curriculum development	
Autonomy_School	.830
Managing school resources	
Problem solving	
Working with parents	
Building relationships with community agencies	
Managing school budgets	

colleagues is neither expected nor taken into account by principals. This is a troubling finding, given that the professional relationships at work are shown to be protective to workers. Principals may have learnt during their rise to the top of the organization that there is little prospect of genuine support from colleagues and/or subordinates and found alternative ways to garner support for what they do. This finding does lend support to the adage that it is indeed lonely at the top.

Consequences: Burnout

Danhof-Pont, van Veen, and Zitman (2011) conducted a meta-analysis of burnout from thirty-one studies. Approximately 10–15 percent of workers in the Netherlands suffer from burnout each year. With principals the level is much higher. In 2011, 45 percent of Australian principals who completed the Australian Principal Health and Wellbeing Survey (Riley, 2012) experienced one or more of the following symptoms of burnout either all the time (13.3%) or a large part of the time (32.5%): felt worn out, physically exhausted, emotionally exhausted, or tired. Principals feel physically and emotionally exhausted almost as much as they feel tired (see Figure 9.1).

Influencers' Impact on Operational Decisions

A number of groups outlined earlier have various levels of influence in the running of schools. Most individuals who have some influence can be

Table 9.3 Pearson product-moment correlations between principals' professional relationships subscales and occupational health and safety subscales

Subscale	2	3	4	5	6	7	8	9	10	11	12	13	14	15
1 Threats of violence	.602**	.200**	-.063**	-.013	.007	-.042	0.01	.026	.196**	.346**	.195**	.236**	.093**	.149**
2 Physical violence		.186**	-.071**	-0.037	-.022	-.022	.015	.051*	.143**	.316**	.133**	.202**	.062**	.104**
3 Bullying			-.141**	-.136**	-.061**	-.090**	.025	.023	.150**	.133**	.228**	.233**	.051*	.242**
4 Autonomy_Staff				.673**	.355**	.196**	.072**	.138**	-.069**	-.108**	-.122**	-.205**	.012	-.217**
5 Autonomy_School					.330**	.225**	.037	.126**	.018	-.060**	-.075**	-.138**	.027	-.163**
6 Confidence to manage staff						.611**	.077**	.053*	-.024	-.095**	-.121**	-.074**	-.076**	-.217**
7 Confidence to manage community and self							.147**	.056*	-.169**	-.186**	-.243**	-.096**	-.162**	-.377**
8 Support from relatives								.259**	-.057*	-.056*	-.094**	-.053*	-.073**	-.168**
9 Support from work colleagues									-0.023	-.018	-.024	-.025	0.01	-.132**
10 Stress: Workload										.424**	.404**	.453**	.457**	.359**
11 Stress: Students											.541**	.519**	.321**	.275**
12 Stress: Conflicts												.590**	.399**	.383**
13 Stress: Staff management													.348**	.296**
14 Stress: HR/Financial														.246**
15 Depressed about job														

** Correlation is significant at $p<.001$ level (2-tailed).

* Correlation is significant at $p<.05$

Table 9.4 Pearson product-moment correlations between COPSOQ-II subscales related to emotional demands of the role, and the physical and emotional outcomes for individuals

	2	3	4	5	6	7	8	9	10	11	12
1 Emotional demands	.450**	.562**	.464**	.359**	.410**	.485**	−.185**	.450**	.059**	−.163**	.212**
2 Hiding emotions		.377**	.320**	.247**	.275**	.309**	−.117**	.293**	−0.007	−.201**	.144**
3 Cognitive demands			.315**	.225**	.160**	.290**	−.052*	.338**	0.024	−0.042	.119**
4 Burnout				.547**	.575**	.737**	−.419**	.592**	.108**	−.278**	.195**
5 Troubles sleeping					.461**	.585**	−.362**	.408**	.068**	−.205**	.162**
6 Depressive symptoms						.693**	−.373**	.423**	.171**	−.263**	.219**
7 Stress							−.404**	.561**	.128**	−.293**	.201**
8 General health								−.313**	−.090**	.179**	−.159**
9 Work–family conflict									.118**	−.268**	.169**
10 Family–work conflict										.033	0.03
11 Influence											−.170**
12 Bullying											

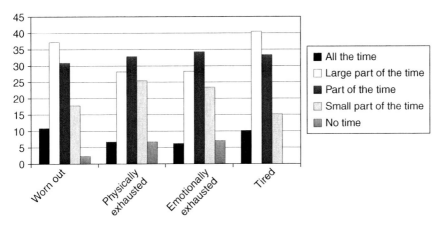

Figure 4.1   Graph showing the responses to the 4 COPSOQ-II burnout scale items. Bars show the percentage of principals in each domain

grouped into one or more of the following: governing board or school council members, state or national educational authorities, formal parent groups, formal teacher groups, formal student groups such as a student representative council, and external examination/accreditation boards. While it would be logical to assume that these groups had particular influence that was logically limited to a subset of school operational decisions such as curriculum and subject choices and school specialization (e.g., a school known for its superior teaching of music, sporting results, or final year student achievement), fundraising activities, or particular expertise (such as legal training), this turns out not to be the case either generally or specifically. An examination of the responses to the following twenty-four items illustrates this point.

For the whole scale Cronbach's alpha coefficient was .713, just within acceptable limits for twenty-four items. However, when these were broken down into their component parts the picture became much less clear. Only three of the four subsets of items related to teaching groups achieved a similar alpha coefficient (see Table 9.4). This suggests that the interrelationship between stakeholder groups' influence in each of the decision areas (staffing, budgeting, instruction, assessment) is both dynamic and wide ranging. Many principals have related that the intended influence from each group is often in opposing directions, making every decision a compromise and with residual bad feelings, hurts, and in the worst case grudges to contend with at a later date. The sense of boundary-spanning is never far from principals' consciousness, as are the micro political implications of nearly all decisions. This also paves the way for inappropriate attempts to influence principals' decisions. Table 9.5 and Table 9.6 display the correlations between influencers and outcomes. What is disturbing is the level of negative influence: bullying by colleagues, parents, and students, along with threats of and actual

Table 9.5   Survey items related to external influences on principals' decision making

Item	
State or national education authorities influence	
1	Staffing decisions
2	Budgeting decisions
3	Instructional content decisions
4	Assessment practices decisions
The schools governing board/councilinfluence	
5	Staffing decisions
6	Budgeting decisions
7	Instructional content decisions
8	Assessment practices decisions
Parent groupsinfluence	
9	Staffing decisions
10	Budgeting decisions
11	Instructional content decisions
12	Assessment practices decisions
Teacher groupsinfluence	
13	Staffing decisions
14	Budgeting decisions
15	Instructional content decisions
16	Assessment practices decisions
Parent groupsinfluence	
17	Staffing decisions
18	Budgeting decisions
19	Instructional content decisions
20	Assessment practices decisions
External examination boards influence	
21	Staffing decisions
22	Budgeting decisions
23	Instructional content decisions
24	Assessment practices decisions

physical violence from students and parents. These represent a great cause for concern and indicate a worrying shift in societal values. From these tables it appears that school principals are suffering considerable hardships.

Important Questions and Future Directions

The important questions that need urgent attention are the underlying causes of principals' suffering revealed in the correlation tables. The multiple

Table 9.6 Cronbach's alpha coefficients for the influences on school operational decisions displaying poor internal consistency

Subscale Items	α
School board	.494
Parent group	.360
Teaching group	.721
Teacher groups influence Assessment practices decisions	
Teacher groups influence Instructional content decisions	
Teacher groups influence Budgeting decisions	
Student group	.453
External examination board/authority	.560

boundary-spanning that principals are constantly engaged with, in a highly charged, high-stakes accountability environment, may hold significant clues to this and are valuable areas to be researched. The new ways of envisioning the work of school leadership as boundary-spanning is likely to be generative of new ways to investigate the complexity of the role along with the positive and negative personal consequences of undertaking it.

We should no longer assume that there will be schools that continue into the future as they have done up till now. The outdated school model based on heroic leadership is unsustainable in today's educational milieu and those who are currently in the role are showing too many signs of strain for the system to remain sustainable.

NOTES

1. "Analysis Terminable and Interminable"
2. Full details are available from www.principalhealth.org.

REFERENCES

Barth, Roland S. 2001. *Learning by heart.* San Francisco: Jossey-Bass.

Berliner, David. 2012. "Confusing assessment with testing and quantification: The overzealous promotion of value-added assessment of teachers." Paper read at the Joint Australian Association for Research in Education and Asia-Pacific Education Research Association Conference World Education Research Association Focal Meeting: Regional and Global Cooperation in Educational Research, Dec 2–6, at University of Sydney.

Bibby, Tamara. 2010. *Education—an 'Impossible Profession'? Psychoanalytic explorations of learning and classrooms.* Hoboken, NJ: Taylor & Francis.

Boden, Rebecca, and Debbie Epstein. 2006. "Managing the research imagination? Globalisation and research in higher education." *Globalisation, Societies and Education* no. 4 (2):223–236. doi: 10.1080/14767720600752619.

Bronfenbrenner, Urie. 1977. "Toward an experimental ecology of human development." *American Psychologist* no. 32 (7):513–531.

Campbell, Donald T. 1976. *Assessing the impact of planned social change.* Hanover, NH: The Public Affairs Center, Dartmouth College.

Danhof-Pont, Marie Bernardine, Tineke van Veen, and Frans G. Zitman. 2011. "Biomarkers in burnout: A systematic review." *Journal of Psychosomatic Research* no. 70 (6):505–524. doi: http://dx.doi.org/10.1016/j.jpsychores.2010.10.012.

Delores, Jacques, Inam Al Mufti, Isao Amagi, Roberto Carneiro, Fay Chung, Bronislaw Geremek, et al. 1998. "Learning: The treasure within." In *Report to UNESCO of the International Commission on Education for the Twenty-first Century.* Paris: UNESCO.

Diamond, Michael A. 1986. "Resistance to change: A psychoanalytic critique of Argyris and Schon's contributions to organization theory and intervention." *Journal of Management Studies* no. 23 (5):543–562.

Egan, Keiran. 2002. *Getting it wrong from the beginning: Our progressivist inheritance from Herbert Spencer, John Dewey, and Jean Piaget.* New Haven, CT: Yale University Press.

Freud, Sigmund, James Strachey, Anna Freud, and Angela Richards. 1953. *The standard edition of the complete psychological works of Sigmund Freud.* 24 vols. London: Hogarth Press.

Gallant, Andrea, and Philip Riley. 2013. "The emotional labour of the aspirant leader: Traversing school politics." In *Emotion in schools: Understanding the hidden curriculum that influences teaching, learning and social relationships,* edited by Melissa Newberry, Andrea Gallant and Philip Riley, 81–97. Bingley: Emerald Group.

Gronn, Peter. 1999. "Substituting for Leadership: The Neglected Role of the Leadership Couple." *Leadership Quarterly* no. 10 (1):41.

———. 2003. "Leadership: Who needs it?" *School Leadership & Management* no. 23 (3):267–291. doi: 10.1080/1363243032000112784.

Kegan, Robert, and Lisa Laskow Lahey. 2001. *Seven languages for transformation: How the way we talk can change the way we work.* San Francisco: Jossey-Bass.

Kelchtermans, Geert, and L Piot. 2013 "Living the Janus Head: Conceptualizing leaders and leadership in schools in the 21st century." In *Back to the Future: Legacies, Continuities and Changes in Educational Policy, Practice and Research,* edited by M. A. Flores, A. A. Carvalho, F. I. Ferreira and T. Vilaça. Rotterdam: Sense.

Kelchtermans, Geert. 2005. "Teachers' emotions in educational reforms: Self-understanding, vulnerable commitment and micropolitical literacy." *Teaching and Teacher Education* no. 21 (8):995–1006. doi: http://dx.doi.org/10.1016/j.tate.2005.06.009.

Kerr, S., and J. Jermier. 1978. "Substitutes for leadership: their meaning and measurement." *Organizational Behavior and Human Performance* no. 22:374–403.

Leithwood, Kenneth, and Christopher Day. 2007. "Starting with what we know." In *Successful Principal Leadership in Times of Change,* edited by Christopher Day and Kenneth Leithwood, 1–15. Dordrecht: Springer.

Mayseless, Ofra, and Micha Popper. 2007. "Reliance on leaders and social institutions: An attachment perspective." *Attachment & Human Development* no. 9 (1):73–93.

Nichols, Sharon L., and David C. Berliner. 2007. "Collateral damage: How high-stakes testing corrupts America's schools." Cambridge, MA: Harvard Education Press.

Oxford University Press. *Oxford English dictionary*. Oxford University Press. Available from http://ezproxy.lib.monash.edu.au/login?url=http://www.oed.com.

Pejtersen, Jan Hyld, Tage Sondergard Kristensen, Vilhelm Borg, and Jakob Bue Bjorner. 2010. "The second version of the Copenhagen Psychosocial Questionnaire." *Scandinavian Journal of Public Health* no. 38 (Suppl 3):8–24. doi: http://dx.doi.org/10.1177/1403494809349858.

Popper, Micha. 2012. *Fact and fantasy about leadership*. Cheltenham, UK: Edward Elgar.

Popper, Micha, and Ofra Mayseless. 2003. "Back to basics: applying a parenting perspective to transformational leadership." *The Leadership Quarterly* no. 14 (1):41–65.

Purkiss, Roslyn B, and Rossi, Robert J. (2007). Sense of community: A vital link between leadership and wellbeing in the workplace. In Alan Glendon, Briony M Thompson, and Brett Myors (eds.), *Advances in organisational psychology* (281–300). Bowen Hills: Australian Academic Press.

Riley, Philip. 2009. "Love teaching or teaching for love? An exploration of unconscious motivation". Paper read at Australian Association for Research in Education Annual Conference: Inspiring Innovative Research in Education Nov 29th–Dec 3rd, at Canberra.

———. 2011. *Attachment theory and the teacher–student relationship: A practical guide for teachers, teacher educators and school leaders*. London: Routledge.

———. 2012. "The Australian School Principal Health and Wellbeing Survey: 2011 results." Paper read at 47th APS Annual Conference: Psychology Addressing the Challenges of the Modern Age, Sept 27–30, at Perth Convention and Exhibition Centre.

Riley, Philip, and Janice Langan-Fox. 2013. "Bullying, stress and health in school principals and medical professionals: Experiences at the 'front-line.'" In *Human frailties: Wrong turns on the road to success*, edited by Ronald Burke, Cary L. Cooper, and Suzy Fox. London: Gower.

Ritzer, George. 1983. "The 'McDonaldization' of society." *Journal of American Culture* no. 6 (1):100–107. doi: 10.1111/j.1542–734X.1983.0601_100.x.

Romi, Shlomo, Ramon Lewis, Joel Roache, and Philip Riley. 2011. "The impact of teachers' aggressive management techniques on students' attitudes to schoolwork." *The Journal of Educational Research* no. 104 (4):231–240.

Sizer, Theodore R. 1984. *Horace's compromise: The dilemma of the American high school: The first report from A Study of High Schools, co-sponsored by the National Association of Secondary School Principals and the Commission on Educational Issues of the National Association of Independent Schools*. Boston: Houghton Mifflin.

Wolcott, H. F. 1973. *Man in the principal's office: An ethnography*. New York: Holt, Rinehart and Winston.

10 Boundary-Spanning Leadership in an Interdependent World

Charles J. Palus, Donna L. Chrobot-Mason, and Kristin L. Cullen

INTRODUCTION

Boundaries in the workplace are experienced in two different ways. They may be experienced as conflict-ridden *barriers* that limit human potential, restrict innovation, and stifle organizational and societal change. Or, boundaries may also be experienced as new *frontiers* at the intersection of ideas and cultures, where breakthrough possibilities reside.

This chapter describes a framework based on research and leadership best practices to illustrate that, under the right conditions, boundaries can be transformed from divisive to productive. This framework is effective at the intersection where, very often, managers and leaders experience boundaries that block progress. For example, it may occur when a team leader finds that she cannot encourage her geographically dispersed managers to form a cohesive and effective group; or, when the director of an inner-city service organization finds that issues around race, culture, and ethnicity get in the way of collaboration. Gone are the days when people work primarily *within* an intact group, in which leaders and followers share interests and identity in a single common culture. Today, one must lead and also participate in shared leadership, *across* groups, at the junctures where wide-ranging experience, diverse expertise, and varied identities intersect (Chrobot-Mason, Ruderman, and Nishii 2013).

In this chapter, we describe a way of understanding such boundary-spanning challenges, and we illustrate this through diverse cases. We provide strategies, practices, and tools that have proven effective in boundary-spanning leadership. First, we describe the emergent challenges of leading in an increasingly complex and interdependent world. Then, we present the five types of boundaries that leaders often face: vertical, horizontal, stakeholder, demographic, and geographic. Following that, we describe the boundary-spanning leadership model and its six practices—buffering, reflecting, connecting, mobilizing, weaving, and transforming—followed by a case study that shows how one company used these practices to achieve what we call the Nexus

Effect—the heart of the boundary-spanning framework. Finally, we provide a set of tools and techniques for anyone confronted with a difficult boundary issue.

The information in this chapter is based on the experiences of leaders who participated in two Center for Creative Leadership (CCL; Greensboro, North Carolina) research projects—the Leadership Across Differences (LAD) project, and survey data from top-level executives who participated in CCL's Leadership at the Peak program. The database for LAD includes over 2,800 survey responses, 289 interviews, and a wide range of secondary data such as media reports and organizational communications from around the world. The goal of the research was to address the following question: What are the leadership processes by which organizations create shared direction, alignment, and commitment across groups of people with very different histories, perspectives, values, and cultures? Data were gathered from six regions: Africa, Asia, Europe, Middle East, North America, and South America.

The second project, involving 128 Leadership at the Peak participants, refined the results of the LAD research. These top leaders were surveyed on pressing trends and challenges, the role of leadership in spanning boundaries, and the types of boundaries leaders face in creating shared direction, alignment, and commitment across their entire organization. The leaders we surveyed believe that strategic boundaries are not being negotiated effectively. Out of the 128 senior executives we surveyed, 86 percent told us that it is "extremely important" that they collaborate effectively across boundaries in their current leadership roles. But just 7 percent of those executives believed they were "very effective" at doing so—a 79 percent gap (Yip, Ernst, and Campbell 2009). Further, 92 percent of senior executives said that the ability to collaborate across boundaries became more important as they moved from middle- to senior-level management. Failure to make this shift can make the difference between success and derailment.

The boundary challenges these executives face include:

- Driving innovation across the organization by cross-fertilizing ideas.
- Aligning resources and actions across groups in matrix structures.
- Coordinating headquarters and regional offices.
- Breaking down silos between enterprises for strategic integration.
- Partnering with clients, constituents, and suppliers to bring new products to market.
- Adapting a new technology that requires new ways of working.

The clear message from the leaders who participated in our research is that within a highly interdependent and flat world, boundary-spanning is the new critical work of leadership.

LEADERSHIP IN AN INTERDEPENDENT WORLD

Globalization continues to connect competitors and collaborators in a single market. The world has become flat (Friedman 2005). Everything and everyone is—or can be—connected. Unfortunately, while the speed of digital communications and the pace of business increase, relational barriers remain mostly unchanged, and humanity continues to experience deep divides. Consider the hurdles faced by those who manage functionally diverse teams across levels of management with a variety of partners in several countries. Their jobs are made easier by technological advances that close gaps in distance, expertise, and knowledge. But at the same time, these leaders are confronted with rifts among organizational silos, bitterness between historical enemies, culture clashes, turf battles, and generation gaps. Such boundaries invite conflict, limit performance, and stifle innovation. On this flat, yet divided leadership landscape, the enormous challenges we face—climate change, war, disease, poverty, injustice—can only be solved by groups working collaboratively. This reality challenges the traditional "leader-follower" paradigm in which a single individual sets goals and followers achieve said goals.

The Center for Creative Leadership defines leadership in terms of three types of outcomes resulting from social processes in a collective (Drath et al. 2008). *Direction* is indicated by agreement on what the collective is trying to achieve. *Alignment* exists when activities are coordinated and integrated in service of the shared direction. *Commitment* is evident when individuals make the success of the collective a priority. Leadership development, in this framework, focuses on building the capability to produce these outcomes.

Boundary-spanning leadership is the capability to create DAC across boundaries in service of a higher vision or goal. By enacting six leadership practices, people work together to create DAC between groups to achieve collective outcomes. These practices are enacted during the interactions of people across groups, teams, functions, units, organizations, and within broader communities and social networks. Boundary-spanning leaders are catalysts of these interactions, and their role is to create the opportunity—the resources, legitimacy, and "headroom" to think and act differently within the broader culture—for these practices to occur (McGuire and Rhodes 2009).

The underlying rationale for mastering these practices is about the need to develop more interdependent forms of leadership (Drath, Palus, and McGuire 2010; Palus, McGuire, and Ernst 2012). There is an evolution in theory and practice underway in which leadership is increasingly understood less in terms of "heroic" individuals (Bones 2011), and more as a process shared by people in a wide variety of ways (Denis, Langley, and Sergi 2012; Drath et al. 2008; Uhl-Bien and Ospina 2012). Leadership happens *among* and *between*—between a leader and a follower, among teammates, between a group and another group or across functional silos, between two organizations working in partnership, and among larger societies or systems seeking to solve problems.

Interdependent leadership is a social system for producing DAC under the guiding belief that leadership is a collective activity requiring mutual inquiry and adaptation in the face of complex challenges. Interdependent leadership can be understood as a later stage in a progression of cultural development, preceded (and informed) by the beliefs and practices of *dependent* leadership (guided by tradition and authority) and then *independent* leadership (guided by expertise and achievement; Palus, McGuire, and Ernst 2012; Torbert 2004).

The organizations we have studied that are developing more interdependent forms of leadership (McCauley et al. 2008; McGuire and Palus 2013) have expanded from *leader* development focused on the character and competence of individuals, to *leadership* development focused on the cultural beliefs and practices for creating direction, alignment, and commitment. Creating shared DAC across boundaries—the art of boundary-spanning leadership—is a key aspect of the broader topic of interdependent leadership development.

THE BOUNDARY-SPANNING LEADERSHIP MODEL: FIVE TYPES OF BOUNDARIES AND SIX BOUNDARY-SPANNING PRACTICES

Based on the experiences of leaders and managers who successfully navigated difficult boundary challenges as well as the latest research and writing on this topic, we have identified five types of boundaries that challenge leaders and six practices that enable boundary-spanning leadership. In this section, we describe how through the six practices, it is possible to transform borders that limit progress into new frontiers that instead facilitate leaders in their efforts to solve problems, create innovative solutions, and transform organizations—skills that are critical in a flat world.

The Five Boundaries

Our research revealed that the five most challenging boundaries involve how we define ourselves and the groups we belong to.

The first type, *vertical* boundaries, are found across levels of hierarchy. Imagine an organization as people living in a house. Vertical boundaries are the floors and ceilings of the house, separating groups according to title, rank, power, and privilege. Common terms within organizations that convey vertical boundaries may include: *span of control, superior/subordinate, top-down/bottom-up,* and *exempt/nonexempt staff.* Span of control, the grouping of lower-level subordinates under a higher-level supervisor, is the traditional approach for managing the boundaries between levels. Yet, today's flat world is transforming vertical boundaries, enabling new levels of interaction up and down the organizational chart. The shifting landscape is redefining the "control" long associated with relationships across vertical boundaries.

The second type, *horizontal* boundaries, are found across organizational functions and units, or when two organizations merge. They are the walls of the organizational house that separate groups laterally according to specialized expertise. Terms within organizations that convey horizontal boundaries include: *division of labor, silos, stovepipes, turf battles, front office/back office,* and *revenue center/cost center.* Managing the boundaries between functional groups originates from the need for division of labor, but is being replaced by the need for integration of labor. Integrating functional groups such as marketing and sales toward a common goal is challenging. Bringing groups together following an organizational merger or acquisition compounds the challenge.

The third type, *stakeholder boundaries,* are the doors and windows of the house, leading outside the organization. Though stakeholders do not reside inside the metaphorical house, they are critical to the success of the organization. In fact, organizations are increasingly tied to a dizzying array of stakeholder groups including but not limited to: shareholders, boards of directors, partners, networks, customers, advocacy groups, governments, and local and global communities. Terms within the organization that illustrate stakeholder boundaries include: *iron curtain, closed doors, enclave, corporate-centric, not our business,* and *insider/outsider.* Stakeholder boundaries have potential to create divides when organizations seek to maximize their individual interests at the exclusion or expense of the interests of their external partners.

Demographic boundaries, the fourth type, are the people living inside the house and represent a variety of social backgrounds and identities, including diversity in gender, race, class, ethnicity, generation, religion, political party, village, and so on. A flat world requires leveraging different knowledge bases and diverse backgrounds as a potent force for value-creating innovation. Demographic boundaries within the organization include: *glass ceilings, generation gaps, diversity divides, ideological battles, identity politics,* and *culture clashes.*

Finally, *geographic* boundaries represent the neighborhood in which the house resides. Such boundaries are defined by physical location and involve groups separated by distance. Terms that suggest geographic boundaries include: *East/West, native/foreign, ecosystems, virtual/face-to-face,* and *regional structure.* Geographic boundaries create constraints when there is a need for collaboration across different locations.

The Boundary-Spanning Leadership Model

In our research we have identified six categories of practices that enable boundary-spanning leadership: *buffering, reflecting, connecting, mobilizing, weaving*, and *transforming*. Three successive strategies for boundary-spanning organize the practices: The initial strategy of *managing boundaries* (featuring the practices of buffering and reflecting) leads to the strategy of *forging common ground* (featuring the practices of connecting and mobilizing), and finally the strategy of *discovering new frontiers* (featuring the practices of weaving and transforming). Figure 10.1, the boundary-spanning model, illustrates the upward spiral of increasing inter-group collaboration. This spiral depicts how the tasks of creating direction, alignment, and commitment (DAC) progress from managing boundaries, to forging common ground, to discovering new frontiers at the nexus between groups.

Through the six boundary-spanning practices, leaders and followers working together with a shared learning mindset can create a Nexus Effect. The Nexus Effect occurs when ideas connect in new ways at the intersection of group boundaries, creating something new, facilitating a significant change, or solving a problem that can only be realized when groups work together. The outcomes thus achieved through inter-group collaboration are greater than what could be achieved if groups worked independently. The Nexus Effect is the ultimate goal of boundary-spanning leadership. When groups collide and feel threatened by their differences, they divide into "us" and "them." The creation of shared DAC becomes further and further out of reach. This effect is so strong and universal that we call it the *Great Divide*. It is the opposite of the Nexus Effect (Figure 10.1) and indicates the

Figure 10.1   The Boundary Spanning Leadership Model

absence or failure of any or all of the six practices. Great Divides can occur along any of the five types of boundaries. Even temporary and arbitrary labels can produce a Great Divide (Chrobot-Mason et al. 2009). It is important to understand that the Great Divide is a perennial part of the human condition and occurs in a variety of situations. However, blaming "them" or "us" for the Great Divide is not productive.

Who we are and how we define ourselves—identity—is at the heart of Great Divides. The identity shared within a group of people serves both to separate them from other groups, and connect members to each other. Identity is formed from the interplay between two basic fundamental human needs—the need for differentiation or uniqueness and the need for integration or belonging (Brewer 2001; Chrobot-Mason et al. 2009). We believe that the reason the five boundaries can be difficult to manage is that they represent differences in identity: not just what people do in their organization but who they are and how they define themselves.

The Six Boundary-Spanning Practices

Boundary-spanning leadership is enabled by the following six practices for producing DAC within and across group boundaries.

Buffering. Buffering is about defining and clarifying group identities *within* each group. It involves the initial shielding or protecting of groups from outside influences or threats. Buffering helps a group define its reasons for being and to develop and maintain a strong sense of identity. The result is that buffering builds *inter-group safety*—the state of psychological security that develops when inter-group boundaries are defined and maintained. People cannot collaborate effectively across boundaries until they first feel protected and safe within their own group. The principle here is to practice differentiation prior to any effort at integration. Many people find this counterintuitive and mistakenly pursue integration before the groups feel sufficiently safe within their own identities. If integration is premature, boundaries become weak or disappear altogether, and the potential contributions from the various distinct identity perspectives are lost. Boundaries serve an important function in organizations and, thus, the first step in boundary-spanning is to manage and clarify boundaries.

One tactic for effective buffering is to deliberately create a unifying team identity. For example, Lisa is a manager at a telecommunications company, tasked with assembling a cross-functional team to roll out a new product line. The new team was frustrated because its members were not sure of the team's purpose or their own roles. Lisa helped the team clarify its mission, inventory their skills and backgrounds, and determine who was responsible for what function or activity. This new clarity helped members feel solid and safe. By buffering the team, Lisa enabled each member to negotiate their work plans with their functional leaders in the organization, facilitating the accomplishment of the team's mission.

Reflecting. This practice enables the experience of seeing each side of a boundary through the vantage point of each of the groups in question. In the same way a mirror casts a reflection for others to see, the practice of reflecting presents each group to the other. It involves sensitizing each group to the others' values and expertise. It illuminates the differences and similarities between the groups and helps each group understand the identity of the other. Groups are able to see the boundary from both sides, come to accept this boundary, and ultimately respect the differences between the groups. The result is *inter-group respect*—a state of inter-group awareness and positive regard that develops when groups understand their similarities and differences. With this practice in place, groups can begin to see common ground in goals and objectives and pave the way for future collaboration.

One tactic for reflecting is to temporarily "stand in each other's shoes" by visiting each others' home turf. Consider the example of Rick Givens, who in 1999 was chairman of the County Board of Commissioners in Chatham, North Carolina. His hometown was experiencing an increase in illegal immigration. Health care and social services were being challenged by the volume of need. Tempers flared and positions polarized. County meetings turned into screaming matches between immigrants and locals. But what happened next changed Rick's view on immigration forever. Rick accepted an invitation to be one of the first participants in a program called the Latino Initiative, which was designed to provide a unique opportunity for educators and community leaders to learn firsthand about Mexican culture. Members actually visited homes and institutions in Mexico. Rick discovered that, like himself and his friends, Mexican immigrants were motivated by the desire to improve the lives of their families. He was genuinely surprised by finding that he shared some deeply held values and beliefs with the immigrants he previously felt were a threat to his family's well-being. Rick returned to North Carolina committed to helping others see what he saw in Mexico. As in this case, reflecting is often a matter of helping the groups really see each other's identities and cultures. Physically visiting each other's locale, and even briefly "standing in each other's shoes," can be very powerful.

Connecting. The practice of connecting creates direct person-to-person linkages. Connecting occurs when individuals temporarily step outside their group identities and step inside a neutral zone where people can interact with one another more directly and personally. When this happens, people suspend, or put on hold, their group identity differences, even if only for a limited time. Over time and sustained interaction, the boundaries that created rigid borders between groups begin to fade into the background. The result is *inter-group trust*—a state of mutual confidence and integrity that develops when boundaries are suspended and new relationships are built.

One tactic for connecting is creating *attractor spaces*. Organizations are full of physical boundaries that divide groups from one another. Physical boundaries organize groups of people with similar work responsibilities in close proximity, but the cost is that they often get in the way of groups that need to be collaborating. To balance these tensions, leaders can create attractor spaces that encourage serendipitous cross-boundary relationships to develop. Take the Googleplex, Google's headquarters in Mountain View, California. Everything from the entry-level town square to the village library beckons employees to leave their computer screens and mingle. Throughout the building, floors are organized into flexible neighborhoods and shared community spaces that make it easy for people to meet across neighborhoods. Employees eat for free in an open cafeteria with a giant whiteboard to capture ideas from emergent conversations.

Mobilizing. This practice seeks to craft common purpose and shared identity across groups. Mobilizing encourages groups to move outside their smaller group identities and to move inside a new, larger, more inclusive shared identity. It enables groups to reframe the differences that divide them in order to work together productively. Leaders reframe boundaries by creating a larger identity (a vision, goal, or task) that is mutually valued and inspires joint action. The result is *inter-group community*—a state of mutual belonging and ownership that develops when boundaries are reframed and collective action taken. Mobilizing is related to connecting in that both practices enable the strategy of forging common ground. The distinction is that connecting builds common ground by breaking down identity differences, whereas mobilizing creates a new and larger identity. Connecting is about suspending the dividing lines between individual group members, while mobilizing is about redrawing the lines to include both groups.

One mobilizing tactic is to craft shared symbols and artifacts to represent "who we are" and "what we believe." Throughout history, symbols, artifacts, and icons have served as powerful media for clans, tribes, cultures, nations, and organizations to represent themselves and express their common identity. Likewise boundary-spanners can draw upon symbolism to create meaning and transcendent purpose. Nelson Mandela forged common ground in many ways as the first president of post-apartheid South Africa. One of his most powerful moves was at the 1995 Rugby World Cup, the year after his election, when racial tensions were profound. International boycotts of the South African rugby team had been inspired by the struggle against apartheid in the country. Mandela, however, instead of using rugby as a stick decided to use it as a carrot. He shocked almost everyone by donning the jersey of the Springboks, the South African national rugby team, when presenting the championship trophy to team captain François Pienaar, an Afrikaner. This simple, yet symbolic, unifying gesture was seen by many as a turning point in national reconciliation.

Weaving. Weaving occurs when group boundaries interlace yet remain distinct. Each group has a unique role or contribution that is integrated in service of a larger whole. To picture weaving, think of an accomplished rug weaver with a loom weaving different threads to create larger patterns and designs. Whereas it is the intersection of colorful threads that enable a weaver to create an intricate rug, it is the nexus where groups collide, intersect, and link that boundary spanners weave a whole new group, while still preserving the integrity of the original threads.

Weaving encourages groups to have their own distinctive identity and purpose ("us" and "them"), and at the same time, to integrate each group within a larger organizational whole ("we"). While weaving meets the need for differentiation by respecting varied experience and expertise, it also meets the need for integration by forming new collaborations across groups with a common purpose. The result is *inter-group interdependence*—a state of collaboration and collective learning that develops when boundaries are interlaced within a larger whole.

Leaders at CRY (Child Rights and You), an organization in India that advocates for underprivileged children, used a weaving tactic to begin transforming their strategy. CRY spans seventeen Indian states and includes vast regional differences in language, ethnicity, religion, and caste. To realize the organizational mission, a new way forward was needed that integrated these variations. In order to unlock unique perspectives and experiences in service of the strategic change the CEO Ingrid Srinath and her team asked people throughout the organization to "bring their differences into the room." Multiple cross-boundary dialogues were held where people representing diverse geographic regions, ethnic and religious groups, and functional groups participated in deep and honest dialogue about the future of the organization. Rather than seen as problems, differences were embraced. This weaving tactic enabled CRY to consider a broader and better range of options to move the organization forward.

Transforming. The sixth and final practice is about *inter-group reinvention*—the state of renewal, alternative futures, and emergent possibilities that develop when inter-group boundaries are crosscut in new directions. It is about what is possible when groups create a new identity and transform the boundaries between them. By crosscutting boundaries, new identities and new possibilities associated with those identities emerge. To crosscut means to cut against the grain or on the bias. Transforming occurs when time and space is provided for members to cut against the grain of their respective boundaries, thereby opening themselves up to change.

When you bring multiple groups together in search of reinvention, each of the tactics described for the previous five practices can be used. Transforming can be thought of as a gestalt, as the integrated totality of the six boundary-spanning practices. It is the explicit intent of transforming that defines it as a practice—to crosscut boundaries of identity in search of new and emergent possibilities. When this occurs, problems that were previously intractable can be resolved, and solutions that felt far beyond reach, become not just viable but fully realizable. This is the Nexus Effect, fully realized.

Butch Peterman, the founder, owner, and president of Abrasive Technology Inc. (ATI), a manufacturer of diamond-based tools, wanted to make his company adaptive to global competition. He also wanted to make it an excellent place to work. His inquiries about the best way to do this led him to transform the company and its culture, from functional silos and a strict division of labor to a customer-focused and process-centered organization based in continuous shared learning. It required asking people at ATI to change how they defined themselves and their company. They tossed out the use of traditional and managerial roles and created nontitled roles around core tasks. All employees were assigned a process and were thought of as associates rather than employees, responsible for both managing the work and developing themselves and others. Today, processes are team-oriented, coach roles have replaced supervisor roles, and horizontal cross training is the norm. ATI has increased performance and customer satisfaction, and decreased turnover rates to near zero. It is a high-performing, adaptive, global business and a great place to work

Developing a More Interdependent Leadership Culture

What if organizations routinely achieved the Nexus Effect to become places where groups confidently collaborate and reinvent themselves within and across all types of boundaries? We have studied a number of organizations developing in this direction. In these organizations, boundary-spanning strategies and practices, and the Nexus Effect itself, are becoming embedded in the cultures of the organizations. As introduced earlier, we call these *interdependent leadership cultures* (McCauley et al. 2008). Sustained efforts at boundary-spanning must move beyond one-at-a-time experiments and become part the organizational DNA. Often this requires transforming the leadership culture (McGuire and Rhodes 2009).

A CASE STUDY OF BOUNDARY-SPANNING IN THE CONTEXT OF DEVELOPING AN INTERDEPENDENT LEADERSHIP CULTURE

To see how the practices can enhance boundary-spanning leadership and begin to transform the leadership culture of an organization, let's look at the case of DriveTime. DriveTime is one of the largest used car retailers in the U.S. (for more information regarding interdependent leadership at DriveTime, see McCauley et al. 2008 and McGuire and Rhodes 2009). In 2002, new owners took control of the company. They saw the potential for long-term value in transforming DriveTime from an old-school used-car company into a well-led, technically excellent, socially responsible, and reliably profitable business. This meant overhauling and integrating a value chain including vehicle sourcing and servicing as well as the financing operation in which DriveTime retains and services each loan. A new CEO, Ray Fidel, was brought in. He and his senior team crafted a vision of a collaborative, interdependent approach to leadership, which they understood as requiring a new mindset and new ways of working for everyone in the organization (Torbert 2004). They regard boundary-spanning and systems integration as keys to the long-term success of the company within a changing and competitive world.

DriveTime has been implementing this vision over a period of years and are now working on a second wave of transformation they call *DriveTime 2.0*. As they move from DriveTime 1.0 to DriveTime 2.0, we talked with Ray and Jon Ehlinger (the CEO and senior vice president) about the lessons they have learned about boundary-spanning leadership. Here are key lessons with respect to each of the six practices.

Buffering: The most basic move in boundary-spanning is to initially strengthen and maintain in-group identity and safety as the foundation for subsequent boundary-spanning. After much experimenting, DriveTime concluded that their performance metrics worked best by primarily rewarding in-group objectives. Attempts to reward people based on companywide or shared metrics were not successful. People tend to be motivated by the metrics which they could achieve through in-group effort. Groups needed to focus on their primary work tasks and basic team-building remained important.

Reflecting: DriveTime co-located Finance and Sales in the dealerships. While each group focuses on their own tasks, their co-location allowed each to see firsthand how the other group functions, and each educates each other regarding their own group. Daily positive interactions led to heightened respect between groups with different objectives and identities.

Connecting: The dealerships used an interactive game called Road Trip to develop employees. Road Trip is a multiplayer business simulation in the form of a board game that engages employees in all aspects of running a DriveTime dealership. By learning side-by-side, in a safe environment, members of each group began to make deeper connections to the other groups, building mutual trust and a shared sense of community and culture.

Mobilizing: DriveTime created a leadership development agenda for all their middle- and upper-level managers called Inside Out. Inside Out is aligned with the business strategy and is about individual and collective leadership development toward a more interdependent culture. Multiday, face-to-face meetings were interspersed with individual and group coaching. The purpose of Inside Out is to engage each person's inner development as a human being ("inside") as an underlying engine of growth and change, and to connect this inner personal development with the new corporate strategy and culture ("out"). According to the CEO, Ray, the intent of Inside Out is "to create free thinkers, bigger minds, and headroom for an interdependent culture." Inside Out regional and national gatherings were the first time that many managers experienced the company as a whole community and not just in terms of their group or region.

Weaving: DriveTime uses an agile project methodology called *Scrum* (see for example www.controlchaos.com). Scrum, originally developed in software development, uses collaborative, cross-functional, rapidly responding teams to develop and implement projects when requirements are complex and shifting. Scrum encourages interdependence by being open to formal and informal testing and revision from all over the organization (www. pmdoi.org). In essence, scrum builds learning and problem solving into daily work. A key innovation at DriveTime was the use of Scrum for all kinds of projects, not just for information technology. The boundary-spanning practice of weaving is how new frontiers in the work are realized, and where innovation occurs.

Transforming: Transforming the company and its leadership culture into a new and better kind of organization had always been the vision of the management team. Yet the vision took time to coalesce and required the shared work of leaders all across the company. The very first steps were more about bookkeeping and housecleaning rather than transformation. A lot of employees were not interested in, nor capable of, this vision of a better kind of used car company. Trust needed to be built, and boundaries needed to be managed, before transformation could be possible. Now, over ten years into the journey, they are in the second big wave of transformation, the movement from DriveTime 1.0 to 2.0. According to Ray and Jon, being at something like version 1.5 or "halfway" is an especially difficult place because the previous beliefs and practices are outmoded, and the new culture and systems have yet to be realized. The preparation for this place of development lies in having gone through the journey all the way from buffering, to reflecting and connecting, to mobilizing the entire community, and reweaving old boundaries. Transformation in the boundary-spanning model is the last phase. It is also the first step. For organizations, having the intentional strategy of transformation at the outset is invaluable in providing direction, alignment, and commitment (DAC) for integrating the strategies and practices of boundary-spanning leadership.

HOW TO SPAN BOUNDARIES: TOOLS AND TACTICS

Now let's talk about putting these ideas into action through the use of tools and tactics.

The first tactic is simply to have a *perspective* of boundary-spanning leadership. Awareness comes before action. It is important to learn to *see* this territory of boundaries, bridges, and frontiers and to pay attention to potential collaborative opportunities with a fresh eye. You should begin to recognize, as visible features in your own communities and organizations, the five boundary types and the three main strategies for spanning them.

Boundary-spanning leadership is a social, participatory process. The tools for boundary-spanning leadership typically require group facilitation, using best practices from the fields of organization development and change leadership (e.g., Burke 2002; McGuire and Rhodes 2009). Begin by identifying a particular challenge in your organization or community that requires boundary-spanning leadership. Such challenges may initially be framed around a variety of inter-group issues or symptoms such as:

- Building respect and trust between groups
- Clarifying goals within and across groups
- Aligning resources and actions across groups
- Blending different work cultures and creating shared values across groups

Next, review each of the boundary types and consider which boundaries are most relevant to your challenge. What levels of hierarchy are key to this challenge? What departments or groups are involved, or need to be? Are there external people such as customers or suppliers who need to be included? Which demographics, and geographies, are relevant?

Based on our research findings, we have created a tool called Boundary Explorer™ to help people understand and begin to apply the concepts of boundary-spanning leadership (Ernst, Reinhold, Palus, and Horth 2010). It helps facilitate an initial experience of the five boundary types, three strategies, six practices, and dozens of tactics for enabling leadership across boundaries. Boundary Explorer is a compact deck of cards providing the concepts as both text and visual images to inspire productive conversations around the strategies, practices, and tactics for spanning boundaries.

Then, identify the boundary-spanning leadership strategies and practices that are most relevant to the challenge. Figure 10.2 provides a diagnostic tool for assessing which practices are strengths and which may need further facilitation and development. Clarify the strategy you need to pursue. Do you need to create safety and foster respect? Then your strategy is to manage boundaries through buffering and reflecting. Is your goal to build trust and develop ownership? Turn to the connecting and mobilizing tactics that help forge common ground. If the foundation has been set, then greater interdependence and reinvention—discovering new frontiers—is possible.

Now that you know which boundaries are involved, and which practice areas need attention, you are prepared to consider specific tactics. These are always customized to the situation (see Table 10.1).

Start simply. Begin with a tactic or two that feels easy to introduce and execute. Don't "launch" a boundary-spanning campaign. Begin where you can, find some allies, tap into the power of networks, and build on your successes. Remember that a particular tactic may not always work with your group or situation. Don't be afraid to experiment. Modify our suggestions or make up your own tactics.

How well are you and your group working across the boundaries associated with this challenge? Please take a moment to reflect on the extent to which you and others in your group take the following actions.

Scale: 1 (To a very little extent), 2 (To a little extent), 3 (To some extent), 4 (To a great extent), and 5 (To a very great extent).

	My Personal Effectiveness	My Group's Effectiveness
Buffering		
Protects the work group from external interference and demands.	1 2 3 4 5	1 2 3 4 5
Appropriately filters communication into and out of the work group.	1 2 3 4 5	1 2 3 4 5
Clearly defines roles and responsibilities of group members.	1 2 3 4 5	1 2 3 4 5
Clarifies boundaries to accurately differentiate the work of different organizational groups.	1 2 3 4 5	1 2 3 4 5
Reflecting		
Sensitizes groups to each other's needs and priorities.	1 2 3 4 5	1 2 3 4 5
Facilitates the exchange of information and viewpoints across group lines.	1 2 3 4 5	1 2 3 4 5
Serves as an ambassador between groups by representing the unique perspective of one group to others.	1 2 3 4 5	1 2 3 4 5
Helps members of different groups surface assumptions and beliefs about one another.	1 2 3 4 5	1 2 3 4 5
Connecting		
Creates links between members of separate organizational groups.	1 2 3 4 5	1 2 3 4 5
Creates a welcoming environment for group members to get to know each other on a personal level.	1 2 3 4 5	1 2 3 4 5
Builds social networks across the organization.	1 2 3 4 5	1 2 3 4 5
Provides opportunities for individuals to discover commonalities across group lines.	1 2 3 4 5	1 2 3 4 5
Mobilizing		
Develops an inclusive vision and shared goals.	1 2 3 4 5	1 2 3 4 5
Pushes groups to set aside their differences and work for the common good.	1 2 3 4 5	1 2 3 4 5

(*Continued*)

	My Personal Effectiveness	My Group's Effectiveness
Acts as a catalyst for collective action.	1 2 3 4 5	1 2 3 4 5
Inspires group members to focus on a unifying vision.	1 2 3 4 5	1 2 3 4 5
Weaving		
Creates opportunities for groups to work interdependently with one another to achieve a common goal.	1 2 3 4 5	1 2 3 4 5
Combines unique contributions of groups as a source for innovation.	1 2 3 4 5	1 2 3 4 5
Creatively reconciles conflict between people to uncover new solutions.	1 2 3 4 5	1 2 3 4 5
Creates opportunities for groups to integrate their distinct resources to achieve greater success.	1 2 3 4 5	1 2 3 4 5
Transforming		
Encourages separate groups to reinvent how they work together when a new direction is required.	1 2 3 4 5	1 2 3 4 5
Actively seeks to transform the way diverse groups work collaboratively across the organization.	1 2 3 4 5	1 2 3 4 5
Is able to transform conflicting groups into collaborative groups.	1 2 3 4 5	1 2 3 4 5
Creates an environment where deeply held values, beliefs, and perspectives are open to change.	1 2 3 4 5	1 2 3 4 5

Scoring: For your ratings, add scores for each item set and place the combined number in the appropriate cell below (Range = 4–20).

	4–8 Area for development		9–14 Area for continuous improvement		15–20 Area of strength	
	Self	Group	Self	Group	Self	Group
Buffering						
Reflecting						
Connecting						
Mobilizing						
Weaving						
Transforming						

Figure 10.2   A Tool for Assessing Boundary-Spanning Leadership.
Source: Adapted from the *Boundary Spanning Leadership Toolkit*. Reinhold, D., C. Ernst, and C. J. Palus. 2012. Greensboro, NC: Center for Creative Leadership.

Table 10.1 Examples of Boundary-Spanning Tactics.

	Vertical Boundaries (Hierarchical levels and ranks)	Horizontal Boundaries (Functions, units, disciplines)	Stakeholder Boundaries (Partners, suppliers, customers, communities)	Demographic Boundaries (Gender, age, culture, ethnicity, education, ideology)	Geographic Boundaries (Locations, regions, languages, markets)
			MANAGING BOUNDARIES		
Buffering— Monitor and protect the flow of information and resources across groups to define boundaries and build inter-group safety.	Remind people of formal vertical communication channels for vital information flows. Hold strong when agendas are competing. Embrace that "No" is not a dirty word. Push back respectfully. Champion the ideas and priorities of your group to senior management.	Prepare a team charter of roles and responsibilities. Share it with others in the organization. Create time and space for your group to define themselves. Develop realistic expectations with other groups about what your group can and can't do.	Specify rules of engagement that specify how your team and an external team will interact during a joint venture. Create communities of practice that include stakeholders.	Sponsor demographic affinity groups so that nondominant and cultural groups have an opportunity to network and share in-group experiences.	Build a buffer between your team and headquarters if agendas are competing. Make decision rights explicit regarding who is the decision maker, under what conditions.

Reflecting—*Represent distinct perspectives and encourage knowledge exchange across groups to understand boundaries and foster inter-group respect.*					
	Initiate a meeting with senior management to facilitate advocating upward the ideas generated by employees. Facilitate a "fishbowl" dialogue with an inner circle of execs talking with each other and an outer circle of managers listening. Report out and reverse the circles.	Meet with other groups for the purpose of sharing your charters (etc.) with each other. Practice "standing in the others' shoes" by asking your group "how would other teams, units, or organizations think about this?"	Arrange field trips for your team to visit customers. Document what is observed as it relates to an organizational challenge. Invite a partner group to "shadow" your organization for a day; then do the same with theirs. Share your observations with each other.	When an issue comes up that involves race, gender, or religion, consider making it a teachable moment in order to learn about differences and unique perspectives. Ask thought-provoking questions to unlock the different values and assumptions between groups.	Encourage international business travelers to add an extra day to their trip to hit the streets and experience the culture. Ask them to share their observations at a team meeting. When traveling to another location, take something from your local area like cheese or chocolate to share with colleagues at their location. Encourage them to do the same when they come to visit.

(*Continued*)

Table 10.1 (Continued)

	Vertical Boundaries (Hierarchical levels and ranks)	Horizontal Boundaries (Functions, units, disciplines)	Stakeholder Boundaries (Partners, suppliers, customers, communities)	Demographic Boundaries (Gender, age, culture, ethnicity, education, ideology)	Geographic Boundaries (Locations, regions, languages, markets)
		FORGING COMMON GROUND			
Connecting— Link people and bridge divided groups to suspend boundaries and build inter-group trust.	Host a lunch picnic to bring people together from different levels of the organization. Pair up individuals who do not know each other.	Create more "third spaces"—corners, conversation nooks, cafes, and meeting places that bring groups together on neutral ground. Link two or three people who don't normally bump into one another, but should.	Rotate meetings with a key vendor between your site and theirs. When visiting their site, request time for "putting names with faces" by having your team walk around and meet people. Network with people in adjacent industries, emerging economies, or as a volunteer in your community.	Mix it up outside the office and get people of different generations, races, or nationalities together for a sporting event. Do a walk-a-thon or build a Habitat house together with staff and families.	Reserve the first 15 minutes of your regular virtual meeting for relationship building—spend time sharing personal milestones, news, or updates of interest. Create a global Facebook page or team blog.

(Continued)

Mobilizing— *Craft common purpose and shared identity acrossgroups to reframe boundaries and develop inter-group community.*	Establish "skip level" meetings for your staff to have conversations with your manager about goals and strategy.	Following a merger, get people from the same functions in the two organizations together and craft a new mission. Collect and share organizational stories that demonstrate shared identity and purpose.	Articulate a goal that your organization and another organization can partner around in order to beat a common competitor.	Identify a core set of organizational values that are inclusive and motivating for all demographic groups.	Install shared organizational symbols, wall hangings, and icons in all your offices that build community and represent your organization at its best anywhere in the world.

DISCOVERING NEW FRONTIERS

Weaving— *Draw out and integrate group differences within a larger whole to interlace boundaries and advance inter-group interdependence.*	Debrief a shared accomplishment by bringing people together across levels to discuss success factors. Continuously implement simple, small-scale projects for divergent groups across levels to gain experience at low-risk interdependent tasks.	Bring together conflicting groups to articulate their differences and then explore ways to creatively reconcile them by integrating their work. Facilitate quick movement of people in and out of project teams as needs arise and priorities shift.	Integrate the unique strengths of your organization and an organization in a different sector (e.g., nonprofit, government agency) to solve a shared problem in your community. Practice "diversity in counsel, unity in command" (Cyrus the Great)—challenge openly, debate furiously, then decide and act as one.	Bring different demographic groups together to talk about market needs and trends within their respective groups, and how the organization could create new products to serve them.	Develop "glocal" solutions—draw and integrate *global* best practices within your company and *local* market knowledge to envision new products, services, or internal processes. Seat members of globally diverse groups at the same tables for a an idea think-tank.

Table 10.1 *(Continued)*

	Vertical Boundaries (Hierarchical levels and ranks)	Horizontal Boundaries (Functions, units, disciplines)	Stakeholder Boundaries (Partners, suppliers, customers, communities)	Demographic Boundaries (Gender, age, culture, ethnicity, education, ideology)	Geographic Boundaries (Locations, regions, languages, markets)
Transforming— *Bring multiple groups together in emergent, new directions to crosscut boundaries and enable inter-group reinvention.*	Bring members of your network together who represent different levels. Facilitate a dialogue about how they see the business and explore unconventional ideas.	Host "alternative future conversations." Invite anyone in the organization to attend; provide no agenda other than to imagine the ideal, transformed organization 5 years from now. Target old boundaries that forever impede collaboration; they deserve to be "nixed" or "reinvented."	Strike a small-scale partnership with your #1 competitor— explore new, collaborative frontiers that could be discovered together.	Create action-learning teams with "maximum diversity" (e.g., age, gender, race, culture, education) to develop business plans of entirely new markets or services than your organization currently offers.	Get the whole system in the room— bring together a large cross-section of key leaders from around the world once a year to envision "game-changing" opportunities.

Adapted from: Ernst, C., and D. Chrobot-Mason. 2010. Boundary Spanning Leadership: Six Practices for Solving Problems, Driving Innovation and Transforming Organizations. New York: McGraw-Hill Professional.

CONCLUSION

Our approach to boundary-spanning requires new behaviors in which to engage and new concepts necessary to understand. Boundary-spanning leadership is generally a change in leadership style for most, if not all, who undertake this approach. We have learned many lessons from our own experiences in organizations and from the participants in our studies. In conclusion, we offer some key lessons here that we hope will serve as guides for those who embark on a program to develop boundary-spanning leadership and more interdependent leadership cultures.

- Focusing on *differences* first seems counterintuitive to achieve boundary-spanning, and yet our work tells us this is critical. Understanding, honoring, and valuing differences must happen first before common ground can be found. Organizations seem to naturally want to focus on common ground first and yet doing so often backfires.
- It can be difficult to step into that space in which groups collide, because this is uncomfortable for most of us; it involves conflict and tension. And yet, this is exactly the place we need to spend time in to achieve greater innovation. Leaders need to step into that uncomfortable space and get more comfortable there. It is important to learn from each attempt at boundary-spanning, and to incorporate those lessons into subsequent efforts. Strategies, practices, and tactics must be shaped by experience. Failures must be taken in stride, without recrimination, and the lessons applied to further efforts.
- This kind of leadership development takes time. The transition to more interdependent leadership through boundary-spanning is not a process that happens overnight.
- Interdependent leadership development requires intentional alignment with the business strategy of the organization. Organizational systems, structures, and processes must be strategically integrated in ways that are supportive of collaborative, interdependent work.
- Finally, we observe that models of leadership emphasizing heroic, independent leadership are pervasive. Although people espouse ideas about shared leadership, they often revert to older and more deeply embedded views and practices. Time and practice are needed to learn the mindsets and skills necessary for boundary-spanning.

ACKNOWLEDGEMENTS

Chris Ernst, David Magellan Horth, Diane Reinhold, Jerry Abrams, the Leadership Across Differences Team, and the Boundary Spanning Leadership Community of Practice for their many contributions to the ideas described in this chapter..

REFERENCES AND ADDITIONAL READINGS

Bones, C. 2011. *The Cult of the Leader: A Manifesto for More Authentic Business.* New York: Wiley.

Brewer, M. B. 2001. "The Social Self: On Being the Same and Different at the Same Time." In *Intergroup Relations: Essential Readings*, edited by M.A. Hogg and D. Abrams, 245–253. New York: Psychology Press.

Burke, W. W. 2002. *Organization Change: Theory and Practice.* Thousand Oaks, CA: Sage Publications.

Chrobot-Mason, D., C. Ernst, and J. Ferguson. 2012. Boundary Spanning as Battle Rhythm. *Center for Creative Leadership White Paper Series.* Greensboro, NC: Center for Creative Leadership.

Chrobot-Mason, D., M. N. Ruderman, and L. Nishii. 2013. "Leadership in a Diverse Workplace." In *The Oxford Handbook of Diversity and Work*, edited by Q. Roberson, 315–340. New York: Oxford University Press.

Chrobot-Mason, D., M. N. Ruderman, T. J. Weber, and C. Ernst. 2009. "The Challenge of Leading on Unstable Ground: Triggers that Activate Social Identity Faultlines." *Human Relations* 14: 1763–1794.

Cross, R., C. Ernst, and W. Pasmore. 2013. A Bridge Too Far? How Boundary Spanning Networks Drive Organizational Change and Effectiveness. *Organizational Dynamics.* 42(2). 81–91.

Denis, J-L, A. Langley, and V. Sergi. 2012. "Leadership in the Plural." *The Academy of Management Annals.* http://dx.doi.org/10.1080/19416520.2012.667612

Drath, W. H., C. McCauley, C. J. Palus, E. Van Velsor, P. M. G. O'Connor, and J. B. McGuire. 2008. "Direction, Alignment, Commitment: Toward a More Integrative Ontology of Leadership." *Leadership Quarterly* 19, 635–653.

Drath, W. H., C. J. Palus, and J. B. McGuire. 2010. "Developing Interdependent Leadership." In *The Center for Creative Leadership Handbook of Leadership Development*, 3rd ed., edited by C. D. McCauley, E. Van Velsor, and M. N. Ruderman, 405–428. San Francisco: Jossey-Bass Wiley.

Ernst, C., and D. Chrobot-Mason. 2010. *Boundary Spanning Leadership: Six Practices for Solving Problems, Driving Innovation and Transforming Organizations.* New York: McGraw-Hill Professional.

Ernst, C., and D. Chrobot-Mason. 2011. "Flat World, Hard Boundaries: How to Lead Across Them." *MIT Sloan Management Review* 52 (Spring): 81–88.

Ernst, C., D. Reinhold, C. J. Palus, and D. M. Horth. 2010. *Boundary Explorer Facilitator's Guide.* Greensboro, NC: Center for Creative Leadership.

Ernst, C., and J. Yip. 2009. "Boundary Spanning Leadership: Tactics to Bridge Social Identity Groups in Organizations." In *Crossing the Divide: Intergroup Leadership in a World of Difference*, edited by T. L. Pittinsky, 89–99. Boston: Harvard Business School Press.

Friedman, T. 2005. *The World Is Flat: A Brief History of the Twenty-First Century.* New York: Farrar, Straus & Giroux.

Johansen, B. 2012. *Leaders Make the Future: Ten New Leadership Skills for an Uncertain World.* San Francisco: Berrett-Koehler.

Lee, L., D. M. Horth, and C. Ernst. 2012. "Boundary Spanning in Action: Tactics for Transforming Today's Borders into Tomorrow's Frontiers." *Center for Creative Leadership White Paper Series.* Greensboro, NC: Center for Creative Leadership.

McCauley, C.D., C.J. Palus, W.H. Drath, R.L. Hughes, J. McGuire, P.M.G. O'Connor, and E. Van Velsor. 2008. "Interdependent Leadership in Organizations: Evidence from Six Case Studies." *CCL Research Report no. 190*. Greensboro, NC: Center for Creative Leadership.

McGuire, J.B., and C.J. Palus. 2013. "Toward Interdependent Leadership Culture: Transformation in KONE Americas." *Lessons in Changing Culture: Learning from Real World Cases*, edited by D. Warrick and J. Mueller. Oxford, UK: Rossi Smith Academic Publishing.

McGuire, J.B., and G. Rhodes. 2009. *Transforming Your Leadership Culture*. San Francisco: Jossey-Bass.

Palus, C.J., J.B. McGuire, and C. Ernst. 2012. "Developing Interdependent Leadership." In *The Handbook for Teaching Leadership : Knowing, Doing, and Being*, edited by S. Snook, N. Nohria, and R. Khurana, 467–492. Thousand Oaks, CA: Sage Publications with the Harvard Business School.

Pasmore, B., and K. Lafferty. 2009. "Developing a Leadership Strategy." *Center for Creative Leadership White Paper Series*. Greensboro, NC: Center for Creative Leadership.

Reinhold, D., C. Ernst, and C.J. Palus. 2012. *Boundary Spanning Leadership Toolkit*. Greensboro, NC: Center for Creative Leadership.

Reinhold, D., C. Ernst and C.J. Palus. 2011. *Boundary Spanning Workbook: Tactics for Success*. Greensboro, NC: Center for Creative Leadership.

Torbert, B., and Associates. 2004. *Action Inquiry: The Secret of Timely Transforming Leadership*. San Francisco: Berrett-Koehler.

Uhl-Bien, M., and S.M. Ospina. 2012. *Advancing Relational Leadership Research: A Dialogue Among Perspectives*. Charlotte, NC: Information Age Publishing.

VanVelsor, E., C.D. McCauley, and M.N. Ruderman, eds. 2010. *The Center for Creative Leadership Handbook of Leadership Development*, 3rd ed. San Francisco: Jossey-Bass Wiley.

Yip, J., C. Ernst, and M. Campbell. 2011. "Boundary Spanning Leadership: Mission Critical Perspectives from the Executive Suite." *Center for Creative Leadership White Paper Series*. Greensboro, NC: Center for Creative Leadership.

11 Boundary-Spanning as Enacted in Three Organizational Functions
New Venture Management, Project Management, and Product Management

David Wilemon

BOUNDARY-SPANNING

This chapter focuses on three organizational positions whose leaders engage in frequent boundary-spanning activities. They are: new venture leaders, project team leaders, and product management. Each performs different roles within their respective organizations. However, a common pattern among these positions is the need for each to engage in boundary-spanning. Boundary spanning is defined here as the process of working across various organizational lines or boundaries to garner support, resources, or information needed to complete assigned tasks. This chapter focuses primarily on boundary-spanning between a team and supporting functional groups, the team's supporters, and external organizations. Interviews were conducted by the author in order to gain additional contextual information regarding how these three positions carried out their tasks as well as the challenges they faced. A convenience sample was derived from personal contacts in several firms. Involved in the interviews were eight new venture team leaders, nine project leaders, and six product managers. Interviews were conducted on-site for approximately half of the positions; others were conducted via telephone. The questions used are part of a larger study of cross-functional teamwork effectiveness involving new venture team leaders, project leaders, and product managers. The interview protocol contained these questions:

1. Briefly describe what you need to do to be successful in your job.
2. How frequently do you need to go beyond your immediate team or department to gain advice, support, and resources?
3. What issues, problems, or opportunities, if any, have you encountered in gaining external resources, support, or advice? External implies beyond your team/group.
4. What advice, if any, would you give to others who need to seek support, resources, or information beyond their immediate team, department, or organizational boundaries?
5. What, if anything, has helped you deal effectively with your managers, others in different departments, and external organizations?

These five questions allowed for additional probes to delve deeper into the experiences of the interviewees. Due to the small sample size of the three positions, no descriptive statistics are presented. Rather, the interview data is used to help the reader understand some of the boundary-spanning methods, challenges encountered, and the contextual milieu of the interviewees. All the venture team leaders and project leaders interviewed were involved with technology-oriented companies. The product managers were split between consumer product and industrial product companies. The interviews lasted about an hour. Several quotes from the interviewees are used so that the reader can "hear" the voices of the various team leaders as they describe their experiences with boundary-spanning. In the following sections a brief discussion of each function and how boundary-spanning functions overall is discussed.

Key Organizational Functions

New Venture Leaders

Corporate venture managers are engaged in bringing about significant change in an organization's products and services (Block and MacMillan 1993; Sharma and Chrisman 1999). The speed and degree to which new technologies and markets change creates the need for more effective approaches to deal with these strategic challenges. Moreover, as industry observers note, globalizations offers as many challenges as opportunities. Organizations are continually wrestling with how best to compete in a rapidly changing competitive landscape. Unfortunately, many organizations are designed for efficiency and not for creating and developing new business opportunities. Too often established organizations are encumbered by cultures, mindsets, and practices that defeat even the best ideas for major new business development opportunities. Several astute companies, however, have discovered that internal corporate venture teams are a useful approach for creating new businesses. Zahra defines corporate entrepreneurship/internal venturing this way (1991, 259):

> Corporate entrepreneurship may involve formal or informal activities aimed at creating new businesses within established companies through product and process innovations and market developments. These activities may take place at the corporate, division, functional, or project levels, with the unifying objective of improving a company's competitive position and financial performance.

Murray and Hoyt describe the role of new corporate ventures this way (2009, 1):

> In today's struggling economy, savvy companies are looking for ways to create new value. To do this, many organizations create internal venture

teams, sometimes referred to as corporate venture groups, corporate entrepreneurs or skunk works operations. These groups are responsible for getting the organization into new businesses. One part start-up, one part venture capital firm, and one part strategic business unit, they play a unique, hybrid role. These explorers are often required to enter new and unchartered territory, and they find themselves with plenty of opportunity and advantages. At the same time, they are faced with numerous unexpected and daunting challenges.

Finally, Block and MacMillan note that corporate venturing has the following characteristics (1995, 14):

- Involves an activity *new* to the organization
- Is initiated or conducted *internally*
- Involves significantly *higher risk* of failure than the base business
- Is characterized by *greater uncertainty* than the base business
- Will be *managed separately* at some point during its life
- Is undertaken for the purpose of increasing sales, profit, productivity, or quality

The venturing process usually begins when management decides that new businesses and new directions are needed by their company. This may result from a study of existing products regarding their maturity, profitability, and competitive position in the market. If the majority of established products are mature and under pricing pressure, companies may realize the need for change and experiment with new ventures (Mason and Rohner 2002; Costello 1984). In other cases, a technology may be developed that does not fit existing markets, the company's organization, or the organization's culture (Burns 2008). At this point, some companies will elect to use an internal venture team to create new business opportunities.

New venture team leaders are often selected by senior management, as the need for growth and innovation comes from the firm's strategic plans (Buckland 2003). Companies experienced in new ventures usually craft a charter for the venture manager, which lays out the expectations of senior management for the venture. In other cases when the senior management does not have experience with venturing, the venture manager has to develop the charter first and then sell it to the management team for agreement. One of the interviewees noted the following example:

The charter is your marching orders. It is what the organization expects for your venture group. Of course, it may change as you move forward. Sometimes management changes the charter, and sometimes you change it, according to what is happening. In one case a competitor beat us to the market. We had to change our entire approach and revise the charter.

> Once our competitor launched their new product, our initial charter was irrelevant.

Once the decision is made to seek new ventures, senior management also needs to design or approve a process for guiding new venture candidates. This entails establishing expectations for the venture, determining major milestones, and deciding how progress will be reported. Budgeting, staffing, and communicating issues to the organization for the purpose of the new venture and its intended benefits must be undertaken. Communicating with the organization about the new venture is important because it allows senior management to share what steps are needed to ensure future success (Burgelman and Doz 2001; Wilemon 2011). Some companies will attempt to engage in new ventures, however, with little or no experience in the venturing process. In one of the interview, a venture manager made this comment:

> Our company did not have a lot of experience with new products, much less new ventures. When I went to the various groups for help, they wondered what I was up to and if anyone was serious about the venture. Initially, it was difficult for our venture team because the organizational environment for a new venture had not been established by our senior management team. The next time I would ask management specifically what they have done to pave the way for new ventures. If the response was nothing, then I had the choice of either backing away or creating our own infrastructure and support system for our new venture.

Once the venture team's charter and the venturing process is established, the next step is often called the "fuzzy front-end" of venturing (Kim and Wilemon 2002). Several ideas may be available and the venture team must winnow these ideas down into one or two for development. In other cases, there may be a technological breakthrough, but no market is known and the venture team must determine if a market even exists (or can be developed) for the new technology. Once an idea has been established as credible, the venture team seeks funding for further development. Most companies provide funding on a step-by-step basis. When a target is reached, the venture group requests additional funding for the next phase in the development. Eventually, a business case is required which details the technology, the markets aimed for, the funds needed, who is part of the venture team, what assistance is needed from other functional areas and external support groups, and what the potential is for spin-offs, etc.

As Block and MacMillan note (1995, 11): "Senior management determines where each venture should be located within the organization and how it should interface with other units." The location of the venture team has a critical impact on the teams' ability to boundary span effectively. For example, in one company the venture team was placed in the company's marketing department. Problems developed when the venture team asked

R&D for help. As the venture leader noted, there was "push back," and requests for assistance were often met with comments such as:

- We will call you once we are ready to look at your requests.
- The bearings are hot for us, so we have limited time to devote to non-R&D problems.
- We need to get approval from our managers before we commit to anything outside our own group's work, and that takes time.

To assist venture leaders and their team's boundary-spanning activities, the team can be helped if it is located at a high level for organizational visibility and clout. In one company, the venture team was actually located on the same floor as the senior managers. This was viewed as a very positive step by the team as it said to the rest of the organization that "new ventures are important to this organization."

The venture team develops the venture and periodically reports to the venture sponsors, i.e., senior management. During the process of developing the venture, many teams are often met with resistance, dysfunctional politics, setbacks in the venture's strategies, and numerous unanticipated challenges (Mason and Rohner 2002). In one case, the venture team lost their key technical contributor to a competitor. This set the development of the new venture back more than two months as they had to recruit someone to fill the void.

Boundary-Spanning by Venture Managers

The issue of boundary-spanning by venture managers is particularly interesting since, in many instances, the venture may require some/all skills beyond the parent or "host" organization. One venture team leader noted:

> This is not a typical job. If you have a problem, in most organizations you can walk down the hall and discuss the issue with a colleague. With new ventures, there may be no one within the organization you can talk to, so you need to get out of you cocoon and find solutions elsewhere. I often tell my group that the biggest challenge we face is that the answers to our problems may not in our group at all.

Other interviewees made similar comments about the lack of an infrastructure to support new ventures in their companies.

Another challenge that venture leaders face is the lack of executive experience in the venturing process. This can lead to a limited amount of coaching along with behavior modeling. One venture manager noted that the major source of information on the venturing process was from venture managers in other companies. Seeking information from others in different organizations about new venture management and its processes is another example of boundary-spanning by venture leaders. One team leader related his experiences at a company that had never engaged in any form of corporate venture management:

> The board of directors hired a new CEO at a time when all of our products were maturing. He had no experience with venturing nor did our company. He knew that revenue from our aging products would soon diminish. So he took us to a company where venturing was part of that company's DNA. They were very gracious and told us how they did the entire process. Of course, we had to make modifications, but it gave us the confidence that we could do it, too. Perhaps the most important outcome of that visit was that our senior managers saw what was required of them, in terms of processes, resources, and commitment.

In terms of venture manager boundary-spanning behavior, several other examples were revealed in the interviews. One venture manager said that he spent nearly half of his time dealing with various senior managers gaining their support to back his venture. Several key senior managers in his company were critical in terms of how much financial support was required. Another venture manager noted that since she required support from various disciplines, she spent much of her time dealing with disciplines beyond her major field of expertise. Some of these disciplines were external to her company. She commented on her boundary crossing activities this way:

> While my background is electrical engineering, I had to deal with people in software development, marketing, mechanical engineering, and ceramics. This was not easy for me. I would try to understand the thought processes of my key interfaces and then ask them the right questions. When I felt that I had an answer, I would go back to my team and discuss what I had learned. It was easier when I had a team member that had similar skills as the person I was dealing with. I would let my team member lead the discussion and get him to help me understand what was being discussed.

One of the characteristics of most venture teams occurs in narrowing down several ideas into one or two ideas worthy of commercialization. Think of the venturing process as a large funnel with the wide end (mouth) on the left. As ideas are evaluated, they move from the left to the right of the funnel. During various evaluations the ideas become more refined, and finally one or two may be selected for commercialization. The mouth of the funnel is sometimes called the "fuzzy front-end" of a new venture (Kim and Wilemon 2002). It is an information rich environment of ideas, concepts, technologies, and personal visions. As ideas are examined, some are dropped from consideration, while others may be shelved. There are noticeable differences usually in boundary-spanning behavior in the front end of the funnel versus the narrow end. In the wide part of the funnel where there are many ideas, boundary-spanning is used to engage a wide assortment of experts. As ideas are narrowed, boundary-spanning often becomes more focused. Before an idea is launched and marketing issues become increasingly important, the venture leader will need to discuss various aspects of the marketing discipline with people knowledgeable about advertising, promotion, distribution, pricing, and competitive strategies. These details are usually not discussed in depth at the front-end of the venture process. One of the venture leaders made this comment while discussing this issue:

> As we gained momentum, we began planning the marketing strategy for our product. I knew that I needed help. My background is technology and marketing is clearly not my forte. So, I talked to several people in our corporate marketing group about our needs, and they convinced me to hire someone who had marketing experience with this type of technology. After some pleading with the senior managers for support, we did hire a marketing person with a technology background who had the skills we needed. It is important to know your limitations and what you don't know.

Another issue that became evident in the interviews is that boundary-spanning by venture managers is often required to protect an emerging new venture. Most organizations have more needs than resources; so if a new venture is formed, a variety of organizational "push backs" can develop. One of the venture leaders explained this behavior in the following manner:

> Okay, so you've got this new idea that you think is the greatest, but many others in your organization will not agree with you. I have been met with so much resistance with this new venture because the other functional department heads say things like, "Oh that's nice; but we tried that five years ago, and it was a bust"; or "we need your funds for our own products which are proven winners. Your technology is still an unknown by the market." So, I have had to do the political thing and go around to each of these decision makers and make my case for scarce resources. If I can't win them over, perhaps I can neutralize a negative vote or at least change a negative attitude when it comes to funding decisions. I see my job as a team leader, a politician, and as an integrator of diverse ideas.

Project Leaders

Project team leaders are responsible for managing a task that has a limited life span within the host organization (Turner and Muller 2003). Typical organizational projects include developing and implementing a major new software program, installing a new financial control system in the organization, managing an acquisition, or developing a new product. The usual case is when an existing product is updated or needs to be modified. While new ventures often deal with revolutionary technologies, project leaders often deal with evolutionary tasks: they build on known ways of doing things. One of the most common uses of project management is in developing new products for existing markets and the extension of current products. We will use new product development as the basis for our discussions regarding boundary-spanning by project team leaders.

Major Characteristics of Project Management

There are several characteristics common to most new product development project teams as follows (Wilemon 1985):

Goal Orientation—Project management is used to solve specific, identifiable goals within stated parameters: for example, cost, schedule, and performance objectives.

Multidisciplinary Emphasis—The nature of many project management tasks requires the contributions of diverse organizational members. Many of the contributors will be beyond the boundaries of the core project team.

Change Orientation—Project leaders deal with various types of change. For example, markets and technologies may change as well as competitive strategies. The ability to adjust to and manage change is considered a key requirement for project success. Other examples of change include dealing with political issues within the organization, views about the project, as well as changing attitudes regarding the desirability of the project.

Responsibility Identification—An effective project management system clearly identifies who is responsible for what tasks and when the tasks must be completed. Without responsibility identification projects are likely to evolve into chaos.

People Involvement—A key to most successful projects is the quality of people involved and their ability to work in a team environment. The issue of people involvement also implies that there will be many times when contributors from other areas of the organization are needed to make the project a success.

Finite Duration—Once the objectives of the project have been achieved, the project team is usually disbanded. One of the major advantages of project management are that it can be designed to be a very results-oriented approach to managing tasks (Mann 2005). A major focus of the team is on task completion. One role of project team leaders (similar to venture teams) is to minimize external distractions that can disrupt the team's progress. Project teams also have the potential to develop synergy from the talents of its various team members.

Often this requires gaining the collaborative effort of core team members as well as those external to the team. In addition, projects offer the opportunity for morale building, management testing, job enrichment, as well as favorable visibility with senior management. Project management also offers the opportunity to gain management's involvement in significant organizational undertakings as well as cross-functional communication (Bartech, Ebers, and Maurer 2013; Hass 2004). Finally, projects have a customer, either internal or external to the organization. Project management is one method to help ensure that the customer's needs are met, and that there is a single point of contact for the customer.

Barriers to Cross-Functional Project Teamwork

There are a number of barriers to effective project teamwork which can affect not only the team but also how the team or its leader interacts with others in the organization as well as with those beyond the company's boundaries. Barriers to teams that are required to span various and often diverse organizational boundaries include (Wilemon 1985):

- Unclear project objectives
- Differing priorities of team members
- Role conflicts within and between groups and teams
- Lack of a clear definition of the team and its structure
- Appointment of a project leader who is not credible to the team members and key support groups/organizations
- Assignment of team members not well suited for the project work
- Lack of commitment to the project by team members
- Internal or external competition over team leadership
- Communication problems within the team and with external support groups
- Perceived lack of support from sponsors and/or senior management

Boundary-Spanning by Project Managers

Project leaders engaged in new product development were asked about their boundary-spanning experiences. The first question was: Briefly describe what you need to do to be successful as a project leader. Some representative quotes include the following:

When I first became a project leader, I thought that I needed more authority to get others in the organization to support the project. I learned, however, that it is not the amount of authority that you have but your ability to involve people in the project and help them get energized about what you are trying to do. All the team members here are highly skilled in their technical specialties, and they love to use their skills. What they don't like are the politics and disruptions that regularly occur within our organization. So, I spend a lot of time with what you might call "working the organization" to shelter the team from the politics here and doing what I can to facilitate their work.

Another project leader addressed the same question this way:

> I spent a lot of time initially building the team and getting people to feel committed to what we were trying to do with the advanced product offering. This product had a lot more bells and whistles than anything we had produced before, and we needed the help of several different groups. One of the groups was an overseas subsidiary. My initial efforts at gaining agreement with all those involved were marginal at best. What was happening? These disparate groups were hearing conflicting messages from our project team which caused major confusion. That's when I learned how important it is to have a cohesive team so that others beyond your team hear the same message versus one individual team member's interpretation of the message. Therefore, if you want to send a clear, cohesive message when you are dealing with various support groups, strengthen your own team first. I spent a lot of up-front time getting my team on the same page.

Another project leader discussed the problems encountered in garnering support for his project as described:

> The biggest problem I've had occurred when we were ready to simultaneously commercialize the product in several countries. I knew this would be a challenge as we had been working with these countries since the middle of our project. I went to the manager in country X and told him about the roll out, and he said, "no problem, we will be ready." Next, I went to our facility in country Y, and essentially they said, "no problem we will be ready when you are." Then on the last leg of my trip; I stopped in country Z, and they gave me the same spiel. But when we were ready to launch, country Z was nowhere near ready to support us. They totally underestimated what was required. What did I learn? I learned how important it is, in one way or another, to have those you are counting on tell you in detail what they will do to fulfill their responsibilities to your team. If they can't do this, it is a clear indicator that they won't be prepared to help you.

It is obvious from this project leader's experiences that boundary-spanning requires communication to assess understanding as well as commitment. In complex projects, this may require multiple attempts in order to achieve clarity about issues and requirements (Hoang and Rothaermel 2010).

Product Management

The most common use of product managers (sometimes called brand managers) is managing existing products within an organization. These managers usually are skilled in marketing and understanding their customers' needs and requirements (Katsanis and Pitta 1995). One of the most widely used areas for product management is in consumer products (Low and Fulleron 1994). Some large consumer goods companies, for example, may have more than a hundred product or brand managers. By contrast, many large companies may have very few venture managers. Like venture managers and project managers, product managers have to engage in considerable boundary-spanning in order to accomplish the demands of their positions (Lysonski 1985).

This section focuses primarily on the boundary-spanning role of product managers in the postlaunch phase of a product (Lysonski, Singer, and Wilemon 1989). Product managers must deal and negotiate with a wide variety of departments or organizations, both internal and external. Examples of product manager responsibilities include the development of a product's marketing strategy, pricing, promotion, and distribution, and the identification of service requirements. In addition, product managers may decide if spin-offs are warranted, along with managing the product's profit and loss, building needed social networks, leveraging the knowledge of those who can facilitate the success of the product, and championing the product both internally and externally to give it the resources needed for market success (Raupiar 1980; Cardile 2002).

One of the product managers interviewed describes how she experienced the differences between dealing with various departments within her company versus the external groups that provide support to her product line:

> I have found that there are major differences between dealing with various departments inside the organization and the companies that are external to the company in terms of providing support for my product. You really have to exert yourself internally in order to gain support. Why? The functional groups are already overloaded with requirements from other product managers. Sometimes, the squeaky wheel does get the grease, and other times departments simply ignore the squeak and keep doing what they are doing. I have learned not to ask my boss to intervene on my product's behalf. To me, that says I cannot do this product manager job. They pay me to get things to work. On the other hand, when I go to an outside design company or an advertising agency, they are very responsive. They see me as a customer, and I control the compensation for the services they provide. I find that external companies are far more responsive to my needs.

In another interview, a product manager who had a great amount of experience with various overseas divisions in his company made this comment about the skills needed to deal with the various cultures in his work environment:

> One of the most important lessons I've earned is that people respond differently, depending on their cultural backgrounds. In North America, people are quite direct in their communications. I am used to straight talk. Some countries in Asia, however, are not quite the same. It may take considerable time to get a yes or no from a colleague there. Eventually, I will hear from one voice, but I understand that there have been many voices that have gone into the one voice that I hear. I have learned to give them more time so they can thoroughly check things out within their organization. This is very different from how we operate in our company. If someone calls me about something, I can usually give them an immediate response or soon thereafter.

In further discussions with this product manager, he discussed dealing with a major distributor in another country. He noted that would spend considerable time negotiating the cost of the product with the distributor. Once the negotiations were over the product manager felt that his work was completed for the next several months. But this assumption would not be the case. Rather, the distributor would find some reason for reopening the negotiations over the price of the product to his company. Thus, it was seen as an ongoing process of negotiating and then renegotiating. He said, "I've learned that there is no universal playbook for negotiating in all markets. Each country has their own quirks when it comes to making and keeping a deal."

Potential Interactions among Functions/Positions

These functions or positions sometimes meld together. For example, a new venture team may develop a major new business or technology and test its market and technological viability. If the venture looks like it will fulfill the organization's desire for growth and diversification, the venture is often turned over to a project team to fully develop it. Some companies will often ask the venture leader to become either a team member or an advisor to the project team. In other cases, the venture manager may become the project leader; but, often, the venture leader's skill set is not suited for the project manager's role. In some cases, one or more venture team members may become a project team member due to their expertise and experience with the venture. If the project is successful, the new product may be managed by a product manager responsible for the commercialization success of the venture. Thus, a venture may migrate from an embryonic idea (new venture) to a project for development (the requirements are generally clear), and finally may be managed by a product manager. Each manager often needs to have different skills in a different environment, yet all are required to engage in boundary-spanning. (Zakaria, Amelinckx, and Wilemon 2004).

BOUNDARY-SPANNING FACILITATORS

This section focuses on some of the major factors which can facilitate the boundary-spanning capabilities of each organizational position. The importance of each facilitator will vary depending upon the environment faced by the manager/team leader as well as the task needing to be accomplished (Tushman and Scanlan1981). Several factors which can facilitate boundary-spanning by each type of manager are noted below (Wilemon 1985). No attempt is made to assess which facilitators are more important to each type of manager discussed in this chapter. The potential facilitators include the following:

> Credibility—If the leader is credible it is more likely he or she will be able to garner the support of others. There are at least two dimensions to credibility: 1) the leader's personal credibility, and 2) the credibility of the task. For example, if the product being developed is not perceived as important and credible, the manager is likely to have more difficulty the manager in gaining support from others. A very desirable outcome occurs when both the manager and project or task are credible. Personal credibility is derived, in part, from successful performance. Task credibility is derived from the perceived value of a project, its supporters, and the perceived likelihood of success. In one of the interviews, a venture team leader noted the following about credibility:

> In my opinion, credibility is the most important quality I possess. If I have high credibility with others, it says they believe me when I say something. They trust me to do what I say. Unfortunately, credibility has to be earned again and again. If I fail, my credibility will be tarnished. So I always protect it to the best of my ability.

> Accessibility—Does the particular manager have access to senior management and to others who support the venture, project, or product? If so, it is more likely that boundary-spanning can be accomplished. Access to management implies that the manager can communicate directly with senior management or supporters. In some instances a venture team leader may report to the CEO or other senior manager. Such access is likely to give the manager clout with those he or she must deal with. When team leaders/managers have low levels of accessibility to senior management, their interfaces will not have a clear idea who is supporting them. A project leader made this comment regarding his accessibility with his company's senior managers:

> When I take on a project management role, I do what I can to negotiate for access to senior management. I can't always get it, but it can make my job much easier to accomplish. I also have learned that this is an

area in which you never want to pretend to have access to senior management when you don't. This can tarnish one's credibility.

Priority—How do various supporting organizations view the project, venture, or product? Is the task a priority to them? Is it a priority to the company? If so, it is more likely that successful boundary-spanning can be effectively accomplished. Priority is how important the organization perceives the new venture, the project, or the product to be. If others perceive that a project is important, they are more likely to give it support. A comment from one of the leaders interviewed follows:

Priority, of course, is important. The main source of it is from senior management. If management thinks and acts like a specific project is critical to the organization, others are likely to view it the same. Unfortunately, for project leaders is that management sees several of projects and ventures in their roles and what is priority today might be smothered by the "next big thing." So, my job is to do my best to make the perception of priority last. I make visits to senior management and renew their interests, and I invite them to a Friday afternoon "show and tell pizza party" to keep the project on their minds. Maintaining priority is a mind-sharing process. Priority helps surpass the noise and the chaos that occurs in any organization.

Visibility—Visibility is the extent to which others know about an organizational undertaking such as a new venture, a project, or a product. If it is a tightly guarded secret, as is the case of some new ventures, the venture's visibility may be very low. As a rule, the more visible the project (if perceived positively), the more likely members of different departments will support the project. Also, a secret new venture may have high visibility with senior management but have low visibility with the employees in the organization. A team leader needs to maintain an appropriate level of visibility when leading organizational tasks.

Interpersonal Skills—Several research studies have noted the importance of interpersonal skills in gaining support for organizational tasks. Some of the key skills needed in gaining support include listening skills, communication skills, demonstrating empathy, and managing conflicts and disagreements. Some team leaders will have excellent interpersonal skills while others may lack these skills but have exceptional technical skills. Sometimes training may help such leaders; and in other cases, they may use team members to cross boundaries for the team.

Organizational Culture—Organizations exhibit different cultures, which can affect the ability of managers to deal with others beyond their immediate boundaries. Some organizations are porous and place a high value on cooperation, teamwork, and openness (Boerner, Schaffner, and Gebert 2012). Others, by contrast, are more rigid and are more like warring tribes. In such organizations, cooperation comes at a high price for the team leader trying to gain cooperation and support from others. There also are differences in cultures between the major functions in organizations. One project team leader discussed the cultural differences between three groups he had to rely on for help (R&D, marketing, and manufacturing) this way:

> You wouldn't believe the differences between what our marketing group values and what our R&D group values. Our R&D group is concerned with doing something new and exciting, perfectly and accurately. They work hard to achieve these goals and have little patience for those who want to hurry their processes. They love novelty and experimenting with different approaches. Our marketing group, on the other hand, always has the customer in mind. What do our customers want? What do we have to do to serve them well? Both of these groups are different from our manufacturing processes group, who are primarily concerned with productivity and volume. All three groups are needed on our project, so you can imagine how the mix of different values and cultures challenges me.

Management's Role in Facilitating Boundary Spanning—One of the most important factors that can facilitate a manager's ability to span organizational boundaries is the tone that management sets for the organization. If senior management values teamwork and cooperation, there is a greater probability that their subordinates will do the same. By contrast, if there is jealousy and protectionism at the highest levels, such behavior is likely to be emulated at lower levels within the organization. In essence, the culture established by management can either facilitate or hinder effective boundary-spanning. One interviewee made this comment:

> Senior management is always preaching teamwork. In fact, it is part of the company's credo. You see the word "teamwork" everywhere in this company. Yet, I know that at their level, there are a lot of disagreements, conflicts, and in some cases withholding of information. At my level, we are aware of this disconnect between what is said and what actually occurs. We have similar conflicts at the product manager level, so we have the "monkey see, monkey do" syndrome. Our managers simply do not model good teamwork in their interactions with each other, and it sends a strong signal to the entire organization.

A PROPOSED BOUNDARY-SPANNING INSTRUMENT

Working with a number of managers and team leaders, I have often observed that some are very capable at boundary-spanning and cross-functional teamwork, while others may be capable but are reluctant to work across boundaries. One reason for this reluctance could be the fear of rejection or encountering conflict. By contrast, some managers are very willing to engage others in different organizations but have difficulty doing it well due to their interpersonal skills. Is there a way to help assess one's capabilities to span organizational boundaries? In this section, an instrument is proposed to help identify those team leaders and team members who are most likely to be effective at boundary-spanning and cross-functional teamwork.

Instrument Description

The purpose of this short self-assessment instrument is to assist those either contemplating their role as a boundary-spanner or to assist those currently in these roles to identify both their potential strengths and weaknesses.

Instructions: Review each question and circle the number that best describes your willingness and ability to seek help and advice from others in different areas of your organization or from those in organizations external to your company who can help you accomplish your goals.

1. I seek help from others in different parts of the organization when it is needed:

   1   2   3   4   5

   Not at All   Usually

2. I have the ability and willingness to converse effectively with others in different disciples/functions:

   1   2   3   4   5

   Not at All   Usually

3. I am empathetic and understand the challenges other groups/organizations face in performing their jobs:

   1   2   3   4   5

   Not at All   Usually

4. I have the ability to explain my job and its requirements to others in different functional areas and organizations and gain their assistance:

   1   2   3   4   5

   Not at All   Usually

5. I am able to adjust to the different working styles of people:

   1   2   3   4   5

   Not at All   Usually

6. I appreciate that the various groups in my organization and external to my organization often have different values and cultures:

   1   2   3   4   5

   Not at All   Usually

7. I try to cooperate with others in the organization who need my help:

          1   2   3   4   5

   Not at All   Usually

8. If one approach doesn't work in gaining cooperation from another person or group, I will try a different approach:

          1   2   3   4   5

   Not at All   Usually

9. In my dealings with other groups, I focus on achieving a win-win outcome:

          1   2   3   4   5

   Not at All   Usually

10. When I deal with others beyond my team I try to get them to see the overall (superordinate) objectives of the organization and how working together can contribute to these goals:

           1   2   3   4   5

    Not at All   Usually

Proposed Scoring

40–50 = High boundary-spanning potential or capability

30–39 = Moderate boundary-spanning potential or capability

<30 = May encounter major boundary-spanning problems. Potential candidate for professional development and skills training.

Obviously, one's score is just one data point, and other important considerations need to be taken into account, such as recommendations of peers, experience, observations, and reports from superiors. It is posited, however, that there is likely to be a high correlation between the results of the proposed instrument with one's capability and willingness to effectively span organizational boundaries.

As noted, the managers of venture leaders, project leaders, and product managers can use this same instrument to help evaluate those who need help in spanning organizational boundaries. Another way to use this instrument is for team leaders to assess a team member and then compare it with the team member's own assessment. For this approach to work, the leader would need some firsthand knowledge of the team member's capabilities. Comparing the results can then become a platform for discussing differences in perceptions and an avenue for possible coaching of the team member. Finally, a team can assess itself with the instrument and point to areas where the team as a whole can improve. This is perhaps the least threatening of the approaches noted for using the instrument.

STUDY CONTRIBUTIONS

This chapter contributes to the literature in four ways. First, it examines how boundary-spanning is enacted by three different positions in organizations, namely, new venture management, project management, and product management. The author is not aware of any studies which have attempted to examine these three functions simultaneously and draw inferences from them regarding how they perform their roles. Second, while small in number, the interviews add insights in the contextual environment of these three positions as they engage in managing their organizational boundaries. While some differences are noted in the interviews, there are many similarities in how these managers experience and develop boundary-spanning activities. Third, an instrument is developed to help those whose roles require boundary-spanning to assess their own strengths and limitations. The instrument also can be used by managers of various organizational positions to evaluate their subordinates who are required to engage in boundary-spanning.

FUTURE RESEARCH SUGGESTIONS

Several suggestions for future research are offered to scholars interested in boundary-spanning behavior and research. In terms of venturing, additional research is warranted on how new venture leaders shield and protect their new ventures from the "host" or parent organization. The contextual interviews gathered for this chapter suggest that considerable boundary-spanning often occurs to protect the new venture from the ongoing needs of the parent organization. Another area that warrants attention is how one's ability to span diverse organizational boundaries affects new venture success. This area of research would require multiple participants and a validated instrument which could assess boundary-spanning capabilities. Additionally, a longitudinal study would be required to assess boundary-spanning capabilities and its relationship to success (Marrone 2010). Studies on the differences between new venture managers with access to internal competencies versus venture managers who must rely almost entirely on expertise beyond the boundaries of the organization could be useful to further understanding the challenges faced in boundary-spanning. Another research area that might prove particularly useful to managers would be to focus on ways to reduce the need for boundary-spanning or make the boundary-spanning process more efficient and effective.

SUMMARY

This chapter examines boundary-spanning from three perspectives; namely, new venture leaders, project leaders, and product managers. While the environmental context and tasks are different, there are several common-alities among these three groups as they seek support and assistance from others within and beyond their immediate organizations. Interviews with a small number of team leaders in each position were undertaken to learn more about their activities and perspectives on working with others. To assist others in understanding how different team leaders dealt with the challenges of boundary-spanning, quotes from the interviews were used. To help assess the skills and capabilities needed in boundary-spanning, an assessment instrument is proposed for use by either team leaders or team members or by those who want to engage in such roles. The instrument also can be used by an entire team to assess its overall capabilities in engaging and working with various support groups. Several suggestions for future research are advanced for these important organizational positions.

REFERENCES

Bartsch, Vera, Mark Ebers, and Indre Maurer. February 2013. "Learning in project-based organizations: The role of project teams' social capital for overcoming barriers to learning." *International Journal of Project Management* 31 (2):239–51.

Block, Zenas, and Ian MacMillan.1995. *Corporate Venturing.* Boston, MA: Harvard Business School Press.

Boerner, Sabine, Melanie Schaffner, and Diether Gebert. May 2012. "The complementarity of team meetings and cross-functional communication: Empirical evidence from new services development teams." *Journal of Leadership & Organizational Studies* 19:256–66.

Burgelman, Robert and Yves L. Doz. 2001. "The power of strategic integration." *Sloan Management Review* 42 (3):28–38.

Burns, Paul. 2008. *Corporate Entrepreneurship: Building the Entrepreneurial Organization.* 2nd ed. New York: Palgrave MacMillan.

Carlile, Paul. July–August 2002. "A pragmatic view of knowledge and boundaries: Boundary objects in new product development." *Organization Science* 13 (4):442–55.

Costello, Dennis. 1985. *New Venture Analysis: Research, Planning, & Analysis:*85–87 Homewood, IL: Dow Jones-Irwin.

Gemmill, Gary, and David Wilemon. 1973. "The product manager as influence agent." *Journal of Marketing* 36 (1):26–30.

Haas, Martine. 2006. "Knowledge gathering, team capabilities, and project performance in challenging work environments." *Management Science* 52:1170–84.

Katsanis, Lea Prevel, and Dennis Pitta. 1995. "Punctuated equilibrium and the evolution of the product manager." *Journal of Product & Brand Management* 4 (3):49–60.

Kim, Jongbae, and David Wilemon. 2002. "Strategic issues in managing innovation's fuzzy front-end." *European Journal of Innovation Management* 5:27–39.

Low, George, and Ronald Fullerton. May 1994. "Brands, brand management and the brand manager system: A critical-historical evaluation." *Journal of Marketing Research* 31 (2):173–90.

Lysonski, Steven, Alan Singer, and David Wilemon. 1988. "Coping with environmental uncertainty and boundary spanning in the product manager's role." *Journal of Services Marketing* 2 (4):15–26.

Lysonski, Steven. Winter 1985. "Boundary theory investigation of the product manager's role." *Journal of Marketing* 49 (1):26–40.

Mann, Leon. 2005. *Leadership, Management and Innovation in R&D Project Teams*. Westport, CT: Prager Publishers.

Markham, Stephen. July–August 2000. "Corporate championing and antagonism as forms of political behavior: An R&D perspective." *Organization Science* 11 (4):429–47.

Marrone, Jennifer. 2010. "Team boundary spanning: A multilevel review of past research and proposals for the future." *Journal of Management* 36 (4):911–40.

Mason, Heidi, and Tim Rohner. 2002. *The Venture Imperative: A New Model for Corporate Innovation*. Boston, MA: Harvard Business School Press.

Murray, Colleen, and Steve Hoyt. 2009. *New Business for Corporate Entrepreneurs*. San Mateo, CA: Jump Publications.

Sharma, Pramodita, and Sankaran J. Chrisman. 1999. "Towards a reconciliation of the definitional issues in the field of corporate entrepreneurship." *Entrepreneurship Theory and Practice*. 23 (3):11–27.

Turner, Rodney, and Ralf Muller. 2003. "On the nature of project management as a temporary organization." *International Journal of Project Management* 21 (1):1–8.

Tushman, Michael, and Thomas Scanlan. 1981. "Characteristics and external orientations of boundary spanning individuals." *Academy of Management Journal* 24 (1):83–98.

Wilemon, David. June 22, 2011. "Inside corporate venture teams: An empirical study of venture managers and their experiences." *Society of Interdisciplinary Business Research Conference* (SSRN). http://ssrn.com/abstract=1869413.

Wilemon, David. 1985. "High performing project managers." *School of Management Working Paper Series*. School of Management, Syracuse University. Syracuse, NY.

Zahra, Shaker. 1991. "Predictors and financial outcomes of corporate entrepreneurship: An exploratory study." *Journal of Business Venturing* 6 (4):259–86.

Zakaria, Norhayati, Andrea Amelinckx, and David Wilemon. 2004. "Working together apart? Building a knowledge-sharing culture for global virtual teams." *Creativity & Innovation Management* 13 (1).

Part IV
Organizations

12 Trusting Across Boundaries

Frens Kroeger and Reinhard Bachmann

Trust has become widely acknowledged as a crucial factor in inter-organizational relationships. It affects a wide range of relationship qualities, from increasing relationship stability to lowering transaction costs for the trusting parties (for an overview, see Zaheer et al. 1998). Accordingly, the literature on inter-organizational trust has burgeoned.

However, there has been little conceptual development to elucidate the exact workings of inter-organizational trust; the role of boundary-spanners in building and maintaining trust between organizations has effectively remained a "black box" in research to date. As Currall & Inkpen (2002) point out, it is common practice in research to use data at the individual level to explain trust at the inter-organizational level, with little or no attempt made at defining the link between them. In their review of literature on inter-organizational trust, Zaheer & Harris (2006) found that of the thirty-eight articles surveyed, twenty do not address the relationship between trust on the individual and organizational levels at all, five point to their status as distinct constructs but fail to address the relationship between them, and seven only "imply" a relationship (2006: 46–53, table 1).

This chapter aims to fill this crucial gap. We will take a closer look at trust building processes in relationships between actors who fulfill boundary-spanning roles in the two organizations. In regard to trust-building processes, too, it is boundary role persons (BRP) who establish the "vital linkages and binding forces between organizations" (Adams 1980: 331; 1976). Our central interest is to examine how these boundary-spanners can translate trust placed in individuals into trust that is placed in organizations as entities in their own right. Furthermore, we will consider how boundary-spanners mediate between intra- and inter-organizational trust, but also the problems and possible conflicts that can arise in these processes.

Two brief definitions/explanations are necessary before we begin. First, following Mayer et al. we conceive of trust as "the willingness of a party to be vulnerable to the actions of another party based on the expectation that the other will perform a particular action important to the trustor, irrespective of the ability to monitor or control that other party" (1995: 712). Second, it should be noted that our observations are based on an institutionalization perspective on trust, as detailed in Kroeger (2012; forthcoming 2013). That is, in short, we assume that modes of trust building can be shared between actors, as they develop and institutionalize repertoires of ways of signaling trust and trustworthiness. This is particularly significant for our observations in this chapter as it helps to explain how trust can move between analytical levels and refer not just to individuals, but also to organizations or teams within them.

BOUNDARY-SPANNERS AND TRANSITORY BOUNDARY SYSTEMS

Three broad classes of functions are fulfilled by boundary role persons (BRP): (1) the more strictly *instrumental* business function (administration of inputs and outputs; also see Bettencourt & Brown 2003: 394–5); (2) a function which, following Aldrich & Herker (1977: 219), can be termed *uncertainty absorption* (encompassing both information filtering and buffering from external pressures); and (3) the *representation* function (which includes not only representing the organization to its environment, but also the environment to the organization; Organ 1971). Especially the latter two are of significance for trust considerations.

Most usually, the ideal-typical BRP dyad is viewed either as negotiating from positions firmly located within their respective organizations, with only their communication crossing these boundaries, or they are supposed to move in a social space in which the two organizations overlap, in principle being temporary members of both (Friedman & Podolny 1992; Gummesson 1996). In contrast, we adopt Adams's idea that the boundary-spanners "constitute, at least transitorily, a boundary social system" (1980: 331). This perspective is able to acknowledge that the transitory boundary system encompassing the actors is more than the sum of its parts. Here, the BRP translate organizational roles and routines into their—often more complex—inter-organizational realities. What is more, this conception is able to accommodate how the BRP do not simply alternate or compromise between their respective organizations' imperatives, but how, as reflexive actors, they can (re)interpret and change this context creatively, constructing a new institutional context that differs from either organization.

Thus, the institutionalization cycle of the transitory boundary system accepts input from and feeds into both institutional contexts (the organizations), but through the creative interaction of the boundary-spanners also partially decouples itself from them. In effect, it stands orthogonal to the organizational institutionalization cycles (see Figure 12.1).

From our point of view, BRP interaction thus creates a system in its own right. Of course, it is only transitory, i.e., it "holds together and functions only so long as people . . . perform the behaviors required to maintain the

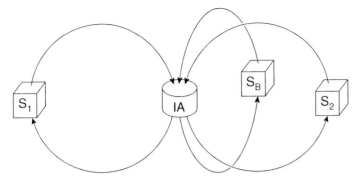

Figure 12.1 Institutionalization perspective—boundary system as orthogonal cycle (Key IA—Interaction S₁, ₂—Structures organizations 1 & 2, S_B—Structure boundary system)

organizational cycles" (Kahn et al. 1964: 13). The boundary system is of course not fully independent of the two organizations. Indeed, with (ideal-typically) only two actors involved it would not qualify as a social system. Its persistence is dependent on the interconnection with third actors within the organizations.

Our conception, as illustrated in Figure 12.1, shows how this simultaneous dependence on and independence of the organizations can be explained—by the existence of three institutionalization cycles which are distinct, but none-theless interconnected. This finding is significant because it reveals the locus of building and institutionalizing trust. It is within this transitory boundary system that BRP engage in symbolic exchange to build trust. Here, they translate (parts of) their respective organizational repertoires into a new, shared context. On this basis, they negotiate and externalize their cognitive symbolic vocabularies and their path toward commonly accepted norms, thus creatively constructing emerging intersubjective realities of trust which can impinge upon the institutional structures of the organizations involved (S_B, S_1, S_2 in Figure 12.1). The boundary system is thus the locus of inter-organizational trust building.

The institutionalization of this trust, in an inter-organizational con-text, has *multiple loci*: it is institutionalized partially in the structure of the boundary system itself, and partially in the structures of the organizations involved. Thus, behavioral forms of trust become anchored in the bound-ary system, but also in the organizations or teams within them. In this way, institutionalized patterns of trusting can be preserved if one or both mem-bers drop out of the boundary system itself. After new actors have taken up their places, the institutionalized patterns can be 'reinjected' into the social system and trust building can continue, not unperturbed or uninterrupted, but within the path established over the history of the institutionalization trust building processes.

FROM INTERPERSONAL TO ORGANIZATIONAL TRUST

Boundary-spanners build interpersonal and inter-organizational trust in these boundary systems. Consequently, we need to examine the exact way in which trust building efforts between individuals can be translated into trust invested in organizations as entities in their own right.

To do so, we will consider whether and in how far trust placed in an organization differs from trust placed in an individual. If there are indeed any significant differences, we will need to inquire into the connections between the two: how do boundary-spanners translate (inter)personal into (inter) organizational trust? In doing so, we will take an "external" perspective (Ancona & Caldwell 1992), considering the organization primarily as an *object* of trust. (For organizations as possible *subjects* of trust, i.e., as trusting entities, see Kroeger 2012.)

Organizational Trust Between Interpersonal and System Trust

Part of inter-organizational trust is that an external actor places their trust in an organization as the trusted object. In the following, we will refer to this aspect as *organizational trust*.

This is an issue regularly touched upon in treatments of inter-organizational trust, but the mechanisms and processes involved have hardly been specified further since Giddens's description of trust in expert systems (1990, 1994). This is itself strongly based on Luhmann's seminal ideas about system trust (1979: ch. 4). On the other hand, trust on the organizational level is frequently described by simple analogies to interpersonal trust (Bigley & Pearce 1998). Consequently, we will locate organizational trust in reference to these two poles.

It is certainly correct that the structure and logic of interpersonal and organizational trust are "essentially similar" (Govier 1994). In both, the trustor makes a decision based on "good reasons" to make themselves vulnerable, thus making a risky investment but reducing complexity by bracketing out the possibility of unfavorable future actions by the trustee. (See the definitions of interpersonal trust by Luhmann 1979, Bachmann 2001, and Möllering 2006.) It has been noted that organizational trust occurs in a medial condition between knowledge and ignorance (Sydow 2006) and often relies on familiarity or familiar typifications in much the same way as interpersonal trust (Apelt 2003).

While these commonalities are widely recognized, the increasing acknowledgement that interpersonal and inter-organizational trust are distinct constructs is typically based only on the empirical observation that one can exist in the other's absence (Doney & Cannon 1997: 35; Jeffries & Reed 2000: 877). The most obvious difference is that organizational trust is trust placed in a social system. Rather than to the motives and likely future actions of an individual, it refers to the institutionalized roles and routines of the respective organization. The trustor "basically assumes that a system is functioning and places his trust in that function, not in people" (Luhmann 1979: 50).

However, counter to a common interpretation (e.g., Lahno 2002), organizational trust is not *purely* system trust. The latter, referring to large overarching social systems such as the economy, is characteristically diffuse (Luhmann 1979: 53). It does not encourage an active search for alternatives, and its degree of taken-for-grantedness is high. Organizations, by contrast, do not appear as "given," but are identifiable as discrete entities. Different degrees of perceived reliability and trustworthiness often constitute a decisive factor in making choices between individual organizations (e.g., as preferred suppliers; Morgan & Hunt 1994). Organizational trust thus lacks the tacit, "automatic" qualities of system trust stressed by Luhmann; its creation involves much higher degrees of reflexivity. Morgner (2008) probes deeper into this important distinction, arguing that organizations, but not the overarching social systems are "addressable" (i.e., attributions have a concrete social referent). As a consequence organizational, but not system trust is "conditionable" (i.e., actors can base their trust decision fundamentally on testing trustworthiness in sequential interactions), pointing toward fundamental differences in their creation. Organizational trust is thus a distinctly *meso-level* form of trust: in important respects it is situated *between* the interpersonal micro- and the systemic macro-level forms.

Adapting a description by Lahno (2002: 3), then, we can define organizational trust as follows:

An actor who trusts an organisation makes him- or herself vulnerable to the actions of others who are guided by the organisation, based on what the trustor knows about the regularities of organisational behaviour and about the behavioural incentives and norms as set by the organisation.

From an institutionalisation perspective, we may say that (inter)organisational trust is enacted as (inter)personal trust in interaction.

This points us towards the interdependencies between the micro and meso levels.

As is widely accepted, trust between organizational representatives is generally at least partially based on organizational trust. The latter "provides a context for interpersonal trust and the relationship between negotiators" (Jeffries & Reed 2000: 874). Existing organizational trust can act as an antecedent facilitating the building of interpersonal trust in interaction, in a fashion similar to but more powerful than the effects of a known organizational reputation (Lorenz 1988). The same is true of system trust: it is not just the more global assumptions of familiarity or "situational normality" (Luhmann 1988; Misztal 2001), but also the fact that the respective social system or subsystem is trusted that can act as a reassuring and trust-facilitating background consideration.

Interpersonal trust can thus build on organizational trust, and both of these in turn will typically build on system trust pertaining to the relevant sector of the life-world. In this sense, the different levels of trust are nested inside one another (also see Shapiro 1987).

To see, then, that interpersonal and organizational forms of trust are indeed mutually facilitating or "recursively related" (Currall & Inkpen 2002; Sydow 1998, 2006), we need to consider ways in which organizational depends on interpersonal trust.

Facework Between Intra- and Extra-Role Behavior

It is undoubtedly correct that without their representatives, organizations would lack any capacity for the reciprocity or even interaction indispensable to trust building (Schweer 2003). It is much easier for individual actors to signal predictability and benevolence (Doney & Cannon 1997; Lui & Ngo 2004). The implication, then, is that these signals—somehow—rub off onto an external actor's image of the organization. But how?

In our view, the concept of "facework" (Giddens 1990: 80) appears the most helpful here. When facework works effectively (which is far from certain; also see below), trust is invested in the person of the representative, but it is "trust qua role," "trust qua group membership" (Lahno 2002: 1, 6), relating primarily to the roles and positions determined by the institutional system of the organization (Ring & Van de Ven 1994; also see Meyerson et al. 1996). It is this role-based connection between individual and organization that facework is anchored in. The transference from interpersonal to organizational trust can occur if the potential trustor regards the behavior of the boundary-spanner as typical of their organization (Sydow 2006: 382; Doney & Cannon 1997: 41)—as directed by trustworthy organizational roles and routines (also see Lyon & Porter 2010). The connection between interpersonal and organizational trust established by facework is thus constituted by role-based trust.

Yet organizational actors are not pre-programmed robots. This draws our attention to one of the distinctive qualities of the role-based trust elicited in facework: in interaction, the "compulsory figures" prescribed by organizational roles and routines are mixed with the "free skate" (i.e., extra-role behavior) devised or improvised by the individual actor. The two may indeed be difficult to tell apart for an external trustor. As Bachmann notes, trustors themselves often find it difficult to determine whether their trust pertains more to their partner or more to the social system that controls the partner's behavior (1998: 308).

Organizational trust arises from this blend of intra- and extra-role behavior. This yields distinctive advantages as well as disadvantages. Of course, a highly competent representative is needed to credibly represent both an organization's values and the roles and routines institutionalized for their implementation. Perceived competence ranks particularly highly as a sign of

BRP trustworthiness (Hawes et al. 1989). Having an inadequate individual represent the organization is likely to erode organizational trust. This may be the case even if the boundary-spanner is perceived as atypical of the organization, as its institutional system may be considered incapable of assigning suitable individuals to important tasks (also see Perrone et al. 2003).

In contrast, a competent organizational representative who displays many of the tactical and communicative abilities called for in an effective boundary-spanner (Williams 2002; Marrone et al. 2007) can be of great value to the organization, as the blurred boundaries between intra- and extra-role behavior may help significantly improve the perception that external actors gain of the organization itself. The intra-/extra-role distinction can be particularly fuzzy in the case of boundary roles, which are often comparatively unstructured (Bettencourt & Brown 2003: 395; Walker et al. 1975: 35). Consequently, positive patterns of conduct, even where largely based on the boundary-spanners individual abilities, can come to be ascribed to the organization and its institutional system. This case represents the clearest example of how interpersonal trust may "rub off" onto organizational trust.

Organizational Trust Between Cognitive and Normative Trust

One fundamental drawback of organizational trust seems to be that it does not typically acquire the same depth as interpersonal trust, but lacks the emotional attachment often found in the latter. It is generally considered much "shallower" or "thinner" (Govier 1994: 239). While this may have a stabilizing influence, because disappointments will likely be felt to be less grave or emotionally consequential, "for the very same reasons [it] cannot offer the same degree of security as genuine trust in personal relationships can" (Lahno 2002: 7).

We can explain this issue in terms of the distinction between cognitive and normative trust. Cognitive trust, as defined here, encompasses predictive trust and competence trust—is the trustee *likely* to behave in the way expected? This includes the question: does the trustor think the trustee is *capable* of carrying out the behaviors? By contrast, normative trust has emotional relevance to the actor holding it (McAllister 1995). It refers not just to competence or likely behavior, but to the goodwill (Dore 1983) that the trustee is perceived to have toward the trustor and their common activity. As such, it refers to the actor's character or "whole disposition" (Dasgupta 1988).

It is only normative or "strong" trust that affords the trustor the full benefit of trusting. It reduces complexity more effectively, thus granting the trustor greater psychological exoneration (Luhmann 1979; Berger & Luckmann 1967). But organizational trust, where it is considered, is typically assumed to be purely cognitive in nature (e.g., Schoorman et al. 2007; Jeffries & Reed 2000).

By contrast, we hold that actors can develop normative trust in an organization. Lepsius (1997: 286–8) points out that actors' trust can relate merely to the material results of an organization's operations, or to the values underlying them. Taking this as a basis, we can define the two different forms as follows. Normative organizational trust refers to the organization's guiding ideas and values (what the organization "stands for," or what it "is all about"). Cognitive organizational trust, by contrast, refers to the predictability of future actions brought about by the roles and routines institutionalized to implement those ideas and values.

Cognitive organizational trust thus includes an assessment of probabilities based on, e.g., organizational interests and the ways in which current circumstances influence them. But it also encompasses a judgment on whether or not the roles and routines adequately fulfill their intended function (similar to competence trust in interpersonal relations). An organization's guiding ideas and values effectively represent an organizational analogue of individual goodwill. Normative organizational trust is thus based on more than a mere probabilistic prediction of likely vs. unlikely future courses of action, but is based on the much broader belief in having formed a correct impression of the organization's normative principles. (In this context also see the idea of "organizational identity"; Gioia 1998.)

This renders relevant not just whether actors *know* about the guiding ideas and values of an organization (and about their actual implementation in practice), but also whether and to what degree they *identify* with them (Tajfel 1982: 2). As Lahno points out, Hart (1961) convincingly explained this as the result of different perspectives.

> Hart distinguishes two different ways how [an actor] may look upon a social rule . . . From an 'external point of view', one perceives the rule as an uninvolved outside observer who does not himself regard the rule as valid and binding. . . . From an 'internal point of view', on the other hand, the social rule is perceived as valid, i.e. as a rule that actually justifies demands and obligations. . . . It is not only that others will most probably act according to the rules; it is also that one wishes this to be the case and considers them somehow to be obliged to act in these ways. (Lahno 2002: 8)

That is, while the organizational trust of an outsider will be purely cognitive in nature, an insider can hold normative trust in an organization. Obviously, one task of facework is to give a more intimate view of the organization. This encompasses, on the one hand, (cognitive) information about the organization, its internal workings, rules, roles and routines. But it also needs to attempt to make the external partner truly understand, and if possible accept, the organization's guiding ideas and values, as institutionalized in organizational culture. That is, facework needs to attempt to transform the external partner from an outsider to an insider. Only if this is successful can the external partner develop normative, and thus stronger and more stable, organizational trust. As Lewicki & Bunker (1996) note, strong inter-personal trust facilitates the adoption of such an insider perspective.

BOUNDARY-SPANNERS BETWEEN INTRA- AND INTER-ORGANIZATIONAL TRUST

Facework is both a highly central and a highly sensitive task. Of course, external trust building is not independent of internal processes (also see Ancona & Caldwell 1992). Indeed, by virtue of their centrality in inter-organizational trust building, boundary-spanners routinely establish "trust chains" that connect trust relations with external to such with internal partners.

Trust Chains

As the pivotal link between intra- and inter-organizational trust relations in these chains we regard the boundary-spanners role autonomy, defined by Perrone et al. (2003: 423) as "the leeway agents have in interpreting and enacting their roles." We do not assume that BRP, in a functionalist vein, necessarily or inevitably have trusting relationships with their constituents, nor that trust is the only way of granting the requisite role autonomy. But boundary-spanners will often have an active interest in building internal trust. Because they typically bundle the outputs of a number of departments, most BRP have to span boundaries *within* their organization too. What is more, they quite typically lack formal authority over their internal partners in a similar way to their external ones (Organ 1971). Consequently, relationship- and trust building are likely to be attractive strategies to them in both intra- and inter-organizational relationships (Nonis et al. 1996).

Furthermore, in some senses boundary-spanners are well placed to engage in trust building. One trait that clearly locates BRP at the boundaries of organizations is the lesser force with which the institutionalized world view of the organization imposes itself on them. They develop a different psychological orientation toward the organization as they face "*outward* upon the world" rather than being oriented primarily toward maintaining the organization's internal equilibrium (Kahn et al. 1964: 99; Adams 1980: 329). That is, to BRP it is particularly salient to be able to "take the role of the other" (Mead 1934), as they need to "understand the social constructions of other actors, and how they 'define the issue in relation to their own values and interests'" (Williams 2002: 110, partly quoting Hosking & Morley). Furthermore, there is a premium on understanding, and being able to use, external partners' symbolic repertoires provided by their respective institutional backgrounds (Organ 1971: 77). The necessary communicative abilities are regularly stressed in the literature and form an important part of the "impossible string of virtues" that are required of the ideal boundary-spanner (Fairtlough, quoted in Williams 2002: 112; Walker et al. 1975: 35).

These requirements sought for in boundary-spanners have a lot in common with abilities that facilitate successful trust building behavior (both within and between organizations). Of course, boundary-spanners do not necessarily have all of these capacities. Recruitment of suitable individuals into these positions can be highly problematic (Hartline & De Witt 2004; Lorenz 2003: 67). At a minimum, however, we may assume that over the time of their role incumbency, boundary-spanners will typically be faced with these requirements more frequently and accumulate more experience in regard to these trust-relevant abilities than organization members whose role has less "boundary relevance" (also see Tushman & Scanlan 1981a; Levina & Vaast 2005).

Our argument here is not that inter-organizational trust is inevitably based on or linked to intra-organizational trust, but merely that boundary-spanners are likely to regard internal trust as a desirable means to obtain the role autonomy they need to engage in inter-organizational trust building, and that their role provides incentives for acquiring some of the requisite abilities.

Ideally, then, intra-organizational trust leads to inter-organizational trust. Conversely, inter-organizational trust will frequently lead to higher performance on the part of the boundary-spanner, which is fit to strengthen internal constituents' trust in them (Tushman & Scanlan 1981a; Williams 2002). Restricting our observations to this relationship of reciprocal facilitation would, however, produce an unduly harmonistic picture of trusting relationships (a problem that is not uncommon in the literature; Kern 1998; Lewicki et al. 1998). We should not neglect that inter-organizational trust can also be *disruptive* of intra-organizational trust.

Inter-Organizational Trust and Intra-Organizational Suspicion

As noted, in order to build trust boundary-spanners routinely need to "take the role of the other," to understand the symbols, interests and values of external partners and their organizations. But many of the same behaviors that facilitate trust with their external partners are likely to arouse suspicion among internal constituents.

Because the understanding that they develop with their trusted counterpart in another organization is highly personalized, it is likely to appear to their own organizational constituents as opaque, difficult to control, or even threatening (also see Tushman & Scanlan 1981b: 290–1). To make matters worse, when constituents encounter the boundary-spanner, the latter will often be trying to fulfill their task to "represent accurately and influentially to his constituents the needs (preference orderings) of the outside organization with which he is dealing, as well as its values and norms" (Adams 1980: 333). These dynamics are liable to arouse suspicion about which goals and norms the BRP may regard as binding. Doubt about their loyalties is one of the "classic" problems BRP are regularly confronted with (Adams 1980; Organ 1971; also see Richter et al. 2006). This is reflected, for instance, in the "common industry practice . . . to have clauses in job contracts that prohibit salespeople from contact with previous customers for a specified period after employment termination" (Jeffries & Reed 2000: 878).

A typical concern of constituents is that a boundary-spanner may increasingly assimilate the values and interests of the partner organization instead of their own (Organ 1971; Friedman & Podolny 1992), i.e., that they may "go native" (Webber & Klimoski 2004; McElroy et al. 2001). We want to argue, however, that this is rather unlikely to arise from trusting relations with another organization's BRP for two reasons.

Firstly, counter to some more essentialist conceptions (e.g. Schweer 2003), in order to build trust actors only need to *respect* the partner's norms and values. They need to understand and tolerate them, but not actually to *share* them or adhere to them outside their common field of interaction. From our perspective, what BRP share with members of other organizations is not norms, but only the *symbols* of those norms. Because part of a symbol's meaning is always supplied by their user, "what is actually held in common is not very substantial, being *form* rather than content. Contents [may] differ widely" (Cohen 1985: 20).

Secondly, the assumption of a straightforward adoption of another organization's norms is simplistic because the norms in question would not actually be those of the partner organization, but those of the boundary system described above. This fact is often reflected in references to boundary-spanners' "dual identity" (Richter et al. 2006). BRP do identify, sometimes strongly, with the behavioral norms of this boundary system. External norms, e.g. those of a professional community common to both BRP, can reinforce this effect (Albert 1998; Lorenz 2003).

Neither of these points is mere quibbling. We are dealing not with norm adoption, but with symbolic exchange. In addition, the symbols used are not simply those of another organization, but have been negotiated between the BRP within the transitory boundary system. Rather than pointing us toward the risk of "going native," these arguments show the potential for an egoistic exploitation of inter-organizational trust relations by individual boundary-spanners.

When discussing facework dynamics, we considered the consequences of BRP competence (or incompetence). Equally crucial, however, is the question of their *willingness* to represent the organization favorably to external partners. (Note that this means that the BRP's behavior needs to exhibit competence and goodwill, i.e., two dimensions that trust can refer to.) Particularly where external partners have few other contacts within the organization, the representative will generally have to signal in one way or another their typicality of and commitment to their own organization. That is, the transfer of trust from the interpersonal to the organizational level will often have to be actively encouraged by the BRP as a part of facework.

At the same time, where business with an external partner is important to the organization (e.g. due to its volume), an individual relationship of trust with that partner may strengthen the BRP's position within their organization. The potential for abuse is, again, connected to the representative's role autonomy. The BRP may take care to keep the partner's trust focused on them as an individual rather than as an organizational representative. If they purposefully present themselves as disconnected from or atypical of the organization, no organizational trust will ensue (Sydow 2006: 390n.). Even distrust of the organization may be engendered if a trusted partner is seen to feel the need to distance themselves from it.

Especially in industries where actors can pursue highly individualized careers and/or where "poaching" among competitors is common (also see below), personalized trust relations with central external partners can be harnessed as internal sources of power (Hanlon 2004; Kroeger 2012). Interestingly, whereas trust tends to be associated with legitimate power only, this use of external trust is likely to generate an illegitimate power source as it directly contradicts organizational norms that demand the representative evoke organizational rather than individual trust.

The power that can be derived from such constellations should not be underestimated. Not only can it be quite considerable, depending on the centrality of the trust relation to the organization's operations, but it can be highly persistent. It is likely to be difficult to address or challenge due to the immensely positive connotations of the trust relation that lies at its surface. Challenging patterns of behavior which are generally acknowledged as productive, prosocial, and altruistic (Uslaner 2002) is much less likely to find the support of other constituents. Beyond that, when particular ways of building trust are institutionalized which effectively favor certain groups or individuals over others, the resulting power relations can be institutionalized with them. Path dependence effects can contribute to perpetuating these power imbalances even beyond the point where their original basis (e.g., the respective trust relationship) has ceased to exist. In the worst case, the illegitimate power relations may undergo "deep" institutionalization together with the corresponding trust patterns. If this occurs, they become taken for granted and gain the particularly effective tacit influence that Lukes (1974) described as the "third face of power." That is, the existence of these power relations comes to be so taken for granted that they become part of the cognitive and normative "locks" that institutionalized repertoires may place on interaction (Campbell 2004).

This possibility, combined with the institutionalization of power behind an innocuous "façade of trust" (Hardy et al. 1998), can make this kind of power highly enduring and resilient. The potential pay-off for a BRP from egoistically using individual trust relations is thus not inconsiderable. Awareness of this potential for exploitation creates dilemmas for both constituents and the BRP themselves.

Role Conflict within the Trust Chain

Constituents tend to be acutely aware of the potential that the boundary-spanners special role offers for egoistic abuse. However, revoking internal trust in the BRP would likely mean restricting the boundary-spanners autonomy and imposing additional monitoring and control mechanisms on them (Ferrin et al. 2007: 477–8; Aldrich & Herker 1977: 226). Constituents are often mindful that these measures are likely to have a negative effect on the representative's ability and/or willingness to engage in effective facework. (Also see Rosen & Adams 1974 on the reluctance of superiors to discipline influential boundary-spanners.)

On the one hand, (perceived) BRP *competence* may be compromised by lacking discretion if external partners come to doubt the BRP has sufficient command over organizational resources (internal clout; see Doney & Cannon 1997: 37–40).

On the other hand, (factual) BRP *goodwill* may be jeopardized if the BRP's organizational commitment suffers from repeated allegations of lacking loyalty or the imposition of further controls. Because close monitoring is typically interpreted as a signal of lacking trust (Kramer 1999: 590–2), there is a significant risk that these measures will function as a self-fulfilling prophecy, affecting the BRP's job satisfaction and organizational commitment, and reducing their motivation to represent the organization favorably to others (Creed & Miles 1996; Goolsby 1992; Bradford et al. 2009). Furthermore, decreased commitment will lead, first and foremost, to the abandonment of positive extra-role conduct (Organ 1988; Jex 1998)—i.e., of precisely those behaviors which we identified as crucial for building organizational trust in facework. This type of "free skate" behavior (and *a fortiori* the individual capacities needed for it) are difficult, if not impossible to enforce (often even to define; Bettencourt & Brown 2003: 395). Constituents are thus faced with a conflict regarding the BRP to which no easy or off-the-shelf solutions seem to exist.

To the boundary-spanners themselves, role conflict—interpreted here as "perceived incompatibility among role expectations and demands" (Bettencourt & Brown 2003: 396)—tends to be part and parcel of their role (Goolsby 1992; Friedman & Podolny 1992). Beyond the potential for conflict inherent in all boundary roles, caused by the often contradictory expectations placed in them by external vs. internal partners, as well as different groups within their own organization (Whetten 1978; Kahn et al. 1964), boundary-spanners can be faced with a dimension of role conflict that is specific to the trust chain at whose center they are placed.

The boundary-spanners' trust and trustworthiness are a "given" neither for external partners nor for internal constituents. The BRP will thus typically need to build and maintain trust actively in both intra- and inter-organizational relations. This is of relevance both to egoistic and organizationally committed, to powerful and less powerful representatives. Even powerful BRP tend to opt for "softer" solutions as long as they can avoid the risks of coercive power use (Nonis et al. 1996; Molm 1997).

We have seen that external partners will generally be alive to indications of the BRP's role autonomy and intra-organizational power. Understanding and respect for the external partner's motives and constraints, commitment to jointly formulated interests, and a capacity to credibly and influentially represent them within their home organization are important factors that external partners will want to see credibly symbolized (Lewicki & Bunker 1996; Kramer 1999). The demands of organizational constituents will regularly be the direct opposite. Particularly if BRP loyalty has already become a matter of suspicion, their constituents may call for clear signals of undiluted commitment and conformity to the home organization's norms, goals, and procedures, with no exceptions or digressions made in favor of external agents.

This conflict is not easily solved by the BRP simply being "a little two-faced" (Organ 1971: 78) and switching behavioral styles between audiences. Rather, we would expect both internal and external partners to look to choices which can be interpreted as reliable signals for either autonomy or conformity because they involve a tangible business decision and/or consequential material stakes. "Close party supervision, for example, increases the press for bargaining and 'hard tactics' by representatives who must demonstrate their loyalty" (Brown 1983: 33; also see Rao & Schmidt 1998). The BRP, too, may thus be faced with a conflict that is difficult to solve in daily business. How both constituents and boundary-spanners deal with this potential for conflict will largely be an empirical question.

EMPIRICAL OBSERVATIONS

Our conceptual perspective on trust building across organizational boundaries needs to be fleshed out empirically. Especially the question of how boundary-spanners as well as their constituents deal with the potential conflicts thrown up by internal and external trust building are in need of empirical clarification. For this purpose, we will draw on empirical evidence collected in twenty-one interviews in the UK book publishing industry in 2008 and 2009. The quotes we will present in the following stem from boundary-spanners (mostly editors and senior executives), who are communicating with authors, professional proofreaders, printing firms etc. (Numbers behind quotes in the form "RS 01" refer to individual respondents. For a methodological description of the study, see Kroeger 2012.)

Interpersonal and Organizational Trust

All respondents in our sample stress the decisive influence of individuals and their personalities. "Personalities are key. . . . They *are* the business"

(RS 20). However, only a small minority maintain that their trust relations are always strictly interpersonal only, insisting that "I deal one on one with people . . ., and if they are in a company that's coincidental" (RS 01).

Overall, our respondents overwhelmingly agree that companies, as entities, can be trusted and regarded as trustworthy or untrustworthy. Furthermore, in many cases it is apparent that trust placed in an organization refers to the roles, routines, or working practices defined directly by the organization. The trust placed in organizational representatives, then, is at least partially role-based. Even a freelance contact who claimed at first that her trust relations were purely interpersonal reflects later: "maybe it's not me they trust, maybe it's the position they trust" (RS 06).

On the other hand, respondents are highly aware of the distinction between the role and its individual incumbent, who may have considerable discretion within it.

> The idea of being the face of [the company]—on the one hand, yes. . . . But on the other hand there's always an awareness that there's a separation between the individual and the firm. It's quite hard to imagine a personality becoming so much the representative of the culture of the firm. (RS 03)

External partners' trust refers to the role as well as the personality within it. This is why "you can have an untrustworthy set of people who are dealing, but the company ethic is sound," or conversely, "you can have somebody dealing on a day-to-day basis that is much more trustworthy" than the overall company (RS 07). The distinction becomes particularly conspicuous when the two objects of trust are separated. One respondent quotes the example of an individual who proved untrustworthy at a previous occasion and who moves between organizations.

> [They] have done something dubious under one company, [and] then they're working for some other company. So then you have to look out in regards to, is the individual more [significant] . . ., or is the fact that they're working for this other organisation now going to be basis enough for the trust? (RS 11)

The respondents' trust is thus founded on "a mixture of the individual relationship . . . and the credibility of [the company]" (RS 03). Obviously, respondents are continually alive to the difference between the role (as defined by the organization) and its enactment (as devised by the role incumbent).

Facework and Beyond

Accordingly, all respondents except one (who voices a strong belief that trust can only ever be interpersonal) confirm that the behavior of individual boundary-spanners is representative of their organizations. One respondent aptly expresses the concept behind facework with the metaphors of "face" and "voice":

> The *face* that you see most of the time represents a . . . company. . . . The *voice* that you hear . . . is based in that company. (RS 16)

Especially during the early stages of trust building, facework can have immense impact. A senior executive points out:

> Because as an outsider you go on very limited information, you exaggerate the import of that information. . . . So if all I know about [a publishing house] is I know three or four people in the company, then for me that's [that publishing house], a hundred percent. (RS 03)

In the eyes of respondents, this principle clearly extends to issues of trust and trustworthiness in which the organization is represented by its boundary-spanners (or, as one respondent puts it in an interesting reversal, "how [the] individuals are presented through an organisation"; RS 12). An editor explains that he will "set out a stall if you like. . . . I will seek to create that trust in them that here's a [publishing house] that's going to do a very good job" (RS 15). That is, he routinely strives to invoke organizational trust.

Although perceptions of individual and organizational trustworthiness can remain separate (see above), most respondents who act as representatives do not reflect much on the transferal of ascribed trustworthiness to their company, but tend to take it for granted as part of their representative function. Consequently, their strategy for representing their company as trustworthy is simply to behave in a trustworthy manner themselves.

The facework dynamics also extend to the ascription of (trust-relevant) values to organizations, based on the conduct of their representatives. These values too, roughly equivalent to an organization's "goodwill," are communicated in routine facework, i.e., in habitual day-to-day interaction: "It's those sorts of small things that you do all the time that reinforce an opinion that you're a decent company and a decent group of people" (RS 08).

This is also mirrored in the respondents' own reactions to the normative facework of partner organizations. Several respondents state that the relationships with external partners depend strongly on the notion of perceived "goodwill" of the organization. A production director, for instance, explains that visits to Singaporean printers convinced her that "they are very decent . . . organisations. I don't have a problem putting work with them" (RS 12). Again, trust based on perceived organizational values is not identical with normative congruence, but the trust refers to the perceived generalized goodwill of the other party (in this case: the other organization) in relation to common future activity. (In this example, the perceived organizational values enable the respondent to trust that the partner company will "not actually harm anyone in Singapore" if she puts work with them.)

As we have seen, in facework boundary-spanners can convince external partners of the organization's trust and/or trustworthiness. At the same time, the above respondent's impression has been formed only partially by facework. While she relies on meetings with representatives at first, she tends to schedule visits to the printers' production facilities later. In order to trust them, she considers it "important to see what they look like and to see how they treat their staff, what kind of people they employ," etc. (RS 12; similar by RS 08). Meeting further relevant members of the other organization is considered particularly important. Thus, trust building often proceeds "beyond facework."

External partners gain "a sense of how the organization works" from organizational representatives who, "first time round, [will] want to explain to them to some extent" (RS 13). But especially in longer-term relations respondents normally strive to form a more thorough impression, looking beyond a single representative's facework. Indeed, this deeper insight into the other organization can be invaluable in correcting misleading impressions resulting from facework (both misleadingly "good" and misleadingly "bad"; RS 10). One respondent relates the example of a potential partner she had never used because he personally did not seem trustworthy to her:

> This was a purely personal instinct, I thought "there's just something about this guy that [isn't right]" . . . And once I went and met with him *in his office* and saw his staff and his operation and things like that, my whole opinion of the operation changed. (RS 11)

Furthermore, the granting of deeper insight to an external partner on the part of the organization can itself serve as a token of trust and trustworthiness, through showing that the organization has "nothing to hide," and relinquishing a source of potential power over the outsider: "The more you're brought into the process, the more you're trusted, [and] the less those new pieces of information that come up are used to put you in your place" (RS 02).

It thus seems plausible that while the significance of facework is unrivalled initially, it can be gradually offset by the deeper and more comprehensive insights into the organization that (may) follow. Because these deeper insights are typically facilitated by representatives, successful facework may progressively render itself redundant.

Internal and External Trust

A clear majority of respondents agrees that the ability to engage in facework and other forms of external relationship building is affected notably by the presence or absence of internal trust between the BRP and relevant internal constituents (especially their superiors). A senior executive explains:

> The editor's got to trust us that we're gonna back up their judgement, and we've got to be confident that the editor's got the right judgement. . . . But if the editor's . . . unsure that we're gonna support their judgement, that's gonna communicate to the author at some level, and he's not gonna be as comfortable in his dealings with the organisation. (RS 13)

An editor unreservedly confirms this, talking about the possibility of lacking internal trust: "Yes, I think undoubtedly it would rub off in less confidence in dealing with [authors] . . . Because I wouldn't be able to make those same promises" (RS 15).

Vice versa, success in external relationships is a crucial factor for BRP in building up the "track record" that underlies much internal trust building too. Another senior executive elaborates on this, speaking from the perspective of the BRP's superior:

> If you're running one of these divisions and you have maybe ten editors reporting to you, you will know that some of them you really really trust, because they have a fantastic track record. And . . . if they come into your office and say "I've found an incredible budget-busting book, and I want to spend two hundred thousand pounds on it," you'll know that the last five times they did that, they were right. (RS 05)

This kind of trust, of course, is largely predictive (i.e., cognitive) in nature. But it is likely to afford the editor considerable discretion in his external dealings. While the above quotes, strictly speaking, pertain only to the connection between internal trust and external *relationships*, this points us toward the question of role autonomy, which may act as a link between internal and external trust building. An editor clarifies this in connection to just the same idea of a "track record": "You can't just do a series of books that [sell small numbers], or you'd be finished, and then you'd have no autonomy" (RS 18).

To appreciate the function of role autonomy in external trust building, we need to consider the import of initiative in extra-role behavior. A production director stresses its potency as a trust signal, describing it as

> demonstrating that you are willing to go the extra mile to help, that it's not purely "you've paid for this and therefore we do that," that people are prepared to pull stops out to help achieve a certain outcome. . . . And that's I think how you build the trust. (RS 12)

A majority of respondents refer to the trust-evoking behavioral signal of "going the extra mile," i.e., of showing commitment to the common aim by proving initiative and "interacting with the project rather than just blindly following instructions" (RS 01), as well as being flexible regardless of the terms dictated by contract (RS 14). (Also see Deakin & Wilkinson's concepts of "flexibility beyond contract" and "flexibility outside contract"; 1998.)

While this is a potent signal of goodwill, underlying it is the ability (in a sense: the "competence") to be flexible. In order to develop trust in an organizational representative, outside partners typically need to "feel they're dealing with someone who's empowered to take decisions and to do things rather than someone who's going to say 'well, I'll have to get that approved'" (RS 13). Perceived in-house "clout" ranks highly as a signal that promises made will actually be fulfilled. Sufficient discretion in the interpretation of their role is thus crucial to the trust building abilities of BRP.

Our data also support the idea that internal trust suggests itself as a solution to this problem. As one respondent emphatically states, "you have a sense of autonomy the more you're trusted, . . . more freedom, . . . more licence to operate" (RS 10). Internal trust, thus, does indeed seem to facilitate external trust. The senior executive quoted above confirms this, asserting that "we've got to trust the editor . . . because otherwise they're making promises we're gonna say no to, . . . which is gonna make the relationship fall apart very quickly, both with the editor and with the author" (RS 13).

With regard to a different interface (*viz.*, relations with freelancers), another respondent emphatically confirms the importance of internal trust.

> It would make my job much harder if [the in-house people] didn't trust me. Because I'd have to justify everything I did. . . . So I couldn't function if they didn't trust me. (RS 06)

Going in a little more detail, she explains how internal trust would impact on external trust and vice versa:

> If they didn't trust me and I had to justify what I sent out to everybody all the time—there are so many unsaid things that happen in the process that would then have to be said. . . . And it means that I would have to be on my guard to make sure that the freelancers *absolutely* did a good job so that I could *then* try and win the trust of the in-house people by presenting them with this good job that somebody's done, so that next time they would know that they could trust me. And that would affect my relationship with the freelancers, . . . it would be harder to trust *them*. (RS 06)

This reaffirms the point that even though internal trust may not be the only conceivable way of granting sufficient role autonomy to BRP to engage in effective external trust building, it is certainly an important one.

BRP Loyalty and Role Conflict

While we will not go too deeply into the more abstract issues connected to the "transitory boundary systems" in which BRP operate, it is worth noting that BRP often conceive of themselves and their external partners as what could be termed a "trans-organizational team." A production director, for instance, is very clear on the relationship with some of their suppliers' staff: "even though they are working for a different company on a different continent, it's more like a team effort" (RS 12; very similar by RS 08). Another production director generalizes this statement further:

> Without being all cosy-cosy about it, the whole supply chain . . . is one big team. Cause . . . we want a product that is where it needs to be at the time when it needs to be there, and of fit-for-purpose quality . . . It's in all of our interests to achieve that, so the supplier, of course, is part of the team. (RS 20)

References to the common task, to shared aims and goals, and to various ways of helping each other out within these "teams" are frequent. The transitory boundary teams can thus gain a high degree of coherence. Accordingly, some external partners are regarded to be "as much part of the company as the people who work here are" (RS 09). A production director confirms: "I always feel that the account controller that happens to work for [our chief printers] is actually our employee within their factory" (RS 16).

Mirroring this, a respondent admits that she enjoys the interaction with her external partners so much that actually, "it's the fitting within *this* organisation that's the most challenging for me" (RS 11).

Given these statements, it is not surprising that a clear majority of respondents affirm that they are constantly alive to potential issues of divided or unclear BRP loyalties, sometimes even wondering: "And who does the [BRP] end up working for, as it were?" (RS 21)

Beyond that, BRP are frequently faced with situations of role conflict in which they are supposed to reveal their "true colors." Respondents report high levels of role conflict as a matter of course. As boundary-spanners, they frequently refer to their role as "always in-between" (RS 05), in the middle between external and different internal partners. "Well, that's what I think our role *is*, essentially" (RS 20).

Internal and External Signaling

Respondents thus agree that external partners are looking for signals of autonomy, that the best way of achieving that autonomy is by getting the trust of—potentially suspicious—internal constituents, and that they, as BRP, are habitually faced with role conflict. With that, all ingredients for the hypothesized signaling conflict are present. The conflict, however, is not. While the above factors would lead us to expect a problematic contradiction between the requirements of simultaneously signaling conformity internally and autonomy externally, there are virtually no indications of this in the data.

Our data suggest two reasons for this, both of which are connected to the BRP's relationship with external partners. Firstly, the respondents frequently emphasize that they can count on their external partners to appreciate the constraints that they operate under. Many external partners are in boundary roles themselves and, accordingly, are likely to be experienced in "taking the role of the other." "It's trying to put yourself in their shoes" (RS 15; very similar by RS 18). The commonalities that exist between most boundary roles are likely to facilitate this identification (also see Lorenz 2003). Whether the external partner is a BRP or not, they share membership in the same boundary system, at the same company interface, and their role is typically either similar or complementary to that of the BRP.

On the part of the external partner, these factors are likely to result in high cognitive familiarity with and normative respect for the boundary-spanners role obligations (or, as another respondent puts it, "that respect for one another and that understanding for one another's businesses"; RS 08). References to the notion of an "understanding" with external partners are highly frequent in our data.

A production director illustrates this understanding:

> The influence that . . . individuals can have over a business will depend on its structure. . . . So if it's [a large multinational corporation] . . ., then they're working within tight parameters. They're still a personality, they're still an individual, we're just putting them into context. You are then clear on the constraints that *they* have to work within. (RS 20)

External partners thus do not require signals of BRP autonomy at the expense of their respective organizations. More than that, the second reason for the absence of the hypothesized signaling conflict, as suggested by our data, is that strong signals of autonomy will often run the risk of indicating disengagement from their "home" organization. Some respondents acknowledge the possibility of distancing oneself from the company to signal autonomy to external partners, and that this does happen at times. Under certain circumstances, BRP are able to "play people off" against each other; but if goodwill trust is to be built, "you can do that . . . only rarely" (RS 15). Overall, respondents agree that it is "not . . . a very productive thing" (RS 14).

Because external partners are aware that the BRP will necessarily need to signal conformity to their organization, distancing themselves from it is likely to be taken as "two-facedness" and thus as a signal precisely of *lacking* trustworthiness. A production director illustrates this with a very clear example.

If . . . they use the phrase "they" about a different department in their organisation being responsible for a hold-up, for instance, I know we're dealing with the wrong person. . . . If they don't use that phrase "we", or you don't feel that they are one and the same with their organisation, then I feel very uneasy about things. And I think my staff do as well. (RS 16)

Organ's assumption that others may be "repelled by the 'hypocrisy' . . . of the boundary agent" (1971: 79) obviously applies not just to constituents (as suggested by Organ), but to external partners too. This is consonant with our assumptions about normative or goodwill trust. To build it, trustors want to be convinced that they have formed a correct impression of the trustee's character. Signaling should thus be consistent between internal and external relations. Perceived inconsistencies are likely to be interpreted as strategic manipulations and thus as signals of lacking trustworthiness on the part of the BRP.

Correspondingly, there is ample data which substantiates that to build trust, the same principles of signaling apply intra- and inter-organizationally. Thus, respondents state that internal trust depends on communication and openness, delivering on promises and building up a track record, establishing an "understanding," and "going the extra mile" much the same way as in external relations, and that this symbolism is of the same tacit kind. Given the need for consistent signaling, it is unsurprising that it should be primarily oriented at the demands of internal (rather than external) partners. External partners are generally understanding of the BRP's constraints, and the most relevant internal partners include superiors who have authority over the BRP.

Both internal and external partners thus expect signals of conformity to the "home" organization. This does not mean, however, that there are no tensions for the BRP between internal and external trust building. They still need to keep a balance between their commitments to internal and external partners. But because the signals need to be "legible" to both parties, the BRP will likely have to alternate between signals indicating commitment to each. At times, they have to "shout the corner" of their external partners within their organization (RS 06), at others they need to manage, e.g., a lowering of expectations of their partners on behalf of their organization (RS 13). They have to "play it by ear" according to the specific situation.

One of the central factors in explaining why respondents do not seem to regard any of these aspects as very serious problems is clearly that they are simply used to dealing with role conflict. They tend to regard it as a normal and everyday part of their role, often to a degree where it is not conceived of as real conflict any more.

Again, this is sometimes reflected in our data when respondents explain they never face role conflict, and only later realize that that is not quite true. As an experienced editor concedes: "Yeah, I suppose there is a conflict there.

I don't know how it's resolved really. But maybe it remains unresolved and you have to keep the faith" (RS 18).

External Trust and Internal Power

The internal trust of constituents in boundary-spanners, on the other hand, can indeed face considerable obstacles. In the following, we will consider some factors that may justify constituents' trust, but also suspicion and lack of trust in BRP. To illustrate our points, we will consider the relationships of editors with authors and with their internal partners, as well as the potential for conflict resulting from the "poaching" of editors.

As our data clearly demonstrate, the trust between editor and author lies at the heart of the business model of publishing. Without it, many respondents would think a successful publishing process inconceivable. This trust is constitutively linked to internal trust relationships.

On the one hand, the author's trust also has to extend to the way in which the editor represents them within the organization. A senior editor points out that this means that trust "is the crucial importance. . . . The author needs to be able to feel confident, although in the knowledge that their editor works with other people, that they have their total loyalty" (RS 18). An author confirms emphatically: "that *is* a question of trust." For instance, "I don't *know* whether he says to [the lady] in the publicity department 'all right, we've given it a big go, let's forget about it now and concentrate on other titles'" (RS 19). Consequently, trust is indispensable.

On the other hand, beyond the editor's external trust relationship with the author, internal trust in the editor can be seen to be (almost) equally crucial to the overall business model of book publishing. First and foremost, this trust pertains to the notion that the editor is competent in selecting and acquiring the right authors. A senior executive underlines its centrality by reminding us that publishing companies have outsourced many of their old functions like printing and distribution: "So what are we? We . . . represent an editorial decision." In commercial terms, then, "it's all about editorial genius, having the taste for what will be the zeitgeist when something is published" (RS 21). Therefore, in a sense, publishing is centrally "about having a faith in that man's [or woman's] judgement" (RS 16).

Acquiring new authors is of course a central element of publishing. But because of the inherent unpredictability of success, it is even more important in commercial terms to retain authors who have already proven profitable and who can be expected to generate further successes. A senior executive emphasizes: "The most commercially successful publishers in the world are those who have a stable portfolio of repeating authors" (RS 21).

The "glue" binding successful authors to the publisher is invariably considered to be a close and trusting relationship with them. "If there's no trust . . ., there's nothing to stop the author just going for the biggest offer every time, and shifting publisher every time" (RS 09). As a consequence, the building of trusting relationships with authors is considered "at the heart of being a good commissioning editor. Absolutely, a hundred percent" (RS 15).

A senior executive likens the case of returning authors to "somebody who's trusting you to be the midwife of their book every year, two years. You want the same midwife, cause you know that they give birth to your books successfully" (RS 21).

One question is central here, however: who exactly is the "midwife"? Who or what is it that the trust binds the author to—the publishing house or the individual editor?

Again, we hold that the answer to this question is best drawn not from "cheap talk," but from concrete commercial and material interaction—in this case, when the editor of one or several successful authors is "poached" by a competitor.

The rationale behind this "poaching" is that, because of their close and trusting relationship, the author(s) will follow the editor to the new publisher.

> If you are [one extremely successful author]'s editor, somebody who hires you if [this author] is out of contract will be able to say "well, maybe I'm buying myself five-hundred thousand hardback copies if I hire this editor." (RS 05)

Indeed, this happens regularly, and authors do often follow the editor. As an experienced editor explains:

> If, let us say, an editor . . . goes to another [company], I don't think it's illegitimate to ask an author to pursue. Or you may not even want to ask . . ., the author may not hesitate to follow. And obviously that happens a fair amount. (RS 18)

These dynamics provide us with a very clear example of a central external trust relation that serves as a source of internal power. This power becomes visible in the agreement of several senior executives that they do everything to retain successful editors.

> We've got one like that here, who's absolutely extraordinary and supreme with authors, and as a result has an amazing stable of best-sellers . . . And you would employ him forever for that, because he is the glue that keeps authors who sell half a million copies on the list. (RS 05)

Other senior executives seem to agree that you "would employ [such editors] forever for that"—they describe high salaries and various other rewards to "keep them happy" and "keep them with you" (RS 09). Another respondent gets to the heart of the matter.

It gives them loads of power . . . These editors carry a lot and lot of personal power because of the fact that they're the ones who hold the relationships, and if they resign or leave they take their list with them. (RS 10)

(Both of these respondents stress elsewhere that trust lies at the heart of this relationship.)

Authors hold different levels of power in their relationships with publishers, depending on their success. Together with highly successful authors, their editors command significant power within their "home" organization because of the constant potential threat of their moving to publishers who may want to "poach" the editor-author team.

In these cases, the author's trust is focused entirely on the editor, rather than on the wider company. Whether intentionally (in order to retain this power) or not, the respective editors have obviously failed to translate this interpersonal into organizational trust through facework.

Counter-Strategies

Thus, our data provide clear evidence that editors can use the external trust relationships with successful authors as an internal power resource. However, as a result the publishing house is at a higher risk of losing some of its most central assets, at least in part because the author's trust in the editor is not transferred to the publisher as an organization, but remains fully interpersonal.

It is not entirely clear whether or not the editors in question *intentionally* obstruct this transfer. But there are some indications that this applies at least to some cases. One respondent points to the egocentric orientation of some editors. Assuming the vantage point of an imaginary editor, she explains:

I'm the one that holds the relationship with [a well-known author], therefore I am special. The fact that [this publishing company] pays my salary, oh that's just a by-the-side. (RS 10)

Returning to an issue previously touched upon, editors may at times try to maintain their individual trustworthiness in the author's eyes at the expense of that of the wider organization. A senior executive mentions that in some of the companies she previously worked for, you could overhear editors blaming the company if they failed to deliver on their promises: "I was incredibly keen, but of course I was stopped by my senior colleagues" (RS 05). Another senior executive, similarly, talks about "political" actions undertaken only to further the editor's own interest. "It's not an untrustworthiness of a really egregious kind, but it's a dubious motivation. . . . I am aware of that as a problem" (RS 03).

On the other hand, the failure to translate interpersonal into organizational trust may be merely an inadvertent omission. Some respondents seem to hold that, while companies can generally be the object of trust, this particular trust relation between editor and author is simply too elusive and idiosyncratic to ever relate to anyone but them individually and personally. "Because it is all to do with creativity and all those intangibles—how authors thrive" (RS 04). The trust relation is based on "synchronis[ing] with an author's imaginative direction" (RS 18), and on "a certain taste or a certain sensibility, or a certain . . . personality" (RS 03). From this vantage point, there seems no alternative but to simply accept the potential for egoistic abuse of external trust relations as a given. ("So just get on with it!"; RS 16).

However, trust is not a zero-sum game. Additional trust relationships can be built without reducing the trust between editor and author. There is no need to reduce the editor's autonomy and thus endanger external trust building. Instead, constituents (in particular the editor's superiors) often strive to embed the author more thoroughly within the company. By going "beyond facework" (see above), they can promote trust building with other members of the organization in order to bind the author to the wider organization rather than to the individual editor only.

After all, within the publisher it is not in fact only the editor who the success of the book depends on. Rather, the team of people that contribute to it include members of different departments, such as art and design, sales and marketing, production and distribution. Consequently, "if you're somebody on their fiftieth novel you kind of know your team, and you know the people that bring your book to market" (RS 21). An editor underscores the significance of this.

> When the author delivers a manuscript that the commissioning editor's delighted with, . . . but you've got a shoddy team around you, then you end up both being very let down . . . You are very dependent on those good people around you for it to be a success. And . . . however good that relationship might be with an author . . . , that relationship can be shattered by failings on the part of other people in the company . . . , or it can be cemented by other people in the company. (RS 15)

Multiple relationships of authors are thus often highly productive. Beyond that, however, they can serve as a safety net against opportunism on the part of the author as described above. A senior executive makes this explicit.

> We also try to make sure that our really important authors have multiple relationships, that they know the sales director, they know me [the managing director], they know the chief executive, they know maybe five or six people around before you can get to the cover designer and the marketing person and the publicist, who of course they always

know. Because the great risk with editors is, . . . they carry value with them . . . So you try to diminish the possibility of editors leaving and taking the value of the business with them by making sure that the author really does have—if they're an important author—a real network of relationships. (RS 05)

Several senior executives confirm that "every year the emphasis is more on teamwork with the publisher" (RS 13). And indeed, several respondents draw attention to the fact that this does often succeed in keeping authors from following the editor.

Their authors don't always follow them. Their authors' allegiance may be to a chequebook, it may be to a company that over many, many years has served them very, very well. It may not be specifically to that editor—they know the sales people very well, they may even know the production people very well. (RS 16)

Apart from purely commercial reasons, then, the relationship with the "team" in the company can be decisive. Of course, we cannot simplistically deduce the presence or absence of trust from this. Authors may follow an editor or refrain from doing so for a variety of reasons. However, the same senior executive who likened publishing an author's book to midwifery (see above) clarifies the significant role of trust.

There are absolutely good examples, recent examples, of somewhere where an editor has moved, and because the company, the team has been solid, dependable, good, and consistent enough, the editor's gone and the authors have stayed. Because they trust that team. (RS 21)

CONCLUSION

In this chapter, we aimed to contribute some much-needed clarifications to the literature on inter-organizational trust by describing the processes through which boundary-spanners build, maintain, and translate trust from the interpersonal to the inter-organizational level. Our findings are as follows.

Organizational representatives interact in transitory boundary systems. These systems are the locus of building trust and one of the loci of its institutionalization (in addition to the organizations involved).

Organizational trust is trust placed in organizations as social systems. It is a form of system trust, is enacted as interpersonal trust and mediated by role-based trust. This mediation or translation takes place in facework, in which the representative enriches organizational role prescriptions with extra-role behavior.

For boundary-spanners, trust with external partners is connected to internal trust relations with their organizational constituents. The key link between these trust relations is constituted by the boundary-spanners' role autonomy. Internal and external trust can facilitate each other, but they can also lead to internal conflict—for the BRP themselves, and for their organizational constituents if the BRP (ab)uses their special position to turn external trust into a source of possibly illegitimate internal power. Especially the latter point was demonstrated empirically with respect to the internal and external trust relations of editors in UK book publishing. While the way the conflict unfolds for boundary-spanners proved different from our theoretical expectations, our data provided an alternative explanation—in short, external partners value consistency over autonomy. Organizational constituents were shown to address their conflicts regarding the boundary-spanner by going "beyond facework" and embedding authors more deeply in multiple relationships within the organization.

Clearly, trust across boundaries deserves further attention, conceptually as well as empirically. We hope that this chapter will provide a fruitful starting point.

REFERENCES

Adams, S.J. (1976). The Structure and Dynamics of Behavior in Organizational Boundary Roles. In Dunnette, M.D. (ed.). *Handbook of Industrial and Organizational Psychology*. Chicago: Rand McNally. 1175–99.

Adams, S.J. (1980). Inter-Organizational Processes and Organization Boundary Activities. *Research in Organizational Behavior* 2: 321–55.

Albert, S. (1998). The Definition and Metadefinition of Identity. In Whetten, D.A. & Godfrey, P.C. (eds.). *Identity in Organizations: Building Theory through Conversations*. London: Sage. 1–13.

Aldrich, H. & Herker, D. (1977). Boundary Spanning Roles and Organization Structure. *Academy of Management Review* 2: 217–230.

Ancona, D.G. & Caldwell, D.F. (1992). Bridging the Boundary: External Activity and Performance in Organizational Teams. *Administrative Science Quarterly* 37: 634–65.

Apelt, M. (2003). Bürokratische Strukturen stützen Vertrauen. *Erwägen Wissen Ethik* 14: 332–3.

Bachmann, R. (1998). Conclusion: Trust—Conceptual Aspects of a Complex Phenomenon. In Lane, C. & Bachmann, R. (eds.). *Trust Within and Between Organizations: Conceptual Issues and Empirical Applications*. Oxford: OUP. 298–322.

Bachmann, R. (2001). Trust, Power and Control in Trans-Organizational Relations. *Organization Studies* 22: 337–65.

Berger, P.L. & Luckmann, T. (1967). *The Social Construction of Reality: A Treatise in the Sociology of Knowledge*. London: Allen Lane.

Bettencourt, L.A. & Brown, S.W. (2003). Role Stressors and Customer-Oriented Boundary-Spanning Behaviors in Service Organizations. *Journal of the Academy of Marketing Science* 31: 394–408.

Bigley, G.A. & Pearce, J.L. (1998). Straining for Shared Meaning in Organization Science: Problems of Trust and Distrust. *Academy of Management Review* 23: 405–21.

Bradford, K.D., Crant, M. & Phillips, J.M. (2009). How Suppliers Affect Trust with Their Customers: The Role of Salesperson Job Satisfaction and Perceived Customer Importance. *Journal of Marketing Theory and Practice* 17: 383–94.

Brown, L.D. (1983). *Managing Conflict at Organizational Interfaces*. Reading, MA: Addison-Wesley.

Campbell, J.L. (2004). *Institutional Change and Globalization*. Princeton, NJ: Princeton University Press.

Cohen, A.P. (1985). *The Symbolic Construction of Community*. Chichester: Horwood.

Creed, W.E.D. & Miles, R.E. (1996). Trust in Organizations: A Conceptual Framework Linking Organizational Forms, Managerial Philosophies, and the Opportunity Costs of Controls. In Kramer, R.M. & Tyler, T.R. (eds). *Trust in Organizations: Frontiers of Theory and Research*. London: Sage. 16–38.

Currall, S.C. & Inkpen, A.C. (2002). A Multilevel Approach to Trust in Joint Ventures. *Journal of International Business Studies* 33: 479–95.

Dasgupta, P. (1988). Trust as a Commodity. In Gambetta, D. (ed.). *Trust: Making and Breaking Cooperative Relations*. New York: Blackwell. 49–72.

Deakin, S. & Wilkinson, F. (1998). Contract Law and the Economics of Inter-Organizational Trust. In Lane, C. & Bachmann, R. (eds.). *Trust Within and Between Organizations: Conceptual Issues and Empirical Applications*. Oxford: OUP. 146–72.

Doney, P.M. & Cannon, J.P. (1997). An Examination of the Nature of Trust in Buyer—Seller Relationships. *Journal of Marketing* 61: 35–51.

Dore, R. (1983). Goodwill and the Spirit of Market Capitalism. *British Journal of Sociology* 34: 459–482.

Ferrin, D.L., Bligh, M.C. & Kohles, J.C. (2007). Can I Trust You to Trust Me? A Theory of Trust, Monitoring, and Cooperation in Interpersonal and Intergroup Relationships. *Group & Organization Management* 32: 465–99.

Friedman, R.A. & Podolny, J. (1992). Differentiation of Boundary Spanning Roles: Labor Negotiations and Implications for Role Conflict. *Administrative Science Quarterly* 37: 28–47.

Giddens, A. (1990). *The Consequences of Modernity*. Stanford, CA: Stanford University Press.

Giddens, A. (1994). Risk, Trust, Reflexivity. In Beck, U., Giddens, A. & Lash, S. (eds.). *Reflexive Modernization*. Cambridge: Polity Press. 184–197.

Gioia, D.A. (1998). From Individual to Organizational Identity. In Whetten, D.A. & Godfrey, P.C. (eds.). *Identity in Organizations: Building Theory through Conversations*. London: Sage. 17–31.

Goolsby, J.R. (1992). A Theory of Role Stress in Boundary Spanning Positions of Marketing Organizations. *Journal of the Academy of Marketing Science* 20: 155–64.

Govier, T. (1994). Is it a Jungle Out There? Trust, Distrust, and the Social Construction of Reality. *Dialogue* 33: 237–52.

Gummesson, E. (1996). Relationship Marketing and Imaginary Organizations: A Synthesis. *European Journal of Marketing* 30: 31–44.

Hanlon, G. (2004). Institutional Forms and Organizational Structures: Homology, Trust and Reputational Capital in Professional Service Firms. *Organization* 11: 187–210.

Hardy, C., Phillips, N. & Lawrence, T. (1998). Distinguishing Trust and Power in Inter-organizational Relations: Forms and Façades of Trust. In Lane, C. & Bachmann, R. (eds.). *Trust Within and Between Organizations: Conceptual Issues and Empirical Applications.* Oxford: OUP. 64–87.

Hart, H.L.A. (1961). *The Concept of Law.* Oxford: OUP.

Hartline, M.D. & De Witt, T. (2004). Individual Differences Among Service Employees: The Conundrum of Employee Recruitment, Selection, and Retention. *Journal of Relationship Marketing* 3: 25–42.

Hawes, J.M., Mast, K.E. & Swan, J.E. (1989). Trust Earning Perceptions of Sellers and Buyers. *Journal of Personal Selling & Sales Management* 9: 1–8.

Jeffries, F.L. & Reed, R. (2000). Trust and Adaptation in Relational Contracting. *Academy of Management Review* 25: 873–82.

Jex, S. (1998). *Stress and Job Performance: Theory, Research, and Implications for Managerial Practice.* Thousand Oaks, CA: Sage.

Kahn, R.L., Wolfe, D.M., Quinn, R.P. & Snoek, J.D. (1964). *Organizational Stress: Studies in Role Conflict and Ambiguity.* New York: Wiley.

Kern, H. (1998). Lack of Trust, Surfeit of Trust: Some Causes of the Innovation Crisis in German Industry. In Lane, C. & Bachmann, R. (eds.). *Trust Within and Between Organizations: Conceptual Issues and Empirical Applications.* Oxford: OUP. 203–13.

Kramer, R.M. (1999). Trust and Distrust in Organizations: Emerging Perspectives, Enduring Questions. *Annual Review of Psychology* 50: 569–98.

Kroeger, F. (2012). Trusting organizations: The institutionalization of trust in inter-organizational relationships. *Organization* 19: 743–63.

Kroeger, F. (forthcoming 2013). How Is Trust Institutionalised? Understanding Collective and Long-Term Trust Orientations. In Bachmann, R. & Zaheer, A. (eds). *Handbook of Advances in Trust Research.* Cheltenham: Edward Elgar.

Lahno, B. (2002). Institutional Trust: A Less Demanding Form of Trust? *Revista Latinoamericana de Estudios Avanzados* 15: 19–58. (Page numbers cited refer to online version, available at http://www.uni-due.de/imperia/md/content/philosophie/kliemt_mat104_005.pdf, accessed 14/07/2007.)

Lepsius, R.M. (1997). Vertrauen zu Institutionen. In Hradil, S. (ed.). *Differenz und Integration: Die Zukunft moderner Gesellschaften.* Frankfurt: Campus. 283–93.

Levina, N. & Vaast, E. (2005). The Emergence of Boundary Spanning Competence in Practice: Implications for Implementation and Use of Information Systems. *MIS Quarterly* 29: 335–63.

Lewicki, R.J. & Bunker, B.B. (1996). Developing and Maintaining Trust in Work Relationships. In Kramer, R.M. & Tyler, T.R. (eds). *Trust in Organizations: Frontiers of Theory and Research.* London: Sage. 114–39.

Lewicki, R.J., McAllister, D.J. & Bies, R.J. (1998). Trust and Distrust: New Relationships and Realities. *Academy of Management Review* 23: 438–58.

Lorenz, E. (1988). Neither Friends nor Strangers: Informal Networks of Subcontracting in French Industry. In Gambetta, D. (ed.). *Trust: Making and Breaking Cooperative Relations.* Oxford: Blackwell. 194–210.

Lorenz, E. (2003). Inter-Organisational Trust, Boundary Spanners and Communities of practice. In Burchell, B., Deakin, S., Michie, J. & Rubery, J. (eds.). *Systems of Production: Markets, Organisations and Performance.* London: Routledge. 60–73.

Luhmann, N. (1979). *Trust and Power*. Chichester: Wiley.

Luhmann, N. (1988). Familiarity, Confidence, Trust: Problems and Alternatives. In Gambetta, D. (ed.). *Trust: Making and Breaking Cooperative Relations*. Oxford: Blackwell. 94–107.

Lui, S.S. & Ngo, H.Y. (2004). The Role of Trust and Contractual Safeguards on Cooperation in Non-Equity Alliances. *Journal of Management* 30: 471–85.

Lukes, S. (1974). *Power: A Radical View*. London: Macmillan.

Lyon, F. & Porter, G. (2010). Evolving Institutions of Trust: Personalized and Institutional Bases of Trust in Nigerian and Ghanaian Food Trading. In Saunders, M.N.K., Skinner, D., Gillespie, N., Dietz, G. & Lewicki, R. (eds.). *Organisational Trust: A Cultural Perspective*. Cambridge: CUP. 255–77.

Marrone, J.A., Tesluk, P.E. & Carson, J.B. (2007). A Multilevel Investigation of Antecedents and Consequences of Team Member Boundary-Spanning Behavior. *Academy of Management Journal* 50: 1423–39.

Mayer, R.C., Davis, J.H. & Schoorman, D.F. (1995). An Integrative Model of Organizational Trust. *Academy of Management Review* 20: 709–34.

McAllister, D.J. (1995). Affect- and Cognition-Based Trust as Foundations for Interpersonal Cooperation in Organizations. *Academy of Management Journal* 38: 24–59.

McElroy, J.C., Morrow, P.C. & Laczniak, R.N. (2001). External Organizational Commitment. *Human Resource Management Review* 11: 237–56.

Mead, G.H. (1934). *Mind, Self and Society: From the Standpoint of a Social Behaviorist*. Chicago: CUP.

Meyerson, D., Weick, K.E. & Kramer, R.M. (1996). Swift Trust and Contemporary Groups. In Kramer, R.M. & Tyler, T.R. (eds). *Trust in Organizations: Frontiers of Theory and Research*. London: Sage. 166–95.

Misztal, B.A. (2001). Normality and Trust in Goffman's Conception of Interaction Order. *Sociological Theory* 19: 312–24.

Möllering, G. (2006). *Trust: Reason, Routine, Reflexivity*. Amsterdam: Elsevier.

Molm, L.D. (1997). Risk and Power Use: Constraints on the Use of Coercion in Exchange. *American Sociological Review* 62: 113–33.

Morgan, R.M. & Hunt, S.D. (1994). The Commitment-Trust Theory of Relationship Marketing. *Journal of Marketing* 58: 20–38.

Morgner, C. (2008). The Distinction between Personal and System Trust. Unpublished working paper, Department of Sociology, University of Cambridge.

Nonis, S.A., Sager, J.K. & Kumar, K. (1996). Salespeople's Use of Upward Influence Tactics (UIT) in Coping With Role Stress. *Journal of the Academy of Marketing Science* 24: 44–56.

Organ, D.W. (1971). Linking Pins between Organization and Environment. *Business Horizons* 14: 73–80.

Organ, D.W. (1988). A Restatement of the Satisfaction-Performance Hypothesis. *Journal of Management* 14: 547–57.

Perrone, V., Zaheer, A. & McEvily, B. (2003). Free to Be Trusted? Organizational Constraints on Trust in Boundary Spanners. *Organization Science* 14: 422–39.

Rao, A. & Schmidt, S.M. (1998). A Behavioral Perspective on Negotiating International Alliances. *Journal of International Business Studies* 29: 665–93.

Richter, A.W., West, M.A., Van Dick, R. & Dawson, J.F. (2006). Boundary Spanners' Identification, Intergroup Contact, and Effective Intergroup Relations. *Academy of Management Journal* 49: 1252–69.

Ring, P.S. & Van de Ven, A.H. (1994). Developmental Processes of Cooperative Inter-organizational Relationships. *Academy of Management Review* 19: 90–118.

Rosen, B. & Adams, J.S. (1974). Organizational Coverups: Factors Influencing the Discipline of Information Gatekeepers. *Journal of Applied Social Psychology* 4: 375–84.

Schoorman, F.D., Mayer, R.C. & Davis, J.H. (2007). An Integrative Model of Organizational Trust: Past, Present, and Future. *Academy of Management Review* 32: 344–54.

Schweer, M.K.W. (2003). Vertrauen als Organisationsprinzip: Vertrauensförderung im Spannungsfeld personalen und systemischen Vertrauens. *Erwägen Wissen Ethik* 14: 323–32.

Shapiro, S. (1987). The Social Control of Impersonal Trust. *American Journal of Sociology* 93: 623–58.

Sydow, J. (1998). Understanding the Constitution of Inter-organizational Trust. In Lane, C. & Bachmann, R. (eds.). *Trust Within and Between Organizations: Conceptual Issues and Empirical Applications*. Oxford: OUP. 31–63.

Sydow, J. (2006). How can systems trust systems? A structuration perspective on trust-building in inter-organizational relations. In Bachmann, R. & Zaheer, A. (eds.). *Handbook of Trust Research*. Cheltenham: Edward Elgar. 377–96.

Tajfel, H. (1982). The social psychology of intergroup relations. *Annual Review of Psychology* 33: 1–39.

Tushman, M.L. & Scanlan, T.J. (1981a). Characteristics and External Orientations of Boundary Spanning Individuals. *Academy of Management Journal* 24: 83–98.

Tushman, M.L. & Scanlan, T.J. (1981b). Boundary Spanning Individuals: Their Role in Information Transfer and Their Antecedents. *Academy of Management Journal* 24: 289–305.

Uslaner, E.M. (2002). *The Moral Foundations of Trust*. Cambridge: CUP.

Walker, O.C., Churchill, G.A. & Ford, N.M. (1975). Organizational Determinants of the Industrial Salesman's Role Conflict and Ambiguity. *Journal of Marketing* 39: 32–9.

Webber, S.S. & Klimoski, R.J. (2004). Client-project manager engagements, trust, and loyalty. *Journal of Organizational Behavior* 25: 997–1013.

Whetten, D.A. (1978). Coping with Incompatible Expectations: An Integrated View of Role Conflict. *Administrative Science Quarterly* 23: 254-71.

Williams, P. (2002). The Competent Boundary Spanner. *Public Administration* 80: 103–24.

Zaheer, A. & Harris, J. (2006). Inter-Organizational Trust. In Shenkar, O. & Reuer, J. (eds.). *Handbook of Strategic Alliances*. London: Sage. 169–98. (Page numbers cited refer to online version, available at http://papers.ssrn.com/sol3/papers.cfm?abstract_id=1256082, accessed 11/02/2010.)

Zaheer, A., McEvily, B. & Perrone, V. (1998). Does Trust Matter? Exploring the Effects of Inter-organizational and Interpersonal Trust on Performance. *Organization Science* 9: 141–59.

13 A Field-of-Practice View of Boundary-Spanning in and across Organizations

Transactive and Transformative Boundary-Spanning Practices

Natalia Levina and Emmanuelle Vaast

BOUNDARY-SPANNING IN AND ACROSS ORGANIZATIONS

There has been a surge of interest among organizational scholars in the notions of boundaries and boundary-spanning. The term "boundary-spanning" is very broad and includes related phenomena of coordination and collaboration, which in turn can be cooperative or competitive in nature (Cohen, Cash, and Muller 2000). Boundary-spanning is certainly not new to social organizing (Merleau-Ponty and Edie 1964; Weber 1978), but recent advancements in information and communication technology (ICT) and globalization have enabled rich and inexpensive communication across a wide set of individuals and organizations and exacerbated the need for boundary-spanning work. For example, there has been an increased emphasis on boundary-spanning across diverse groups of experts as a key process in producing organizational innovation (Leonard and Swap 1999; Carlile 2002; Dougherty 1992; Hargadon and Sutton 1997). In addition, modern ways of organizing increasingly rely on spanning organizational boundaries in the context of strategic alliances (Gulati and Singh 1998), supply-chain integration efforts (Cousins et al. 2006), user-centered innovation initiatives (von Hippel 1988), and outsourcing of products and services (Levina 2005; Levina and Vaast 2005; 2008; Kellogg, Orlikowski, and Yates 2006). Increased globalization of organizations and markets has created a need for simultaneously spanning multiple cultural, institutional, temporal, and spatial boundaries (Hinds and Kiesler 1995; Levina and Vaast 2008; Espinosa, DeLone, and Lee 2007). Organizational initiatives such as "a single face to the customer" rely on the idea that through the use of ICTs organizations will be able to bridge boundaries across functionally diverse and geographically-distributed units and enable seamless integration of business processes. ICT is also enabling online production systems where users and producers of information goods collaborate on product designs (Lee and Cole 2003; Ciborra and Andreu 2001) and scientists can solve problems outside their domain of expertise (Jeppesen and Lakhani 2010).

In the broadest sense, boundary-spanning happens when actors deliberately or inadvertently relate entities separated by a boundary. While modern technology and globalization are enabling much boundary-spanning, it is not solving key sociological problems associated with the differences in practices, interests, and understandings of people coming from diverse backgrounds and lacking a common history of interaction. Organizational theorists have long been aware of the acute problems created by cross-boundary work and have argued that while diverse expertise may be very valuable on projects, inefficiencies of working across boundaries may overweigh the benefits (Polzer, Milton, and Swann 2002; Reagans and Zuckerman 2001). Much work has been done in sociology and organizational theory in trying to understand the nature of boundaries and the challenges that they pose to boundary-spanning work (Abbott 1995; Carlile 2004; Montgomery and Oliver 2007; Levina and Vaast 2008). These problems have been associated with differences in knowledge as well as with issues of power (Carlile 2002; Levina and Vaast 2005; Swan et al. 2007). While many diverse perspectives have been used to understand boundary-spanning including social networks, information processing, coordination theory, social identity theory, and small group research, a practice perspective has a specific emphasis on understanding issues of knowledge and power together and provides unique insights into boundary-spanning phenomena (Carlile 2002; Levina and Vaast 2005; 2008; Kellogg, Orlikowski, and Yates 2006; Bechky 2003).

In this chapter we adopt a practice perspective, specifically drawing on Bourdieu's practice theory (Bourdieu 1977; Bourdieu and Wacquant 1992) to advance the development of a theory of boundary-spanning. Focusing in particular on Bourdieu's concept of field-of-practice we are going to address two gaps in the literature on boundary-spanning.

First, the literature on boundary-spanning has largely discussed the differences between parties involved in boundary-spanning activities rather than on the *shared* context in which these activities take place. The notion of a field-of-practice allows us to both describe the differences between agents involved in boundary-spanning as well as to depict the shared social space in which these differences, including power relations and expertise, get established and sorted out. We will argue that all practices, including boundary-spanning practices, take place in fields, and therefore that even the boundary itself needs to be understood in relation to a particular field of practice.

Second, while Carlile (2002; 2004) has pointed out that boundary-spanning is associated with power struggles and negotiation when agents face novel situations, little has been said about how these power struggles are shaped by existing power relations produced by existing institutional fields. Carlile (2004) points out that artifacts play a critical role in such negotiations, but argues that the role of boundary-spanners (agents) is less important in these situations than in less novel situations involving translation of knowledge. Levina and Vaast (2005) argue that such power negotiations take place in a new joint field of practice that emerges from boundary-spanning, but again largely ignore the wider institutional forces. Finally, Levina and Orlikowski (2009) propose that in conditions of novelty and ambiguity wider institutional fields do not determine power relations and that entrepreneurial agents may strategically employ discourse to negotiate new power arrangements or renegotiate old ones. However, their work does not speak directly to the role of shared artifacts or the nature of boundaries involved. In this chapter, we will use the notion of existing and emergent fields of practice to discuss how power relations are produced, reproduced, or transformed through two different modes of boundary-spanning practices.

In what follows, we first show how Bourdieu's practice theory conceptualizes the relationships among the notions of practice, boundaries, and fields-of-practice in a way that acknowledges the importance of power relations, the role of human agency, and the mutual constitution of institutions and actions. Then, pursuing and advancing Carlile's (2004) conceptualization, we posit that novelty, based upon agents' actions and perceptions, is an essential component *and* outcome of boundary-spanning practices rather than an "input" into them. We distinguish two modes of boundary-spanning depending upon whether its practices preserve or transform the shared fields of practice in which they take place: transactive and transformative. The theoretical distinction between these two modes helps us further unpack different roles played by agents (boundary-spanners) and artifacts (boundary objects) when they are used in each mode of practice. We draw implications of our new conceptualization of boundary-spanning practices for organizational design, coordination theories, institutional entrepreneurship, and theories of the firm and its boundaries.

BOURDIEU'S PRACTICE THEORY: FIELDS OF PRACTICE, BOUNDARIES, AND PRACTICES

Here we briefly overview key concepts of Bourdieu's theory of practice as they pertain to understanding boundaries and boundary-spanning. Bourdieu's theory of practice associates the emergence, institutionalization, and transformation of socio-structural properties with the micro-level social interactions of people within the context of their everyday practices (Bourdieu and Wacquant 1992). Enacted structural properties constrain social activity, but they can also be transformed through agents' actions. Power relations arise as agents do not share equal access to three fundamental types of capital, which are enacted resources acquired and maintained through social relations. These types are economic capital (money, time, access to technology), cultural capital (professional expertise, education, ownership of information), and social capital (networks of interpersonal relations which an agent can draw upon). There is also symbolic capital, which refers to agents' ability to improve their position due to social recognition of their current privileged positions. Symbolic capital, such as prestige, honors, and attention, can be attached to any species of capital.

Practices can be seen as socially and historically situated actions and perceptions (dispositions) of agents. Through their practices, agents are constantly engaged in shaping *fields of practice* as well as the *boundaries* that separate these fields. Boundaries delimit fields and arise from differences in practices that are differentially recognized and rewarded across fields. Simultaneously, fields of practice emerge as constellations of relations among agents who share unique sets of practices and interests while producing their own unique form of capital. While agents in a field are united by their common pursuits, they are also divided as they have differential access to the capital of their field. Within fields of practice, dynamics depend upon the positions and relationships among various agents, with relative "haves" and "have-nots'" acting toward the reproduction or transformation of the structural properties of the field.

More generally, in fields of practice, power dynamics originate from the relative positions of different agents (Bourdieu and Wacquant 1992). Agents who have accumulated more capital than others are able to influence others and maintain their own privileged positions. Moreover, fields of practice and relations taking place in them can, and in modern societies typically do, become institutionalized. Whereas in primitive societies power relations were embedded in interpersonal relationships among specific agents, in modern societies objects such as titles, codes, forms, and procedures are used to objectify relations and allow different individuals to enact the same practices time after time. Thus fields become institutionalized through the objectification of practice (Bourdieu 1977). Bourdieu's practice theory has been an inspiration to the institutional theory of organizational fields (DiMaggio 1991; DiMaggio and Powell 1983). It especially helped in understanding how institutions that carry symbolic capital can constrain agents' practices as well as how, through their practices, agents can engage in building and reproducing existing institutions (DiMaggio 1991; DiMaggio and Powell 1983).

For example, management academia is a field of practice with its own unique set of power relations uniting agents around the production of cultural capital in management studies and dividing them on the basis of differential ability to attain stakes in these fields (e.g., publications in top journals, titles, awards, etc.). Over time many practices in this field have been institutionalized, whereby norms and expectations about the actions of senior scholars (e.g., journal editors) and junior scholars (e.g., Ph.D. students) are taken for granted.

Also, fields are not entirely autonomous and are themselves defined in relation to other fields (Bourdieu 1996). Over time, fields of practice may become nested or fragmented and/or overlap according to the changing practices of agents and the resources they acquire in the process (Abbott 1995). The embeddedness of various fields provides a complex and ambiguous set of conditions in which individual action is no longer determined by a particular institutional norm because multiple, potentially conflicting norms apply (Levina and Orlikowski 2009). This opens up room for individual agency.

For instance, management academia is divided into multiple subfields of interest while also overlapping with many other fields such as industries, other professional fields, the field of higher education, etc. It is itself also a subfield of the field of academia. The practices of a management professor who teaches a business course are therefore situated within a constellation of fields of practice; and the professor may accumulate more or less capital in these different nested and overlapping fields. If, for example, this professor was to win a teaching award at the university level she would be able to accumulate capital in at least four fields: business academia, the business school, the university, and academia more generally.

Boundaries between fields and subfields become pronounced in a dynamic process. Such boundaries can only be understood in relation to a shared, wider field. For example, when one talks about a boundary between interpretivist and functionalist management scholars, the very notion of this boundary is defined in relation to the field of social research (Burrell and Morgan 1979; Deetz 1996). Thus, practices, boundaries, and fields are mutually constituted; none is given theoretical dominance.

Yet, in the literature on boundary-spanning, the notions of practices and boundaries have been more prominent than the notion of fields, partially because many practice-focused studies of boundary-spanning have investigated small groups rather than larger institutions (Carlile 2002; Bechky 2003; Levina and Vaast 2005). Still, according to Bourdieu all practice is situated within fields. Thus, boundaries and boundary-spanning practices are also situated within a field of practice. For instance, a management researcher who decides to apply concepts from genetics and theories of evolution to investigate organizational phenomena (e.g., treating routines in organizations as genes) acts as a boundary-spanner by relating existing resources from another academic field to his original, primary field (as proposed, for example, by Nelson and Winter 1982). Whether and how the "new" theory will be received in the management field depends on the ability of this researcher to associate her insights with cultural capital in her primary field, as well as on the relative institutional position of management and genetics in the field of academia. Over time, conferences, journals, and courses may be created, new researchers may be trained, and new language created around this new theory, giving way to the emergence of a new academic subfield, combining genetics and management (e.g., evolutionary economics). This new subfield is embedded within its parent fields, which means that actions taken by an agent in the new field also may shift or reinforce their positions in related parent fields.

Considering boundary-spanning practices as situated within fields of practice raises important questions: Which fields provide the context in which boundary-spanning activities are situated and in which boundaries are defined and negotiated? Do these fields exist *a priori* as wider institutions, or do agents create them in a given situation? What are the different ways in which agents span boundaries in practice and what are their impact on the power dynamics in existing and new fields? We follow Carlile's (2004) theory of knowledge integration across boundaries to propose that the notion of novelty is central to understanding these questions.

NOVELTY AND MODES OF BOUNDARY-SPANNING PRACTICE PRODUCTION

In novel situations, issues pertaining to power relations among interacting agents become particularly visible because agents do not have a clear expectation of each other's behavior and lack clear status hierarchy, welcoming political battles (Levina and Orlikowski 2009; Carlile 2004). In the context of knowledge work studied by Carlile (2004), novelty is related to a relative lack of common knowledge across groups involved. Carlile (2004) focuses on novelty as a key dimension differentiating the boundary-spanning situations and boundaries involved. He argues that novelty is a more relevant property than "uncertainty" because the latter has to be assessed from the outside as an external property of the environment; whereas, the former "underscores the participatory and relational nature of what an actor needs to share and to assess when all is not known" (ibid., 557). When the degree of novelty between two or more actors is low, then boundary-spanning is a matter of either transferring or translating the knowledge across a well-defined, unproblematic boundary (ibid., 558). When the novelty between actors in the boundary-spanning situation is high, the knowledge used by the more powerful actors in the past may no longer be as relevant, opening up room for power renegotiation. Boundary-spanning in this case relies on transforming knowledge-in-practice and associated power relations.

We further develop Carlile's relational thinking about novelty by arguing that the degree of novelty involved in a boundary-spanning situation is an emergent property that depends on people's actions and perceptions, in particular, regarding the shared context in which their interaction takes place. If actors perceive each other as belonging to a shared context and engaging in reproducing practices in that context, their main challenge may be to transfer and translate across diverse languages and practices. They would readily draw on that shared context (a joint field in which they all practice) for routines, norms, and mutual expectations in the interaction.

We will draw on Carlile's (2004) new product development (NPD) example in automotive manufacturing to illustrate this point. In this example four types of engineers were working in advanced vehicle design group:

vehicle styling, engine/power train, climate control, and safety. Each group had its own interests and practices: styling engineers wanted to create an aesthetically distinct vehicle design, engine/power train group wanted to meet horsepower requirements and fuel economy constraints, climate engineers needed to make sure that that the vehicle stays cool in the summer and warm in the winter, and the safety group worried about bumper placement and the location of the engine to limit collision damage. Carlile studied the development and implementation of a computational tool that was meant to help these diverse groups engage in joint problem solving. He described two phases of the project: the first one, in which the tool was developed and implemented in two vehicle redesign efforts, and the second one, in which the use of the tool had to be renegotiated to allow more input from safety engineers (compared to traditionally more powerful groups such as style and power train engineers).

Carlile illustrates transfer- and translation-focused boundary-spanning work by showing how all four groups of engineers establish a common lexicon to specify the size, shape, geometry, and other parameters of the new vehicle (2004, 562). The leader in charge (Bill Knox) developed and later implemented a computation tool to enable communication across boundaries. It was relatively straightforward for project participants to use the new computational tool to represent what each group wanted from the new design and how their choices depended on each other. Bill's major role was in translating across context through common terms encoded in the tool. It is easy to see from Carlile's case study that all engineers involved drew on the norms, expectations, and routines already established in the field that they shared, namely the field of modern vehicle design. An easy way of seeing the institutional influence of this field is to imagine a new, but experienced, style engineer joining the project. He or she should know exactly what style, size, and geometry of the vehicle mean and how they relate to power train, climate, and safety issues.

The case used by Carlile continues to show how in the first phase of the project a common taxonomy was used by project participants to understand each other and how the manager in charge was able to translate the concerns of all parties involved without renegotiating relations among them. In this way, participants not only drew on the institutionalized practices in the shared field of vehicle design but also reproduced those practices and associated power relations (e.g., safety engineers' concerns were least important in the first stage of the project).

Carlile's story continues to discuss the second phase of the project, where safety engineers' concerns eventually acquired high prominence, as the vehicle was subpar in terms of safety performance. As a result a new practice was created around the computational tool that allowed safety engineers to express their concerns. This new practice transformed existing relations in the field of modern vehicle design. Carlile argues that the latter situation corresponded to a higher degree of novelty (style engineers had to learn more about safety engineering and its concerns and had to change their practice to accommodate). We propose that the degree of novelty involved in the boundary-spanning situation did not change in and of itself over the lifetime of the project: in both stages, relative knowledge (or lack thereof) among engineers about their colleagues' interests and practices was the same. However, in the first phase of the project the situation was treated as rather familiar and part of established practices in the shared institutional field. In the second stage of the project it was clear that shared practices themselves had to be transformed. The actions that incorporated the concerns of climate engineers as critical in the design thus transformed the practice in the shared institutional field.

In our interpretation of Carlile's NPD example, we see the degree of novelty as an emergent property of the situation perceived and enacted by agents involved in boundary-spanning. We thus propose that the nature of boundary-spanning practices is the primary concept in understanding boundary-spanning work, while the degree of novelty is a secondary concept emergent from the nature of practices. We differentiate two modes of boundary-spanning on the basis of whether they preserve existing relations in shared institutional contexts or transform them: transactive and transformative boundary-spanning. This preservation or transformation may be deliberate or inadvertent as agents are often unaware of the nature of the relations in fields of practice (Bourdieu and Thompson 1991). We argue that the degree of novelty can be viewed as an output of these practices and defined based on the extent to which transformation in the field was actually achieved. For example, it is possible, and often the case, that agents decided to engage in a collaboration so as to create something new and learn each other's practices, but end up following old norms and reenacting old practices, thereby reinforcing prior relationship without much novelty (Levina and Vaast 2005). Let us briefly overview each mode of boundary-spanning practice before expanding on how various boundary-spanning mechanisms, such as objects and roles, are involved in each.

In the case of the transactive mode of boundary-spanning, existing relationships among agents in shared fields of practice are reproduced. Agents who carry out the boundary-spanning activity engage in a salient shared field or fields guiding the interaction, with taken-for-granted norms and expectations. These shared contexts allow participants to exchange information or translate across diversity (across subfields or overlapping fields) because in order for any translation or exchange to take place some shared meaning must exist. Because of the taken-for-granted nature of practices in the shared field, the relations in these fields tend to be reproduced over time. This mode is relatively efficient since the different parties involved know what to expect from the transactions. Agents leading such practice help others share information and translate across boundaries by relying on shared practices in the joint field. Objects in this case are also used to translate the needs of the different parties as well as to combine outcomes of work (e.g., in a repository). The early phase in the project investigated by Carlile exemplifies this transactive mode of boundary-spanning: the four types of engineers knew what to expect from the project and their relative interests and competences were communicated through a computational tool in the project that helped express and reproduce but not change their respective relationships.

The transformative mode of boundary-spanning entails changes in the relations and relative positions of the parties involved. In this case, agents with separate interests and resources jointly negotiate changes in their respective practices and as a result in the nature and value of their capital in the joint endeavor. In this case the joint context for their interaction is either unclear or inadequate in satisfying their individual and joint needs. Thus, for example, in Carlile's case, the field of modern vehicle design was still the most salient field in which agents engaged, but existing relationships that marginalized the contribution of climate engineers were insufficient to produce new vehicle designs of value to the organization in question. Moreover, we can argue that these agents shared a number of other fields. For example, their joint organization's field of practice (Beta Motors) with its own institutionalized routines, norms, and expectations set another context that could have helped in addressing the group's needs, but that was in fact not sufficiently supportive. In Carlile's case study, the transformation was facilitated by an able leader who helped recognize and define the pragmatic, relational problem at stake and further developed the computational tool that helped other engineers better understand and become invested in the safety engineers' issues. The use of the tool facilitated the production of the new practice—a new design process transforming relationships in the joint field of modern vehicle design within this organization.

Notably, when agents from diverse backgrounds collaborate for the first time they may not only transform power relations and related knowledge-in-practice in existing fields, but also create new joint fields. This is the situation described by Levina and Vaast (2005), in which diverse professionals participating in new information systems (IS) development and implementation projects created new (unique) sets of practices, capital, and boundaries in which they related to each other's practices. In creating this new field they also transformed power relations in shared fields (institutions) in which they were already engaged such as their organizations, industries, and professions.

BOUNDARY-SPANNERS, BOUNDARY OBJECTS, AND BOUNDARY-SPANNING DYNAMICS

We elaborate the implications of this new theorizing on two key concepts that have been shown as essential for boundary-spanning practices to emerge: boundary-spanning roles and boundary objects. With our focus on fields of practice and associated power relations, we propose that boundary-spanning individuals and objects play different roles depending on whether they are involved in reproducing or transforming existing power relations in relevant fields-of-practice.

Boundary-Spanners and Boundary Objects

People who span boundaries of various fields have long been identified in the organization literature as boundary-spanners (Tajfel 1978; Tushman and Scanlan 1981; Lysonski and Johnson 1983; Friedman and Podolny 1992). These are people who have been designated and/or who de facto reach beyond group boundaries in order to build common ground between separated parties (Hargadon and Sutton 1997; Allen and Cohen 1969; Cross and Parker 2004). These individuals are often asked to play one or more roles including, among others, that of a representative, gatekeeper, advice or trust broker, scout, or ambassador (Aldrich and Herker 1977; Ancona and Caldwell 1992; Leifer and Delbecq 1978). Given their multiple, possibly contradictory roles and their participation in diverse, sometimes conflicting groups, boundary-spanners often suffer from acute stress and may fail to fulfill the many roles they are charged with (Dubinsky et al. 1992; Singh, Verbeke, and Rhoads 1996; Lysonski 1985). This is particularly true when they are expected to create novelty by transforming existing relations (Levina and Vaast 2005). This is why the literature often points to the critical role of shared artifacts, which can be easily extended over time and space and do not experience stress, in aiding transformative boundary-spanning.

Boundary objects have been defined as artifacts that "are plastic enough to adapt to the local needs and constraints of the several parties employing them, yet robust enough to maintain a common identity across sites" (Star 1989, 393). Examples of boundary objects include: prototypes (Carlile 2002; Bechky 2003), maps, forms, repositories (Star and Griesemer 1989), use-case scenarios and wire frames (Levina and Vaast 2005; Bodker 2000), accounting ledgers (Briers and Chua 2001), and even abstract objects such as narratives (Bartel and Dutton 2001) and shared concepts (Kim and King 2000). As suggested in the above definition of the concept, boundary objects are by nature ambivalent. As with the notion of boundary-spanners, research on boundary objects has highlighted multiple, at times conflicting, properties and functions that they may embody. Specifically, properties of boundary objects such as their degree of abstraction have been described as desirable in some studies (Henderson 1991; Kim and King 2000) and not desirable in others (Bechky 2003; Carlile 2002). With regard to their functions, research has identified relatively common situations in which some objects that had been designated to be used to span the boundaries between two parties ended up being used superficially or remained unused, or even reinforced existing boundaries (Schultze and Boland 2000; Newell, Scarbrough, and Swan 2001; Levina and Vaast 2005, 2006; Barrett and Oborn 2010).

Carlile (2004) has argued that boundary-spanning individuals are critical for translating across boundaries while being less so for transforming practices, where shared artifacts (boundary objects) play a more prominent role. We draw on multiple studies of boundary-spanning in-practice to claim that boundary-spanners are as, if not more, crucial in transformative boundary-spanning practices. In fact, Star and Griesemer's (1989) seminal study that helped coin the term "boundary object" pointed out the crucial role of a boundary-spanner (in this case, a museum curator) for addressing the pragmatic concerns of diverse groups (scientists, collectors, and general public) and creating a new field of practice (associated with the new zoological museum). Negotiation scholars have also argued that boundary-spanners have a crucial political function including brokering trust and negotiating relations among conflicted groups (Friedman and Podolny 1992).

Perhaps it is often hard to recognize the work done by boundary-spanners in transforming relations among groups and associated knowledge-in-practice because many individuals, and sometimes groups, may be involved in accomplishing this goal. For example, in a vivid illustration of such transformation described by Bechky (2003), a leading assembler helped other assemblers and engineers transform their understanding through the use of a prototype; however, this transformation involved all three individuals changing their views and relations. Similarly, in Bechky's ethnographic study, a whole group of professionals (technicians) was charged with spanning the boundary between engineers and assemblers.

Furthermore, we argue that boundary objects, and not just boundary-spanners, are crucial for transferring information or translating across boundaries, while preserving power relations in shared fields. Indeed, when collaboration is spread across time and space, the ability of boundary-spanners to translate is limited and they must rely on objects to help them in the process. Objects such as shared repositories of information, maps, prices, drawings, and forms are constantly used to transact across boundaries of diverse fields. These objects are, however, produced within a shared field where they acquire a common identity and meaning, thereby allowing for translation across diverse fields to take place.

Fields-of-Practice View on Boundary-Spanners and Boundary Objects

While both boundary objects and boundary-spanners play a crucial role in transactive and transformative practices, the actual use of these objects and roles is quite different between these two modes of practice production. Table 13.1 summarizes the different uses of these boundary-spanning "mechanisms" in different modes. We will elaborate on each of them below.

In the transactive mode, boundary-spanning involves mapping diverse practices onto a shared practice produced within a joint field. In this case, boundary-spanners act as translators who help to define the mapping.

Table 13.1   Modes of boundary-spanning production

Transactive mode	Transformative mode
Boundary-spanners act as translators	**Boundary-spanners** act as translators and negotiators, transforming existing and/or building new joint practices
Objects of exchange are used to transfer information or translate from one context to the other	**Boundary objects** are used to represent differences among groups and shared identities across groups
Transactional production of work: Reflecting on and adding to the work of others	**Collaborative production of work:** Reflecting on and challenging the work of others
Relational Implications: Existing relations among agents are reproduced	**Relational Implications:** Novel relations among agents are produced

According to Levina and Vaast (2005), for designated actors to fulfill boundary-spanning roles in practice, they need to understand practices in both fields and how they relate to each other (via a common context), meaning that they need to be legitimate peripheral participants in each. In a simple case of natural language translation, a translator needs to know both languages and be able to tie words to common concepts by shared human practices across cultures.

By contrast, in contexts in which boundary-spanners exert a transformative role on the boundary and the situation of the other agents, they need not only to translate but also to negotiate relations among practices. In natural language translation, this would be the job done by dictionary creators who translate new words and propose better translations for the old ones. Sometimes this negotiation happens on the basis of an existing shared field where mapping between practices in diverse fields is already established and boundary-spanning is a matter of renegotiating existing relations and knowledge-in-practice. This was the case in Carlile's NPD example, in which the project leader charged with the creation of the computational tool was able to help safety engineers elevate their concerns in the established shared field. Other times, however, in renegotiating old relationships new fields are created. The possibility of creating new fields to allow agents to break away from existing power structures (in which they may be dominated) was a crucial way in which Bourdieu proposed to break "the iron cage of structuralism" (Bourdieu 1996). Levina and Vaast (2005) illustrated how in an IS development project, diverse professionals could not break away from the existing power relations within the institutional field of management consulting until they created a new joint field around a particular consulting project with its own distinct practices, interests, and capital. Boundary-spanners were crucial in facilitating the creation of this joint field-of-practice. In this case, individuals who became boundary-spanners-in-practice were not only legitimate peripheral participants in the practices of each party and in the joint field of management consulting, but were also invested with symbolic, cultural, economic, and social capital necessary to renegotiate old practices and create new ones. They basically had to have an understanding of everybody's needs and the power to act and make decisions on behalf of others. Over time, they also had to draw others into the new joint field of practice that they had created.

There has been much debate in the literature on what constitutes and does not constitute a "good" or "true" boundary object (Kellogg, Orlikowski, and Yates 2006; Hsiao, Tsai, and Lee 2012; Levina and Vaast 2005; Barrett and Oborn 2010). We believe that part of this debate has to do with the different uses of shared artifacts depending on the mode of boundary-spanning practice involved. Drawing on Levina and Vaast (2006), we clarify the confusion by proposing that those boundary objects that are used in transactive practices be termed "objects of exchange." These objects are not contested and negotiated, but rather are defined to accomplish the work of exchange or translation across diverse fields. They are produced with a clear salient shared context and used to map/translate separately produced work into that shared context. In the natural language case, a dictionary is clearly such an object when we talk about everyday, nonprofessional translation. In Carlile's (2004) NPD case, the computational tool documenting the size, geography, and other parameters of a vehicle was such an object. In a simple case of information exchange, shared document repositories serve such a function.

Alternatively, agents can use boundary objects to represent differences in practices and interests in diverse fields as well as common stakes, thereby helping to transform power relations among agents involved. IT-enabled transformation efforts often deliberately put digital artifacts at the center of the renegotiation of relations. For example, in Carlile's NPD case, the computational tool was specifically created to address these differences and facilitate *joint*—as opposed to separate—problem solving. Boundary objects (like objects of exchange) belong to the shared context of practice where their "common identity" (Star 1989) is defined. However, unlike objects of exchange whose meaning in the shared context, albeit minimal, is taken for granted, the shared identity and meaning of boundary objects-in-practice is continuously contested and emergent. Moreover, these objects are not merely functional means of communication and connections but also symbolic representations of power (Bourdieu and Thompson 1991). For example, Levina and Vaast (2005) describe a case of an insurance company that developed and implemented a new intranet Web site for the purpose of facilitating sharing of best practices among its mobile sales force. This Web site was initially seen as a "corporate evil" and hardly used by sales agents (Levina and Vaast 2005). It took a tremendous negotiation effort by the boundary-spanner (corporate headmaster of the site) to convince insurance agents both symbolically and pragmatically that the site was a "helpful repository of useful tips."

Objects of exchange can, and often, do become part of depersonalized practice, that is, it is no longer necessary to engage the same agents who created them in using them. Indeed, they are often part of the institutionalized practice in the shared field. Forms are a typical example of such objects, where many diverse agents accomplish simple translation tasks without forming personal relationships with others who process their forms (e.g., in a passport application process). However, in the case of transformative practices, boundary-spanners are personally involved in negotiating separate and common meaning of boundary objects. Note here that when we say "interpersonal" we do not really mean that all agents are individuals, which would be inconsistent with Bourdieu. Agents can be groups, organizations, and even countries. Following Bourdieu we see the interpersonal or "embodied" mode of practice production as that which relies on the same agent and their joint history for its reproduction (replace actors A and B with actors C and D and the meaning of the practice will be lost). On the other hand, the objectified mode of practice is the one in which replacing agents with others will not change its nature because relations have become depersonalized (see Levina and Vaast 2006, for an extended discussion).

Dynamics of Boundary-Spanning in Fields-of-Practice

We next outline different types of entanglements between agents and objects as they engage in different modes of practice production for the purpose of preserving or transforming emergent and existing fields.

Depending on the mode of boundary-spanning, the dynamics of agents' engagement with objects and with each other is quite different. In the case of transactive boundary-spanning, agents share and reflect upon objects of exchange but do not challenge the work done by others. Depending on how institutionalized and routine their interaction is, they may need to engage in discussions to create a clear mapping between their diverse practices and may even communicate continuously; however, they will not be "undoing" the work done by others. For example, in the first phase of Carlile's case study, there was much communication about the design, but diverse engineers simply used a new computational tool to build on each other's prior work and decisions. A vivid example of this is also provided by Levina and Vaast (2005), where the most powerful group of consultants (strategists) developed Web site design through wire frames (schematics of information layout). Strategists did so hoping to communicate to graphic designers functional requirements for the Web site. However, graphic designers did not feel empowered to challenge strategists in any way and simply added colors and fonts on top of mediocre designs produced by strategists, resulting in a poorly designed Web site. Their interaction was shaped by institutionalized practices of Web development in prior firms where they had previously worked. These examples illustrate that transactive practice may involve a lot of communication and close working relationships (it does not mean the "arms-length" relationship symbolically associated with this term). However, the reproduction of power relations among agents is the same as if they were throwing things over the wall or working on an assembly line. We call this mode of interaction among agents and objects "transactional."

In case of transactive boundary-spanning, relative power positions and relations are renegotiated and different, novel practices emerge. In this case, boundary-spanners create and use boundary objects to symbolize and accomplish change. They also draw others to join them in boundary-spanning (and, in turn, to become boundary-spanners themselves). In this mode, the use of these objects must involve some degree of undoing work done by others and challenging practices established in the shared and possibly separate fields. In Carlile's NPD example, during the second phase, the computational tool was used to challenge the approach of stylist engineers and undo some of the design choices they made to accommodate climate engineers. In Levina and Vaast's (2005) case, clients were able to challenge consultants' approach to the Web site's functionality design by disagreeing and pushing back on use case scenarios that consultants developed. Following the literature on multi-party collaboration we call this mode of interaction between agents and objects "collaborative" because it allows both parties to synergistically integrate their practices and knowledge-in-practice. Carlile (2002, 2004) and Levina and Vaast (2005, 2006, 2008) have argued extensively that such integration cannot be accomplished without a change in power relations among agents.

In the case of transformative boundary-spanning, as we have argued earlier, agents may deliberately or inadvertently engage in the production of a new joint field of practice. The creation of new fields involves new practices, forms of capital, and power relations. While Levina and Vaast's earlier writing (2005, 2006) has focused on the necessity of the emergence of such field novelty to be produced through boundary-spanning, a more careful examination of the concept of shared fields of practice challenges that position. Indeed, it does not appear in Carlile (2004) or Bechky (2003) that new fields necessarily emerged. Rather these cases seem to be indicative of the transformation of existing fields. However, Levina and Vaast (2005) field studies indicate that sometimes agents cannot "break away" from their established, routinized ways of acting without creating a new field. In this case, boundary-spanners are engaged in producing boundary objects that help them define the identity and represent the capital of the new field, as well as delineate its boundaries. Agents then use boundary objects to draw others to join the new field. For example, in the creation of new academic fields, such as the field of Information Systems, specific researchers from such fields as accounting, computer science, strategy, and management could not fit their research interests into the frames of existing institutional fields in which they practiced. They thus created new inter-disciplinary research centers (e.g., the famous University of Minnesota MIS Research Center created by then accounting professor Gordon Davis), conferences (ICIS and AMCIS), associations (AIS) boundary objects (e.g., the new research journal *MIS Quarterly*, specific research models and theories, textbooks), and PhD programs. In doing so, they challenged conventions in the related research fields and the relations between agents (in this case academic disciplines) in business school academia (a new agent entered the field and shook up established resource allocation).

Finally, it is important to note the relationship between the transactive and transformative modes of boundary-spanning. As Carlile's (2004) framework, we see the transactive mode as being a necessary part of the transformative mode. Indeed, without translation across practices it is impossible to negotiate change. Moreover, as agents produce these diverse practices they may move from one mode to the other both intentionally as well as inadvertently. It appears to us that in Carlile's (2004) case, agents started with an explicit goal of addressing a knowledge integration problem (thus, in fact, they wanted to transform practices and achieve novelty). However, their initial actions were transactive and not transformative of practices. Subsequently, they recognized the pragmatic problems at stake and moved to the transformative mode of practice production. In Levina and Vaast's (2005) case of an insurance company's intranet implementation, agents also started with transactive thinking in mind (assuming the sales force would just adopt the tool and incorporate it into its existing practices), but ended up transforming practices. On the other hand, in the case of the Web development consulting project, agents started with the idea of "revolutionizing the industry" and producing lots of novelty, but ended up in a transactive mode mostly because none of the individuals nominated to boundary-spanning roles was able to fulfill those roles in practice.

IMPLICATIONS

This chapter makes four primary theoretical contributions to the literature on boundary-spanning practices. First, it points out the importance of shared, typically institutionalized, contexts (or fields of practice) in which any boundary-spanning practice takes place. Second, it proposes that novelty can only be defined in relation to the impact of boundary-spanning practices on these shared fields rather than simply as an input determining the choice of such practices. Moreover, we draw on Bourdieu to propose that the impact of practices on the shared field is best understood through the notion of power relations among agents (individuals, groups, or institutions) in that field. Third, we propose two modes of boundary-spanning practices (transactive and transformative) defined on the basis of how the practice impacts relations in shared fields of practice. Fourth, we clarify different roles that the use of boundary objects and the engagement of boundary-spanners play in different modes of boundary-spanning practice. We propose that in transactive practices, boundary objects become objects of exchange and boundary-spanners act as translators helping to share information and map practices across fields. In this case they draw on shared practices in existing shared fields to accomplish boundary-spanning work. In transformative practices, boundary-spanners act as both translators and negotiators, using boundary objects to represent differences among practices and negotiate new relations within existing shared fields, and possibly in newly produced joint fields of practice.

The distinctions we draw in this chapter have direct implications to organizational design issues. First, we agree with Carlile's (2004) basic logic that organization designers may want to tailor structural elements involved in boundary-spanning to the type of boundary-spanning that is desired. However, Carlile proposed that the degree of novelty in the situation is guiding the choice of practice. Our theory suggests that the desired degree of novelty to be achieved by agents through their action should guide the choice. Second, we suggest that as organizations design such practices they use both shared artifacts and boundary-spanning roles but of different nature and for different aims. Unlike Carlile's initial argument, we believe that agents play a crucial role in transformative boundary-spanning and that boundary objects' use and usefulness is defined by such agents' actions. Third, we point out the importance of boundary objects of a "limited" type, which we termed "objects of exchange" in designing transactive boundary-spanning. Many such objects have been described in the literature. For instance, IT-based artifacts such as document repositories that do not look like full-fledged boundary objects-in-practice but rather look like trading zones serve as objects of exchange (Kellogg, Orlikowski, and Yates 2006; Levina and Vaast 2006).

On a related note we suggest to organizational designers that while morphing the two modes of boundary-spanning is a natural part of the practice and is typically desirable so as to balance exploration and exploitation in organizational life (March 1991), unintentional morphing or rather "slippage" from one type of practice to the other may be detrimental to some or all of the concerned parties. This is particularly the case because a) transforming power relations may unintentionally hurt the positions of agents involved, leading to discontent and possible break-up of the effort and b) the transformative mode of practice is more "expensive" in a sense that when agents challenge each other and undo prior, taken for granted, approaches they use more resources. For example, when a company decides to outsource part of its design process to another company assuming that the vendor will follow its client's lead on what to do and how to do it (in a transactive mode) but the vendor instead tries to suggest new approaches and pushes back, not only do projects typically take longer, but the relations between the two parties as well as within the clients' firm are transformed (Levina and Vaast 2008; Levina and Orlikowski 2009).

A related implication of our research concerns organization design issues typically driven by coordination theories (Crowston 1997; Crowston, Rubleske, and Howison 2006). We suggest that the robust machinery developed by coordination theory that talks about different types of interdependencies (pooled, sequential, reciprocal) (Thompson 1967) and different types of cross-boundary mechanisms (interpersonal vs. codified) (Lawrence and Lorsch 1967) misses an important aspect of boundary-spanning that has to do with power relations in practice. It is mostly oriented at transactive boundary-spanning and not at transformation. Codifying coordination practices, for example, has not only functional roles (to map and translate across diverse parties) but also symbolic ones when power relations are at stake. Thus, for transforming relations and creating new fields a new theory of "coordination" needs to be developed.

Our work also draws more heavily on institutional theory than prior work on boundary-spanning and has implications for research on institutional entrepreneurship. Following the work of Maguire, Hardy, Lawrence (Maguire, Hardy, and Lawrence 2004; Phillips, Lawrence, and Hardy 2000), and others we see institutional entrepreneurship as situated within existing fields of practice while also facilitating the creation of new fields. Our work characterizes two critical roles of boundary-spanners as institutional entrepreneurs—the role of translators and the role of negotiators. We have argued previously that these two roles are very hard to fulfill in practice as they require legitimate peripheral participation in multiple fields, the legitimacy to represent and negotiate on behalf of these fields, and symbolic, cultural, economic, and social capital endowments to help create new fields (Levina and Vaast 2008). Our contribution is in a) enriching our understanding of these roles based on years of research on boundary-spanners and b) pointing out the important role of boundary objects that such agents create and use in the process.

Last, but by no means least, our framework allows us to enter long-standing debates on firm boundaries and the nature of the firm. There is mixed evidence on whether firms actually have superior boundary-spanning capabilities (or what Kogut and Zander 1992, termed combinative capabilities). The very nature of these capabilities has been left quite open-ended and the argument that firms have superiority over markets challenged (Foss 1996; Grandori and Kogut 2002). Indeed, relying upon our framework and evidence from research on boundary-spanning (Levina and Vaast 2008), we see that transformative and transactive boundary-spanning can take place equally well within or across firm boundaries. Our insights on this debate stem from the recognition of the role played by the shared organizational fields of practice in enabling transformative boundary-spanning. While transactive boundary-spanning can proceed efficaciously in any shared context (including within professional fields or industries), in order to renegotiate power relations within shared fields and create new joint fields of practice boundary-spanners need to be endowed with significant amount of symbolic and other resources. Through their hierarchical structures (positions, titles, and budgets), organizations can endow boundary-spanners with the necessary (economic, intellectual, and social) resources and with symbolic legitimacy within multiple groups. Thus, a CEO by virtue of her position can span boundaries between marketing, sales, and engineering, transforming relations among these groups and possibly creating new fields, and capital, in the process (e.g., cross-functional teams). Across organizations this becomes harder to achieve because belonging to an organization means accessing the symbolism of positions and roles in these organizations.

CONCLUSION

To conclude, our conceptualization sheds new light onto existing practice-based theorizing of boundary-spanning and opens up new doors for integrating this theorizing with other organizational theories: organizational design, coordination, institutional entrepreneurship, and firm boundaries. Our theory also benefits from and adds to a tradition of cumulative scholarship. In the last forty years much has been written on boundary-spanners and boundary objects, and much of the more recent literature has acknowledged the importance of practice theory. We relied upon and further developed these late developments, integrated diverse empirical findings onto our theoretical framework and, overall, proposed a lens on boundary-spanning that reconciled prior accounts while advancing theory.

REFERENCES

Abbott, Andrew. 1995. "Things of boundaries." *Social Research* no. 62 (4):857–882.

Aldrich, Howard, and Diane Herker. 1977. "Boundary spanning roles and organization structure." *Academy of Management Review* no. 2 (2):217–230.

Allen, T. J., and S. I. Cohen. 1969. "Information flow in research and development laboratories." *Administrative Science Quarterly* no. 14 (1):12–19.

Ancona, Deborah, and David Caldwell. 1992. "Bridging the boundary: External activity and performance of organizational teams." *Administrative Science Quarterly* no. 37:634–665.

Barrett, Michael, and Eivor Oborn. 2010. "Boundary object use in cross-cultural software development teams." *Human Relations* no. 63:1199–1221.

Bartel, Caroline A., and Jane E. Dutton. 2001. "Ambiguous organizational memberships: Constructing organizational identification in interactions with others." In *Social identity processes in organizational contexts*, edited by Michael A Hogg and Deborah J Terry, 115–130. Philadelphia, PA: Psychology Press.

Bechky, Beth. 2003. "Sharing meaning across occupational communities: The transformation of understanding on a product floor." *Organization Science* no. 14 (3):312–330.

Bodker. Susanne. 2000. "Scenarios in user-centered design-setting the stage for reflection and action." *Interacting with Computers* no. 13 (1):61–75.

Bourdieu, Pierre. 1977. *Outline of a theory of practice*. Translated by Richard Nice. Cambridge: Cambridge University Press.

———. 1996. *The state nobility: Elite schools in the field of power*. Translated by Lauretta C. Clough. Stanford, Calif.: Stanford University Press.

Bourdieu, Pierre, and John B. Thompson. 1991. *Language and symbolic power*. Cambridge, Mass.: Harvard University Press.

Bourdieu, Pierre, and Loïc J. D. Wacquant. 1992. *An invitation to reflexive sociology*. Chicago: University of Chicago Press.

Briers, Michael, and Wai Fong Chua. 2001. "The role of actor-networks and boundary objects in management accounting change: A field study of an implementation of activity-based costing." *Accounting, Organizations and Society* no. 26 (3):237–269.

Burrell, Gibson, and Gareth Morgan. 1979. *Sociological paradigms and organisational analysis: elements of the sociology of corporate life*. London: Heinemann.

Carlile, P. R. 2004. "Transferring, translating, and transforming: An integrative framework for managing knowledge across boundaries." *Organization Science* no. 15 (5):555–568.

Carlile, Paul Reuben. 2002. "A pragmatic view of knowledge and boundaries: Boundary objects in new product development." *Organization Science* no. 13 (4):442–455.

Ciborra, C. U., and R. Andreu. 2001. "Sharing knowledge across boundaries." *Journal of Information Technology* no. 16 (2):73–81.

Cohen, A. L., D. Cash, and M. J. Muller. 2000. "Designing to support adversarial collaboration." Paper read at ACM 2000 Conference on Computer Supported Cooperative Work, at Philadelphia, PA.

Cousins, P. D., R. B. Handfield, B. Lawson, and K. J. Petersen. 2006. "Creating supply chain relational capital: The impact of formal and informal socialization processes." *Journal of Operations Management* no. 24 (6):851–863.

Cross, Robert L., and Andrew Parker. 2004. *The hidden power of social networks: understanding how work really gets done in organizations*. Boston, Mass.: Harvard Business School Press.

Crowston, K. 1997. "A coordination theory approach to organizational process design." *Organization Science* no. 8 (2):157–175.

Crowston, K., Rubleske, J., and Howison, J. 2006. "Coordination theory and its application in HCI." In *Human-Computer Interaction in Management Information Systems Foundations, Advances in Management Information Systems Series*, edited by Ping Zhang and Dennis Galletta, 120–138. Armonk, NY: M. E. Sharpe, Inc.

Deetz, S. 1996. "Describing differences in approaches to organization science: Rethinking Burrell and Morgan and their legacy." *Organization Science* no. 7 (2):191–207.

DiMaggio, Paul J. 1991. "Social structure, institutions, and cultural goods: The case of the United States." In *Social theory for a changing society*, edited by Pierre Bourdieu and James Samuel Coleman, 133–155. Boulder, NY: Westview Press; Russell Sage Foundation.

DiMaggio, Paul J., and Walter W. Powell. 1983. "The Iron Cage revisited: Institutional isomorphism and collective rationality in organizational fields." *American Sociological Review* no. 48:147–160.

Dougherty, Deborah. 1992. "Interpretive barriers to successful product innovation in large firms." *Organization Science* no. 3 (2):179–202.

Dubinsky, Alan J., Ronald E. Michaels, Masaaki Kotabe, Chae Un Lim, and Hee-Cheol Moon. 1992. "Influence of Role Stress on Industrial Salespeople's Work Outcomes in the United States, Japan, and Korea." *Journal of International Business Studies* no. 23 (1):77–99.

Espinosa, Alberto, William DeLone, and Gwanhoo Lee. 2007. "Virtual Team Boundary Complexity: A Team Coordination Perspective." Paper read at the Academy of Management Annual Meeting, August 3–8, at Philadelphia, PA.

Foss, Nicolai J. 1996. "More critical comments on knowledge-based theories of the firm." *Organization Science* no. 7 (5):519–523.

Friedman, Raymond A., and Joel Podolny. 1992. "Differentiation of boundary spanning roles: Labor negotiations and implications for role conflict." *Administrative Science Quarterly* no. 37 (1):28–47.

Grandori, Anna, and Bruce Kogut. 2002. "Dialogue on organization and knowledge." *Organization Science* no. 13 (3):223–231.

Gulati, R., and H. Singh. 1998. "The architecture of cooperation: Managing coordination costs and appropriation concerns in strategic alliances." *Administrative Science Quarterly* no. 43 (4):781–814.

Hargadon, Andrew, and Robert I. Sutton. 1997. "Technology brokering and innovation in a product development firm." *Administrative Science Quarterly* no. 42 (4):716–749.

Henderson, Katherine. 1991. "Flexible sketches and inflexible data bases: Visual communication conscription devices, and boundary objects in design engineering." *Science, Technology, & Human Value* no. 16 (4):448–473.

Hinds, P., and S. Kiesler. 1995. "Communication across boundaries—work, structure, and use of communication technologies in a large organization." *Organization Science* no. 6 (4):373–393.

Hsiao, Ruey-Lin, Dun-Hou Tsai, and Ching-Fang Lee. 2012. "Collaborative knowing: The Adaptive nature of cross-boundary spanning." *Journal of Management Studies* no. 49 (3):464–491.

Jeppesen, L. B., and K. R. Lakhani. 2010. "Marginality and problem-solving effectiveness in broadcast search." *Organization Science* no. 21 (5):1016–1033. doi: Doi 10.1287/Orsc.1090.0491.

Kellogg, Katherine C., W. J. Orlikowski, and JoAnne Yates. 2006. "Life in the trading zone: Structuring coordination across boundaries in postbureaucratic organizations." *Organization Science* no. 17 (1):22–44.

Kim, Jeffrey Y., and John L. King. 2000. "Boundary instances in heterogeneous engineering teams: Trouble management in the dram manufacturing process." *Research on Managing Groups and Teams* no. 3:79–98.

Kogut, Bruce, and Udo Zander. 1992. "Knowledge of the firm, combinative capabilities, and the replication of technology." *Organization Science* no. 3 (3):383–397.

Lawrence, Paul R., and Joy W. Lorsch. 1967. "New management job: the integrator." In *Harvard Business Review* no. 45 (6): 142–151.

Lee, G. K., and R. E. Cole. 2003. "From a firm-based to a community-based model of knowledge creation: The case of the Linux kernel development." *Organization Science* no. 14 (6):633–649.

Leifer, Richard, and Andre Delbecq. 1978. "Organizational/environmental interchange: A model of boundary spanning activity." *Academy of Management Review* no. 3 (1):40–50.

Leonard, Dorothy, and Walter C. Swap. 1999. *When sparks fly: Igniting creativity in groups*. Boston, Mass.: Harvard Business School Press.

Levina, Natalia. 2005. "Collaborating on multiparty information systems development projects: A collective reflection-in-action view." *Information Systems Research* no. 16 (2):109–130.

Levina, Natalia, and Wanda J. Orlikowski. 2009. "Understanding shifting power relations within and across organizations: A critical genre analysis." *Academy Management Journal* no. 52 (4):672–703.

Levina, Natalia, and E. Vaast. 2008. "Innovating or doing as told? Status differences and overlapping boundaries in offshore collaboration." *MIS Quarterly* no. 32 (2):307–332.

Levina, Natalia, and Emmanuelle Vaast. 2005. "The emergence of boundary spanning competence in practice: Implications for implementation and use of information systems." *MIS Quarterly* no. 29 (2):335–363.

———. 2006. "Turning a community into a market: A practice perspective on IT use in boundary-spanning." *Journal of Management Information Systems* no. 22 (4):13–38.

Lysonski, Steven. 1985. "A boundary theory investigation of the product manager's role." *Journal of Marketing* no. 49 (1):26–41.

Lysonski, Steven J, and Eugene M Johnson. 1983. "The sales manager as a boundary spanner: A role theory analysis." *The Journal of Personal Selling & Sales Management* no. 3 (2):8.

Maguire, S., C. Hardy, and T. B. Lawrence. 2004. "Institutional entrepreneurship in emerging fields: HIV/AIDS treatment advocacy in Canada." *Academy of Management Journal* no. 47 (5):657–679.

March, James G. 1991. "Exploration and exploitation in organizational learning." *Organization Science* no. 2:71–87.

Merleau-Ponty, Maurice, and James M. Edie. 1964. *The primacy of perception: and other essays on phenomenological psychology, the philosophy of art, history and politics*. Evanston, Ill.: Northwestern University Press.

Montgomery, Kathleen, and Amalya L. Oliver. 2007. "A fresh look at how professions take shape: Dual-directed networking dynamics and social boundaries." *Organization Studies* no. 28 (5):661–687.

Nelson, Richard R., and Sidney G. Winter. 1982. *An evolutionary theory of economic change*. Cambridge, Mass.: Belknap Press of Harvard University Press.

Newell, S., H. Scarbrough, and J. Swan. 2001. "From global knowledge management to internal electronic fences: Contradictory outcomes of intranet development." *British Journal of Management* no. 12 (2):97–111.

Phillips, N., T. B. Lawrence, and C. Hardy. 2000. "Inter-organizational collaboration and the dynamics of institutional fields." *Journal of Management Studies* no. 37 (1):23–43.

Polzer, J. T., L. P. Milton, and W. B. Swann. 2002. "Capitalizing on diversity: Interpersonal congruence in small work groups." *Administrative Science Quarterly* no. 47 (2):296–324.

Reagans, R., and E. W. Zuckerman. 2001. "Networks, diversity, and productivity: The social capital of corporate R&D teams." *Organization Science* no. 12 (4):502–517.

Schultze, U., and R. J. Boland. 2000. "Knowledge management technology and the reproduction of knowledge work practices." *Journal of Strategic Information Systems* no. 9 (2–3):193–212.

Singh, Jagdip, Willem Verbeke, and Gary K Rhoads. 1996. "Do organizational practices matter in role stress processes? A study of direct and moderating effects for marketing-oriented boundary spanners." *Journal of Marketing* no. 60 (3):69–86.

Star, S.L., and J.R. Griesemer. 1989. "Institutional ecology, 'translations' and boundary objects: Amateurs and professionals in Berkeley's Museum of Vertebrate Zoology 1907–39." *Social Studies of Science* no. 19 (3):387–420.

Star, Susan Leigh. 1989. "The Structure of Ill-Structured Solutions: Boundary objects and heterogeneous distributed problem solving." In *Readings in distributed artificial intelligence*, edited by M. Huhn and L. Gasser, 37–54. Menlo Park, CA: Morgan Kaufman.

Swan, J. A., Mike Bresnen, M. Robertson, and S. Newell. 2007. "The object of knowledge: The role of objects in interactive innovation." *Human Relations* no. 60:1809–1837.

Tajfel, Henri. 1978. *Differentiation Between Social Groups: Studies in the Social Psychology of Intergroup Relations*. London: Academic Press.

Thompson, James D. 1967. *Organizations in action; social science bases of administrative theory*. New York: McGraw-Hill.

Tushman, Michael L., and Thomas J. Scanlan. 1981. "Boundary spanning individuals: Their role in information transfer and their antecedents." *Academy of Management Journal* no. 24 (2):289–305.

von Hippel, Eric. 1988. *The sources of innovation*. New York: Oxford University Press.

Weber, Max. 1978. *Economy and society*. Edited by Guenther Roth and Caus Wittich, 2 vols. Berkeley: University of California Press.

14 Hospital Culture and Infection Control

Acceptance, Compliance, and Complications across Boundaries

Peter N. Rosenweg and Janice Langan-Fox

INTRODUCTION

The often impenetrable nature of professional boundaries demonstrates the need for people with the interorganizational skills who can effectively span professional, political and commercial interests in an ambassadorial, coordinating or empowering capacity (Drach-Zahavy 2011, 89).

The aim of this chapter is to illustrate the benefit and indeed the essential requirement for the personal skills needed to overcome barriers to engagement and cooperation held by groups, where variously retention of privilege, advantage, or reputation maybe at stake. The case of compliance with the hand hygiene protocol in hospitals is taken here as a critical example shaping the behavior of staff and the outcomes for patients. The almost reluctant response to the hygiene protocols by experienced and learned practitioners is depicted in the current reports of observed compliance by nurses and doctors for Australia, emphasizing the continuing problem with compliance. The possibility of an alternative perspective for a fail-safe solution is also discussed for the hospital environment, where unseen pathogens can swiftly kill the vulnerable.

Nowhere has this been demonstrated more aptly than in the health services and by the case in point regarding the evidence that hospital acquired infections (HAIs) are generally spread from patient to patient on the hands of doctors and health-care workers (HCWs) in hospital settings and continue to do so today. The history and development of controls for HAIs proposed by various professionals in their time has demonstrated the extreme difficulty of penetrating protected professional bodies from both inside and outside to effect change and advance care in saving lives. As an example, the documented observation of the transmission of puerperal fever first published in 1843 by the American doctor and subsequent Dean of Harvard Medical, Oliver Wendell Holmes Sr. (Wikipedia, December 15, 2012), advocated burning the towels, linen, and even the surgeons clothes after attending patients with the fever, but without any real expectations that surgeons would comply with his suggestion to burn their clothes. Several years later in a Viennese hospital in 1847, Ignaz Semmelweis experienced the same problem in getting his findings about infection across to his colleagues, despite demonstrating success in reducing the transmission of the frequently fatal puerperal fever (Best et al. 2004). It seemed that the simple mechanism of washing hands between patients with a solution of chloride of lime (Lindberg et al. 2011, 60) was too simple hence unlikely and that Semmelweis clearly much too ignorant. The protective reactions of the medical profession in each case represented something more than doubt about things that were still invisible to the naked eye at the time. Their responses showed a threat sensitivity and reactiveness in defending the class in the profession by attacking the integrity of the doctor involved for proposing 'such nonsense.' Semmelweis was subsequently consigned to a mental asylum when he refused to recant and step back from his findings. Semmelweis was unsuccessful in propagating his theory and the evidence of his observations was ignored. Penetrating the boundaries of conservatism and elitism of the profession of medicine in Vienna was met with abject rejection. Correspondingly it was no easier for Snow, a London doctor (c.1855), who had subsequently approached the profession on a similar matter and at a time when the elitist nature and the elevation of the profession in Britain was boosted further when that occupation was legislated restricting entry and licensing by examination in 1858 (Hall 2005, 189). The status and self-importance of the profession having been further improved, effectively reduced the ability for external developments in medicine to span their professional boundary. The European medical establishments went on to resist and refuse any endorsement of Semmelweis's means of infection control through hand washing, ignoring or countering the vociferous and reputedly messianic nature of the "unknown Hungarian doctor in Vienna," by deprecating the evidence of his greater survival rates. Thus the medieval view that infection was spread by the miasma, a kind of epidemiological fog, continued to be tolerated by the profession for a little longer. Semmelweis was not alone in being publically criticized for his views on the transmission of infection. John Snow (c. 1855), a London doctor, had come to the notice of his colleagues after successfully localizing the source of an outbreak of cholera in London to a single drinking tap in one location, receiving adverse criticism from *The Lancet*, a medical journal at the time, and his colleagues for his various comments regarding the spread of infection (Sandler 2000). Semmelweis was subsequently vindicated, as was Snow, once the weight of evidence had become irrefutable through the concurrent work of the British surgeon Lister (1827–1912) and the French chemist Pasteur (1822–1895) (DePaolo 2012), the mounting evidence resulting in the necessary paradigm shift in thinking about infections.

The critical need for the capacity and means to span professional and other boundaries became singularly important some eighty years after Semmelweis's attempts, on the accidental discovery of a substance that killed bacteria, *Penicillium notatum*, in 1928 by Fleming, a Scottish biologist. Realizing the importance of the discovery, Florey, Chain, and Heatley in

1941 (ACS 1999) subsequently worked on producing the mechanism for its production. However, despite a dire need for a powerful antibiotic effective against the large number of combat-related infections returning from numerous fronts in the 1941–1943 years of war, the Florey team were unable to span the competitive boundaries of science, commercial interests, and the British war office, finally having to relinquish the patent rights to American interests so as to obtain large-scale production of the antibiotic in 1944. Florey's team were reportedly required to buy a license so as to continue to work on the antibiotic they had developed.

In the period following 1945 and up to 2004, scientific research and discovery delivered further notable milestones in medicine, but had little impact in spanning the entrenched silo-like professional boundaries that remained. In the same period there had been only gradual improvements or advancements in infection control in the face of increasing infection rates and in preventing the transference of serious life-threatening infections in hospitals, beyond the use of gloves, masks, gowns, chlorhexidene, and iodine (Klein, Smith, Laxminarayan 2007). The barriers to interprofessional teamwork may have contributed to this slowness in developing effective protocols, as each health-care profession has its own culture. Up to the middle of the twentieth century the profession of medical doctors was still largely male dominated and patriarchal with a tendency to inhibit cross-boundary collaboration and cooperation with other associated hospital workers. Doctors continued to feel that it was unnecessary to listen to the 'doctors' helpers,' the nurses (Hall 2005, 188). The period saw the rise of hospital-acquired infection (HAIs) to epidemic proportions in some places and the development of drug-resistant strains or clones of the major infections.

THE PRESENT STATE OF INFECTION CONTROL

"Nosocomial infections," or HAIs, are defined as those infections acquired while being treated for another condition in a hospital. Initial claims of the national annual estimates of preventable incident mortality rates of HAIs in Australia, the UK and the USA, numbered around 7,000 in Australia (Victorian Quality Council report 2007), 40,000 in the UK, and 90,000 or more from the USA (Best et al. 2004). The magnitude of the problem became more public, thus compelling more attention on how HAIs are being transferred in hospitals and adopting the simple remedy demonstrated by Semmelweis in 1847 as a standard protocol. The rates of infection of the three reference countries mentioned here have fallen significantly since 2005 but remain puzzlingly high, having achieved a seeming incident plateau, similar to that experienced with occupational health issues in other industries (Donald and Canter 1993, 5–8; Geller 2001, 101), where in the industrial context the causes may be more easily attributed to the system of work, human factors, lack of cooperation, and availability of resources.

INCREASE IN THE SCOPE AND URGENCY
OF THE AUSTRALIAN PROBLEM

The magnitude of the opportunity for adverse nosocomial or HAIs in Australian hospitals compares with the size of the increase in the service provided, illustrating the urgent and desperate need for more effective remedies to the problem of HAIs. The potential growth in the problem of HAIs compares with the rise of admissions to hospitals. In the 2004–05 period there were about 4.3 million hospitalizations involving 759 public hospitals and 42.6 million occasions of service to nonadmitted patients in that period (AIHW statistics 2007). By 2011 those figures had reached 8.9 million hospitalizations and 50.7 million emergency and outpatient services (AIHW statistics 2010–11). Each visit to a hospital could thus be either an opportunity to transmit or acquire an infection from patients or from the environment within the hospital.

HOSPITAL CULTURE AND COMPLIANCE

It has been argued by Schein (2004, 12–13) and Collins (2000, 135) that cultural influences act as the social glue that holds the organization together, defines acceptable behavior, and gives it its own unique face. One definition is that "the safety culture of a hospital can be generally seen in the product of individual and group values, attitudes, perceptions, competencies and patterns of behaviour that demonstrate the commitment to, and the style and proficiency of the management of an organization's health and safety" (ACSNI 1993). While culture from the integrationist perspective (Collins 2000, 135) is a useful descriptive framework with which to explain situationally specific instances and the means to relate to both the macro and the micro contexts in the workplace, hospital culture may be more accurately seen as a collection of subcultures, reflecting a differentiationist perspective. An environment in which coexisting and multiple agendas compete (Collins 2000, 137), as reflected by the health-care professions, would likely impede cross-boundary cooperation (Bate 2000).

The accusation of a 'poor safety culture' has been a popular media response to hospitals and organizations experiencing catastrophes or other adverse events (Langan-Fox and Vranic 2011a; 2011b), such as wrong-site wrong-surgery, medication misidentification, the revelation of the magnitude of preventable fatalities by Baggoley (2008) or, more industrially, those resulting in great publicity and loss of life (e.g., BP Deepwater Horizon Oilrig disaster in 2010, Texas City Refinery explosion in 2006, and Pike River New Zealand in 2010). Catastrophes such as these have been commonly cited as a consequence of failure in safety leadership. However, it is conceivable that since any response by an organization is dependent on the information it receives, that catastrophes can occur anywhere cooperation and collaboration between professional units is ignored and remain silo-like, self-protective, uncommunicative, and complacent (Singhal et al. 2009).

Occupational specialization is a characteristic differentiator within organizations. Hall (2005, 188) has argued that the base values of hospital groups and occupations may be the same but the specialization that emanates from different technical languages, technology, and systems separates them from other groups. It could be argued that the inherent problem, outside of methodological issues with changing the safety culture in an organization, is the variability and diversity of individual motivation it contains. It could also be asserted, notwithstanding evidence for exceptions to the contrary, that essentially, individuals have their own agendas and come to work for their own purposes. In general, outside of nationalistic and strongly hierarchical organizations such as the military, there appears to be little evidence to show that simply by coming together as a group, individuals are imbued or aligned with any organizational patriotism or zeal desirable for the attainment of corporate objectives outside of their own work or that of professional groups. Pittet (2004) exploring specific behaviours related to hand hygiene compliance found a similar lack of uniformity of determinants at the behavioural and cognitive level that would identify specific predictive behaviours in compliance concluding that successful compliance could be better explained as occurring due to multiple influences acting on the person. It may also be argued that he found multiple and disparate motivations coexisting in a group consistent with nonaligned views.

It could be assumed from the culture literature that any intra-group alignment of purpose is more feasible where the group has a clear identity (i.e., doctors, psychologists, nurses). Thus it could be argued that the further the role a person has from the main identity of the organization, and the lesser the stake, engagement, and a shared mental model there is in its purpose, the more likely it is that motivation is more practical, less altruistic, and focused on the expectation of a pecuniary reward. It is therefore not surprising that studies have shown only marginal success achieved in actually changing organizational behavior as there may be fewer cross-boundary connections or values that can be addressed across dissimilar occupational groups. Investigating the disparity between intentions and results of culture-change projects, Smith (2003) reported a small 19 percent success rate in a review of some 210 like-change projects, consistent with the poor results previously found by Carr et al. (1996) and Kotter (1995) in similar projects, ranging from a high of 32 percent to a low of 10 percent.

The resilience with which group norms can act as boundaries was also evident in Bate's (2000) study involving an attempt to improve the cooperation between conventional hospital units, at a 'greenfield' hospital site in the west of England. He was not able to improve cross-boundary cooperation by changing the typical hierarchical hospital structure to a more networked form, where group boundaries were designed to be less distinct. He found that embedded prerogatives, tribal-like mindsets, and competing subgroup cultures made the spanning of boundaries problematic. He concluded that simply changing structures did not alter or avoid the problems of tribal-like competing subcultures.

PRESENT STATUS OF COMPLIANCE
WITH INFECTION CONTROL METHODS

There has been significant success globally since 2004 in controlling infection in most hand hygiene (HH)–engaged hospitals. In general, almost every young doctor and trainee nurse now knows about the work of Semmelweis and the history of blind resistance to advances in that understanding. There remains a resilience in noncompliance and a barrier or plateauing of achievement in full eradication of the three most serious infections. The most lethal of these easily transmitted pathogens, MRSA (methicillin-resistant *Staphylococcus aureus*) and the various hospital and community clones of the disease, C-Difficile (*Clostridium difficile*), and VRE (Vancomycin-resistant *enterococci*) are made even more threatening due to their ability to survive for long periods outside of humans. (Kampf and Kramer 2004, 867).

Achieving full compliance with the HH protocols at each patient contact depicted in the "five moments model" has hovered at around 40–70 percent both in Australia (HHA 2012), the USA (Keller 2011), and the UK (Creedon et al. 2008), showing that some hospital groups are characteristically less aligned. The differences appear most consistently where the authority and identity gradient is steepest, for example, between doctors and nurses, including allied health groups. By contrast, Lankford et al. (2003) found that in a comparative study of an old and a new hospital environment that HCWs in proximity to a medical staff person or peer who did not wash hands were significantly less likely to wash their own hands, suggesting that HH compliance can also be influenced by the behavior of other HCWs.

Stepping beyond organizational behavior, the epidemiological explanation often cited for this resilience in eradication is that one person in ten may be a natural carrier of an MRSA or other pathogen, hence the problem is impossible to eradicate. A behaviorally oriented alternative explanation suggests that staff, including nurses, doctors, and support personnel, contextually in the train of a routine or because of mental overload may unthinkingly choose to ignore or rationalize failure to adhere to the HH protocol after each and every contact, enabling the omission in HH practices to propagate to other risk-related acts, such as not discarding contaminated gowns and gloves after patient contact and acting with a lack of awareness when touching both soft and hard contaminated surfaces (bed clothing and metal rails) in the vicinity of patients.

A third explanation for noncompliance lies with the expectations of performance and the system of work. Public hospital wards can be busy places. Patient volumes and staff-patient ratios have a significant impact on operating costs. A 'cost-accounting' rationale to maximize patient through-puts and bed availability may encourage the presumption that staff peak performance can be expected throughout a shift. The resultant workload on HCW's underlines the need for a better understanding of the capacities and human limitations involved in a consistent delivery of the ideal fully compliant service. The added complexity of new procedures, medication regimes, equipment, and various patient-management protocols, can act to further compress the underlying priorities of ward life; which are made even more difficult in old-building-design, and in hospitals with fewer or less convenient facilities. The load on staff in those instances can potentially stretch personal resilience to the point where the cognitive load and growing fatigue with multiple responsibilities (Winwood et al. 2006, 438; Samaha 2007, 221) could impact the capacity to maintain attention and vigilance, short-term memory and recall of intentions, and, significantly, the motivation to avoid shortcuts and comply with all necessary protocols. However, the contamination of already vulnerable patients with HAI pathogens is not inevitable if the transference of pathogens can be controlled.

The revelation of the magnitude of the global HAI problem drew attention to the cognitive-behavioral circumstances in which actual noncompliance with the HH protocols often occurs. A strategy involving patient contact events resulted in the establishment of the five moments model by the World Health Organization (Figure 14.1) (WHO 2006).

At the operational level the WHO model links systematic cued or prompted behaviors at each stage of the process of individual patient care or contact, to address the normal limitations of prospective memory (remembering intentions) in the face of distractions, disruptions, and unscheduled deferments of tasks, as frequently occurs when responding to immediate patient calls for attention.

The connection between HCWs, as one means of transmission of infection, has also prompted more attention on training methods and compliance reinforcement techniques so as to combat the natural entropy of motivation and habituation with the compliance message over time. The work of Marian Zeitlin and Jerry Sternin cited in Lloyd, Buscell, and Lindberg (2008, 15) highlights the sustained success of the Positive Deviance Initiative (PDI) program, which was initially implemented in six 'beta hospitals' in the United States and is now used in some forty countries, in the reduction of transmission of all infections including MRSA and C. difficile. The Positive Deviance Initiative can be likened to other teamwork-based strategies as in the 'Morning Huddles' (Creedon et al. 2008), replicating 'toolbox talks' used in general industry.

The effectiveness of the PDI process may be due in some part to its boundary-spanning characteristics. Buscell (2008), reviewing the method, suggested PDI as a means to improve compliance and to effect culture change at the participant or operator level. The form of the methods were described as resembling the 'integrationist' perspective of culture as cited

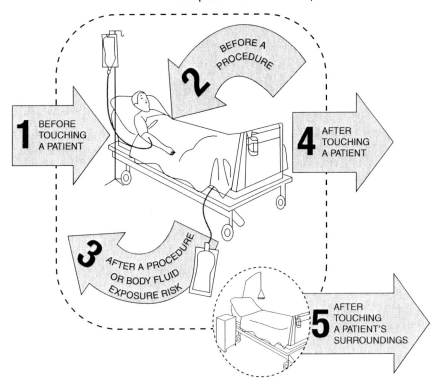

Figure 14.1   The five moments model of hand hygiene
Source: WHO, 2006

by Collins (2000, 135), drawing on the work of Martin (1992) and Schein (1992, 2004) through mapped social networks. A significant aspect, according to proponents, is the positive stance used in the method to amplify what is going right rather than fixing what is not working in an organization (Buscell 2008, 41). PDI employs the notion of mapping the connectivity and pattern of interaction of exceptional individuals (and groups) to inform and promote the issues to others in their network and across professional boundaries (Holley, 2007).

It is suggested by proponents that the bottom-up leadership of the PDI program generates greater mindfulness, acceptance, shared responsibility, and identification within the group. Once achieved to a target level in the PDI program, the motivational aspects of compliance as described by Buscell (2008) are transformed to being of a much higher value than before and worthy of aspiration. Positive deviance involves those individuals who already follow the HH and other infection control protocols to encourage others (within and across organizational units or boundaries) to imitate the required positive behaviors. The social mechanisms in the process are stated in general to include: assisting others to identify the inhibiting problems and engaging groups to develop a solution where noncompliance is apparent, as well as assisting in spreading the PDI practices.

Results from the PDI program at John Hopkins and elsewhere have been reported as very positive, delivering a progressive 60 percent reduction in infections over an eighteen-month period (Buscell 2008). Culture change projects are not easy to measure, hence the use of a social network approach makes it possible to survey and generate the changing social maps within an organization to assess results. It has also been suggested that HCWs' perception of their role as caregivers may be enhanced through the PDI model by shifting the preoccupation of HCWs from executing 'tasks' to a more patient-centered perspective. The evidence based on observations for HH compliance in some studies indicates that male doctors are the least compliant group (HHA 2012; Keller 2011; Creedon et al. 2008); little of the PDI literature or programs specifically mention their contribution or assimilation of the process.

BOUNDARY-SPANNING AS A MECHANISM IN MAINTAINING AND STRENGTHENING PDI

Considering the potential vulnerabilities of adherence to hand hygiene compliance, there is a need to examine mechanisms to promote hand hygiene programs. One such approach could be through encouraging specific team boundary-spanning activities. "Team boundary spanning involves a deliberate strategy by a team to communicate frequently with those outside the team in order to promote the team, secure resources, and protect the team from interference" (Ancona and Caldwell 1992, 8).

In our research context in hospitals, medical teams, e.g., nurses, doctors, auxiliaries, and so on, who are actively engaged in hand hygiene activities could engage in boundary-spanning tasks which might be more effective in achieving team goals—the patient-centered perspective of health care, and delivering high adherence to hand hygiene protocols. For instance, recent research by Meyer et al. (2011) investigating the boundary-spanning functions of nurse managers was able to determine key characteristics of boundary-spanning in hospital teams. Span (reporting relationships), time in manager-staff contact, transformational leadership, nurse-supervisor satisfaction, and operational hours comprised the research variables.

The boundary-spanning tendencies of the medical team will be influenced by the various national cultures of its members, the culture of the unit (i.e., hospital ward), and, more importantly, the culture of the hospital that enforces procedural compliance to prescribed safety routines.

VARIABILITY IN COMPLIANCE

Despite the preponderance of views and subsequent effort to diminish infections, noncompliance with defensive protocols persists as an ever-present shadow of risk and as a plateau of resistance preventing elimination, or at least a sustainable reduction, of HAIs. The paradox in this is that noncompliance with the defensive protocols by HCWs typically occurs in a presumably more uniformly aligned environment or culture than can be found elsewhere, where as previously argued, the background commitment to a high level of care and safety for the individual is assumed to be the norm.

More recent figures of compliance with the hand hygiene protocol as indicated by observations of "the five moments" protocol was obtained from some 377 hospitals in 2010 and 629 hospitals in 2012 in the public and private sector in Australia. The method of monitoring appears to have improved since the figures were first gathered in 2003, and while observation methodology is inherently problematic, the underlying movement has demonstrated a positive trend. More specifically, the initial Victorian hospital hand hygiene compliance rate as reported by Nicol, Watkins, and Plant (2007) at 66 percent has improved further, and Victoria continues to lead slightly against other regions. Changes in reporting statistics in the National Hand Hygiene Observation Compliance Rate have shown improvements to an average of 73.8 percent to date (see Table 14.1), still short of the ideal

Table 14.1 Compliance percentage rates by observation moment audit period 1 (Hand Hygiene Australia 2012)

Nature of Risk		Mean Compliance Rate Overall & by Moment at Collection Period 1		
		2010	2012	Change
	Overall Average Annual Rate	64.0	73.8	+9.8
1. Before touching a patient	Infection transferred to patient from elsewhere	56.9	69.3	+12.4
2. Before a procedure	Patient internally contaminated via wounds or veins	60.6	74.4	+13.8
3. After a procedure	HCW exposed to patients internal infection	75.3	83.2	+7.9
4. After touching a patient	Externally located infection transferred to HCW	73.9	80.7	+6.8
5. After touching patients area	Infection caught and carried from ambient surfaces	56.6	66.2	+9.6

Table 14.2   Percentage differences in HCW compliance rates by observation moment audit period 1

	HCW Mean Compliance Rate Percentage Differences by Audit Period 1						
	Doctors			Nurses/Midwives			Between Group Compliance Difference
	2010	2012	Within Group Change	2010	2012	Within Group Change	
Mean Audit Period 1	49.3	59.6	10.3	69.9	78.3	8.4	+18.7 Nurses
1. Before touching a patient		54.3			73.4		+19.1 Nurses
2. Before a procedure		63.4			76.5		+13.1 Nurses
3. After a procedure	n/a	71.1	n/a	n/a	85.2	n/a	+14.1 Nurses
4. After touching a patient		69.6			83.8		+14.2 Nurses
5. After touching patients area		50.3			73.5		+23.2 Nurses

Data Source: Australian hospital statistics 201011 (http://www.hha.org.au)

100 percent rate but significantly greater than the 40 percent or less reported in 2003. However, when considering the updated figures, the residual of noncompliance leaves on average one person in four as noncompliant. Or perhaps from another view, each monitored person is compliant only 73.8 percent of the time and that compliance varies to reflect the accumulation of fatigue over both daily and weekly shift durations.

The variability in compliance on tasks in patient management has been similarly addressed by using the five moments of contact (WHO 2006) model (see Table 14.1). While encouraging, the data show that the risk level of becoming a potential carrier of a life-threatening nosocomial infection by a HCW must still be at an unacceptable 27.2 percent, an especially disturbing figure when coupled with Baggoley's (2008) statement that 70 percent or more of the HAIs resulting in fatalities in the past may have been preventable.

THE OVERALL CHANGE IN COMPLIANCE OVER TWO YEARS IS 9.8 PERCENT, IN GENERAL SHOWING THAT:

- Doctors are less compliant than nurses by 18.7 percent.
- Doctors are more likely to introduce infections from elsewhere into a patient's area.
- Doctors perceive the hands-on phase of their contact as only relevant to already identified infection.

- Nurses are more aware than doctors of the pre- and postcontact risk of contamination.
- Doctors are more likely to spread infection during their short contact with patients than nurses, who may be in constant contact with patients.

The observation of compliance shows an average improvement of 9.8 percent over the previous period. However, doctors show a significant difference in lagging approximately 18.7 percent behind that of other HCW's, suggesting a degree of complacency or only a partial acceptance of the risks involved. The pattern of noncompliance events could indicate that some doctors perceive the risk of infection as emanating from the patient themselves, hence doctors may be mindful of infection while in contact and in coming away from patients, but less mindful of the risks of being a carrier in transporting infections to patients from elsewhere in the ward.

The significant difference of observed compliance with the "five moments" model in the observations between nurses and doctors suggests a lesser impact of cross-boundary influences, or that hand washing has not been fully established as critical in the doctors' system of work involving bedside interventions, ward rounds, consultations, and follow-up visits.

For most hospitals, the experience of managing infection control includes reaching an unstable plateau of achievement, with rates of infection resistant to further sustained reduction despite best efforts, a phenomenon first mentioned by Donald and Canter (1993) as the incident plateau.

The incident plateau, as an asymptotic trend, has been seen to be a common feature throughout hospitals and is evident in their own contexts in other industries (Figure 14.2), generally frustrating the achievement of sustainable near-zero hospital infection, incident, or accident rates; the phenomenon is suggestive of an absence of any reinforcement spanning organizational boundaries.

The Donald et al. (1993) "incident plateau" has become a common reference to the resilience of noncompliance and incidents to a program of

Figure 14.2 The Incident Plateau
Source: Psyfactors Pty Ltd. Permission to reproduce obtained Dec 15, 2012

sustained reduction. The plateau shows that the residual of incidents or non-compliance depicted in the area below the graph (Figure 14.2) drops elastically only to rebound back to some original level over time.

Comments by researchers relevant to the resilience of the incident plateau and human error in general include that of Key Dismukes, chief scientist in Human Factors at NASA (2001 2006), who after reviewing some 20,000 incidents in the ATSB database concluded that "trained conscientious people routinely make mistakes." Another perspective suggests, that when it comes to prediction that "safety incidents are probabilistic and elimination pathways may reduce the severity of events and their frequency, but their ultimate likelihood can only be delayed by vigilance, understanding and through an active projection of the possible," as in Endsley's definition of situational awareness (Jones and Endsley 1996, 507). This emphasizes that in the hospital context, the incident plateau may be a stark reflection of human limitations in which the circumstances for failure in compliance with the HH protocol find an opportunity, rather than a reflection of generally willful or aberrant behavior by HCWs.

The diminishing return from implementations of various technologies and interventions, resulting in a plateauing of incidents, depicts the historical universality of the resilience of mistakes and errors making up incident rates. The incident plateau has not received the attention it deserves as an indicator of a boundary between safety performance and failure. The development of credible perspectives, theory, and evaluative tools have proceeded to provide a better understanding of the functional bridge between human and system interactions. Cognitive task analysis (Jenkins et al. 2009; Strater 2005), as an example, provides better metrics of task-related human performance and the required level of fault tolerance (Hollnagel, Woods, and Leveson 2008, Ch 11; Woods et al. 2010, Ch 12) for sustained performance.

CONCLUSION

In summary, the issues presented in this paper on compliance with hand hygiene (HH) infection control methods have touched on the cultural resistance to compliance, spanning professional boundaries, inconsistency of application of the HH methods, cross-industry limitations in achievement, and the innovative training developed to address the problems with a means for fuller engagement by health-care workers (HCWs).

First, in considering the history of the search for agents and methods to eliminate hospital-acquired infections (HAIs), at the functional level, there has been a natural and persistent attempt to reduce the complex into the simple, with the purpose of adding certainty, safety, and consistency in infection-control performance to the hospital workplace, by placing hand-wash sanitizers at every necessary location in the ward. Whilst the hand wash has been demonstrated as highly effective as a germicidal agent, infection control remains variable because of the human potential for noncompliance (Table 14.2). The ongoing question and search for 'the one thing' that will make the difference in managing infections suggests a need for a rationalization or normalization of the problem. Reducing complexity could be achieved as it is elsewhere by reducing the 'many to many' relationships of the elements involved in preventing the transfer of infection to a more simplified form of a 'fewer to many' relationship. An example of a reduction using a simplified model to achieve a more rigorous infection control strategy is sometimes used in intensive care units, where a 'barrier' model isolating the patient to all direct hand contact is used and which, arguably, relies on the perception if immediate and personal risk to reinforce compliance. Another possibility may exist in factoring in a robust tolerance for mistakes through a redesign of tasks, system of work, and the environment, while maintaining the precision and consistency of task application required in hospitals. A context where lives are at risk may prove to be initially difficult and sensitive to alter, but this challenge is not necessarily insurmountable. Engineering such resilience into the process of ensuring safety of patients may simply mean operating in a zone where any deviation due to human error is trapped before it has any impact or so that it has little or no consequence.

Second, it is also argued here that what is required to achieve increased and sustained compliance is a wider understanding of the behavioral dynamics of the workplace that embraces both the top-down effect of organizational imperatives as culture as well as the bottom-up needs of HCWs. Culture change and compliance interventions based on HCW motivation will likely continue to deliver poor results, as would be expected from the history of such approaches. Since doing the same thing over and over and expecting the results to be different is reputedly futile, a shift in perspective may be necessary. A different system of work that engages staff more and makes team interaction more effective and purposeful, such as the Positive Deviance Initiative, shows considerable promise for expansion, coming as it does with already widespread reports of acceptance and success. Furthermore, staff training in boundary-spanning approaches could help focus the attentions and efforts of medical personnel to work across levels of status and expertise to advance the rate of compliance with infection control methods.

Third, it is suggested that within-group performance should not be the only focus. The history of failure in avoiding harm to patients in hospitals has demonstrated the critical nature and importance of minimizing barriers to cooperation and acceptance because of both professional and structural or hierarchical reasons. Nowhere is this more important than in hospitals, with their multiprofessional structures. In recognition of this and as an example of a method in progress, the Positive Deviance Initiative already makes mention of cross-boundary objectives in various implementations.

The need to span boundaries laterally could usefully also address or span upward to vertical hierarchies of management, the traditional keepers of all resources and policies, to diminish the complacency borne by the 'morality of altitude' that sometimes exists in larger organizational hierarchies. Directly confronting policy with critical outcomes may help to expedite action aimed at the reduction or even elimination of preventable deaths.

ACKNOWLEDGEMENTS

The present chapter was inspired and/or supported by two research projects: the Ph.D. work of the first author and funding obtained by the second author for "*Preventing Adverse Events in Hospitals,*" a Linkage National Competitive Grant from the Australian Research Council, Canberra. Application number: LP0989878

REFERENCES

ACS (1999). American Chemical Society International Historic Chemical Landmarks. Discovery and Development of Penicillin.1999. http://portal.acs.org/portal/PublicWebSite/education/whatischemistry/landmarks/flemingpenicillin/index.htm (accessed December 15, 2012).

Advisory Committee on the Safety of Nuclear Installations (ACSNI) (1993). Study group on human factors, Third report: Organising for safety. London: HMSO cited by Gadd.S, Collins. A.M. (2002) Safety Culture: A review of the literature. HSL/2002/25 website http://www.hse.gov.uk/research/hsl_pdf/2002/hsl02–25.pdf (Accessed December 15, 2012)

AIHW (2007) Australian Institute of Health and Welfare & Australian Commission on Safety and Quality in Health Care 2007. *Sentinel events in Australian public hospitals 2004–05. Cat. no. HSE. 51 Canberra: AIHW.*

AIHW (2012). Australian hospital statistics 2010–11. http://www.aihw.gov.au/publication-detail/?id=10737421633 (accessed December 15, 2012).

Anat Drach-Zahavy (2011). Interorganizational teams as boundary spanners: The role of team diversity, boundedness, and extrateam links, *European Journal of Work and Organizational Psychology*, 20:1, 89–118. http://dx.doi.org/10.1080/13594320903115936 (Accessed December 15, 2012).

Ancona, Deborah G.; Caldwell, David F. (1992). Bridging the boundary: External activity and performance in organizational teams, *Administrative Science Quarterly*, Dec 1992, 37:4, 634–665.

Australian Commission on Safety and Quality in Health Care (2010), Windows into Safety and Quality in Health Care 2010, ACSQHC, Sydney. http://www.safetyandquality.gov.au/wp-content/uploads/2010/11/Windows-2010-Web-version.pdf (Accessed December 15, 2012).

Baggoley, C. "Reducing harm to patients from healthcare associated infections," media release, July 23, 2008, The Australian Commission for Safety and Quality in Health Care.

Best. M, Neuhauser. D. (2004). Ignaz Semmelweis and the birth of infection control, *Quality Safe Health Care*, 13, 233–234.

Bate, P. (2000). Changing the culture of a hospital from hierarchy to networked community, *Public Administration* 78(3): 485.

Buscell, P. (2008). Pathways to Prevention, *Strategist*, Autumn 2008, 41–45.

Carr, D.K., Hard, K.J., Trahant, W.J. (1996), *Managing the Change Process: A Field Book for Change Agents, Consultants, Team Leaders, and Reengineering Managers*. New York, NY: McGraw-Hill. Cited in Smith, M. (2003) Changing an organisation's culture: correlates of success and failure, *Leadership & Organization Development Journal*, 24, 5.

Collins. D (2000) *Management Fads and Buzzwords. Critical-Practical Perspectives*, 135–145. London: Routledge.

Creedon, S.A, Slevin. B, DeSouza. V, Mannix. M, Quinn. G, Boyle. L, Doyle. A, O'Brien. B, O'Connell. N, Ryan. L, (2008) Hand hygiene compliance: exploring variations in practice between hospitals, *Nursing Times*, 104:49, 32–35. http://www.nursingtimes.net/hand-hygiene-compliance-exploring-variations-in-practice-between-hospitals/1944149 (Accessed December 15, 2012).

DePaolo, C. "The Victorian web. Pasteur and Lister: A Chronicle of Scientific Influence. "http://www.victorianweb.org/science/health/depaolo.html (Accessed December 15, 2012).

Dismukes, R. Key. (2001). Rethinking crew error: Overview of a panel session, *Research and Technology Report. Moffett Field, CA: NASA Ames Research Center*.

Dismukes, R.K., Berman, B., Loukia Loukopoulos. San Jose State University/NASA Ames Research Center. *CRM/HF Conference Denver, Colorado* 16–17 April 2006.

Donald, I., and Canter, D. (1993). Attitudes to safety: Psychological factors and the accident plateau. *Health and Safety Information Bulletin 215*, November, 5–8.

Geller, E. S (2001). Behavior-based safety in industry: Realizing the large-scale potential of psychology to promote human welfare, *Applied & Preventive Psychology* 10:87–105.

Hall, P. (2005). Interprofessional teamwork: Professional cultures as Barriers. *Journal of Interprofessional Care*, Supplement 1: 188–196.

Hand Hygiene Australia. (2012). National Data Period One, 2012 http://www.hha.org.au/LatestNationalData/national-data-period-one-2012.aspx (Accessed December, 15 2012).

Holley, June.(2007). Charting Pathways to Change: Mapping the Positive Deviance MRSA Prevention Networks at the VA Pittsburgh Healthcare System's Acute Care and Long-Term Care Facilities Shows Promise, *Plexus Institute*, August 2007. http://www.positivedeviance.org/pdf/Projects%20healthcare/Social%20 Network_Mapping_Analysis_VAPHS%20(2).pdf

Hollnagel, E., Woods, D.D., Leveson, N. (2006). *Resilience Engineering: Concepts and Precepts*. Aldershot, UK: Ashgate.

Jenkins, D. P., Stanton, N. A., Salmon, P. M., Walker, G. H. (2009). *Cognitive Work Analysis: Coping with Complexity*(Human Factors in Defence). Farnham, UK: Ashgate.

Jones, D.G., Endsley, M.R. (1996). Sources of Situation Awareness Errors in Aviation, *Aviation, Space and Environmental Medicine*, 67:6, 507–512.

Kampf. G and Kramer. A. (2004). Epidemiologic background of hand hygiene and evaluation of the most important agents for scrubs and rubs, *Clinical*

Microbiology Reviews. 2004 October; 17:4, 863–893. http://www.ncbi.nlm.nih. gov/pmc/articles/PMC523567/ (Accessed December 15, 2012).

Keller, D. M. (2011). Hand hygiene compliance poor and self-assessment unreliable, Cited in *Medscape Psychiatry and Mental Health News* Oct. 26, 2011, http:// www.medscape.com/viewarticle/752281 (Accessed December 15, 2012).

Klein, E., Smith, D.L., and Laxminarayan, R. Hospitalizations and deaths caused by methicillin-resistant *Staphylococcus aureus*, United States, 1999–2005. *Emerging Infectious Diseases.* 13 (2007):1840–6. Available from http://www.ncbi.nlm.nih. gov/pmc/articles/PMC3044510/ (Accessed December 15, 2007).

Kotter, J.P. (1995). Leading change: why transformation efforts fail, *Harvard Business Review* 73, no. 2, March–April 1995: 59–67

Langan-Fox, J., and Vranic, V. (2011a). Intern coping, stress and patient-adverse events: the human, hospital and system cost of developing medical expertise. In J. Langan-Fox and C.L. Cooper (Eds). *Handbook of Stress in the Occupations.* Cheltenham, UK: Edward Elgar Publishing.

Langan-Fox, J., and Vranic, V. (2011b). Surgeon stress in the operating room: error free performance and adverse events. In J. Langan-Fox and C.L. Cooper (Eds). *Handbook of Stress in the Occupations.* Cheltenham, UK: Edward Elgar Publishing.

Lankford. M. G, Zembower. T. R, Trick. W. E, Hacek. D. M, Noskin. G. A and Peterson. L. R. (2003). Influence of Role Models and Hospital Design on the Hand Hygiene of Health-Care Workers. Emerging Infectious Diseases Vol. 9, No. 2, February 2003 http://wwwnc.cdc.gov/eid/article/9/2/02–0249_article.htm (Accessed December 15, 2012).

Lindberg. C, Norstrand. P, Munger. M. T, DeMarsico. C, Buscell. P. (2011). Letting Go, Gaining Control: Positive Deviance and MRSA Prevention. *Plexus Institute.* http://www.plexusinstitute.org/?page=complexity3 (Accessed December 15, 2012).

Lloyd, J., Buscell, P., & Lindberg, C. (2008). Staff-Driven Cultural Transformation Diminishes MRSA, *Prevention Strategist*, Spring, 10–15.

Martin. J. (1992). *Cultures in Organizations: Three Perspectives.* New York: Oxford University Press.

Meyer M.N., O'Brien-Pallas L., Doran, D., Streiner D., Ferguson-Pare, M., Duffield C. (2011). Front-line managers as boundary spanners: effects of span and time on nurse supervision satisfaction, *Journal of Nursing Management*, 19, 611–622.

Nicol. P.W., Watkins. R.E., and Plant. A.J. (2007). Infection Control in the Acute Care Setting: Time for a change of perspective, *Australian Infection Control*, 12:4, 118–126.

Oliver Wendell Holmes (1843), cited in http://en.wikipedia.org/wiki/Oliver_Wendell_ Holmes,_Sr.#Medical_reformer.2C_marriage_and_family (Accessed December 15, 2012).

Pittet. D. (2004). The Lowbury lecture: behavior in infection control. *Journal of Hospital Infection*, September 2004, 58:1, 1–13

Samaha E, Lal, S., Samaha, N., and Wyndham, J. (2007). Psychological, lifestyle and coping contributors to chronic fatigue in shift-worker nurses, *Journal Of Advanced Nursing*, 59:3, 221–232.

Sandler. D.P. (2000). John Snow and modern-day environmental epidemiology, *American Journal of Epidemiology* (2000) 152: 1, 1–3. doi: 10.1093/aje/152.1.1.

Schein, E.H. (1992). *Organisational Culture and Leadership.* 2nd ed. San Francisco: Jossey-Bass.

Schein, E.H. (2004). *Organisational Culture and Leadership*, 12–13. 3rd ed. San Francisco: Jossey-Bass.

Singhal. A., McCandless. K., Buscell. P., Lindberg. C. (2009). Spanning silos and spurring conversations: Positive deviance for reducing infection levels in hospitals, *Performance*, 2:3, 78–83. http://www.plexusinstitute.org/resource/collection/0F1D2212–2F8A-4C6B-80CA-5DC016A5C683/Singhal-Arvind-etal-SpanningSilos.pdf (Accessed December 15, 2012).

Smith, M. (2003). Changing an organisation's culture: correlates of success and failure. *Leadership & Organization Development Journal*, 24, 5.

Strater. O. (2005). *Cognition and Safety: An Integrated Approach to Systems Design and Assessment*. Farnham, UK: Ashgate

Victorian Quality Council. (2007). http://www.rch.org.au/washup/index.cfm?doc_id=4770

WHO. (2009). WHO Facts File. http://www.who.int/features/factfiles/patient_safety/en/index.html (Accessed December 15, 2012)

Winwood, P.C., Winefield, A.H. and Lushington, K. (2006). Work-related fatigue and recovery: The contribution of age, domestic responsibilities and shiftwork, *Journal of Advanced Nursing*, 56:4, 438–449.

WHO. (2006). World Health Organization, "My 5 moments for Hand Hygiene." http://www.who.int/gpsc/5may/background/5moments/en/index.html (Accessed December 15, 2012)

Woods, D. D., Dekker, S., Cook, R., Johannesen, L., Sarter, N. (2010). *Behind Human Error*. 2nd ed. Farnham, UK: Ashgate.

15 The Role of Organizational Controls and Boundary-Spanning in Software Development Outsourcing
Implications for Project Performance[1]

Anandasivam Gopal and Sanjay Gosain

INTRODUCTION

Software development outsourcing is a multifaceted and complex activity in which clients and vendor interact in many different ways to produce and deliver the software services required. Most outsourced software projects involve significant technical activities combined with a social process of acquiring and integrating knowledge from various stakeholders such as users, project managers, developers, and clients. In such a context, appropriate organizational controls are vital in reconciling the interests of stakeholders and improving project performance. Little work has explicitly studied the effect of the controls on project performance. Indeed, a recent meta-analysis (Narayanaswamy, Henry, and Purvis 2007, 2) points out that the "focus has been on identifying the factors that lead to the choice of controls and not the results that come from the use of controls. Even when performance outcomes are considered, the relationship to the use of various forms of control is often not clear." This study tries to address this gap in the literature by studying the effect of organizational controls on project performance.

In studying the impact of controls in the context of outsourcing, there are two organizational interfaces that appear in outsourced projects. The first interface lies between the vendor project management and the vendor development team. The second interfaces lies at the organizational boundary between vendor and client organizations. While prior research on controls in outsourcing hints at these multiple interfaces (Choudhury and Sabherwal 2003, Kirsch et al. 2002), they are not explicitly separated in theoretical treatment. The second difference from prior research on control is in recognizing that vendors and clients in outsourcing arrangements may have radically different knowledge domains and expertise (Levina 2005). Vendors have strong technical knowledge but typically lack business domain knowledge, while clients possess strong business domain knowledge but not deep technical knowledge and do not directly engage with technical artifacts. Therefore, in order to successfully manage an outsourced project, it is important for both parties to collaborate on sharing this knowledge across knowledge boundaries, thereby necessitating boundary-spanning (Carlile

2002). Explicating the role of boundary-spanning across the client-vendor organizational interface in shaping the effectiveness of controls applied at the management-vendor team interface is an important contribution of our study.

Boundary-spanning has emerged as an important concern in the context of knowledge sharing across fields of practice (Carlile 2002). In outsourced projects, it is necessary to not only span geographical and cultural boundaries but also the more relevant boundary of knowledge domains. Boundary-spanning plays a particularly significant role in enabling the vendor organization to apply control more effectively to manage the development team. The extent of boundary-spanning between the vendor and the client allows the vendor to institute controls that are more effective for the specific context and to effectively leverage relevant control parameters. The distinction between the two organizational interfaces inherent in outsourcing is thus captured; boundary-spanning *between* vendor and client significantly moderates the relationship between formal controls and project performance *within* the vendor organization. This approach bridges prior work studying controls in in-house development (Kirsch 1996, 1997) and boundary-spanning in software outsourcing (Levina and Vaast 2005, Levina 2005) into one parsimonious model of project performance.

In outsourced projects, the most commonly observed performance parameters are software quality and team efficiency. Quality, i.e., *product performance*, is a key outcome of software development activities (Henderson and Lee 1992). Additionally, adherence to budgeted cost and schedule, i.e., *process performance*, represents an important outcome measure (Wallace, Keil, and Rai 2004). The work reported provides a quantitative analysis of the link between controls and product and process performance. We tested our hypotheses on data from a sample of ninety-six offshore software projects, collected using a questionnaire and company databases, from software outsourcing vendors in India. We confirm that boundary-spanning between the client and the vendor significantly moderates the efficacy of formal controls instituted within the vendor organization to direct the project team.

BACKGROUND THEORY

Our research model, shown in Figure 15.1, is rooted in organizational control theory, which posits that four main modes of control may be employed in managing economic activity—behavior-based controls, outcome-based controls, clan-based controls, and self-control (Ouchi 1979, Eisenhardt 1985). In outcome-based controls, the controller specifies the parameters of the desired outcome; the controllee's rewards are based on the observed outcome. In contrast, behavior-based controls are used when specific rules and procedures are established for the controllee to follow, thereby leading to the desired outcome.

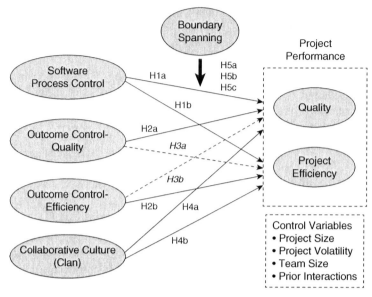

Figure 15.1   Empirical Research Model

In contrast to formal control, *informal* controls, i.e., clan and self-control, are based on social strategies that stress interpersonal and individualistic dynamics. Clan controls are implemented by promoting a set of common values and beliefs within the organization such that the agent's desire to be identified as a valid member of the "clan" induces the desired behavior. Clan controls include undocumented but socially accepted methods of activity, informal codes of conduct with respect to vendor-client relationships, and accepted behaviors that facilitate desired working conditions within the firm (Ouchi 1980). Our work in this chapter considers a specific type of clan control, *collaborative culture*, which refers to a value-based system, emphasizing shared purpose in working towards common goals.

While the focus on much of the controls literature in software development research has been on establishing the choice of control portfolios, there is little by way of establishing the impact of chosen controls on project performance (Narayanaswamy, Henry, and Purvis 2007). Behavioral controls can be likened to software processes in that both require adherence to a set of prescribed activities and methods to develop and maintain software (Paulk et al. 1993, Kirsch 1996). Thus, some of the existing research of the positive effect of processes on outcomes (Krishnan et al. 2000, Gopal et al. 2002) could be seen as indicative of the positive effects of behavioral control. Similarly, some existing work that attests to the beneficial impacts of strong incentives on vendors to achieve quality and efficiency targets is suggestive of the positive effects of outcome-based controls (Gopal et al. 2003, Banerjee and Duflo 2000). However, the aggregate effects of these different forms of controls have not been studied together in a holistic manner in the outsourcing domain. It is possible that they have differing effects on dimensions of performance when evaluated together—this represents another gap in the literature.

The preceding discussion suggests three unexplored avenues in the literature on controls. First, work pertains to in-house software development. The increasing prevalence of outsourcing would indicate a need to extend the study of controls to outsourced projects. Second, most existing work has studied the performance implications of software processes and incentives in isolation. Third, extending controls to outsourcing requires recognition of the two interfaces that exist in most software outsourcing engagements. We thus augment the conceptual model of control by incorporating the impact of the interactions between the client and the vendor, which we treat as manifestations of *boundary-spanning*, on the performance implications of different types of controls examined together.

Boundary-Spanning

Software development is a knowledge-intensive activity wherein firms' competitive advantage emerges from their unique ability to recombine individual and organizational knowledge. The effectiveness with which firms are able to collate, share, and build on individual knowledge bases depends upon the scope and the flexibility of the knowledge integration activities (Grant 1996). Thus, successful firms are able to create and manage inimitable and flexible models for knowledge sharing.

In software outsourcing, the vendor is a repository of both declarative and procedural technical knowledge (Pressman 2001). However, the vendor requires extensive knowledge about the business domain that the system will support (and be embedded in) from the client. The client's business domain contains large amounts of tacit knowledge that may not be adequately captured in the declarative knowledge elements traditionally used, such as functional specification documents. A large part of the typical outsourcing relationship revolves around knowledge integration activities between the vendor and client, aimed at bridging the gap between their respective knowledge domains, i.e., boundary-spanning (Carlile 2002). Empirical work studying boundary-spanning activities has focused on three important facets: boundary-*spanners*, boundary *objects*, and boundary-spanning *processes* (Carlile 2002, Star 1989). Boundary-spanners refer to individuals who are responsible for ensuring that the required knowledge is able to flow across the boundaries. Spanners "facilitate the sharing of expertise by linking two or more groups of people separated by hierarchy, location or function" (Levina 2005). Boundary objects that can be used to share knowledge are needed. Star (1989) defines boundary objects as "objects that are plastic enough to adapt to local needs and constraints of several parties employing them yet robust enough to maintain a common identity across sites." In the

IT context, boundary objects can refer to document archives, software code, and design artifacts (Levina 2005, Pawlowski and Robey 2004). Finally, Carlile (2002, 2004) describes the need for a process using which members across knowledge domains can share information bidirectionally in order to integrate, transform, or apply existing knowledge to the activity at hand. Our definition of boundary-spanning in the outsourcing context thus draws from these three building blocks of boundary-spanning—spanners, objects, and processes.

Effect of Formal Controls

Behavioral control involves managers prescribing appropriate procedures that have to be followed by agents in carrying out their activities. The reasoning for instituting such control is that adherence to prescribed behavior norms will lead, under the right contingencies, to higher performance. In the outsourcing context, appropriate behavior controls can include development methodology specification (Choudhury and Sabherwal 2003; Necco, Gordon, and Tsai 1987), clearly defined procedures and documentation related behaviors (Kirsch 1997). Research has shown that controlled and disciplined processes, analogous to strict behavior controls, have resulted in higher quality for in-house software products (Krishnan et al. 2000). We extend this reasoning to the outsourcing domain and test for similar effects of behavioral control on project outcomes. To the extent that adherence to process and methodologies within the project team on the vendor side are associated with better quality, we propose:

> H1a: *Higher levels of behavioral (process specifications-based) control will be associated with higher levels of software quality.*

Software development is an uncertain activity with a high degree of risk surrounding the causal relationship between input and output (Pressman 2001). Therefore, it is possible to have all requisite inputs into the development process and still experience technical or managerial issues during the project that adversely affect the ability to complete project on time or within budgeted costs. Behavioral controls aim to mitigate this inefficiency by encapsulating appropriate planning templates and development practices most suited to the industry context. Hence, we propose:

> H1b: *Higher levels of behavioral (process specifications-based) control will be associated with higher levels of project efficiency.*

Organizations implementing outcome control specify desired goals and employees are rewarded based on the extent to which they meet these goals. A behavioral view of outcome control indicates that once the controllee has been provided information about desired outcomes, his/her incentives should ensure appropriate behavior to meet these goals (Kirsch 1997). This view is supported by agency theory wherein the presence of incentive alignment between the principal and agent leads to better outcomes by enabling the appropriate agent behavior (Jensen and Meckling 1976). In software outsourcing, appropriate outcomes used in predicating agent control or rewards include software quality. It is possible for vendor managers to stipulate quality benchmarks for the project and hence incentivize appropriate actions from the development team. Software project participants can then be rewarded or sanctioned based on their individual or team's performance in meeting these goals. Hence:

> *H2a: Higher levels of quality-based outcome control will be associated with higher levels of software quality.*

Agents may be incentivized along different dimensions in their activities (Jensen and Meckling 1976, Allen and Lueck 1999). Certain projects can be heavily incentivized along quality for mission-critical applications, while for other projects, time to market or time to delivery are more critical. Therefore, the dimension along which the outcome control is deployed will also play a role in determining outcomes, while the other dimension of performance should not be impacted. Efficiency-based controls are often applied in offshore settings (Thibodeau 2004). Research has shown that appropriate incentives for developers can lead to motivation of developer performance in software developer settings (Kirsch 1997). Therefore, we expect that variance in the level of efficiency-based outcome controls will be associated with associated with differing levels of efficiency.

> *H2b: Higher levels of efficiency-based outcome control will be associated with higher levels of project efficiency.*

An interesting but unexplored implication of outcome-based controls that we consider in this study is the effect of one type of outcome-based control on the other dimension of performance. Specifically, we consider the spillover effects of *quality*-based outcome controls on *efficiency* and vice versa. What issues draw such attention as well as the consequent actions by the manager is a function of the context in which the manager is embedded (Ocasio 1998) and the limited information and capacities available to him/her. Thus, a focus of managerial attention on quality as an outcome and the resulting quality-based controls could lead to inadequate attention (whether intentionally or otherwise) paid to efficiency parameters on the project. This would imply a negative effect of quality-based outcome control on efficiency and vice versa. We thus postulate the following hypotheses:

> *H3a: Higher levels of quality-based outcome control will be associated with lower levels of project efficiency.*

H3b: Higher levels of efficiency-based outcome control will be associated with lower levels of software quality.

Effect of Informal Control

Clan control operates when all members of the work group embrace the same values, adopt similar problem-solving approaches, and commit to achieving group goals (Ouchi 1979). A *collaborative* team culture can be seen as an important specific manifestation of clan control. Collaborative culture leads members to freely share resources and ideas with others. Since the success of work conducted in software teams depends on how well team members collaborate (Hoegl and Gemuenden 2001), a collaborative team culture will facilitate the achievement of project objectives. Due to likely heterogeneity in skills and expertise within a project team, with collaborative exchanges, the team can leverage the competence of each member in their area of expertise and bring it to bear upon relevant task activities. Thus, we propose:

H4a: Higher levels of collaborative culture based clan controls will be associated with higher levels of software quality.
H4b: Higher levels of collaborative culture based clan controls will be associated with higher levels of project efficiency.

Moderating Influence of Boundary-Spanning

Client organizations possess knowledge of the business domain relevant to the project. This knowledge is marshaled through a requirements definition process that converts the requirements to functional specifications. However, the process of acquiring the specific knowledge, needed for creating functional specifications, is often inefficient and open to contingencies that unfold over time (Pressman 2001, Thibodeau and Rosencrance 2002). Therefore, even after requirements elicitation, continued dialogue with the client is necessary to address open issues about the business domain for vendor managers (Gopal, Mukhopadhyay, and Krishnan 2002). From the vendor side, vendors possess deep technical knowledge required for making decisions about technology choices for the project. In most cases, the relevant knowledge about the technological details has to be shared with the client to make informed decisions throughout the project. Thus, there is clearly a need for sustained bidirectional knowledge sharing across respective knowledge domains of the client and the vendor. Thus, the importance of the boundary-spanner in this role is crucial to the process of knowledge sharing.

There are significant benefits to knowledge sharing carried out through boundary-spanning. Important project-level information necessary for successful execution of the project is shared between the vendor and the client. This includes *operationalizing* the control parameters for the specific project context and *instantiating* controls to the specific context of the project. In addition, this interaction will also provide vendor management with an enhanced understanding of both the technical issues surrounding the project as well as the touch points between the technical and the business aspects. This enhanced understanding of client requirements will enable vendor managers to translate this knowledge into a more fine-tuned set of control parameters and facilitating conditions that can be applied to the development team. These artifacts (prototype code, design documents), viewed through the lens of boundary-spanning, are highly instrumental in enabling the fine-tuning of behavioral control since they enable higher-order knowledge to be shared between clients and vendors (Pressman 2001).

With behavioral control, enhanced knowledge sharing from boundary-spanning could result in more appropriate methodologies and procedures applied to the team. Boundary-spanning activities enhance communication and coordination between the vendor and the client, which leads to quicker resolution of open issues (Gopal, Mukhopadhyay, and Krishnan 2002) as well as allows for adjustments to the behavioral specifications that are instituted as the context evolves (Kirsch 2004, Krishnan et al. 2000). Therefore, we propose

> H5a: *Boundary-spanning activities between the vendor and the client will positively moderate the relationship between behavioral control and project performance.*

In the case of outcome controls, boundary-spanning provides vendor managers with two benefits. First, it helps vendor management choose the right outcomes in the project and link these outcomes to the appropriate business-level metrics required for the project. In many cases, the outcome benchmark changes over the course of the project as more knowledge between the vendor and the client is shared and a clearer shared mental model emerges of the required software (Choudhury and Sabherwal 2003, Levina 2005). Second, it enables the vendor to create the appropriate outcome control that reflects the trade-off between quality and efficiency (or cost) in the project. The use of outcomes controls is thus enhanced by the use of appropriate boundary objects that emphasize the right attributes and thereby apply the right incentives. Thus, we propose the following:

> H5b: *Boundary-spanning activities between the vendor and the client will positively moderate the relationship between quality-based outcome control and software quality.*
>
> H5c: *Boundary-spanning activities between the vendor and the client will positively moderate the relationship between efficiency-based outcome control and project efficiency.*

RESEARCH DESIGN AND ANALYSIS

In order to capture information on modes of control and boundary-spanning observed in software outsourcing, we felt that a field study in a single organization (cf. Ethiraj et al. 2005) may not capture adequate variance reflective of the industry. On the other hand, a broad-based survey targeted at the industry as a whole generally results in low response rates. Therefore, we chose a focused survey methodology; data was collected from a small set of organizations using structured surveys administered personally onsite. We draw upon Indian firms in collecting data for this study. From a database of about 600 software firms maintained by NASSCOM (an industry-level software services trade association), a total of 267 software companies were first short-listed. From these 267 companies, 45 firms were randomly selected and senior management at these firms was contacted with a request to participate in the research study. Once they agreed to participate, the executives were requested to provide us with a list of projects completed in the previous six months. All projects chosen were outsourced in entirety to the vendor firm and were carried out by the vendor firm. A total of twenty-three firms finally agreed to participate in our research for a response rate of 51 percent. These firms employed on average 3,200 employees, with the smallest firm employing 450 employees at the time of data collection. To ensure coverage of a broad range of projects from each organization, we retained only projects from firms where we had at least four or more projects. Our final sample for this study consisted of a total of ninety-six projects from ten

Table 15.1 Sample description, n = 96

Project Characteristic	Sample Description
Software Domain[1]	Application (65.1%) System (16.9%)
Client Industry[2]	Biotech/Healthcare (10.8%) Finance (8.4%) Information Technology (34.9%) Automobile, transport & Logistics (10.8%) Manufacturing (8.4%) Retail (4.8%)
Project Type[1]	New Development (51.8%) Maintenance (19.3%) Reengineering (18.1%)
Platform[2]	Mainframe (16.9%) Unix Variants (31.3%) Windows (30.1%)

[1] Remaining projects could not be clearly classified into one of these categories
[2] Remaining projects belong to additional categories

firms. Table 15.1 provides a descriptive summary of our sample, showing the breakdown of the sample by client industry, software domain, type of project, and the technical platform used.

The questionnaire used for data collection was created by adapting scales from prior research. The objective data, such as project-level metrics on project efficiency and project size, were obtained from the company databases. The questionnaire was pretested in two ways. First, the questionnaire was presented to a set of quality auditors certified by the Software Engineering Institute (SEI). Their comments on the questionnaire were elicited and incorporated into the questionnaire. Second, a Web-based version of the questionnaire was created and a pilot survey was conducted using fifteen software organizations (not in final sample). Respondents to the pilot were asked to fill out the survey, and their feedback was incorporated into the final survey. The specific questionnaire items for the constructs used are shown in Table 15.2, with their respective sources listed. Additional details on the constructs and their validation are available in Gopal and Gosain (2010). Table 15.3 provides summary statistics and interconstruct correlations for the variables in the analysis. For multi-item reflective constructs, the composite reliabilities are indicated and all are above the 0.70 threshold. All constructs show composite reliabilities higher than 0.50, thereby establishing their reliability. Divergent validity is confirmed as the average variance extracted (i.e., the average variance shared between a construct and its measures, AVE) is greater than the variance shared with other constructs in the model (Fornell and Bookstein 1981).

As a first step in establishing the psychometric properties of our measures, we subject the reflective constructs to an exploratory factor analysis using varimax rotation and a threshold eigenvalue of 1.0. Each set of items pertaining to an underlying construct loaded well together on the construct. A more stringent test of scale validity is to use oblique rotation techniques that allow individual factors to be correlated (Ford, MacCallum, and Tait 2006). While the oblique rotated factor structure is typically harder to interpret, it is a more accurate representation of real-world complexity of the examined variables. We conducted factor analysis on our scales using maximum likelihood extraction and applying promax rotation. The analysis provides us with five distinct factors capturing collaborative culture, overruns, quality, behavioral control, and a composite factor that accounted for both quality-based outcome control and efficiency-based outcome control. In other words, the higher inter-item correlation between the items capturing the outcome-based controls did not separate out as expected. This is not entirely surprising since it is possible that a firm that implements outcome-based controls along the quality dimension will have a higher probability of implementing outcome-based controls along efficiency as well. This factor analysis procedure, however, attests to the scale validity of our other constructs and suggests that our measures meet the psychometric properties

Table 15.2   Questionnaire items and sources

	Questionnaire Items (Variable Name)	Sources—*Dimension*
Behavioral Control— *Reflective*	• The project followed documented processes for software development (Behcon1)	Kirsch (1996)
	• Project estimates (such as project size, cost, and schedule) were documented regularly for use in planning and tracking the project (Behcon2)	Adapted from Krishnan et al. (2000) and Gopal et al. (2002b)
	• Changes to software system requirements resulted in appropriate changes to project plans and schedules (Behcon3)	Krishnan et al. (2000)
	• The project's actual results on the project plan were compared regularly with estimates in the project plan (Behcon4)	Krishnan et al. (2000)
	• Corrective action was taken proactively when actual results deviated from the project plan (Behcon5)	Krishnan et al. (2000)
	• All project members agreed to the commitment of their time as per the project plan (Behcon6)	Gopal et al. (2002b)
Outcome Control— Quality *Reflective*	• Software quality was assessed and compared to the quality goals in the project plan (Outq1)	Krishnan et al. (2000)
	• The project had measurable and quantified goals for the quality of released software (Outq2)	Krishnan et al. (2000)
	• Software quality was used as a basis for rewards for project members (Outq3)	Ravichandran and Rai (2000, 411, Quality Orientation of Reward Schemes)
	• Software quality measures like defect rates were taken into account in rewarding project members (Outq4)	Ravichandran and Rai (2000, 411, Quality Orientation of Reward Schemes)
	• User satisfaction with software quality was an important factor in determining rewards for project members (Outq5)	Ravichandran and Rai (2000, 411, Quality Orientation of Reward Schemes)

(Continued)

Table 15.2   (*Continued*)

	Questionnaire Items (Variable Name)	Sources—*Dimension*
Outcome Control— Efficiency *Reflective*	• To the best of your knowledge, how often was development effort tracked on this project? (1 – very infrequently to 7 – very frequently) (Outeff1)	Gopal et al. (2002b)
	• To the best of your knowledge, how often was project schedules tracked on this project? (1 – very infrequently to 7 – very frequently) (Outeff2)	Gopal et al. (2002b)
	• Timely achievement of project goals was used as a basis for rewarding project members (Outeff3)	Ravichandran and Rai (2000, 411, adapted replacing quality with costs and schedule)
	• Completing the project on time was an important factor in determining rewards for project members (Outeff4)	Ravichandran and Rai (2000, 411, adapted replacing quality with costs and schedule)
	• The project's performance on cost was used as a basis for rewarding project members (Outeff5)	Ravichandran and Rai (2000, 411, adapted replacing quality with costs and schedule)
	• Adherence to planned schedule was used as a basis for rewards for project members (Outeff6)	Ravichandran and Rai (2000, 411, adapted replacing quality with costs and schedule)
Collaborative Culture— *Reflective*	• People in the project team were supportive and helpful (Collab1) • There was willingness to share responsibility for failure (Collab2) • There was willingness to collaborate across different groups (Collab3)	Harley and Hult (1998)
Boundary- spanning— Roles	• One or more members of the project team had been formally designated to facilitate coordination with client • One or more members of the project team informally facilitated coordination with the client	Adapted from Levina and Vaast (2005)

(*Continued*)

Table 15.2   (Continued)

	Questionnaire Items (Variable Name)	Sources—*Dimension*
Boundary-Spanning—Process	Project planning meetings Status review meetings	Adapted from Gopal et al. (2002a) and Carlile (2002)
Boundary-Spanning—Objects	Code inspections Design reviews	Adapted from Gopal et al. (2002a) and Carlile (2002)
Software Quality—*Reflective*	Response time Flexibility Usability Reliability	Adapted from Szejko (1999).
Project Efficiency—*Reflective*	Measured using actual project performance compared to budget: Schedule overruns Cost overruns Effort overruns	Adapted from Gopal et al. (2002a)
Project Volatility—*Formative*	Employee turnover from the project team was a major problem (Turnover) Requirements significantly fluctuated over the course of the project (Req Instability) It was difficult to retain employees with the skills required in this project within the organization (Retention)	Adapted from Gopal et al. (2003)

required for further analysis. To further verify the factor structure of our reflective constructs, we subjected the data to confirmatory factor analysis using LISREL. All the hypothesized paths from the indicator variables to the hypothesized latent variables were significant at $p < 0.05$.

We used PLS to estimate the research model used to test our hypotheses. Since moderation models require the use of interaction terms, we use the approach recommended by Chin et al. (1996) in this chapter. For interactions involving reflective indicators, we centered indicators for the main and moderating constructs and created all pair-wise product indicators where each indicator from the main construct is multiplied with each indicator from the moderating construct. For interactions involving formative constructs, we used the following suggested two-step process. The first step entails using the formative indicators in conjunction with PLS to create underlying construct scores for the predictor and moderator variables. Step two consists of

Table 15.3 Descriptive statistics, composite reliability, and correlations among constructs

	Mean	S.D	C.R.	(1)	(2)	(3)	(4)	(5)	(6)	(7)	(8)	(9)	(10)	(11)
1. Quality	5.862	0.645	0.84	0.756										
2. Project Efficiency	–17.118	20.578	0.92	0.070	0.888									
3. Behavioral Control	5.300	1.039	0.87	0.495	0.130	0.758								
4. Outcome Control—Quality	4.773	1.227	0.84	0.555	0.019	0.656	0.730							
5. Outcome Control—Efficiency	5.862	0.645	0.85	0.434	0.026	0.481	0.622	0.629						
6. Collaborative Culture	5.590	0.819	0.88	0.540	–0.026	0.494	0.455	0.350	0.773					
7. Boundary-Spanning	0.00	1.000	–	0.174	0.327	0.161	0.052	0.031	0.240	0.799				
8. Project Size	9.430	6.973	–	–0.096	–0.137	0.014	–0.146	0.014	0.043	0.071	1.000			
9. Project Volatility	3.267	1.299	–	–0.295	–0.267	–0.222	–0.213	–0.140	–0.240	0.163	0.166	0.677		
10. Team Size	15.783	21.845	–	–0.094	0.052	0.097	0.106	–0.044	–0.114	–0.026	–0.058	0.240	1.000	
11. Prior Interactions	0.000	1.000	–	0.142	0.085	0.102	0.153	0.165	0.091	–0.031	–0.133	–0.143	–0.012	0.948

Notes:
1. diagonal elements show the square-root of Average Variance Extracted for each construct
2. Boundary-Spanning is a formative construct with three dimensions: Process (Mean = 27.23), Objects (Mean = 5.11) and Boundary-Spanning Roles (Mean = 5.11)
3. Project Volatility is a formative construct with three dimensions: Requirements volatility (Mean = 4.08), Personnel Turnover (Mean = 2.65), and Retention (Mean = 3.06)
4. Prior Interactions is a formative construct with two dimensions: Prior Projects (Mean = 22.487) and Concurrent Projects (Mean = 3.650)

Table 15.4 Model estimation, PLS

	DV = Software Quality			DV = Project efficiency		
	Controls	Main Effects	Main Effects and Interactions	Controls	Main Effects	Main Effects and Interactions
Behavioral Control		0.098	0.106		0.270ᵛ	0.260ᵛ
Outcome Control (Quality)		0.269*	0.272**		−0.212**	−0.239***
Outcome Control (Efficiency)		0.097	0.092		0.022*	0.032**
Boundary-Spanning		0.099***	0.045		0.303ᵛ	0.043
Behavioral Control X Boundary-Spanning			0.102ᵛ			0.188**
Outcome Control (Quality) X Boundary-Spanning			0.049*			
Outcome Control (Efficiency) X Boundary-Spanning						0.098ᵛ
Collaborative Culture	−0.412***	0.275*	0.281**	−0.088	−0.035*	−0.050**
Project Volatility	−0.065	−0.122	−0.123	−0.121***	−0.206	−0.214
Project Size	0.090	−0.058ᵛ	−0.056	0.073	−0.104	−0.128ᵛ
Prior Interactions	0.024	0.025	0.031	0.059	0.037	0.039*
Team Size		−0.068	−0.066		0.081***	0.075***
Firm Controls	Yes	Yes	Yes	Yes	Yes	Yes
R²	0.191	0.457	0.494	0.033	0.208	0.248
N	96	96	96	96	96	96

ᵛp < 0.10, *p < 0.05, **p < 0.01, ***p < 0.001

taking those single composite construct scores to create a single interaction term. The results of the PLS analysis are shown in Table 15.4. The path coefficients in the model were assessed using the jackknife routine.

RESULTS AND DISCUSSION

The results from PLS shown in Table 15.4 provide broad support for the impact of organizational control on project performance. We discuss results for the main effects in the quality model first. These are displayed for quality in the first two columns of Table 15.4. Our results show no significant effect of behavioral control on quality, indicating no support for Hypothesis 1a. Hypothesis 2a pertains to the direct effect of quality-based outcome control on quality in the project and receives some support in our analysis. Although we do not formally hypothesize a direct effect of boundary-spanning, the results indicate a significant and positive effect of these activities on quality. Knowledge sharing between the client and vendor teams eliminates gaps in understanding requirements and ensures clarity of expectations, thereby improving the client team's ability to deliver to functional requirements.

With respect to the project efficiency model, shown in the appropriate columns of Table 15.4, the direct effect of behavioral control on project efficiency is marginally significant, showing some support for Hypothesis 1b. Hypothesis 2b postulated a direct effect of efficiency-based outcome control on project efficiency and we see support for this hypothesis. While the effect is significant, the magnitude is small, suggesting that further research is needed to confirm if this finding can be effectively applied in practice. Similar to the quality model, we see a direct effect of boundary-spanning on project efficiency significant at the $p<0.10$ level, indicating the value accruing from boundary-spanning.

Hypotheses 3a and 3b postulated that outcome-based formal controls focused on a certain outcome dimension will have negative externalities with respect to other dimensions of outcomes. We see that, in accordance with Hypothesis 3a, quality-based outcome controls are associated with a decrease in project efficiency, thus suggesting that formal controls may have unintended consequences that may dampen their overall utility. There is no such corresponding effect in the effect of efficiency-based outcome controls on quality. Our analysis shows that instituting outcome controls focused on one dimension may have negative effects on other outcome dimensions in the outsourced project; this effect has not been highlighted or established empirically in extant literature and has implications for the use of formal outcome-based control in outsourcing engagements. Hypothesis 4a and 4b pertained to the influence of the collaborative culture observed in the teams on project outcomes. Our results with respect to collaborative culture show mixed results; while collaboration enhances the quality in the project, it also leads to reduced project efficiency.

To test Hypotheses 5a through 5c, pertaining to the moderating influence of boundary-spanning, we followed a hierarchical process where we compared the results of models with and without interaction constructs (Carte and Russell 2003). The significance of the interaction terms is assessed using a pseudo F-test (Chin, Marcolin, and Newsted 1996). The f^2 statistic is computed based on the R^2 difference calculated as $(R^2_{full} - R^2_{excluded}) / (1 - R^2_{full})$. The pseudo F statistic is calculated as $f^2 * (n-k-1)$, with 1, $(n-k)$ degrees of freedom when n is the sample size and k is the number of constructs in the model. These results, shown in Table 15.5, confirm that boundary-spanning activities interact with both behavioral and outcome control in impacting quality and project efficiency.

Hypothesis 5a pertains to the positive moderating effect of boundary-spanning on the relationship between behavioral control and project performance; we see partial support for this hypothesis in the columns with interaction results in Table 15.3 for both quality and project efficiency. The interaction of boundary-spanning and behavioral control is statistically significant in enhancing project efficiency. However, based on tests of moderation, we do not see evidence of a significant interaction effect of behavioral control and boundary-spanning in impacting quality. Hypotheses 5b and 5c pertain to the moderation effect of boundary-spanning on

Table 15.5 Tests of moderation effects

Boundary Spanning as Moderator of	Included Model R^2	Excluded Model R^2	F^2	Pseudo-F (1, 88)	Conclusion
Behavioral Control → Software Quality	0.458	0.457	0.002	0.162	Not Significant
Behavioral Control → Project Efficiency	0.243	0.208	0.046	4.069	Significant ($p < 0.05$)
Outcome Control-Quality → Software Quality	0.482	0.457	0.048	4.247	Significant ($p < 0.05$)
Outcome Control-Efficiency → Project Efficiency	0.233	0.208	0.033	2.868	Significant ($p < 0.10$)

the relationship between outcome control and performance and are both strongly supported. Boundary-spanning positively moderates the effect of quality-based outcome control on quality and the effect of efficiency-based outcome control on project efficiency. We graph the interaction results holding all other variables at their means, as shown in Figure 15.2. Interestingly, in the low boundary-spanning case (where the aggregate boundary-spanning construct is held at one standard deviation below the mean), the total direct and indirect returns to formal controls are small in the case of quality and almost nonexistent in the case of efficiency. However, in the high boundary-spanning case, the effect of formal control on quality and efficiency is significantly higher. These results indicate that boundary-spanning activities

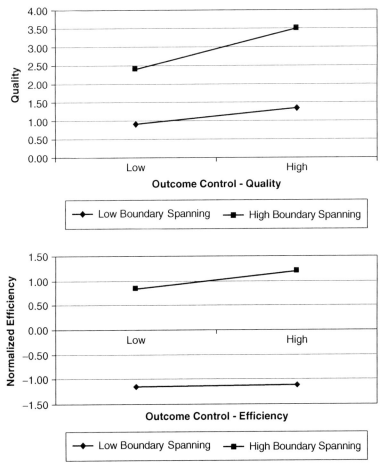

Figure 15.2 Interactions of Outcome-Based Controls and Boundary-Spanning on Software Quality and Project Efficiency

are important facilitators for the efficacy of formal outcome controls; our analysis provides clear pointers to inform the current debate about how the efficacy of formal controls in outsourced projects (Narayanaswamy, Henry, and Purvis 2007) may be enhanced.

It is noteworthy that behavioral control does not appear to have a significant impact on quality as an outcome but affects project efficiency. One reason for this dichotomy could be the relative ease with which it is possible to establish appropriate behavioral control with respect to schedules, costs and effort in a project. The benefits of boundary-spanning allow the vendor to better align project plans and costs with understanding of the business domain, thereby leading to a stronger moderating effect. On the other hand, establishing such behavioral norms and methodologies for quality is much harder. Software development is comparable to R&D for the uncertainty that exists in the development process (Pressman 2001). In such uncertain contexts, prior research shows that it is hard to monitor or indeed establish behavioral control with respect to quality or even establish behavioral norms that can be rigorously enforced (Ravichandran and Rai 2000). In such contexts, any additional knowledge gained from boundary-spanning does not appear to make a significant difference in quality.

CONCLUSION

A key contribution of this chapter is in integrating the control perspective with prior research in boundary-spanning, particularly focusing on integration of knowledge from disparate domains. We find that outcome-based controls are effective in addressing the outcomes of choice positively but have possible negative implications for other outcomes. We also find that boundary-spanning moderates the impact of outcome control on respective outcomes as well as the impact of behavioral control on project efficiency. In the process, we are also able to develop a measure for boundary-spanning based on extant research on boundary-spanning in both software development and product development literatures (Levina and Vaast 2005, Carlile 2002).

Apart from contributing to the literature by showing the link between control and project outcomes, our work has practical implications for managers seeking to leverage outsourcing. It suggests that while upfront attention to the design of appropriate control mechanisms is important, it is also critical to have effective liaisons, boundary objects, and interaction processes at the interface between client and vendor organizations on an ongoing basis to make sure that control is finely tuned to the unfolding contextual conditions. While anecdotal evidence of boundary-spanning exists in the practitioner press, we specifically recommend that managers strategize about boundary spanners and objects "in practice" (Levina and Vaast 2005) and institutionalize them in ongoing projects. While the appropriate choice of objects and spanners is a question that we have not considered in this chapter, this clearly reflects an avenue for future research. We argue that a deeper understanding of the relevance of the individual pieces of boundary-spanning in specific contexts is necessary. For instance, in what sorts of knowledge work are boundary spanners and objects of particular importance? Does the importance of spanners and objects increase in proportion to the intangible nature of the activity or the particular attributes of the knowledge boundaries that require spanning? Much of the current work in boundary-spanning in technology-mediated settings has used a deep, qualitative approach (Levina and Vaast 2005). However, a more broad-based approach rooted in hard data would help managers and researchers quantify the specific benefits that accrue boundary-spanning activities and more importantly, also identify conditions under which the costs of boundary spanners, processes and objects may not be necessary.

Finally, a large literature in current research on technology-mediated contexts such as outsourcing has addressed the use of process models such as the ISO and the Capability Maturity Model. However, it is interesting to note that many of the specific processes within these models actually pertain to what we would refer to here as boundary-spanning processes and the manipulation of boundary objects. Part of our objective here was to act as a bridge between the engineering literature, which often recommends processes as "critical success factors" or "key process areas," and the management literature which uses terms such as *boundary-spanning process* and *objects* for the same artifacts or activities. A certain level of boundary-spanning across these research domains in itself appears necessary so that as a community, we understand the synergies and complementarities across these apparently dissimilar research communities. In this chapter, we address this specifically in the IT outsourcing context; it is our hope that a similar "bringing together" of boundary-spanning research across other domains will pay rich dividends in terms of insights and managerial recommendations.

NOTE

1. Originally published: Gopal, A., and S. Gosain. 2010. "The Role of Organizational Controls and Boundary Spanning in Software Development Outsourcing: Implications for Project Performance." *Information Systems Research* no. 21 (4): 960–982.

REFERENCES

Allen, D.W., and D. Lueck. 1999. "The role of risk in contract choice." *Journal of Law, Economics, and Organization* no. 15 (3):704–736.
Banerjee, A.V., and E. Duflo. 2000. "Reputation effects and the limits of contracting: A study of the Indian software industry." *The Quarterly Journal of Economics* no. 115 (3):989–1017.

Carlile, P.R. 2002. "A pragmatic view of knowledge and boundaries: Boundary objects in new product development." *Organization Science* no. 13 (4):442–455.

Carlile, P.R. 2004. "Transferring, translating, and transforming: An integrative framework for managing knowledge across boundaries." *Organization Science* no. 15 (5):555–568.

Carte, T.A., and C.J. Russell. 2003. "In pursuit of moderation: nine common errors and teir solutions." *MIS Quarterly* no. 27 (3):479–501.

Chin, W.W., B.L. Marcolin, and P.R. Newsted. 1996. A Partial Least Squares Latent Variable Modeling Approach for Measuring Interaction Effects: Results from a Monte Carlo Simulation Study and Voice Mail Emotion/Adoption Study. *Proceedings of the Seventeenth International Conference on Information Systems.* December 16–18, 1996. Cleveland, OH.

Choudhury, V., and R. Sabherwal. 2003. "Portfolios of control in outsourced software development projects." *Information Systems Research* no. 14 (3):291–314.

Eisenhardt, K.M. 1985. "Control: Organizational and economic approaches." *Management Science* no. 31 (2):134–149.

Ethiraj, S.K., P. Kale, M.S. Krishnan, and J.V. Singh. 2005. "Where do capabilities come from and how do they matter? A study in the software services industry." *Strategic Management Journal* no. 26 (1):25–45.

Ford, J.K., R.C. MacCallum, and M. Tait. 2006. "The application of exploratory factor analysis in applied psychology: A critical review and analysis." *Personnel Psychology* no. 39 (2):291–314.

Gopal, A., and S. Gosain. 2010. " The role of organizational controls and Boundary Spanning in software development outsourcing: implications for project performance." *Information Systems Research* no. 21 (4):960–982.

Gopal, A., M.S. Krishnan, T. Mukhopadhyay, and D.R. Goldenson. 2002. "Measurement programs in software development: Determinants of success." *Software Engineering, IEEE Transactions on* no. 28 (9):863–875.

Gopal, A., T. Mukhopadhyay, and M.S. Krishnan. 2002. "The role of software processes and communication in offshore software development." *Communications of the ACM* no. 45 (4):193–200.

Gopal, A., K. Sivaramakrishnan, M.S. Krishnan, and T. Mukhopadhyay. 2003. "Contracts in offshore software development: An empirical analysis." *Management Science* no. 49 (12):1671–1683.

Grant, R.M. 1996. "Toward a knowledge-based theory of the firm." *Strategic Management Journal* no. 17:109–122.

Henderson, J.C., and S. Lee. 1992. "Managing I/S design teams: a control theories perspective." *Management Science* no. 38 (6):757–777.

Hoegl, M., and H.G. Gemuenden. 2001. "Teamwork quality and the success of innovative projects: A theoretical concept and empirical evidence." *Organization Science* no. 12 (4):435–449.

Jensen, Michael C., and William H. Meckling. 1976. "Theory of the firm: Managerial behavior, agency costs and ownership structure." *Journal of Financial Economics* no. 3 (4):305–360. doi: 10.1016/0304-405x(76)90026-x.

Kirsch, L.J. 1996. "The management of complex tasks in organizations: Controlling the systems development process." *Organization Science* no. 7 (1):1–21.

Kirsch, L.J. 1997. "Portfolios of control modes and IS project management,." *Information Systems Research* no. 8 (3):215–239.

Kirsch, L.J. 2004. "Deploying common systems globally: The dynamics of control." *Information Systems Research* no. 15 (4):374–395.

Kirsch, L.J., V. Sambamurthy, D.G. Ko, and R.L. Purvis. 2002. "Controlling information systems development projects: The view from the client." *Management Science* no. 48 (4):484–498.

Krishnan, M.S., C.H. Kriebel, S. Kekre, and T. Mukhopadhyay. 2000. "An empirical analysis of productivity and quality in software products." *Management Science* no. 46 (6):745–759.

Levina, N. 2005. "Collaborating on multiparty information systems development projects: A collective reflection-in-action view." *Information Systems Research* no. 16 (2):109–130.

Levina, N., and E. Vaast. 2005. "The emergence of boundary spanning competence in practice: implications for implementation and use of information systems." *MIS Quarterly*:335–363.

Narayanaswamy, R.S., R.M. Henry, and R.L. Purvis. 2007. Understanding the Effect of Control on Information Systems Project Performance via Meta-Analysis. In *Academy of Management Annual Meeting*. Philadelphia, PA.

Necco, C.R., C.L. Gordon, and N.W. Tsai. 1987. "Systems analysis and design: current practices." *MIS Quarterly*:461–476.

Ocasio, W. 1998. "Towards an attention-based view of the firm." *Strategic Management Journal* no. 18 (S1):187–206.

Ouchi, W.G. 1979. "A conceptual framework for the design of organizational control mechanisms." *Management Science* no. 25 (9):833–848.

Ouchi, W.G. 1980. "Markets, bureaucracies, and clans." *Administrative Science Quarterly*:129–141.

Paulk, M.C., B. Curtis, M.B. Chrissis, and C.V. Weber. 1993. "Capability maturity model, version 1.1." *Software, IEEE* no. 10 (4):18–27.

Pawlowski, S.D., and D. Robey. 2004. "Bridging user organizations: Knowledge brokering and the work of information technology professionals." *MIS Quarterly* no. 28 (4):645–672.

Pressman, R.S. 2001. *Software engineering: A practitioner's approach.* 5th ed. New York: McGraw Hill.

Ravichandran, T., and A. Rai. 2000. "Quality management in systems development: an organizational system perspective." *MIS Quarterly* no.24 (3):381–415.

Star, S.L. 1989. "The structure of 111-structured solutions: Boundary objects and heterogeneous distributed problem solving." *Distributed Artifidal Intelligence* no. 2:37–54.

Thibodeau, P. 2004. "More IT Jobs Go Offshore." *Computerworld* no. 38:13.

Thibodeau, P., and L. Rosencrance. 2002. "Users losing billions due to bugs." *Computerworld.*

Wallace, L., M. Keil, and A. Rai. 2004. "How software project risk affects project performance: An investigation of the dimensions of risk and an exploratory model." *Decision Sciences* no. 35 (2):289–321.

Contributors

Vikas Anand is an associate professor of management at University of Arkansas. He received his Ph.D. from Arizona State University, and an MBA in international business from the Indian Institute of Foreign Trade. He also holds a bachelor's degree in engineering and a master's degree in physics. He has published and presented his work on business ethics and knowledge management in several research and practitioner outlets such as the *Academy of Management Review*, *Research in Organizational Behavior*, *Organization Science*, *Academy of Management Executive*, and so on. Prior to his academic career, he was a manager in two large multinational corporations and worked extensively on marketing and strategic planning in various parts of Africa and Asia. His research has included working with several large multinational corporations with respect to business process outsourcing and intercultural issues. He currently serves as the faculty director of the Walton College MBA Programs.

Reinhard Bachmann is professor of strategy and director of the Centre for Trust Research (CTR) at the University of Surrey. He has published widely on the role of trust in business contexts. His work appeared in leading journals, including *Organization Studies*, *British Journal of Sociology*, *Cambridge Journal of Economics*, and *European Societies*. He is coeditor of various books and journal special issues on trust. Also, he serves on the editorial board of *Organization Studies* and is deputy editor-in-chief of the *Journal of Trust Research*.

Preeta M. Banerjee is an assistant professor of strategy at the International Business School at Brandeis University. Her research focuses on the management of technology and innovation and the evolution of individuals, technology, firm, and industry in entrepreneurial endeavors. Banerjee's research has appeared in *Technovation*, *International Journal of Strategic Change Management*, *Technological Forecasting & Social Change*, *IEEE-TEM*, and *R&D Management*. She is a recent recipient of the IBM Innovation Award for her work with serious games in the classroom, the Aspen Institute Rising Star Finalist, and the Fulbright-Nehru to study frugal innovation and entrepreneurship in India. She received her Ph.D. from the Wharton School, University of Pennsylvania, and her B.S. from Carnegie Mellon Tepper School and Mellon College of Science.

Fiona Buick is a research project manager at the University of Canberra. Fiona was awarded a Ph.D. in management from the University of Canberra in June 2012. Her thesis focused on the impact of organizational culture on joined-up working in the Australian Public Service. Prior to commencing her Ph.D., Fiona worked as a human resources practitioner in the public service. Her qualifications are a masters of HRM, graduate diploma in employment relations and bachelor of applied psychology. She is currently the research project manager of the Strengthening the Performance Framework project.

Thomas Stephen Calvard is a lecturer in organization studies and HRM at the University of Edinburgh Business School. Dr. Calvard's research interests include effective team-working, diversity management, and organizational theory development. He is an active member of the Academy of Management, Chartered Institute of Personnel and Development, and the British Psychological Society's Division of Occupational Psychology. Dr. Calvard completed his Ph.D. investigating issues of diversity, team-working, and perspective taking in international MBA teams and mult-iteam systems in the British Royal Navy.

Donna L. Chrobot-Mason is an associate professor and director of the Center for Organizational Leadership at the University of Cincinnati and is an adjunct research scholar at the Center for Creative Leadership. Donna conducts research in leadership, diversity, workplace harassment, and inclusion. She has published in numerous journals and serves on editorial review boards. With Chris Ernst, she coauthored *Boundary Spanning Leadership: Six Practices for Solving Problems, Driving Innovation, and Transforming Organizations*. She holds a Ph.D. and M.A. in applied psychology from the University of Georgia.

Rafael A. Corredoira is assistant professor of management and organization at the Robert H. Smith School of Business, University of Maryland. He received a Ph.D. in Strategy and International Management from the Wharton School, University of Pennsylvania, and an MBA from Drexel University. His research focuses on embedded exploration: how networks—those originating from social ties, market dynamics, and institutional arrangements—constrain or enable firms' entrepreneurial search for innovative solutions. His papers have appeared in leading journals such as *Strategic Management Journal, Academy of Management Journal*, and *Journal of International Business Studies*. His work also received the 2007 International Management Division Best Paper Award from the Academy of Management. His current research examines the flow of knowledge through mobility ties in the semiconductor industry, how public-private institutions and social networks drive upgrading capabilities in the wine and auto-part industries in developing economies, and how cognitive constraints shape technological evolution.

Kristin L. Cullen is a postdoctoral research fellow at the Center for Creative Leadership. She conducts research in leadership, interpersonal influence, organizational networks, and change. Kristin has published in several journals and is currently coleading an applied research project that aims to integrate boundary-spanning leadership and organizational network content within a learning and development program in order to improve collaboration across key boundaries within client organizations. She holds a Ph.D. and M.A. in industrial/organizational psychology from Auburn University.

Anat Drach-Zahavy is an associate professor at the Faculty of Health and Welfare Sciences at the University of Haifa, Israel. She received her Ph.D. degree in the Department of Industrial Engineering and Management at the Technion, Israel. She is the head of the research center for the study, implementation and assimilation of Evidence-Based Practice Her research is focused on health-care organizations, and particularly in the areas of teamwork, safety, and employee health.

Susan Gasson is an associate professor in the iSchool at Drexel University, Philadelphia, USA. Following an early career as a systems designer and consultant, she obtained her MBA and Ph.D. from Warwick Business School in the UK. Dr. Gasson was awarded a prestigious NSF Early Career Award in 2004. Her research explores boundary-spanning group processes and has appeared in journals such as *Information, Technology & People*, the *European Journal of Information Systems (EJIS)*, and the *Journal of Computer-Mediated Communication (JCMC)*.

Anandasivam Gopal is an associate professor of information systems at the Robert H. Smith School of Business, University of Maryland College Park. He received his Ph.D. in information systems from Carnegie Mellon University. His research interests include software engineering economics, entrepreneurship, innovation and venture capital, and technology platforms. He is an associate editor at *Information Systems Research* and a guest associate editor at *Management Science*.

Sanjay Gosain is employed in a technology strategy role with Capital Group Companies, Inc., a privately held investment organization. Prior to his current role, Sanjay was an assistant professor of information systems at the Robert H. Smith School of Business, University of Maryland. He completed his Ph.D. in business administration at the Marshall School of Business, University of Southern California. Sanjay's research broadly addresses the drivers of effective information technology (IT) design, use, and value leverage in corporate settings.

Sharon Grant is a senior lecturer in psychology at Swinburne University of Technology with research interests in organizational psychology and personality psychology. Sharon has published in topic areas including managerial styles; personality, occupational stress, coping and strain; entrepreneurship, including occupational stress in entrepreneurs; the 'Big Five,' health and well-being; personality assessment, skill acquisition, teamwork in organizations; and workplace deviance. Sharon's current work focuses on obesity bias in organizational decision making.

Linda Hobbs is a Senior Lecturer of Science Education at Deakin University. Dr. Hobbs lectures in primary science education. Her research explores issues around out-of-field teaching in secondary schools, focusing on teacher identity. Other research explores the aesthetic dimensions of teaching and school-based pedagogies in teacher education.

Frens Kroeger is lecturer in organization studies at Surrey Business School, and Deputy Director of the *Centre for Trust Research* (CTR), the first research center worldwide to focus entirely on the topic of organizational and interorganizational trust. Frens received his Ph.D. from Cambridge University in July 2011; his first paper in a highly ranked journal was published in November 2011. Frens's research interests revolve around the issue of trust within and between organizations, a topic which he approaches from a strongly conceptual, sociologically informed, and broadly neo-institutionalist perspective.

Janice Langan-Fox is professor of management and an industrial/organizational psychologist at Swinburne University of Technology. Janice has a Ph.D. from the University of Melbourne, a masters of philosophy from the University of Nottingham, and a bachelor of education from the University of East Anglia. She has held positions at Monash University, RMIT, and the University of Melbourne. Currently, as chief investigator, Janice leads an Australian Research Council research team finalizing an investigation into adverse events at three major Australian hospitals. Janice has more than 130 refereed publications: monographs, edited books, book chapters, teaching tools and texts, international peer-reviewed journal articles, and conference proceedings, and has served on editorial boards of *Journal of Personality and Social Psychology, Australian Psychologist, Stress & Health, Journal of Occupational and Organisational Psychology, International Journal of Selection and Assessment,* and *European Journal of Work and Organisational Psychology*. Grants awarded to Janice are around $2 million, with funds coming from the Australian Research Council, International Grants for Research, universities, philanthropic foundations, and industry.

Natalia Levina is an associate professor in the Stern School of Business, New York University. Dr. Levina focuses on understanding how people produce and span organizational, professional, cultural, and other boundaries in the process of developing and using technology. She has studied cross-functional IS development, IS outsourcing, open innovation, and crowdsourcing. Currently she investigates the role of shared contexts in enabling open innovation. Her research was published in *Information Systems Research (ISR)*, *MIS Quarterly*, *Academy of Management Journal*, and *Organization Science*, among others. She currently serves as senior editor at *ISR*.

Charles J. (Chuck) Palus is a research scientist and senior faculty member in research, innovation, and product development at the Center for Creative Leadership. He conducts research on interdependent leadership and creates new knowledge for the Center's organization leadership development practice. He has been widely published on leadership and is coauthor of the book *The Leader's Edge: Six Creative Competencies for Navigating Complex Challenges*. Chuck is also coinventor of the Visual Explorer™, Boundary Explorer™, and Leadership Metaphor Explorer™ tools for facilitating creative dialogue. He holds a Ph.D. in developmental psychology from Boston College.

Philip Riley is a senior lecturer at Monash University. Dr. Riley researches the overlapping space of psychology, education, and leadership. He coordinates leadership award courses and principal development programs at Monash University in Melbourne and conducts *The Australian Principal Health and Wellbeing Survey* annually. Phil's research applying adult attachment theory to the relationship between teachers, students, and school leaders was recently showcased in United States (*The International Handbook of Research on Teachers and Teaching*, Norwell, Massachusetts: Springer) and the UK with the publication of his first book, *Attachment Theory and the Teacher-Student Relationship* (London: Routledge). He has authored or edited more than eighty publications, and been awarded over $2 million in competitive research funding.

Peter N. Rosenweg is a registered psychologist, educated at Swinburne and RMIT Universities, with forty years' experience in aviation, mining, hospital, health care, and manufacturing enterprises. He is the author of the Situational Safety Awareness test presently in wide use in mining. He has a Ph.D. thesis in progress focused on safety compliance in hospital infection control. His psychological practice strives to improve the understanding of safety and performance through a better understanding of the problem of achieving sustained performance through improved resilience, the system of work, evaluation of human risk factors and specific training mechanisms that help to penetrate the incident plateau.

Anit Somech is an associate professor at the University of Haifa and is the head of educational leadership program at the Faculty of Education, and the president's advisor for the Advancement of the Status of Women at the University of Haifa, Israel. She received her Ph.D. degree in the Department of Industrial Engineering and Management at the Technion, with an emphasis on behavioral sciences and management (1994). Her research focuses on teamwork, participative management, and organizational citizenship behavior.

David Wilemon is Emeritus Professor of Innovation Management at Syracuse University Whitman School of Management. He served as the Earl V. Snyder Professor of Innovation Management & Entrepreneurship from 2000 to 2010. He was the cofounder of both the Innovation Management Program and the Entrepreneurship and Emerging Enterprises Program at Syracuse University. Dr. Wilemon's research focuses on innovation management, the management of technology, corporate entrepreneurship, and corporate venturing. His work has been published in the *Journal of Product Innovation Management, R&D Management Journal, Academy of Management Journal, Journal of Marketing, R&D Management, California Management Review, Transactions on Engineering Management, Journal of Innovation Management, Sloan Management Review, Technology and Strategic Management*, and *Engineering Management Review*.

Emmanuelle Vaast is an associate professor at McGill University. Dr. Vaast's research explores how social practices emerge and change with the implementation of various new technologies and how these new practices lead to new social dynamics. She has investigated the knowledge and learning dynamics within and across different social levels such as community and network of practices. Her research was published in *Information Systems Research* (ISR), *MIS Quarterly, European Journal of IS*, and *Organization Science*, among others. She serves as an associate editor at *MIS Quarterly*.

Jacob D. Vakkayil is an assistant professor at IESEG School of Management at Lille and Paris. He teaches organizational behavior, human resource management, and associated subjects to graduate and undergraduate students. His research focuses on issues concerning cross-boundary interactions within and across organizations.

Index